LISTENING
FOR AMERICA

ALSO BY ROB KAPILOW

All You Have to Do Is Listen: Music from the Inside Out

What Makes It Great? Short Masterpieces, Great Composers

LISTENING FOR AMERICA

*Inside the Great American Songbook
from Gershwin to Sondheim*

ROB KAPILOW

LIVERIGHT PUBLISHING CORPORATION

A Division of W. W. Norton & Company

Independent Publishers Since 1923

NEW YORK · LONDON

For information about permission to reproduce selections from this book, write to
Permissions, Liveright Publishing Corporation, a division of W. W. Norton & Company, Inc.,
500 Fifth Avenue, New York, NY 10110

For information about special discounts for bulk purchases, please contact
W. W. Norton Special Sales at specialsales@wwnorton.com or 800-233-4830

Manufacturing by Sheridan
Book design by Ellen Cipriano
Production manager: Anna Oler

Library of Congress Cataloging-in-Publication Data

Names: Kapilow, Robert, author.
Title: Listening for America : inside the great American songbook
from Gershwin to Sondheim / Rob Kapilow.
Description: First edition. | New York : Liveright Publishing Corporation, 2019. |
Includes bibliographical references and index.
Identifiers: LCCN 2019026121 | ISBN 9781631490293 (hardcover) |
ISBN 9781631490309 (epub)
Subjects: LCSH: Popular music—United States—History and criticism. | Songs—United
States—20th century—History and criticism. | Songs—United States—20th century—
Analysis, appreciation. | Musicals—United States—20th century—History and criticism.
Classification: LCC ML3477 .K363 2019 | DDC 782.421640973—dc23
LC record available at https://lccn.loc.gov/2019026121

Liveright Publishing Corporation, 500 Fifth Avenue, New York, N.Y. 10110
www.wwnorton.com

W. W. Norton & Company Ltd., 15 Carlisle Street, London W1D 3BS

1 2 3 4 5 6 7 8 9 0

This book is dedicated to anyone who has ever sat in
a darkened theater and felt themselves transported to
another world by that uniquely American art form:
the Broadway musical.

"Songs make history, and history makes songs."

—IRVING BERLIN

CONTENTS

PREFACE

I cannot imagine a more unlikely book for me to write than this one. When I began my career at the age of twenty-four as the conductor of the Yale Symphony Orchestra and an assistant professor of music at Yale, my sole focus was conducting, performing, and teaching the core repertoire of classical music. Though I grew up loving Broadway musicals and could play practically every show tune I had ever heard on the piano (and would do so for anyone whom I could force to listen), for the six years I spent teaching and conducting at Yale, classical music was my life.

In 1981, however, I was fortunate enough to become the conductor of the Tony Award–winning musical *Nine*. The thrill of conducting a live Broadway show with spectacular performers, superb pit musicians, and sold-out audiences was electrifying. Unlike my experiences in the concert hall, I felt an immediate connection with the audience, who clearly had a far greater understanding of Broadway's musical language than they did of Beethoven's. It was exhilarating. I realized how much I wanted to create the same kind of connection between classical music and its audience that I felt on Broadway, so I started a decade-long series of programs on NPR's

Performance Today called "What Makes It Great." Each week I took the radio audience deep inside a short segment of music—often no more than a few measures—to help them hear what made it tick and what made it great. I wanted listeners to notice all of the rich details that might normally fly right by them. I wanted them to learn the language of classical music, one measure and one great piece at a time.

I gradually expanded these radio programs into live, full-length performances in concert halls around the country. Each evening explored a single piece of classical music through discussion and demonstration with the hope that listeners would hear the music's richness with new ears. One of the most ardent supporters of these programs was Lincoln Center's Great Performers series, and after several years of six classical presentations a season, the producers of their American Songbook series approached me about doing something similar with Broadway repertoire. Though I had adored the music all my life, I had never thought to look closely to see what made it great. But after listening to the songs of composers like Gershwin, Porter, Kern, and Arlen as if they were written by Schubert, I was stunned. Not just by how superbly crafted they were, but by how much I had missed in songs that I had known by heart since I was twelve years old. I was sure that, like me, audiences were missing just as much in this music as they were in Beethoven symphonies. As I began hosting "What Makes It Great" programs that looked closely—word by word, chord by chord, and measure by measure—at four or five songs of Gershwin or Kern, I discovered that audiences were as amazed by the sophistication of these songs as I was.

For the next decade, alongside the classical "What Makes It Great" programs I was performing, the books and CDs on classical music I was writing and recording, and the new classical pieces I was composing, I chose one major Broadway composer to focus on each season. I analyzed hundreds of that composer's songs in order to create a single, evening-length program on their music. One year, I focused on Gershwin, followed by a year on Berlin, then Porter, Kern, Arlen, Rodgers, Bernstein, and Sondheim. In addition to immersing myself in each composer's music, I delved into their biographies, and each year the scope of my research widened. As I began to investigate cultural and historical context as well, I saw how deeply the American Songbook reflected—often in not immediately apparent ways—the times in which it evolved.

Combining a close-focus musical reading with a wide-angled historical point of view brought classic songs like "Over the Rainbow" or "Let's Do It" to life as if they were brand new. Like dusty Old Master paintings that had suddenly been cleansed of years of dirt and grime. Audiences seemed to be as amazed as I was to meet these great songs again as if for the first time: both as extraordinary music and as striking reflections of their contemporary worlds.

In writing this book, I have chosen to explore sixteen songs by eight of the greatest Broadway songwriters, from Kern to Sondheim—fourteen from Broadway shows and two from film musicals. Obviously, with so many songs to choose from, twenty more books could be written using different and equally great songs from each composer. I have chosen ones that speak most directly to me and ones that I feel can most deeply benefit from a close musical reading while also being put into some larger cultural context. When Irving Berlin's "White Christmas" became a symbol of American values for homesick GIs during World War II, Berlin explained that "songs make history, and history makes songs."[1] Focusing on the intersection between history and music—looking at these songs as both extraordinary musical compositions as well as deeply meaningful reflections of an evolving America finding its voice—is at the heart of this book.

A large portion of the music I will explore comes from a period that is often referred to as the Golden Age of the Broadway musical—roughly the years from the 1920s through the 1950s. The age of Kern, Berlin, Porter, Gershwin, Arlen, and Rodgers. Though this might seem to suggest a uniform, Edenic, static musical era, the period was actually bursting with dynamism. Much like America itself, Broadway was being invented moment-by-moment, song-by-song, scene-by-scene, show-by-show. As America emerged out of Europe's shadow and onto the world stage after World War I, the country tried to find an artistic voice of its own, and the Broadway musical was one of the first places this voice emerged. Painters, architects, writers, and composers were all listening for America, for the country's shape, texture, look, and sound. For its stories and its voice. And if we look at the songs of its greatest theater composers from the right angle, we too can listen for America inventing its identity as the country responded to the mind-boggling transformations of the Roaring Twenties, the Depression, World War II, and the postwar and Cold War years.

In a discussion of her book *Draw Your Weapons*, author Sarah Sentilles compares her approach to writing to that of Fred Wilson's 1992 art exhibit "Mining the Museum," in which he provocatively put disparate objects like a fine silver pitcher and goblet in a display case alongside a set of slave's shackles. Sentilles says that, like Wilson's exhibit, her book "tried to put pieces together that you wouldn't otherwise put together . . . [as] an invitation to think, and not a polemic."[2] Similarly, in my book I juxtapose the biography of the real Annie Oakley and Frank Butler with the version presented in *Annie Get Your Gun*, the reality of Depression-era America with the version presented in Gershwin's *Girl Crazy,* the advertisements of 1920s "girlie magazines" with the envelope-pushing morality of Cole Porter, and the actual facts about Puerto Rican gangs in 1950s New York City with *West Side Story* as an invitation to think, and not a polemic. Each chapter is an attempt to put pieces together that you wouldn't otherwise—to listen for America as it was being created out of the imaginations of these extraordinary songwriters.

It is my hope that in looking at these eight composers and sixteen songs through both ends of the telescope, so to speak—zooming in to focus closely on music and zooming out to a broader cultural perspective—that they will emerge as dazzlingly new for you as they have for me. These songs tell us about America then, but also about all of us now. They sing about our hopes and dreams, our longing for love, and the pain of loss. Faulkner says "the past is never dead, it's not even past." I hope that this book takes these classic songs out of a safe, comfortable, Golden Age past, and makes them as vibrantly alive as they were when their creators and the country were inventing who we are. When they were all listening for America.

A NOTE ON TECHNOLOGY AND AUDIENCE

For centuries, an author of a book on music had only two, equally problematic choices. If a book included musical notation, it eliminated readers without the training to read the notation. But excluding musical notation made any detailed discussion impossible. Something like writing a book about painting without pictures. Today, thanks to new technology, this is happily no longer the case. Though there are many musical examples in this book, *absolutely no knowledge of music whatsoever is necessary to read it.* Listeningforamerica.net provides recordings of every example synced to a moving scroll bar that lets you know exactly where you are. Comments and descriptions are written right onto the music, so that you can hear and understand precisely what is happening as it occurs.

I have also tried to avoid using confusing jargon; however, in order to make the book equally interesting for musicians or people with significant musical training, I have put more detailed technical explanations in footnotes or endnotes so as not to interfere with the narrative for the general reader. It is my hope that this book can be enjoyed by a casual listener with no prior musical knowledge as well as a musical-theater aficionado with extensive musical background. In the end, all you have to do is listen.

LISTENING
FOR AMERICA

Prologue
Nothing Comes from Nothing

Richard Rodgers wrote two new songs for the 1965 film version of *The Sound of Music*—"I Have Confidence," which the young nun Maria (Julie Andrews) sings to convince herself she's ready to serve as governess to the von Trapp children, and "Something Good."* Maria, unable to cope with her love for Captain von Trapp (Christopher Plummer), leaves the family under the advice of the jealous Baroness Elsa Schraeder (Eleanor Parker). Upon Maria's return to the convent, Mother Abbess learns that she is trying to escape her problems rather than face them, and encourages her to find a life beyond the walls of the abbey. Maria is heartbroken to learn that the Captain is going to marry the Baroness, but when it becomes clear that Maria is the one he loves, the Baroness gracefully ends the engagement. Astonished by her good fortune, Maria tries to imagine what she must have done to be worthy of such a man. She concludes that, since "nothing comes from nothing," and "nothing ever could," their love

---

* Oscar Hammerstein II, his writing partner of seventeen years, died in 1960, so the responsibility of writing the material fell entirely on Rodgers's shoulders.

could only be the result of some moment in her life when she "must have done something good."

These simple words—nothing comes from nothing—are of course a fundamental truth of all history, and represent one of the overarching themes of this book. Although we begin with music of the 1920s, a decade that saw America looking for an identity that could both reflect and distract from the unnerving realities of a bewildering, postwar world, everything occurs within a context. As radically new as the music of the Roaring Twenties was, it didn't come from nothing. We should therefore start with a quick overview of the "something" that came before it—the theatrical forms of the nineteenth and early twentieth centuries, as well as the African American influences that helped to shape America's evolving musical voice. (For those who want to skip this overview and dive right into the Great American Songbook—the heart of the book—you may jump to Chapter 1 and refer back to the Prologue as needed.)

MINSTREL SHOWS

"We must respect the past, remembering that once it was all that was humanly possible," wrote Spanish-born American philosopher George Santayana in 1940.[1] But parts of the past are easier to respect than others. There are some eras that require almost superhuman amounts of historical empathy, moments when it seems impossible to believe that we weren't morally capable of better. There is probably no greater error in the study of history than to bring the perspective of the present to the world of the past, but the appalling racism of white America during the eighteenth and nineteenth centuries is almost impossible to understand from a morally neutral point of view. Yet however distasteful and shockingly racist it might seem for white men to "cork up" (that is, use the burnt cork from a wine bottle to blacken their faces) before performing in minstrel shows, it represented an enormously popular phenomenon and helped pave the way for much of what was to come in vaudeville and musical theater.

For nearly a half century, from the 1840s to the 1890s, minstrel shows were the most popular form of entertainment in America.[2] They began with performances at the Bowery Theater in New York City during the 1842–43 season by a group of white entertainers known as Dan Emmett's Virginia Minstrels.[3] Although men had been performing in blackface for many years—including Thomas Dartmouth Rice's famous impersonation of Jim Crow—the Virginia Minstrels were the first group to create a full-length evening of entertainment where white northerners in blackface depicted southern, black plantation life through songs, dances, and skits. The idealized version of plantation life imagined in minstrel shows, in which happy black slaves loved their masters and spent their time singing, dancing, and joking, of course bore absolutely no resemblance to reality. Many white northerners, however, had no other contact with black reality, and the offensive caricatures of foot-shuffling, eye-rolling, illiterate, uppity, "happy-go-lucky darkies" would last perniciously well into the twentieth century.

Shortly after Emmett created the Virginia Minstrels, E. P. Christy launched the Christy Minstrels, which quickly became the most popular troupe in the country and gave the minstrel show its three-part structure. The action centered around Mr. Interlocutor—a pompous master of ceremonies—and his two End Men, Mr. Bones and Mr. Tambo, who provided comic interruptions and verbal repartee that anticipated many later comic duos like Laurel and Hardy, Abbott and Costello, and the Smothers Brothers. After a set of musical numbers interspersed with comic exchanges, the second part—called the olio—was essentially a miniature variety show filled with songs and novelty acts that could include everything from acrobats, jugglers, and dogs, to dancers, monologues, or even someone playing tuned water glasses. The third part usually involved a plantation-based skit mixing songs, dances, and dialogue, and sometimes a parody-lecture on a topic of the day (a "Negro Lecture on Locomotives," for example, was an early feature of the Emmett repertoire), followed by a walk-around, during which the cast would hold hands, sing, and dance the cakewalk[4]—an elaborate, high-stepping dance that, by the 1880s, had replaced the waltz as America's favorite dance. (In 1859, Emmett wrote his most famous song, "Dixie," for the Bryant's Minstrels' walk-around, and it eventually became an unofficial anthem for the Confederacy during the Civil War.)

Though everything about the minstrel show was unquestionably racist, looking at the origins of the cakewalk* gives us a sense of the complexity and subtlety of the relationship between blacks and whites in the minstrel tradition. The dance form actually began with slaves peeking through their masters' ballroom windows to watch them dance their marches, polkas, and waltzes. To make fun of the way they looked, the slaves imitated and exaggerated their masters' movements. This mimicry eventually became its own dance—the cakewalk. Their white masters then watched the slaves dancing and were so entertained that they started to copy their slaves' movements, not realizing they were copying a dance that was a parody of themselves. Whites, in effect, were imitating blacks who were imitating whites! As ironic as this was, it was only the first strand of minstrelsy's complex web of influence. Blacks, having seen whites' blackface imitation of them, thought they could do better. As the nineteenth century progressed, blacks started putting together their own minstrel troupes. But the only way whites would permit them on stage—they didn't want to see actual black skin—was if they corked up. This led to black men in blackface in black minstrel shows imitating what white men in blackface were doing in white minstrel shows, thereby perpetuating their own demeaning stereotypes and creating an absurd situation where blacks in blackface were imitating whites in blackface who were themselves imitating blacks who were imitating whites! At heart, these minstrel shows allowed white northerners who had no contact

---

* The dance was originally known as the "prize walk" with the prize being an elaborately decorated cake, hence the term "cakewalk."

with black people to reinforce their sense that they were fundamentally different from and inferior to whites. The version of blacks that they saw represented by minstrel shows allowed whites to dismiss all blacks as the uneducated, lazy, sly, cowardly stereotypes they saw on stage, and it would take years to alter these images in any significant way.

Though the musical instruments commonly used in minstrel shows—banjo, fiddle, tambourine, and bones (castanet-like clappers modeled on a plantation rhythm instrument made out of cows' ribs)—did have some connection to life on a southern plantation, the music itself did not. Audiences might have thought they were listening to America, but in fact they were listening to Europe. Nearly all of the music heard in minstrel shows was based in some way on European or European-derived music. Stephen Foster (1826–64), the most famous composer of the minstrel-show tradition, wrote for the Christy Minstrels for much of his short life. The first American composer to make his living solely from composing, Foster wrote songs and dance music that became a kind of American folk music. In spite of Foster's iconic American status, his music was influenced by Scottish and Irish dances, British ballads, Italian opera, German lieder, as well as by European parlor songs and folk songs. The themes, lyrics, and sentiments were American, the instrumentation in his minstrel-show music was African American, but the musical roots and influences were European.

As Foster's career illustrates, though the minstrel shows were profoundly racist, they had an undeniably positive side as well. Because of their enormous popularity and wide geographical appeal, they were pivotal in creating and promoting a popular repertoire of American-themed songs for America's first national audience. Minstrel shows went wherever there was a railroad station, and troupes brought their music with them to far-flung locales in a way that had previously been unimaginable. On a practical, commercial level, minstrelsy also developed the basic procedures and techniques necessary to produce, promote, and tour that would become the central foundation of vaudeville, and big-time American show business. Finally, and most ironically, a racist genre based on demeaning the entire African American race offered thousands of African Americans the opportunity to become singers, dancers, songwriters, and comedians at a time when those opportunities were reserved exclusively for whites. After the Civil War, freed slaves put on blackface, formed their own minstrel companies, and were able to make a living and somehow find a creative outlet within a belittling, demeaning genre. Eventually, this would lead to original music and shows written and composed by blacks—and the emergence of a black voice at the heart of twentieth-century popular music.

VAUDEVILLE

From the 1880s until the end of the 1920s, when radio and movies with sound captured the public's fancy, vaudeville (from the French *voix de ville*, or "voice of the city"[5]) was probably the most popular form of entertainment for most Americans. It offered something for everyone: shows included an enormous variety of short, unrelated acts (clearly derived from the olio portion of the minstrel shows) ranging from jugglers, magicians, animals, and acrobats, to dancers, comedians, dramatic recitations, and singers. A typical show—or bill, as they were called—would feature about a dozen different performances, repeating several times a day for about a week before moving on to a new town. Having some kind of unusual talent was the key to success in vaudeville, and a really fantastic short act could travel for years. One of the most unusual acts was Hadji Ali, "the Amazing Regurgitator," who swallowed objects like watermelon seeds, coins, and peach pits and then regurgitated them one by one on request from his audience.[6] Because no single performer had to sustain an audience's interest for more than ten minutes, vaudeville became a training ground where performers could practice their craft and develop their talent. Many of Broadway's biggest stars—

performers like George M. Cohan, Al Jolson, Bill "Bojangles" Robinson, and Danny Kaye—got their starts in vaudeville.

Historians generally credit the beginning of vaudeville to Tony Pastor, who opened his legendary vaudeville house in New York City on 14th Street in 1881.[7] Pastor's idea was to create a kind of variety entertainment that middle-class families could attend with their children, a clean show that would be a step above the vulgar entertainment seen in saloons and burlesque houses at the time. A clear sense of the theatrical environment of the times and the new role Pastor wanted to fill can be seen in the famous banner above his theater door. It read, "Entertainment Clean Enough for Women and Children," and promised that there would be no drinking, smoking, or swearing by the performers. Most important, pistols were to be checked at the door.

Pastor's preferred form of entertainment quickly caught on, and at the end of the nineteenth century, before recordings and radio entered the picture, vaudeville was the primary showcase for a songwriter's talents. Songwriters and publishers would convince leading vaudeville performers to sing their songs, and in turn performers would come to publishers and songwriters looking for fresh material. The entire popular-music industry—theater owners, performers, composers, and music publishers—worked together to create hits that would benefit them all. Their hope was that an audience member would hear a song he liked in a vaudeville show, purchase the sheet music at a music store, and play it on the piano for his friends at home, thereby expanding the reach of the song, the performer, the show, and the theater.

By the turn of the century, promoters had bought or built nationwide chains of vaudeville theaters, and by the time of World War I there were more than 2,000 vaudeville theaters stretching across the country.[8] This provided an unprecedented degree of stability for performers, who could now sign a contract for an entire year of employment on a given vaudeville circuit. There were white vaudeville circuits and black vaudeville circuits (the Theatre Owners Booking Association, or the Chitlin' Circuit), and some white circuits even allowed for a black act as well, particularly those employing black children. Vaudeville often provided an escape from the horrific working conditions in urban nineteenth-century sweatshops, and for child stars like George M. Cohan and Eddie Cantor, who started performing at an early age, the theater offered a far-more-attractive alternative financially and socially to the lives they would otherwise have been forced to lead. Silent films, radio, and finally talking pictures put an end to vaudeville, but long before it actually died, it had already largely been subsumed and replaced by another important form, Irving Berlin's favorite—the revue.

REVUES

Until Rodgers and Hammerstein changed the basic template of musical theater in the 1940s and '50s, revues were one of the most popular theatrical forms on Broadway. Revues made no attempt to integrate their songs into an ongoing plot, though occasionally there might be some kind of overriding theme to unify the evening. This made it easy for performers to shuttle back and forth between Broadway revues and vaudeville since, like vaudeville, each performance in a revue was fundamentally a self-contained act. This also made revues far easier for producers to assemble than book musicals. Without the constraints of plot, character development, or unity of tone, it was easy to change the order of songs or even to substitute other songs at a moment's notice. (A particularly generous investor could even be rewarded for his financial assistance with a song for his aspiring-actress girlfriend or mistress. It was newspaper magnate William Randolph Hearst who convinced Florenz Ziegfeld to give Marion Davies, an unknown chorus girl at the time, a role in Ziegfeld's *Follies*.) A revue might have several different composers, with new ones brought in if the original songs didn't work. Because of this, revues provided a crucial point of entry into the theatrical world for inexperienced songwriters not yet ready to write a full-length musical. They offered many young songwriters their first chance to get a song into a show, and a single successful song interpolated in a high-profile revue could launch an entire career. Perhaps equally important to songwriters, a revue offered them the opportunity to create a song with no ties to any particular character or situation. A song that could stand on its own as an independent work and be sung outside the context of the show in any situation whatsoever.

During the 1920s, nearly 120 different revues opened on Broadway.[9] Irving Berlin created a series of *Music Box Revues* for his own Music Box Theatre from 1921 to 1924. The dancer George White started his *George White's Scandals* in 1919 using a single composer for each of his thirteen yearly presentations. Earl Carroll produced eleven editions of his titillating *Earl Carroll's Vanities,* which featured almost completely nude showgirls in probably the raciest of all the Broadway revues. All-black revues like the *Blackbirds* brought some of the most important black talent of the era to Broadway. Rodgers and Hart got their start in a 1925 revue, the *Garrick Gaieties*, which gave them their first hit song, "Manhattan." But the most important revues of them all were the legendary revues of Florenz Ziegfeld: The *Ziegfeld Follies*.

Florenz Ziegfeld's *Follies*, which ran annually from 1907 to 1927, raised the form of the revue to its highest and most exquisite level. His extravagant revues had the most elaborate costumes, the most stunning sets, the most beautiful women, the most gifted comedians, the finest dancers, and the most expensive acts in show business. Inspired by the Parisian *Folies Bergère* but actually named after a New York newspaper column called "Follies of the Day," Ziegfeld's *Follies* set the standard for theatrical glamor on Broadway. Though he had no actual knowledge or skill as a writer, composer, designer, or director, Ziegfeld had superb taste, an uncanny sense of what made a production work, an obsessive focus on detail, an innate feel for what his audiences wanted, and a phenomenal gift for publicity.

One of his first clients was the German strongman Eugen Sandow, whom Ziegfeld brought to the 1892 Chicago World's Fair, touting him as the world's most perfectly proportioned male. Business was weak until Ziegfeld tricked a prominent Chicago socialite into touching Sandow's bicep and having the photograph circulated in the Chicago newspapers.[10] He also managed to convince New York audiences that his wife Anna Held, a Hungarian Jew, was a quintessential French beauty who bathed daily in milk. After the milkman brought a libel suit against her for claiming he supplied her with sour milk, Ziegfeld used the publicity to save her first show, *A Parlor Match*.[11] In addition to his gifts for publicity and spectacle, he had vision and courage, hiring the brilliant comedian Bert Williams in 1910 to become the first black man to costar on Broadway with white performers. Ziegfeld's business card referred to him as "Impresario Extraordinaire," and in many ways he created the template for the modern superstar producer.

The list of performers he hired for the various *Follies* productions included nearly every star of the era—Marilyn Miller, Eddie Cantor, Fanny Brice, Nora Bayes, Billie Burke, Will Rogers, W. C. Fields, Ann Pennington, and Sophie Tucker. Ziegfeld described his mission as "glorifying the American Girl,"[12] but perhaps a more accurate description would be "inventing the American Girl." At a time when magazines like the *Ladies' Home Journal* were setting new standards for what Americans' homes should look like, how they should dress, and what they should read, Ziegfeld was setting a new standard of female sexuality and creating an image of a refined ideal of female beauty that would last for years to come.

Ziegfeld's fall was as spectacular as his rise. His fortune was nearly wiped out by the stock market crash of 1929, and his health soon began to deteriorate. Several final projects failed dismally, and he died in 1932, penniless and disgraced. But the theatrical form he had done so much to elevate and perfect—the revue—would live long after his death and have a major impact on how songwriters, directors, and producers thought about their craft.

OPERETTA

Before World War I, the theater scene in America was incredibly diverse, with a wide variety of musical presentations vying for different kinds of audiences. There were vaudeville houses all over the country, while on Broadway there were revues, musicals with plots (though interpolated songs often rendered these plots superfluous), musicals with little or no story whatsoever, and operettas. Before America began finding its own voice, it adopted one from Europe, inspired by the comic operettas of Offenbach, Gilbert and Sullivan, Lehár, and Johann Strauss. Many of these were brought over intact, translated, or lightly adapted, but home-grown imitations quickly followed. (Victor Herbert, the dean of American operetta, wrote more than forty.) For the first two decades of the twentieth century, operetta was unquestionably one of America's most popular forms of musical theater.

Nearly everything about these European operettas—their music, lyrics, settings, performers, and orchestrations—was antithetical to the newly emerging American voice. Their plots tended to take place in non-American settings—exotic European locations, fictitious countries, or romanticized pasts—and involved non-American characters—kings, princes, duchesses, Gypsy girls, and the like. The subject matter and the language of dialogue and lyrics was the opposite of colloquial American English, filled with romantic, highly sentimental diction like these lines from Lehár's popular 1905 operetta *The Merry Widow*: "The night is romantic and I am alone. / In vain through my window the moonlight is thrown. / 'Oh, Vilia my Vilia!' Oh yes, that's the tune, / The song of the shepherd who cried for the moon." Characters spoke in a language filled with words like "evermore," "nigh," and "betide," and the lyrical, lushly romantic music was filled with European-style waltzes and marches. The string-dominated orchestra invariably included a harp, and the performers were almost always classically trained singers, as opposed to American musical-comedy singers like

George M. Cohan, who made up for his lack of musical training with enormous charisma and communicative ability.[13]

At the beginning of the twentieth century, most of the imported operettas and the models for American imitations came from England or France, but the phenomenal success of Franz Lehár's *The Merry Widow* in the 1907–8 season—the show ran for 416 performances—shifted the focus to Vienna, inspiring a number of imitation Viennese operettas for the next seven years. For audiences who found burlesque and vaudeville too lowbrow and the world of opera too highbrow, operetta offered the perfect middle ground. An escape into a sentimental world of romance and fantasy with relatively sophisticated music and language that was lighter, entertaining, and more immediately accessible than opera. Operetta's popularity, however, was abruptly brought to an end by the onset of World War I. Suddenly, saccharine, mawkish love stories about European princes and duchesses seemed grotesquely inappropriate when so many people were being killed on the battlefield. And as Germany more and more became the hated enemy, banishing Viennese operettas and their clones from American theaters became almost a patriotic act. In a behavior that eerily anticipated the Bush-era foolishness that turned French fries into freedom fries, World War I turned sauerkraut into liberty cabbage and hamburgers into liberty sandwiches.

By 1917, European operettas had vanished from Broadway stages, giving Americans like Jerome Kern and Irving Berlin an opportunity to fill the void with authentically American productions in an authentically American idiom. But shortly after the Armistice ending the war was finally signed, a wave of nostalgia for the imagined good-old days, as well as a desire to escape from war and postwar realities, swept over the country, and operetta made a surprising comeback during the 1920s. European émigrés Rudolf Friml, who came to New York from Prague in 1906, and Sigmund Romberg, who arrived from Bucharest in 1909, composed a string of phenomenally successful operettas in the 1920s, often working with Oscar Hammerstein II on productions like *Rose-Marie* (1924), *The Desert Song*

(1925), and *The New Moon* (1927–28). That these romantic throwbacks to a Eurocentric age could be so successful at the same time that Kern, Gershwin, Berlin, and Rodgers and Hart were inventing an American voice—one expressly designed to reject everything operettas stood for—should serve as an important reminder that history is never neat and tidy. The simple stories we tell ourselves rarely do justice to the messiness of the real world.

RAGTIME

Though ragtime may have entered many people's consciousness with the phenomenal success of Irving Berlin's "Alexander's Ragtime Band" in 1911, Berlin never claimed that he was writing genuine ragtime. In fact, he said he never discovered what ragtime really was. Because the fluid borrowing of music was such an important feature of the black-white dialogue of the twentieth century, precisely defining musical styles like ragtime, blues, jazz, swing, rhythm and blues, and rock and roll can be challenging, if not impossible.

Though black pianists began playing ragtime in brothels and wherever they traveled in the 1890s, the idea began much earlier. "Ragging" referred to a particular way of performing a piece of music, altering and syncopating a preexisting song. In a travelogue published in 1876, the Georgia-born poet Sidney Lanier remarked, "Syncopations are characteristic of Negro music. I have heard Negroes change a well-known melody by adroitly syncopating it . . . so as to give it a bizarre effect scarcely imaginable."[14] In the same way that eighteenth-century performers of Baroque music would elaborately decorate and ornament preexisting pieces, black performers would rag preexisting melodies. Taking an improvised tradition and freezing it in notated form is a practice as old as music itself. It can be seen in the development of Baroque and Javanese gamelan music, as well as ragtime, jazz, and blues. Bach's contemporaries complained that he stifled creativity by writing out all the ornaments and decorations in his music, leaving no room for performers to improvise. In a sense, that is what happened to ragtime as well. Once this kind of freely improvised ragging became a familiar sound, pieces began to be composed in a ragged style. Composers wrote syncopations and decorations into their music rather than allowing performers to improvise them freely. But even after rags were published in sheet music form, professionals continued to improvise on, or "fake," the pieces themselves (the origin of the term "fake book"), resulting in what was really an early form of jazz.

Many Americans heard ragtime for the first time at the 1893 Chicago World's Fair, and by 1899, when Scott Joplin published his wildly popular "Maple Leaf Rag," more than one hundred piano rags had been published. By 1900, lyrics were being added to these ragtime pieces, and the largely racist, demeaning language of these new songs made them extremely popular with whites. In 1911, Irving Berlin's "Alexander's Ragtime Band" took a genre that had started in brothels and dives and made it respectable and stylish. In what would become a recurring phenomenon throughout the century, whites took music that started in the black community and disseminated it in a domesticated form, making it an essential component of mainstream America's musical voice.

Ragtime brought with it a completely new kind of dancing as well. Before ragtime, the waltz, both as a dance and a kind of song (think "Bicycle Built for Two" or "The Sidewalks of New York") dominated the musical landscape. Though the waltz had itself been risqué when it replaced the minuet early in the nineteenth century, by 1900 it had become as old-fashioned as the minuet once was, and the difference between its smooth, romantic, European gentility and the shocking American physicality of the ragtime dances coming out of the black community was nothing short of staggering. The Charleston, the Black Bottom, the Turkey Trot, and the Grizzly Bear were primal, sexual in a way that scandalized (and excited) not just those with Victorian inhibitions but even "modern" New Yorkers. A New Jersey woman was given a fifty-day prison sentence for dancing the Turkey Trot,[15] and politicians and newspapers throughout the country railed against these dances' vulgarity, certain they would corrupt the nation's youth. But the power of the music was overwhelming, and it eventually overrode all inhibitions. This too began a pattern that would repeat throughout the century, in which nearly every popular style of music originating from the black community—ragtime, jazz, blues, bebop, swing, rock and roll, and rap—would initially be condemned by whites who feared it would corrupt their children, only to be embraced, appropriated, and ultimately assimilated into the mainstream.

BLUES

Scott Joplin's death in 1917 is often used as a convenient date to mark the end of the ragtime era, but by then, many of ragtime's essential musical features were already being absorbed into a new style called jazz. At the same time, another great contribution of the black community, the blues, was also entering America's consciousness. Like ragtime and jazz, the blues too would be modified, domesticated, and ultimately absorbed into the musical language of the Broadway musical and American popular song.

The blues began in the rural South and was brought north as part of the Great Migration, when a half-million African Americans moved to northern cities like New York, Chicago, and Detroit during and immediately after World War I. (Historians generally put the total figures of the Great Migration at approximately 1.5 million for the first wave of migration from 1916–1940, and more than 6 million between 1916 and 1970.) The roots of the blues were oral, but its spread to the culture at large really began when the music began to be notated, most famously by W. C. Handy, the so-called Father of the Blues, whose "Memphis Blues" of 1912 and "St. Louis

Blues" of 1914 started a fad that inspired large numbers of songwriters to publish their own bluesy pieces.

The appropriation of the blues by whites began quickly; the first jazz record ever made, the "Livery Stable Blues," was produced by a white group, the Original Dixieland Jazz Band, in February 1917. Many other white imitations followed, like the "Limehouse Blues" and the "Birth of the Blues" (not to mention Gershwin's *Rhapsody in Blue*), and eventually black versions of the blues were recorded as well. In 1920, Mamie Smith's first blues recording, "Crazy Blues," convinced producers that there might be a market for what were then called "race records"—records made exclusively for blacks but that were often bought by whites as well. Her recordings, along with those of other black women like Ma Rainey, helped spread the blues to white listeners throughout the 1920s.

Aside from the simplicity of the basic 12-bar, three-chord format, what drew songwriters and America to the blues was the power and authenticity of its expression. On the simplest level, the blues told the story of a black man or woman who had the "blues." A woman like the woman in the "St. Louis Blues," who sings:

> *I hate to see that evening sun go down*
> *I hate to see that evening sun go down*
> *'Cause my lovin' baby done left this town. . . .*

> *I got those St. Louis blues, just as blue as I can be*
> *Oh, my man's got a heart like a rock cast in the sea*
> *Or else he wouldn't have gone so far from me.*

The blues was a wail, a lament, an outpouring of sadness that came straight from the heart. It told stories of trouble and pain in an honest, unsentimental, world-weary, often sexual way, and all the striking musical features of the blues that white songwriters ultimately appropriated for their own purposes—the shouts, the flattened blues notes, the bent pitches, slides, and vocal cries—grew directly out of a deep emotional heartache at the music's core. The blues brought a profoundly new kind of emotional expression and style of speech to popular music from a source that was utterly American in origin and completely independent of any musical or verbal association with Europe. Like ragtime, the blues was American, and it was the foundation for much of the popular music that would follow.

JAZZ

If Irving Berlin made ragtime respectable, Gershwin did the same for jazz. Howard Pollack's biography of Gershwin quotes the avant-garde composer Henry Cowell's witty 1931 description of jazz as "Negro minstrel music as interpreted by Tin Pan Alley New Yorkers of Hebrew origin,"[16] and though almost none of the music written by the composers in this book could legitimately be called jazz, the influence of jazz on the language of popular song was immense. Gershwin, Arlen, and later Leonard Bernstein had considerable firsthand experience hearing great black jazz artists perform, but most white songwriters' knowledge of jazz was really only second- or thirdhand. In spite of the fact that F. Scott Fitzgerald famously called the 1920s "the Jazz Age," no one seemed able to agree on what that meant or what was or wasn't real jazz. Like ragtime and blues, indefinite origins, blurred genre lines, and the mixing of different musical styles make any single definition of jazz nearly impossible, but there is no doubt that the jazz of black musicians helped give the Broadway musical a language and identity that was independent of Europe and authentically American.

Though jazz originally grew up in New Orleans out of a complex mixture of black spirituals, gospel songs, blues, ragtime, and marches, the same massive black migrations that brought the blues north and west around the time of World War I brought jazz along as well. According to jazz historians Hasse and Lathrop, the earliest officially authenticated use of the word "jazz" in print was in a San Francisco newspaper in 1913, and multiple spellings of the word—"jas," "jass," "jaz" or "jazz"—coexisted until 1918. Adding to the confusion, until the 1920s many New Orleans musicians called what we today would refer to as early jazz, ragtime. In yet another case of whites appropriating black musical culture, jazz first became widely known through the popular recordings of the aforementioned, all-white Original Dixieland Jazz Band, beginning in 1917. It was not until 1923 when King Oliver's Creole Jazz Band began to make their first recordings for Gennett Records, followed by Louis Armstrong's legendary Hot Five and Hot Seven recordings for Okeh Records from 1925 to 1928, that black jazz began to reach the general public. (In another example of the fluid, complex, black-white relationship of musical influence, King Oliver actually owned a large collection of the Original Dixieland Jazz Band's recordings.) Though King Oliver's and Armstrong's recordings—like those of Duke Ellington, Bessie Smith, and Jelly Roll Morton that followed—were originally considered race records and sold only in black markets, they eventually broke through to white markets as well. Initially, jazz spread through a combination of sheet music, player-piano rolls, and the early recordings of the late teens and twenties. However, after an initial reluctance to air jazz due to its supposed inappropriateness, it was the explosion of radio as a mass medium in the middle of the 1920s that ultimately brought jazz to listeners everywhere and made it a truly national phenomenon. For many white Americans, hearing Duke Ellington's performances at the Cotton Club broadcast on the radio was their first exposure to both black performers and "authentic" jazz. The 1920s also took jazz overseas to an enthusiastic European audience, and during the swing era of the 1930s, jazz would enjoy perhaps its widest mainstream exposure. The swing craze would bring performers and audiences of all races together in numbers that remained unequaled before the arrival of rock and roll. The era would also see the transformation of many earlier popular songs into jazz standards, giving them a new and different life and challenging our fundamental conception of what constitutes a song.

Though jazz had an enormous influence on popular songs, their histories are fundamentally different, and the gap between popular music and genuine jazz grew larger and larger as time passed. But in the 1920s, jazz provided the characteristic sound of the era, and the two forms came as close together as at any moment in their histories. Jazz musicians played in Broadway pit orchestras, and Broadway composers wrote music for black performers at the Cotton Club. Jazz's defining instrument, the saxophone, replaced the European sound of the violin as the dominating sound of the popular-music orchestra. It was sensuous, earthy, and enormously emotional, and it changed the entire expression and sound of American orchestras. Jazz said "no" to an Old World European sense of romance and "yes" to the new world of the flappers, bathtub gin, and the Roaring Twenties. Though no one might have been able to precisely define just what jazz was— white bandleader Paul Whiteman called it "the folk music of the machine age"[17]—its sound was in the air. Its spirit spread throughout the culture. If something was a little dull or behind the times, the antidote was to "jazz it up a bit." It was a noun. It was a verb. It was everywhere, and though most of the Broadway music of the 1920s and '30s was more "jazzy" than jazz, it was inescapably shaped by this brash, vital, energetic sound sweeping the country and emerging as a defining element of America's newly invented voice.

1

Inventing America

Jerome Kern's "Can't Help Lovin' Dat Man"

The 1946 film version of Jerome Kern's life, *Till the Clouds Roll By*, is essentially told in flashback form. It begins on the opening night of *Show Boat*, Kern's legendary 1927 musical, with a magnificent, if truncated, *Reader's Digest* version of the premiere. After recounting his pre–*Show Boat* career for nearly two hours, the flashback segment of the film ends with a melodramatic scene in which Kern, lost in thought, walks along the banks of the Mississippi River in Memphis, Tennessee. As the camera focuses more and more closely on Kern's face, he says with increasing intensity and emotion:

> I walked along the river that night with the river wind in my face and the taste of it on my lips, and I stood there listening.
>
> *A tiny scrap of "Ol' Man River" is heard murkily in the low brass. The music of, "You an' me, we sweat an' strain, body all achin' an' racked wid' pain."*

A sudden excitement—thrilling for me—listening to the sound of a river that makes its way right through the heart of America. And the voice of that river with the laughter and the tears and the joys and sorrows and the hopes of all America's people.

> *The musical fragment starts to clarify itself and rises in pitch, louder now, as if the beginnings of an idea are forming in Kern's imagination. Suddenly a majestic show boat with smoke billowing out its smokestacks floats into the frame—a riverboat that looks suspiciously like Cap'n Andy's* Cotton Blossom *on the cover of Edna Ferber's novel* Show Boat. *As the music rises still louder and higher, trumpets and full orchestra enter triumphantly with the opening phrase of "Ol' Man River" underlining Kern's final speech as if the idea for* Show Boat *came from the river itself.*

As the music fades, the two-hour flashback ends, and the film returns us to reality: Kern, played by Robert Walker, in a taxicab with a driver named Joe (wittily the name of the character who sings "Ol' Man River") is on the way to *Show Boat*'s opening night party at the Waldorf Astoria. The scene in which the idea for the show comes to Kern as he walks along the banks of the Mississippi River and happens to see a riverboat pass by has a satisfying if highly melodramatic logic. Its intensity feels appropriately climactic, as it concludes one of the film's central dramatic arcs.

One of the principal characters in the film is Jim Hessler, Kern's lifelong mentor and musical companion. During the flashback, we see Kern as a beginning songwriter come to Hessler's home asking for advice. Though Hessler is initially dismissive of the young composer, a performance of one of his early songs convinces Hessler that Kern has the potential to become a famous songwriter. The two become close friends, and Kern becomes "Uncle Jerry" to Hessler's young daughter Sally. After the appropriate period of trials and tribulations that every young composer must undergo in a film biography,

Kern becomes a success, while Sally turns into an aspiring actress and singer. Kern, who has been helping her career along, gives her her first big break—the title song in his new musical, *Sunny*. But when the producer assigns the song to Marilyn Miller instead, Sally is heartbroken, quits the musical, and ends all contact with both her father and Kern. Shortly afterward, Hessler dies of heart failure, and in a poignant deathbed scene, Kern promises to search for Sally, reestablish contact, and make sure that she's all right.

Hessler's death, as well as his guilt over the break with Sally, plunges Kern into a deep depression, and he loses all will to compose. Oscar Hammerstein II visits and brings along Edna Ferber's novel, *Show Boat*, which he enthusiastically suggests they turn into a musical, but Kern is unable to even feign interest. Time passes; Kern continues to be lost in despair, until one day he learns that Sally is singing in a nightclub in Memphis—the Club Elite. He immediately travels to Memphis, makes peace with Sally backstage, and with his deathbed pledge to his friend fulfilled, his depression lifts. He leaves the nightclub and walks along the Mississippi River. With his personal problems resolved, his creativity is restored, and the idea for "Ol' Man River" and *Show Boat* rises triumphantly out of the moment and the Mississippi River itself.

Though the scene is enormously satisfying emotionally, unfortunately, every aspect of it, and for that matter nearly everything else in the film, is completely fictional. Jim Hessler, Kern's mentor, musical comrade, and constant companion throughout the film never existed (though in some small way he might have been modeled on the Broadway arranger Frank Saddler, a close friend and frequent orchestrator of Kern's shows). Hessler's daughter Sally, also never existed, while Kern's actual daughter, Betty, receives no mention in the film whatsoever. But most important, the entire scene on the banks of the Mississippi River—the supposed genesis of "Ol' Man River" and *Show Boat*—is complete invention. Neither Kern nor Oscar Hammerstein II ever actually saw the Mississippi River. Nor did Edna Ferber, who wrote the novel that the musical is based on. She wrote the book while in Spain at the Golf Hotel,[1] and

Kern wrote the music to this quintessential depiction of early American life on the banks of the Mississippi River from his studio in Bronxville, New York.

It's ultimately not that surprising that this romanticized view of life on the Mississippi River was created by three people who never actually saw it.[2] The South has continually been the source of reinvention both for actual southerners—like Margaret Mitchell, whose *Gone with the Wind* invented a Civil War South that existed only in her imagination—as well as for northerners like George Gershwin and Irving Caesar, who created their banjo-strumming, mammy-waiting Dixie in "Swanee," having never been farther south than the southern tip of Manhattan. (For a country with no ancient history, this kind of mythical southern past has often served as something like an American, pastoral version of a before-the-Fall Garden of Eden.) It takes an enormous amount of artistic self-confidence to create works like *Gone with the Wind*, "Swanee," *Appalachian Spring, Billy the Kid, Show Boat, Oklahoma!* and "White Christmas" purely out of one's imagination, yet it is exactly this kind of self-confidence that was at the heart of America's ability to invent its own musical voice in the twentieth century. That this voice developed at this particular moment in America's history was no accident. The emergence of music that sounded distinctly American, particularly in the realm of the Broadway musical, was deeply connected to historical, political, economic, social, cultural, and technological developments occurring in America at the time. Placing the music of this era in this kind of rich context allows us to listen to this music and our history in new and surprising ways.

Like so many of the songwriters of the Great American Songbook, Jerome Kern was Jewish. But unlike most of them, he was neither poor nor born on the Lower East Side of New York City.[3] His father, Henry Kern, was a prosperous German business owner, and the family was part of a kind of new Jewish American aristocracy. The Germanic culture of Kern's parents would remain a lifelong influence, and Kern's music had a refined elegance and Old

World gentility that clearly distinguished it from the brash, upbeat, hard-edged sound of Gershwin and Irving Berlin. In many ways, Kern, a patrician New York Jew, seems like an unlikely candidate to be the motivating force behind the first truly successful, racially integrated musical on Broadway, not to mention a musical that deals with racial bigotry and includes black performers who play nonstereotypical, three-dimensional characters.

Unlike Berlin and Gershwin, whose careers were launched in meteoric fashion by the spectacular success of a single song—"Alexander's Ragtime Band" for Berlin and "Swanee" for Gershwin—Kern found his voice slowly. Though he had more formal training than many of his fellow songwriters (with studies in theory, harmony, counterpoint, and piano at the New York College of Music and in Germany), like so many other aspiring songwriters, he began his career as an accompanist and song plugger—a pianist or singer hired by a music publisher to demonstrate, or "plug," a publisher's songs to performers, managers, and producers. At the time, America's voice in the musical theater was largely a European one, with foreign plays and operettas dominating the musical landscape throughout the first two decades of the twentieth century. The comic operettas of Gilbert and Sullivan and Offenbach served as models for countless imported and Americanized versions, and it was in this world that Kern first found his voice.

Unlike true operettas, which typically took place in exotic European locales in a fantasy realm of kings, princes, duchesses, and Gypsy girls, British musicals at the turn of the century were concocted out of a mixture of Gilbert and Sullivan, continental operettas, and vaudeville. They replaced the operetta's world of dukes and duchesses with a more realistic, recognizable world of shop owners and chorus girls. For almost a decade, Kern frustratingly interpolated nearly a hundred songs into thirty of these musicals with only modest success. In a sense, it was World War I that gave both Kern and America an opportunity to find their voices: "They Didn't Believe Me" from *The Girl from Utah* gave Kern his first big hit in 1914. Yet nothing in this song's lovely mixture of Old World European sophistication and American innocence, or the famous Princess Theatre shows of the next five years,[4] nor even in his hit shows of the early 1920s like *Sally* and *Sunny* gave any indication of what was to come in *Show Boat*.

Having spent many of his formative years as a songwriter in London, Kern had quickly become a master at mimicking the language of contemporary English musicals. Though this British influence would always remain a part of his voice, like many American artists in the teens and twenties, Kern was interested in finding an American voice. Having initially been founded as a British colony, our earliest cultural identity was predominantly British (still visible in the English spelling Americans tend to use when referring to musical "theatre" as opposed to "theater"), but once independence had been declared, we were cast adrift with no traditions or body of culture that had been handed down from generation to generation for centuries. Though there was of course a rich, ancient, indigenous Native American culture, it largely existed in its own parallel universe, and little attempt was made to integrate it into mainstream American artistic life. What culture did exist was largely a mixture of fragments of diverse immigrant cultures that the continual waves of new settlers kept bringing to America with them, and of course African American culture.

In the absence of a centuries-old musical heritage, African American music became perhaps America's most vital, authentic, homegrown musical source. For decades prior to World War I, white America created mainstream versions of African American forms of cultural expression, beginning with minstrel shows. As the twentieth century progressed and composers began searching for an American voice that could serve as an alternative to the Eurocentric operettas and musicals that dominated Broadway stages, multiple forms of black music became key source material. Black religious music—spirituals, hymns, and gospel songs—as well as blues, ragtime, and jazz all became important, largely uncredited influences on the emerging American musical. *Show Boat* broadly and "Can't Help Lovin' Dat Man" in particular are inextricably bound up with African American music and culture as refracted through a northern white American's eyes.

෨෨

Show Boat was not only the greatest achievement of Kern's theatrical career, it was and is a landmark in the history of the American musical theater. In much the same way that the birth of Jesus can divide chronological time into B.C. and A.D., the timeline of musical theater has traditionally been divided into before *Show Boat* and after *Show Boat*. The show radically widened the dramatic range of the Broadway musical with a story line that dealt with serious issues like miscegenation, alcoholism, racial injustice, compulsive gambling, and desertion. Its plot was utterly unlike the light, escapist plots of other contemporary musicals, and its approach to character development was more like that of a novel or play. Musically speaking, *Show Boat* was an extraordinary mixture of an operetta and a musical. Kern's score managed to mix a wide variety of American vernacular styles ranging from nineteenth-century minstrel shows, historical pastiches, and operetta-like waltzes and ballads; to blues, work songs, jazz, and 1920s popular song. The show was not only dramatically and musically groundbreaking, it was culturally groundbreaking as well, as it was the first musical to present a black and white chorus singing together on a Broadway stage. In short, *Show Boat*'s seriousness of tone and expanded sense of dramatic possibility created a precedent that ultimately allowed other revolutionary musicals to follow.[5]

Race is a central theme in *Show Boat* in ways that were startling for its time. It featured major black characters, and racial issues were central to the plot as well as to the music. "Can't Help Lovin' Dat Man" actually turns on the relationship between black music and white music. The published sheet music begins with an unusual tempo marking that directly reflects Kern's and other white composers' appropriation of black music. Mixing Italian and English words, the marking reads, "Tempo di Blues." That is, tempo of the blues. Europe meets America. Both Hammerstein's lyrics *and* Kern's music attempt to imitate black vernaculars. From the very beginning, the *Show Boat* sheet music listed the song titles in dialect as "Ol' Man River" and "Can't

Help Lovin' Dat Man." But the theater programs and theater critics used more "correct" spellings—"Old Man River" and "Can't Help Lovin' That Man." In a sense, the question of whom this music belongs to is what the song and plot are all about. "Can't Help Lovin' Dat Man" not only begins in the "Tempo di Blues," it actually begins with a white composer's version of the 12-bar blues.

The 12-bar blues began as a southern black form—a wail, a complaint—which was then appropriated, notated, and made mainstream by white musicians. It is the foundation for a great deal of early rock and roll; Elvis Presley's "Hound Dog" is a great example. Though the form eventually became richly decorated and varied, at heart the 12-bar blues uses only three simple chords in a fixed sequence that you might call "home," "away," and "farther away." (In musical terms we call them I, IV, and V because they're based on the first, fourth, and fifth degrees of the scale.) I've sketched the basic pattern in Example 1.1: 4 measures of I (home), 2 measures of IV (away), 2 measures of I (home), 2 measures of V (farther away), and then 2 measures of I (home). In short: I–I–I–I–IV–IV–I–I–V–V–I–I. A home-centered form of 12 measures with two brief journeys away. Home–away–home–farther away–home. (In rock and roll, the 2 measures of V are often replaced by 1 measure of V and 1 measure of IV for variety, as in mm. 9 and 10 of Ex. 1.1.)

Example 1.1 12-bar blues form

Like so many blues singers throughout history, Julie La Verne, the leading lady aboard the *Cotton Blossom* showboat, is complaining about love while somehow accepting the inevitability of the pain it brings. Magnolia Hawks, an aspiring singer and eighteen-year-old daughter of the boat's owner, Cap'n Andy Hawks, has just met and instantly fallen in love with a handsome riverboat gambler, Gaylord Ravenal. Julie warns her of the dangers of falling for this kind of riverboat stranger, to which Magnolia replies that if she discovered he was no good, she would simply stop loving him. Julie tells her that it's not so simple to stop loving someone. No matter what happens (and tragic events will in fact soon happen), Julie will always love her husband, Steve Baker. She simply "can't help lovin' dat man of mine."

The key to "Can't Help Lovin' Dat Man" is the fact that, with one tiny variation, its verse is a perfect 12-bar blues. (Since the basic form starts with 4 bars of the same chord, Kern, like many composers, decorates the pattern in the second measure for variety. See Ex. 1.2)

Example 1.2 12-bar blues in "Can't Help Lovin' Dat Man"

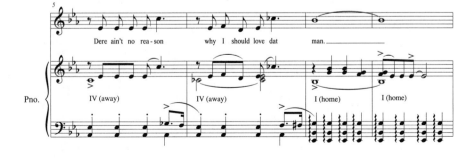

Example 1.2 12-bar blues in "Can't Help Lovin' Dat Man" (*continued*)

But it's not only the harmonic pattern that comes directly from the blues; the melody also uses classic blues notes—flatted notes—borrowed directly from rural, southern blues. Without blues notes, the opening phrase would sound bland and generic, as in Example 1.3A. But it's the blues notes on "sis-" and "Mis-" that make it great (see Ex. 1.3B). They particularize the

Example 1.3A "Can't Help Lovin' Dat Man," Kapilow version

Example 1.3B "Can't Help Lovin' Dat Man," Kern version

relationship between Julie and her "sister" and show the pain and mixed emotions aroused by her "Mister."

Underneath the vocal line, the piano gives the music warmth, the unique mixture of love and pain at the heart of the blues, showing how Julie feels about her "Mister man"—her husband and the troupe's leading man. In Example 1.4A, I've stripped out the blues notes. As a result, the accompaniment lacks all feeling, even though the melody is unchanged. It's Kern's dissonances in the piano part that give the music its emotional power (see asterisks highlighting the descending line in the right hand in Ex. 1.4B).

Details are everything. The difference between a good song and a great one is both enormous and infinitesimal. It's hundreds of small, inspired choices made by a songwriter and lyricist, note by note, word by word, rhythm by rhythm, chord by chord. Kern, for example, could easily have kept the voice

Example 1.4A "Can't Help Lovin' Dat Man," Kapilow version

Example 1.4B "Can't Help Lovin' Dat Man," Kern version

Example 1.5A "Can't Help Lovin' Dat Man," Kapilow version

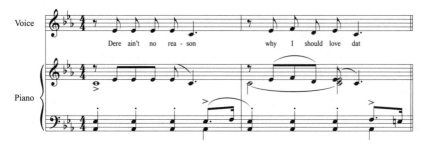

Example 1.5B "Can't Help Lovin' Dat Man," Kern version

blandly in the low register for "Dere ain't no reason why I should love dat" (Ex. 1.5A). But the leaps up on "reason" and "love dat" plus the blues note on "dat" are what make it great and show what loving "dat man" feels like (Ex. 1.5B).

Blues notes are the key to the ending as well. Once again, compare my cheery, upbeat, homogenized version without blues notes (Ex. 1.6A) to Kern's poignant, resigned version with blues notes (Ex. 1.6B).

It's not only Kern's music that draws from African American sources but Hammerstein's lyrics as well. Replacing the flowery language of European operetta with African American vernacular speech (or "white" versions of that speech) became a common technique for songwriters searching for an authentic American voice, and Hammerstein's use of "imitation-black" speech—"Dere ain't no reason, why I should love dat man"—can also be found in Arlen's "Stormy Weather," Gershwin's *Porgy and Bess*, and countless other songs of the period. But what is crucial to understand here is

Example 1.6A "Can't Help Lovin' Dat Man," Kapilow version

Example 1.6B "Can't Help Lovin' Dat Man," Kern version

that this imitation of black musical and verbal language is central to the plot of the entire song. Julie is actually part black, but because she is so light-skinned, she has managed to pass as white. Eventually her secret is uncovered, and since her mixed-race marriage to Steve was illegal in the South, she has to leave the *Cotton Blossom*—an event that starts her on a long downward spiral toward ruin. However, at this point in the show, no one knows her racial status, and when she sings the song, Queenie, the black cook on the ship, recognizes it as a song that only black women sing and is surprised that Julie, a white woman, knows it. It is the fact that Julie is singing a 12-bar blues with blues notes and vernacular African American lyrics that gives her away.

However, Julie is part black and part white, and the song is as "mixed race" as Julie. The verse, as we have just seen, comes from the black world of the blues, but the chorus that follows comes straight out of the white

Example 1.7 "Can't Help Lovin' Dat Man," A section

world of musical theater. It is an absolutely textbook, 32-bar, Broadway song form[6] that begins with the classic, 8-bar A section in Example 1.7.

Rhythm brings the music to life. Compare the stodgy, inert feel of my square, unsyncopated version (Ex. 1.8A) with Kern's (Ex. 1.8B), which brilliantly syncopates only the two key action verbs in the phrase—"swim" and "fly."

Example 1.8A "Can't Help Lovin' Dat Man," Kapilow version

Example 1.8B "Can't Help Lovin' Dat Man," Kern version

Also notice the perfect matching of music and lyrics. The melody has the simplicity of an axiom. It starts with three repeated notes, leaps up to three repeated notes, then returns to the opening three repeated notes. It has a kind of simple inevitability, as does the simple, straightforward, first-year-theory-textbook harmony, which is what the words are all about. "Fish got to swim and birds got to fly." It's just the way things are.

He then copies the 2-measure idea lower to cement it in our ears, but notice the wonderfully dissonant, dark chord under "die" in "I got to love one man till I die" (Ex. 1.9).

The punch line, with its long melody notes, feels almost like a hymn,* and with traditional harmony like the one I have supplied in Example 1.10, that's exactly how it would have sounded.

Example 1.9 "Can't Help Lovin' Dat Man"

* For musicians: the 7–6, 9–8 dissonances in the piano part under "Can't help" help create this hymnlike feeling.

Example 1.10 "Can't Help Lovin' Dat Man," Kapilow version

But listen to the way that Kern wrote "lovin dat man," with the only unusual chord in the phrase (Ex. 1.11).* In his hands, we feel just how strange and unexpected love can be.

Following the standard 32-bar form, the music of the A section repeats with new words, and the B section manages to tell an entire story in only 8 measures (Ex. 1.12). The first 4 bars are all about her man going away— "When he goes away, Dat's a rainy day"—but the last 4 are all about his return—"And when he comes back dat day is fine, / De sun will shine." The music depicts this journey in a direct and powerful way. As she anticipates her man's return, the music climbs up a scale always moving by step, and then finally when he "returns" on the word "fine," the vocal line leaps for the only time in the entire phrase to the highest note of the entire song. And

Example 1.11 "Can't Help Lovin' Dat Man," Kern version

---

* An augmented 6th chord.

Example 1.12 "Can't Help Lovin' Dat Man"

that note—his imagined return—gloriously brings out the sun and leads to the return of the opening music of the chorus.

The song finishes with an exact repeat of the A section, which is rare. Even in a standard AABA, 32-bar Broadway song like this one, there is usually some slight alteration for the conclusion. A melody that goes up and finishes on a high note, or some other kind of change at the end. But here, it is as if what she's telling is so timelessly true, so utterly and simply human, that it has an almost fable-like quality. This is how it is and how it's always been. No alteration is needed. It's a simple universal truth. "Can't help lovin' dat man of mine."

INVENTING AMERICA

Since the invention of photography and later of cinema, we have become more and more able to convincingly portray reality. Yet ironically, as our ability to portray reality has increased, our interest in imaginative versions of reality seems to have diminished. Today we live in an era that is obsessed with authenticity and historical accuracy in its depictions of the past. If a twenty-first-century musical were being written about life on a nineteenth-century Mississippi River showboat, the process would surely begin with extensive historical research on the part of the creative team. No effort would be spared to make sure that every hemline, fish fork, set piece, linguistic accent, and dialect would be reproduced exactly as it was. Historians would be consulted, experts would advise, and the importance of historical accuracy would be taken for granted.

However, neither Kern nor Hammerstein were remotely concerned with historical accuracy. They felt no more need to visit the Mississippi River at the heart of *Show Boat* than Jack Norworth and Albert Von Tilzer felt the need to see a baseball game before writing "Take Me Out to the Ball Game." Like so many writers, artists, composers, and poets, Kern and Hammerstein were inventing America, and they invented it purely out of their imaginations. They took their source material wherever they could find it and modified it without the slightest concern for authenticity. Hammerstein adapted Ferber's novel with astonishing freedom. In the book, for example, Steve and Julie disappear after being forced to leave the *Cotton Blossom*, but in the musical, Julie returns in Act II to play a pivotal role helping Magnolia's career get started in Chicago. Gaylord Ravenal, the compulsive riverboat gambler who marries and then deserts Magnolia, dies in the novel but remains alive in the musical (as does Cap'n Andy) in order to reappear in a Broadway-style reconciliation and happy ending that completely violates the novel's spirit.

Kern was equally free in the way he reimagined his wide variety of source materials to suit his own theatrical purposes. He took African American work songs and spirituals as a model and filtered them through his northern, white sensibility to create his own work song/spiritual, "Ol' Man River." In "Can't Help Lovin' Dat Man," he merged his appropriated version of the blues, with a mainstream, 32-bar, Broadway song form which ultimately became a dance that harked back to the minstrel-show cakewalk. When pressed by the plot to literally evoke an earlier era, Kern simply plucked an actual song from the past, "After the Ball," like a found object and inserted it into his score. Somehow, through the force of Kern's musical personality, all of these reimagined, American sources are able to stand next to songs like "You Are Love" pulled straight from the world of operetta. Even "Bill," originally written for his 1918 Princess Theatre show, *Oh Lady! Lady!* and blithely inserted into *Show Boat*'s second act, somehow manages to feel appropriate in its new context.

Like America itself, Kern and Hammerstein created their *Show Boat* universe out of the rich diversity of sources at hand. In the end, what links Kern, Hammerstein, Norworth, Von Tilzer, and so many other artists of the time was enormous self-confidence and a remarkable belief in the power of the imagination. As America emerged triumphantly from World War I and took a leading place on the world stage, a newfound pride and sense of importance was felt throughout the country. With its economy humming, innovative technologies promising unprecedented levels of prosperity, and skyscrapers growing taller every year, America began to replace Europe as the center of the new. Unencumbered by centuries of European traditions, artists felt free to invent a voice for this rapidly changing country, and new modes of communication—radio, recordings, and the movies—allowed this invented voice to be disseminated not only to America as a whole but to Europe as well. A country that had declared its independence politically in 1776 was only now beginning to declare its independence artistically, and it would be artists like Kern and Hammerstein, Porter and the Gershwins, and Irving Berlin who would help give the newly emerging world power its distinctively American voice.

2

The New Sexual Morality

Cole Porter's "Let's Do It"

While Jerome Kern and Oscar Hammerstein II were working to create their pathbreaking 1927 musical, *Show Boat*, Cole Porter was finishing a decade of licking his wounds in Paris after the humiliating failure of his first Broadway production, *See America First* (1916). When he finally got up the nerve to return to America in 1928, he reintroduced himself to Broadway with the musical *Paris*, featuring the hit song "Let's Do It." What Porter brought to the world of the Broadway musical can be summed up in a sense by the title's deliciously ambiguous pronoun—*it*. Everyone of course knew that "it" referred to sex. William McBrien, Porter's biographer, recounts an amusing anecdote about a man who asks his young daughter to sing "Let's Do It" with him, to which she says, "Daddy, if you don't want me to do 'it,' why do you want me to sing about 'it'?" The whole song in fact depends on the audience hearing the word "it" four times in each verse as directly referring to sex:

> *Birds do it, bees do it,*
> *Even educated fleas do it,*
> *Let's do it, let's fall in love.*

Only with the final four words of each verse—the punch line—does the meaning become more traditional and more respectable: let's fall in love. Of course the double double-entendre, so to speak, is the fact that the only "it" that birds, bees, and fleas actually do is have sex. As far as we know, they don't fall in love. What makes the lyrics so quintessentially Porter is that none of this is ever stated overtly. The reference is understood but never named, and the contrast between the titillation of the implied meaning and the cliché is what the song is all about.

Sex is everywhere in Porter's songs, and it was everywhere in the Roaring Twenties. Living as we do in a twenty-first-century world where, sexually speaking, anything goes, it can be difficult to grasp the extraordinary revolution in morality and sexuality that swept through America in the 1920s. World War I had an enormous impact on America's psyche, and it put an end to a kind of reflexive, optimistic, Victorian belief that society and the world would continually get better. Writers referred to themselves as the Lost Generation, and there was a powerful sense that traditional morality was no longer relevant in the new, disillusioned, postwar world. Victorianism and Puritanism now were exclusively associated with prudery, pomposity, sanctimoniousness, and self-righteousness.

Americans in the 1920s, rejecting conventional religious and moral precepts, became obsessed with sex. Sex in the form of scantily clad, beautiful women was at the core of theatrical entertainments like the *Ziegfeld Follies*, *George White's Scandals*, and the *Cotton Club Parades*, and it was central to newspaper tabloids like the *New York Daily News*, the *New York Daily Mirror*, and the *New York Evening Graphic*, which fed the public a daily diet of salacious news about sex and crime. "Girlie pulp" magazines like *Flapper Experiences, Snappy Stories,* and *Paris Nights*—the *Playboy* magazines of the era—filled their pages with readers' stories such as "My First Kiss" and "My Greatest Sorrow," as well as romantic fiction with titles like "Love and Nothing But" and "The Nightie Before Christmas." Titillating covers proclaiming "Bathing Beauties—and Nothing Else But!" lured readers into page after page of bathing suit photographs. In a precursor of today's online dating profiles, flappers (the nickname for stylish women in the 1920s who behaved unconventionally, wore short skirts, bobbed their hair, smoked, listened to jazz, and liked to talk about sex) posted photographs of themselves in these magazines—almost always in their bathing suits—with a note asking the reader to write and "please include 12 cents." In the back pages of the magazine, you could find listings of men and women in your area, an aid to meeting members of the opposite sex remarkably similar to today's personal ads.[1]

Magazines like these give a vivid picture of the revolution in morals and manners that transformed postwar America during the Roaring Twenties. Women's fashion underwent a remarkable change. Dresses grew shorter, revealing parts of the body that had never been seen before in public. Flappers not only wore thin dresses without corsets, but also dresses that were often short-sleeved, or even sleeveless. Stockings were rolled below the knee. Along with skimpy clothes came the freedom of short hair. The bobbed, close-cropped look we now associate with the era became standard by the end of the decade. The Victorian ideal of the full-figured, corseted, Rubensesque woman with long flowing hair in a full-length dress or gown was replaced by something completely new, centered around short skirts, boyish forms, and straight, long-waisted dresses.

And for the first time in American history, women were openly using cosmetics. Rouge and lipstick, once associated exclusively with prostitutes and women of questionable morals, were now worn by women everywhere. Frederick Lewis Allen's brilliant *Only Yesterday: An Informal History of the 1920s*, colorfully describes the rise of the new cosmetic industry.

> The vogue of rouge and lipstick, which in 1920 had so alarmed the parents of the younger generation, spread swiftly to the remotest village. Women who in 1920 would have thought the use of paint immoral were soon applying it regularly as a matter of course and making no effort to disguise the fact; beauty shops had sprung up on every street to give "facials," to apply pomade and astringents, to make war against the wrinkles and sagging chins of age, to pluck and trim and color the eyebrows, and otherwise

to enhance and restore the bloom of youth; and a strange new form of surgery, "face-lifting," took its place among the applied sciences of the day. Back in 1917 . . . only two persons in the beauty culture business had paid an income tax; by 1927 there were 18,000 firms and individuals in this field listed as income-tax payers. The "beautician had arrived."[2]

The growth of the cosmetics industry was astounding. Some estimates put the amount of money spent on cosmetics in 1930 as high as $2 billion. In order to propel the sales of these new goods and services, the advertising industry exploded in parallel. By some estimates, the total advertising volume in America grew from about $200 million in 1880 to nearly $3 billion in 1920,[3] and the new openness toward sex was central to advertisers' messages. Ads for products like Wanetta-Beauty-Face-Wash promised to help women acquire "entirely new complexions, wonderfully clear, fresh and beautiful," complexions "that will attract attention." In a reaction to the enormous popularity of the films of sex symbol Rudolph Valentino (*The Sheik*), ads touted products like "Sheik Lure"—a "new imported perfume sensation"—claiming that "Just a touch on the skin and the haunting romantic fragrance thrills and lingers for days. Everybody adores it."[4]

Though a great deal of the girlie pulp magazines of the 1920s focused on the appearance of the flappers, like *Playboy*, they covered lifestyle as well. One of the most common themes found everywhere in their pages was the image of the flapper as a strong, thoroughly modern, independent woman no longer willing to submit to traditional concepts of morality or gender roles. The Nineteenth Amendment gave women the right to vote in 1920, and a new desire for equality was transforming the way women conceived of their place in society. They no longer wanted to simply be housekeepers and breeders of children but productive members of society as well. New inventions like the electric iron, the electric washing machine, and the vacuum cleaner liberated women from much of the daily routine that had previously dominated their lives, and having worked during the war in order to replace the men overseas in munitions factories, as railway guards, postal workers, firefighters, bank tellers, and clerks, they had developed a newfound sense of economic and personal independence with aspirations that went beyond the traditional role of housewife.*

Also, Prohibition, which ran from 1920 to 1933, had a major impact on relationships between men and women in the twenties. Despite the ban on alcohol, liquor flowed freely. The speakeasy broke down the separation of the sexes, offering a place where men and women could drink and socialize together in public for the first time. The late-afternoon cocktail party developed into an institution, and in small cities, suburbs, and summer resorts, the country club became the center of social life. Men and women not only drank together, they smoked together. Though as recently as 1904 a woman had been arrested for smoking on Fifth Avenue in New York City, millions of women took up smoking in the 1920s. Between 1918 and 1928, the total production of cigarettes in the United States more than doubled.[5] The days of the men going off to their separate room after dinner to smoke became a thing of the past.

Taboos were being lifted everywhere. The divorce rate exploded from 1 per 18 marriages in the 1880s to 1 per 6 in 1920. It was no longer a badge of shame, and the number of remarriages began to increase as well. Frank public discussion about sex and contraception both inside and outside of marriage was possible for the first time. It wasn't until about 1910 that the words "syphilis," "gonorrhea," and "prostitution" could even be used in public, and the ignorance that resulted from this complete lack of openness had helped the spread of these diseases. Ironically, it was the overwhelming occurrence of syphilis and gonorrhea among soldiers in World War I (the United States was the only military force during the war that *did not* supply condoms to its troops) that forced the military to bring the topic out into the open as part of a desperately needed educational campaign. Though contraception or even the distribution of contraceptive information other than

---

* According to the 1920 census data, the number of married women who were "gainfully employed" had essentially doubled from 4–5 percent in 1890 to 9 percent in 1920. By 1930, more than 10 million women had jobs.

for medical conditions was technically illegal at the time—Margaret Sanger was immediately arrested after opening the first birth control clinic in the United States in 1916—by the 1920s, "birth control" had become a routine phrase in everyday speech, and condoms and diaphragms were widely available, helping to lower the birth rate by 20 percent between 1920 and 1930.[6]

Threats to traditional morality came from everywhere as sex invaded nearly every aspect of life in the twenties. Dating, which had traditionally been a chaste affair conducted in chaperoned living rooms and porches, could now take place in the privacy of the back seat of one of the newly closed cars that became ubiquitous during the twenties. The massive growth of the automobile industry throughout the decade people were now on their own and could drive wherever they liked, including to parties where innocent, traditional dances like the waltz had been replaced by slow fox trots, with partners sensuously glued together in ways that would have been unthinkable a decade earlier.

There was, of course, considerable resistance to this assault on traditional values. In Utah, legislators tried to pass laws that would fine and imprison women who wore skirts higher than three inches above the ankle. In Ohio, lawmakers wanted to limit décolletage to two inches.[7] The Catholic Church was a central player in the fight against legalizing contraception, and there were campaigns against indecency throughout the country. Attempts were made to ban books and suppress films, but ultimately these efforts failed. Attitudes had changed. The war had destroyed a belief in a secure future, and the result was a new kind of *carpe diem* approach to life, a feeling that with no guarantee of tomorrow, living for today was the only thing that made sense.

Everything and everyone was focused on the now. People bought things on the installment plan. Broadway was crammed with show after show, nearly all with short runs. Fads like flagpole sitting, wing walking (stunt walking on airplane wings), mahjongg, dance marathons, cigarette holders, and dance crazes came and went at the speed of light. Hedonism was the ethos of the decade. Anything that got in the way of instant gratification had to be abolished. An uninhibited sex life was considered the key to happiness.

Nice girls now smoked, drank, wore lipstick, necked, and petted. Words like "damn" or "hell" were heard in the theater for the first time. The sensuous saxophone had replaced the romantic violin. Modesty was no longer in style, and chivalry, if not actually dead, was clearly on artificial life support.

It was not without reason that the 1920s are often referred to as "The Decade of Bad Manners." No one wanted to be good. They wanted to be sophisticated, modern, and a little bit shocked, and Cole Porter was happy to oblige. When *Paris* first began its out-of-town tryouts,* the song that received the most attention was "Let's Misbehave." Its title perfectly caught the spirit of the decade and of Porter's sensibility. The song's lyrics immediately made it clear what kind of misbehaving Porter was referring to: "We're all alone, no chaperone / . . . Can get our number." And with everyone else asleep, hidden from view in the newly popular closed cars, it was the perfect time to misbehave.

Nearly as explosive as the growth of the automobile during the 1920s was the growth of the telephone. In 1900 there was only 1 telephone for every 66 people, but by 1925 it had become almost universal with 1 telephone for every 7.[8] Like the automobile, telephones allowed young people to communicate and interact directly, free from their parents' supervision, and Porter uses imagery drawn from the decade's two exploding technologies to give his lyrics a contemporary feel. Thanks to the automobile, "we're all alone," and "no chaperone can get our [phone] number," so "Let's misbehave." The automobile supplies the image for "My poor heart aches on, Why keep the brakes on?" as well.

The 1920s was a decade determined to wake a "world in slumber." And the way to do it was to break the rules and flout conventional morality, which is exactly what the song's lyrics do, not only in their sexual suggestiveness but in their vocabulary. Worried that their love affair will be discovered, the singer defiantly declares: "Somebody's sure to tell, / But what the *hell* do we care?" Swear words like "damn" and "hell" were simply not acceptable

---

* Broadway shows at the time were usually taken to out-of-town locations like Boston, New Haven, or Philadelphia to be rehearsed, refined, and performed for local audiences before being brought to Broadway.

vocabulary for a song before the 1920s, and the bluntness of "Let's Misbehave" was problematic for out-of-town audiences during tryouts. But Porter
would create even more controversy with the song that replaced it. Before
Paris opened in New York on October 8, 1928—less than a year after *Show
Boat*—Porter included one of his most famous songs: "Let's Do It."

It is probably safe to say that no Broadway songwriter of the period had
more confrontations with censors than Cole Porter. Throughout his career,
he pushed the envelope of what was permissible in the theater, and his lifelong battles with censorship began with the title of *Paris's* new hit song.
Censors found the implied sexual reference unacceptable[9] and demanded
that the punch line, "Let's fall in love," be included in the title.* Though the
added phrase clarifies its meaning, it sanitizes it as well, removing the deli-
cious ambiguity and suggestiveness at the heart of the song. Not knowing
what "it" refers to for the first 5 measures was what the song was all about.
This kind of misbehaving on Porter's part was what audiences loved about
his music.

The song tested the limits of propriety in more ways than one. The original opening phrase of the chorus was offensive in a completely different way:

> *And that's why Chinks do it, Japs do it,*
> *Up in Lapland, little Lapps do it,*

Even Porter realized how inappropriate these lyrics were and changed
them to the now familiar, "Birds do it, bees do it, / Even educated fleas do it,"
but his willingness to push the envelope of what was acceptable and the reac-
tive pushback from outraged censors would continue throughout his career.

---

* Even today, the song's title can be found in three different versions. "Let's Do It," Let's Do It, Let's Fall in Love," or with parentheses, "Let's Do It (Let's Fall in Love)."

Some of his battles with the censors were relatively minor and easily resolved. When his 1932 Broadway show, *Gay Divorce*, was turned into a film in 1934 and ran up against the Hays Code, the title had to be changed to *The Gay Divorcee*, as the idea that divorce could be a happy event was unacceptable to the censors in Hollywood. But some of Porter's challenges to conventional morality were far more provocative. One of his most astonishing, boundary-defying songs, "Love for Sale," written two years after *Paris* for the musical *The New Yorkers*, tells the poignant story of a prostitute: "Love for sale, / Appetizing young love for sale." Utterly direct (she describes herself as "still unspoiled" and only "slightly soiled"), without apology, and with no comedy to blunt its expression, the song provoked outrage and condemnation. Its lyrics were banned from the radio for many years, and Porter's reaction to the song's critics offers a remarkable window onto the sensibilities of the times. In the original staging of the scene, a white prostitute, Kathryn Crawford, sang the song in front of Reuben's, a popular local restaurant, with three white backup singers. To make the scene more acceptable to white audiences, the song was transferred to a "colored girl," Elisabeth Welch, who now sang the song in front of the Cotton Club in Harlem. (Somehow, a white prostitute singing in front of a popular white restaurant was unacceptable, but a black prostitute singing in front of a Harlem club was fine.) Porter remained dumbfounded at the reaction to the song throughout his life, and later chose it as his favorite, saying, "I can't understand it. You can write a novel about a harlot, paint a picture of a harlot, but you can't write a song about a harlot."[10]

Porter had far greater success attacking the morality of the time with comic songs like "Let's Do It," and the reaction of the critics to *Paris* was, in the words of the *New Yorker*, "ecstatic." Though Porter was in Europe working on another show at the time and did not attend the opening, perhaps because he was terrified of failing in his return to Broadway, the *New York Herald Tribune* still called him "the flaming star of the premiere of *Paris*." *The New Yorker* said the songs were "up to Mr. Porter's best and there is no better," and, most perceptively, "No one else now writing words and music knows so exactly the delicate balance between sense, rhyme, and tune."[11]

In a 1998 article in the *New York Review of Books*, Brad Leithauser articulates a commonly held view that a weakness of Porter's songs is that "they were text driven." As evidence, he quotes a well-known passage in which Porter describes his working methods:

> I like to begin with an idea and then fit it to a title. I then write the words and music. Often I begin near the end of a refrain, so that the song has a strong finish, and then work backwards.

Leithauser then goes on to say:

> There are many cases, among his more forgettable tunes, where the tune serves as little more than a frame on which to hang the words. Unlike George Gershwin, Porter was no inexhaustible melodist. . . . The flashing word play, the unexpected rhyme, the inspired double-entendre—these often outlast the tunes they garnish.[12]

Because so many of Porter's famous list songs like "Let's Do It" are filled with some of the most extraordinarily witty, sophisticated, virtuosic lyrics ever written, it is indeed tempting to think that their music is simply a frame on which to hang the words. To think that, like the Gilbert and Sullivan patter songs that were Porter's inspiration, his music would have to be seen as basically Gilbert with little more than a Sullivan frame. In other words, you'd have to believe that music and lyrics can be separated in a meaningful way. But what this viewpoint misses is precisely what the *New Yorker* understood so well in 1928: what makes Porter's songs so unique is their "delicate balance between sense, rhyme, and tune." In a great song, whether the words or the music was written first, it is the combination that counts. Though the words might be satisfying on their own, and though the music might be satisfying on its own, once the two elements join to make a song, the lyrics cease to have a purely literary meaning, and the music ceases to have a purely musical meaning. Both music and words become part of a new unit; they cannot be fully understood independently. Porter's sophisticated lyrics, with their elaborate rhymes and imaginative imagery, *are* spectacular in and of themselves, but it is the way they combine with music that makes them unforgettable.

To show how inseparable Gilbert is from Sullivan—how lyrics and music work seamlessly together—I have written a numbingly boring version of the opening 8-bar phrase (Ex. 2.1). It keeps every one of Porter's fantastic words as well as his basic melodic shape and harmony.

This version is not only boring musically, it actually removes all of the wit from the song's lyrics. With this music as the frame on which to hang the words, Porter's lyrics fall flat. Let's look closely at the difference between my version and the original (Ex. 2.2) to see how melody and rhythm bring Porter's titillating lyrics to life. My version begins with a long, two-beat

Example 2.1 "Let's Do It," Kapilow version

Example 2.2 "Let's Do It," Porter version

note on "birds," while Porter starts with a quarter note—a short, one-beat note—followed by a rest. This seemingly insignificant difference utterly transforms the world of the song. A longer note on "birds" makes the vocal line melodic and tuneful, and because a sustained vowel requires the singer to carry over its final consonant to the next word, the rhythm makes the lyric more difficult to understand. Porter's version instead gives a casual, speech-like feel to the song. The word is far easier for the singer to articulate and for the audience to understand.

This difference between the two versions is small but important, but it is the next two notes that are really crucial. The words "do it," with their sexual suggestiveness and ambiguity, are the fundamental source of the song's humor. In my version, "do" and "it" are both on-the-beat, Puritanical quarter notes. They're square in every sense of the word. Porter's version, however, has an impish, naughty syncopation on "it" that forces the performer to sing the two eighth notes quickly—quick enough to slide by the censors.

At the same time, the melody reinforces the rhythm every step of the way. My version begins with an F in the melody—a weighty, grounded, traditional note that fits conventionally with the B♭ chord underneath. Porter's first note is a G—a note that is subtly, insouciantly dissonant to the chord underneath—followed by a naughty, chromatic* slide in syncopated rhythm from G♭ to F. The rhythm, melody, and dissonance in this measure are not simply "a frame on which to hang the words," but rather a perfect musical equivalent to the words—suggestive, titillating, sophisticated, and witty.

This one measure is the key to the entire song. Repetition is central to the memorability of so many of Porter's songs, and it is astonishing how much this one relies on its opening measure. Half of the first 8 bars (measures 1, 2, 5, 6) repeat this tiny melody—G–G♭–F—exactly, and measure 4 repeats the same gesture, only higher. Since this song is a classic AABA Broadway song, its opening phrase (A) repeats three times (we will look at the small changes in the repeats in a moment), which means that we ultimately hear this little three-note melody, either in its original or transposed form, fifteen times. The song is so obsessed with the idea that it actually permeates the B section as well, adding four more repeats, bringing the total to nineteen (see Ex. 2.3).

As crucial as the many repetitions of this opening measure are to the song's overall effect, they are only part of what makes it great. What happens in the measures that *do not* repeat this opening idea is what holds the listener's interest. Once again rhythm and melody work together seamlessly. "Birds do it" and "bees do it" have the identical rhythm and the identical melody. The two measures, like the "birds and the bees," are a pair. After beginning both measures with a note on the downbeat, my version (Ex. 2.1) continues the pattern and starts the third measure—"Even educated"—with another downbeat note. Porter (Ex. 2.2), however, brilliantly starts his third measure with an unexpected rest, as if a light bulb had gone off and

---

* For nonmusicians, chromatic motion is motion by half step—the smallest interval on a piano. The distance between any note and the next nearest note—black or white—on the keyboard.

Example 2.3 "Let's Do It," B section

the next idea sprang to mind—not just birds and bees, but "even educated fleas do it." And the excitement of the new thought is perfectly captured by the tumble of fast notes the image engenders—twice as many notes in measure 3 as in measures 1 and 2—notes that now rise dizzyingly up the scale to the highest note and climax of the phrase—the C on "fleas."

The excitement of the new thought culminates with the repetition of the song's opening idea, transposed higher in measure 4. The music here is anything but a mere frame. It is what brings Porter's lyrics to life. My version falls flat. Music and lyrics are inseparable, coequal partners in Porter's sophisticated universe. They cannot be understood in isolation.

Once the phrase has reached its climax, Porter returns in measures 5 through 7 to the melody and rhythm of measures 1 and 2, but with a modified bass line to keep the plot moving forward. A long note on "love" finishes the phrase and allows us to contemplate the entire sentence. Porter makes sure that the listener has time to process both words and images as well as entire phrases, and his long notes, rests, and pauses are crucial to the intelligibility of his complex, sophisticated lyrics. But he is also careful to pause only as long as necessary. The second A section repeats the music of the first A section almost exactly. He could easily have held the long note on "love" for all of measures 7 and 8 and then begun the next section on the downbeat of measure 9. To keep the musical plot from losing energy, Porter instead cuts off the long note after five beats and adds three wonderful pickup notes in measure 8—"In Spain, the"—to elide the two phrases beautifully and keep the musical momentum moving forward.

In Spain, the best upper sets do it,
Lithuanians and Letts do it,
Let's do it, Let's fall in love.

Porter not only finds a seemingly infinite number of witty new lyrics for each verse; he also finds lyrics that are witty in new ways. In the first verse the syncopation repeatedly fell on the words "do it," which conformed to normal speech patterns. However, in the second verse, the accent on "upper" is willfully awkward—the musical equivalent of accenting the wrong syl-LA-ble. This kind of purposeful misaccentuation brings a whole new level of humor to the song. In addition, brilliantly capitalizing on the homophones "Letts" and "Let's" allows Porter the unique opportunity to repeat the same three words twice in a row with two different meanings, "Letts do it, Let's do it."

Rather than simply relying on ever-more-clever lyrics to carry the song, Porter moves the plot forward musically until the final note. The B section develops the opening idea both melodically and harmonically, and Porter carefully controls the pacing of the section's fantastic new lyrics. He begins with two purposely nonspectacular images—"The Dutch in old Amsterdam do it, Not to mention the Finns"—and then seems to begin a third ordinary image— "Folks in Siam do it"—all to set up the spectacular punch line—"Think of Siamese twins." Everything is designed to make the brilliant punch line land.

After the B section's punch line, Porter returns to the A section one final time (Ex. 2.4). The first 2 measures copy the earlier A sections exactly, and Porter could easily have copied the rest of the section as well. But in a final fantastic stroke, he alters every one of the song's final 6 measures in a spectacular way. We have already talked about the wonderful surprise rest at the beginning of the third measure in each verse: the rest before "even educated fleas do it," and the rest before "Lithuanians and Letts do it." He could have done exactly this in the final verse and written, "People say in Boston beans do it." Instead, he removes the rest and adds two extra notes, along with the word "even," so that the phrase now starts on the downbeat: "People say in Boston, *even* beans do it." The extra notes push the scale higher and higher. Up to this point C had been the highest vocal note of the song. Now, Porter does the opening motive on D♭ for "beans do it," then still higher on D♮ for "let's do it," and even higher, to the highest note of the entire song—E♭—for the final "let's fall in love."

Example 2.4 "Let's Do It," ending

At this point, we've heard the final words, "Let's do it, let's fall in love," many times. What makes them spectacular here is the music. Far more than simply "the frame on which to hang the words," they are what make the moment great. The song bursts free from its restricted rhythmic pattern and its limited melodic range, as Porter's words and music burst free from America's conventional moral code and Puritanical past. Joyously, exultantly, rising higher and higher in pitch they proclaim the era's new sexual freedom—"Let's do it, Let's fall in love."

෨෧

In 1881, Tony Pastor opened his legendary vaudeville house in New York City with the goal of creating a kind of variety entertainment that middle-class families could attend. Listening to the America of the 1880s, he realized that there was a desire on the part of the public for a clean show that would be a step above the vulgar entertainment seen in saloons and burlesque houses at the time. He promised no drinking, smoking, or swearing by the performers, with pistols to be checked at the door. By the time *Paris* opened on Broadway in 1928, vaudeville was in its final death throes, and Porter was listening to a completely different America. Porter's America was the Roaring Twenties and the Decade of Bad Manners. A more urbane America focused on the here and now dominated by a new sense of morality, freedom, and openness. Though Porter's elite, upper-class status was light-years removed from that of most mainstream Americans, he was able to give them a voice they could aspire to. A voice that was sophisticated and articulate, able to effortlessly spin out high-brow virtuosic rhymes intermixed with casual, lowbrow diction and slangy contractions ("Electric eels, I might add, do it, Though it shocks 'em I know"). A voice that was modern and up to date, as well as titillating, provocative, slightly amoral, and suggestively sexual. He took the concerns, desires, and sensibilities of the times and gave them an urbane, witty, upper-class sheen. Almost exactly one year later, the decade's extraordinary bubble would burst with the stock market crash of 1929, but with Porter's first hit, "Let's Do It," the Roaring Twenties had found its anthem, its purpose, and its voice.

3

Airbrushing the Depression

George Gershwin's "I Got Rhythm"

Ira Gershwin, George Gershwin's brother and the lyricist for nearly all of his greatest songs, describes the painstaking creative process he went through to create the lyrics to "I Got Rhythm."

Filling in the 73 syllables of the refrain wasn't as simple as it sounds. For over two weeks I kept fooling around with various titles and with sets of double rhymes for the trios of short two-foot lines. I'll ad-lib a dummy to show what I was at: "Roly-poly / Eating solely / Ravioli, / Better watch your diet or bust. // Lunch or dinner, / You're a sinner. / Please get thinner. / Losing all that fat is a must." Yet no matter what series of double rhymes—even pretty good ones—I tried, the results were not quite satisfactory; they seemed at best to give a pleasant and jingly Mother Goose quality to a tune which should throw its weight around more. Getting nowhere, I then found myself not bothering with the rhyme scheme I'd considered necessary (aaab, cccb) and experimenting with non-rhyming lines like (dummy): "Just go forward; / Don't look backward; / And you'll soon be / Winding up ahead of the game." This approach felt stronger, and I finally arrived at the present refrain with only "more–door" and "mind him–find him" the rhymes. Though there is nothing remarkable about all this, it was a bit daring for me who usually depended on rhyme insurance.[1]

Though this remarkable description of the pains Ira took to create these seemingly spontaneous lyrics paints an indelible picture of the self-aware, self-critical craftsman he was, perhaps what is most fascinating is what he neglects to mention about the actual content of these lyrics and their relationship to the era in which they were written.

Girl Crazy opened on Broadway on October 14, 1930, at the Alvin Theater, almost exactly a year after Black Thursday, the day that precipitated the stock market crash and subsequently led to the Great Depression of the 1930s. During that time, the number of unemployed people in the United States almost tripled from 1.5 million in 1929 to 4.3 million in 1930. By 1932 that figure would grow to 12 million people, or nearly a quarter of the labor force.[2] This unprecedented economic decline, combined with the rise of talking pictures and radio, had a massive impact on Broadway. It became increasingly difficult to raise money for shows, and the number of productions on Broadway fell from 264 in the 1927–28 season to only 187 in *Girl Crazy*'s 1930–31 season. Broadway had averaged almost 45 new musicals a year during the 1920s, but by the 1933–34 season, that number had dropped to only 13.

Expensive, extravagant shows like the famous *Ziegfeld Follies* were among the first casualties of the collapse. The 1931 edition of the *Follies* was Ziegfeld's last, and he would die almost destitute a year later. Two-thirds of New York's playhouses were shut down around that time, and movie houses began to dominate the Theater District, replacing expensive Broadway musicals with cheap talking pictures. Major theater owners like the Shuberts were nearly wiped out. Imagine watching then-unknown Ethel Merman, about to become a Broadway star, stepping on stage amid all this economic turmoil to belt out her anthem of optimism, "I Got Rhythm," declaring, "I got rhythm, I got music, I got my man, who could ask for anything more?" It was striking, yet utterly appropriate, that the only things she seemed to require for her happiness—rhythm, music, her man, daisies, green pastures, starlight, and sweet dreams—all turned out to be free!*

Eight of the songs in this book were composed during the 1930s, a remarkable decade for the Broadway musical. If you were to listen to them without knowing anything about history, you might have no idea that the Depression ever happened. These songs seem to inhabit a kind of alternate universe where rich, elegantly dressed people dance "Cheek to cheek" to the music of "the Beguine," declaring, "You're the top," or "I wish I were in love again." The dire straits of the millions of unemployed workers—Dust Bowl migrants, apple sellers, Hooverville residents, and drought-stricken farmers—seem to play no part in the imaginary world of these musicals. But it's not quite that simple.

Elisabeth Kübler-Ross suggests that, in response to life-altering events, people tend to react by cycling through a series of emotional stages, beginning with denial and anger and ending in acceptance. This continuum of responses to a perceived threat is not only physiological, but artistic as well, and one of the most striking aspects of 1930s culture was that artistic reactions to the Depression came from both ends of the Kübler-Ross spectrum.

On the one hand, there were artists who both accepted and engaged directly with the realities of the Depression, producing some of the decade's most enduring books, movies, plays, musicals, and art. Novels like John Steinbeck's iconic *Grapes of Wrath* (1939) depicted in fictional terms the real-life plight of migrant farmers heading west. James Agee and Walker Evans's *Let Us Now Praise Famous Men* (1941) depicted "the daily living and environment of an average white family of tenant farmers" in words and

---

* We find the exact same sentiment in Gershwin's "I Got Plenty o' Nuttin'" from *Porgy and Bess*—"I got plenty o' nuttin' / And nuttin's plenty for me"—and Irving Berlin's "I Got the Sun in the Morning" from *Annie Get Your Gun*—"Got no diamond, got no pearl / Still I think I'm a lucky girl."

photographs. Images like Dorothea Lange's *Migrant Mother* (1936) became poignant, human symbols of the Depression. Paintings like those of Edward Hopper captured the period's sense of grim alienation, and Hopper explicitly stated that "the province of art is to react to it [life], not to shun it."[3]

Broadway, on the other hand, almost exclusively chose flight over fight. Only a few musicals during the Depression chose to engage directly with its reality: Blitzstein's *The Cradle Will Rock* (1937), a parable set in Steeltown, USA, depicting corporate greed and corruption; *Pins and Needles* (1937), a musical written by and for the members of the International Ladies' Garment Workers' Union, about a real-world feud between the American Federation of Labor and the Congress of Industrial Organizations; and Gershwin's three satirical musicals, *Strike Up the Band* (1930), the Pulitzer Prize–winning *Of Thee I Sing* (1931), and *Let 'Em Eat Cake* (1933).* The Depression's single-most iconic popular song—the musical equivalent of *The Grapes of Wrath* and *The Migrant Mother*—was the Jay Gorney/ Yip Harburg song from the 1932 musical revue *Americana*, "Brother, Can You Spare a Dime." The song, like Steinbeck's novel and Lange's photograph, grew out of a specific, contemporary, historical incident—President Hoover's merciless routing of the so-called Bonus Army of World War I veterans from Washington, D.C.—but expressed something far more universal. Through Harburg's words and Gorney's music, it ultimately became a kind of grim anthem of the Depression itself.

By and large, however, Depression-era Broadway musicals (and Hollywood films) chose escapism over engagement. Instead of dealing with the period's terrifying reality, Broadway offered entertainment designed to distract people, even if only for a moment, from their daily economic anxieties. The intensity of the Broadway musical's desire to provide an escape from reality, however, is itself a reflection of the kind of paralyzing anxiety the

---

* The Rodgers and Hart musical *I'd Rather Be Right* featuring George M. Cohan as FDR, and Harold Arlen's antiwar musical *Hooray for What!*, both from 1937, are two more significant, topical musicals that spoke directly to contemporary Depression-era realities.

Depression produced. We avoid what we cannot bear to look at, and the over-the-top absurdity of the plots of so many 1930s musicals and screwball comedies is a direct reflection of and reaction to Depression-era realities. Even a simple board game like Monopoly, which was invented and quickly became a craze during the 1930s, was its own poignant form of escapism. It allowed millions of people who were unable to afford a meal the chance to acquire a fantasy fortune unimaginable in their daily lives.

Escapism took many different forms during the period. Miniature golf, for example, far more affordable than real golf for Depression-era families, became enormously popular. Invented in the late 1920s, by 1930 there were 30,000 courses throughout the country.[4] In fact, sports as a whole became one of the most significant forms of diversion. In 1900, newspapers did not have sports sections, yet by the 1930s an enormous radio audience had developed for major sporting events like the World Series, college football games, and championship boxing matches. As popular as these radio events were, however, none could compare with the most popular radio show of all, the inimitable *Amos 'n' Andy*. Broadcasting nightly throughout the 1930s, the show had a listenership of 40 million—almost a third of the population! Though essentially an updated minstrel show, with its two white creators, Freeman Gosden and Charles Correll, imitating two black men, the program managed to transcend its own racist, minstrel-show stereotypes through characterizations of real depth and humanity that emphasized universal values of friendship and hard work. It became so popular that NBC ordered its staff to avoid interrupting the show for anything less than a national emergency.[5]

Sometimes the difficulties of the present were imaginatively transposed and projected onto the difficulties of another time and place. In Pearl Buck's Pulitzer Prize–winning 1931 novel *The Good Earth,* set in a fictional prewar China, the Wang Lung family dealt with famine and drought as well as a host of other calamities that made Depression hardships seem minor in comparison. Kenneth Roberts's 1937 historical novel *Northwest Passage* transported Depression-era readers to a colonial past through the trials and tribulations of the Rogers' Rangers, who fought during the French and Indian War. Most famously of all, Margaret Mitchell's wildly popular 1936 novel *Gone with the Wind* projected the difficulties of the Depression onto the tumultuous past of Clayton County and Atlanta, Georgia, during the Civil War and Reconstruction.[6]

The Depression led to actual physical escape as well. As the clouds darkened and the drought worsened, thousands of actual farmers, like the fictional Joads of *The Grapes of Wrath,* headed westward, leaving behind the horrific reality of the Dust Bowl for the imaginary Promised Land of California. Broadway composers made a similar journey, hoping to find stability and financial success in Hollywood's new world of talking pictures. But once they arrived, most were disappointed. Richard Rodgers and Lorenz Hart spent several unrewarding years there before fleeing back to Broadway. Oscar Hammerstein, Harold Arlen, Irving Berlin, Vincent Youmans, Buddy DeSylva, and Cole Porter all went back and forth between Broadway and Hollywood throughout the decade, and though the Gershwins were among the last to arrive, George would never see New York again, dying tragically of a brain tumor in Cedars of Lebanon Hospital in Los Angeles at the age of thirty-eight in 1937.

Gershwin and other Broadway composers of the 1930s managed to create an imaginary world in their musicals that, at least on the surface, bore no resemblance to the real world, but their desire to engage in fantasy—to airbrush the unacceptable—ran much deeper. It went to the heart of Gershwin's personal and musical self-invention, a process that began literally with his own name.

൭ඵ

George Gershwin was both Jewish and the son of immigrant parents. Musical theater historians have estimated that 75 percent of the lyricists and 50 percent of the composers responsible for Broadway's finest songs were

Jewish, and of the so-called Mighty Five—Kern, Berlin, Rodgers, Porter, and Gershwin—only Porter was not Jewish. Like Irving Berlin, Gershwin's parents were Russian, and George's father, Moishe Gershowitz, came alone from St. Petersburg to America in 1890.* His mother, Rosa Bruskin, also came to America from St. Petersburg, but with her entire family in 1892. Moishe and Rosa were married in New York in 1895; they were naturalized in 1898, the year of George's birth. Moishe changed the family name from Gershowitz to Gershvin, and finally, at George's insistence, to Gershwin. At each step, the family's Jewish, immigrant past was replaced with an invented American present. Jacob became George, and Israel became Ira.

Americanizing immigrant names was of course common at the time. Hyman Arluck became Harold Arlen, and Israel Beilin became Irving Berlin, but George went even further with his self-invention, airbrushing his entire biography. Though he loved to paint himself as a poor boy who rose from the gutter, his family was actually middle-class, with enough money to have a maid, a piano, and a record player. And in spite of his attempts to portray himself as a kind of idiot savant with almost no musical education, he actually received a substantial amount of musical training from a variety of teachers. Though Gershwin himself was always vague on details, according to biographer Howard Pollack he began piano lessons at the age of twelve with a teacher, Miss Green, who was first hired to teach Ira. He then continued his lessons with a Hungarian immigrant, Professor Goldfarb, followed by further study with the excellent pianist and composer Charles Hambitzer, the teacher Gershwin called the greatest musical influence in his life.

Though this was already more training than most Broadway songwriters received, George went even further, studying harmony and orchestration with the distinguished composer, violinist, and theorist Edward Kilenyi,

---

* The basic biographical facts about Gershwin in this chapter are drawn from Howard Pollack's definitive Gershwin biography, *George Gershwin: His Life and Work,* University of California Press, 2006.

and taking summer music courses at Columbia. This in no way diminishes the greatness of his work or the remarkable fact that he was able to compose *Rhapsody in Blue* only fourteen years after his first piano lesson, but it does make his musical achievements far more comprehensible. It also provides useful context for the 1919 hit that catapulted him to fame: "Swanee."

In 1914, at the age of fifteen, George, like Irving Berlin and Harold Arlen, left high school without graduating. Almost immediately he became the youngest song plugger in New York, first at Remick's publishing house and then in 1918 at T. B. Harms.* After his first complete show, *La La Lucille,* established his credentials as a bona fide Broadway composer in 1919, "Swanee," written that same year, turned him into an overnight sensation. First written by Gershwin and Irving Caesar as a stand-alone number, independent of any theatrical context, the song was an attempt to capitalize on a fad for songs with a Middle Eastern or Asian feel, like the popular Oliver Wallace/Harold Weeks one-step, "Hindustan." "Why don't we write an American one-step?"[7] was Caesar's prompt to Gershwin. In place of an imaginary Asian or Middle Eastern setting, they concocted an American one, borrowing from Stephen Foster's "Old Folks at Home" ("Way down upon de Swanee Ribber")—the Deep South. Like Kern and Hammerstein's version of the Mississippi River in *Show Boat*, Gershwin and Caesar's Deep South in "Swanee" was pure invention. Caesar stated almost proudly that when they wrote it, "We had never been south of Fourteenth Street. . . . After the song became a hit, we took a trip down south and took a look at the Sewanee River. Very romantic, muddy little river. Very nice, nothing against it, but it's a good thing we wrote the song first and used our imagination."[8] Gershwin claimed it took them about an hour to write it.

The song made almost no impact when it was first heard in the revue *Demi-Tasse*, which opened in New York in 1919. But when Gershwin

---

* Ira, always more academically inclined than George, made it through high school and two years of City College before dropping out after his sophomore year.

played the song at a party, Al Jolson, the most popular performer of the day (another reinvented Russian Jew, born Asa Yoelson), heard it and liked it. At the time, Jolson was performing in a show called *Sinbad*, and after inserting "Swanee" into the show, he recorded it for Columbia Records in January 1920. As Gershwin put it, "After that, 'Swanee' penetrated the four corners of the earth."[9] In figures that seem almost impossible to believe today, the song sold a million copies of sheet music and 2 million records. It was number one on the charts for eighteen weeks and turned out not only to be Gershwin's first hit and the song that made him famous, but also the greatest hit of his entire career in terms of sales. Biographer Howard Pollack beautifully sums up the complex interweaving of invention and history that make this song such a fascinating cultural document; he describes it as a "minstrel song, a remnant of a dying style reinvigorated by a Jewish boy from the Lower East Side put across by a Russian-born Jew pretending to be a black man."*

In many ways, "Swanee" not only kicked off Gershwin's career but the entire decade of the Roaring Twenties, an ebullient decade in America and on Broadway. Gershwin dominated with shows like *Lady, Be Good!* (1924), *Oh, Kay!* (1926), and *Funny Face* (1927). He also wrote five editions of *George White's Scandals* (a yearly revue designed to challenge the *Ziegfeld Follies*), as well as landmark classical compositions like *Rhapsody in Blue* (1924), the *Concerto in F* (1925), and *An American in Paris* (1928). Though Gershwin's Broadway shows during the 1920s lightly referred to some of the issues of the day—Prohibition and rum runners in *Oh, Kay!*, and Lindbergh and psychoanalysis in *Funny Face*—their plots were essentially bubbly, high-spirited, musical comedy romps that did nothing more than serve as props for great songs and dances by the likes of Fred and Adele Astaire.

---

* Jolson had actually been part of one of the last minstrel troupes to tour the country, *Lew Dockstader's Minstrels*, and he would continue the minstrel tradition of performing in blackface into the 1920s, long after it had become a cultural embarrassment.

And when *Girl Crazy* kicked off the 1930s and the Depression replaced euphoria, nothing seemed to have changed onstage.

෴

Girl Crazy takes place in Custerville, Arizona, an imaginary town that has the dual distinction of having had only a single woman within its limits for fifty years—Molly Gray, the local postmistress—and a tradition of regularly killing off its sheriffs. But even though the paper-thin plot seems to exist in a kind of bubble, disconnected from Depression-era reality, elements of the real world manage to sneak into the story.

As the show opens, one group of cowboys pass the time doing a crossword puzzle while four others form a quartet and sing the lazy opening number, "Bidin' My Time": "But I'm bidin' my time, / Cause that's the kinda guy I'm."* Other people may "grow dizzy" with all the activity that keeps them "busy," but "I'm bidin' my time." Though the song is clearly meant to depict a Custerville where nothing much of significance has ever happened or is likely to happen anytime soon, it is hard not to think that the song is equally, if not mainly, about Herbert Hoover maddeningly "bidin' his time," waiting till "next year, next year" when "somethin's bound to happen" to get the country out of the Depression. Even the crossword puzzle leaks in from the outside world. (How likely is it that Custerville cowboys would be doing a crossword puzzle?) Simon & Schuster published the first crossword-puzzle book in 1924, initiating a crossword-puzzle fad that reached such manic levels that for a time the B&O railroad provided crossword-puzzle dictionaries in all their cars for their fanatic, puzzle-addicted passengers.[10] And in Depression-era New York City—where an average salary for a cook was about $24 a week, for a doctor $60 a week, and for a factory worker $35 a week—what must theatergoers have thought when the show's principal character, Danny Churchill, a rich New York playboy sent by his father to

---

* A classic witty Ira Gershwin rhyme.

the family's remote ranch in the hopes that a two-year exile might change his ways, arrives by taxi with a $742.30 fare? (Not to mention, a taxi driven by a Yiddish-speaking cabdriver named Gieber Goldfarb?)

We now know that the Depression that began with the stock market crash in 1929 would continually worsen and last throughout the 1930s, but in October 1930, when *Girl Crazy* opened, this would have seemed inconceivable. For most Americans, hard times did not instantaneously follow the crash. Even at the peak of the bull market in 1929, only about 2 percent of the population had enough money to own stocks,[11] and though the effects of the crash steadily rippled throughout the economy, unemployment didn't hit rock bottom for more than three years. Most workers actually held onto their jobs, though frequently with reduced pay and reduced hours. The rich, at least for the first few years of the Depression, were barely disturbed at all. Hoover was continually reassuring the country that the economic downturn was a temporary crisis, and almost no one believed it would last. In a list created by the National Economic League in 1930 of the top problems facing the United States, unemployment was ranked 18.[12]* It was therefore still possible to laugh at, rather than be horrified by, Danny Churchill's frivolous display of wealth.

In typical "let's put-on-a-show" fashion, Danny decides to turn the family property into a slick dude ranch featuring women, gambling, and alcohol—a perfect Prohibition-era solution.† Kate Fothergill, or Frisco Kate (played by Ethel Merman), an out-of-work saloon singer from San Francisco, is hired to provide the entertainment. Like so many out-of-work migrants during the Depression, Kate and her husband Slick are willing to travel any-

---

* According to the National Economic League, the top five problems facing America in 1930 were (1) Administration of Justice, (2) Prohibition, (3) Lawlessness, Disrespect for Law, (4) Crime, (5) Law Enforcement.

† Though *Girl Crazy* takes place in a mythical Western setting in an imaginary Custerville, Arizona, the characters are all recognizable Broadway types. Putting them in a remote location allows them to engage in musical-comedy hijinks that would have seemed inappropriate in a Depression-era New York setting, and a fictional town had no need to concern itself with unemployment, failing banks, or an economy in free fall.

where for a job, even to Custerville, Arizona. The plot features innumerable cases of disguise and mistaken identities, and though it can be dangerous to read too much into this kind of light entertainment, some musical-theater historians have seen the cross-dressing in this and other shows of the period as a reflection of an emerging gay sensibility in the theater.[13] And featuring Gieber Goldfarb, the Jewish taxicab driver, in a principal role allowed Jewish humor and the Yiddish language to leave behind the circumscribed Second Avenue world of the Yiddish theater and enter the mainstream world of Broadway.

The plot not only makes room for gay and Jewish sensibilities, but Native American ones as well. In one of the funniest scenes in the show, Slick mistakes a highly educated Indian named Eagle Rock (played by an actual Indian, Chief Rivers) for the cabdriver, who had been pretending to be a stage Indian, and the two exit speaking Yiddish to each other! These two minorities, in a sense pranking a white mainstream America, create a surprisingly powerful cultural resonance even in this lightweight farce. Having Gieber Goldfarb—played by Willie Howard, one of the first openly Jewish performers on the Broadway stage—walk out speaking Yiddish, a dying immigrant language and the language of Gershwin's parents, to an actual Native American in a very small way gives a sense of the role the Broadway musical was able to play in creating opportunities for minorities to have a voice in mainstream American culture.

Girl Crazy not only gave voice to Jews and Native Americans but to newcomers as well. The show most famously turned the twenty-two-year-old Ethel Agnes Zimmerman—who according to the opening night playbill, "less than a year ago was pounding a typewriter in an auto appliance plant in Long Island City"—into Ethel Merman, the Broadway star. Though she was not quite as unknown a performer as legend would have it, she had almost no stage experience, and the story of how she got involved in the show is the kind of story normally found only in a Broadway musical. During the summer of 1930, only a few months after quitting her job as a stenographer,

Merman was singing at the Brooklyn Paramount movie theater. Vinton Freedley, *Girl Crazy*'s producer, heard her and raced backstage to introduce himself. Freedley dragged her, still covered in stage makeup, to Gershwin's apartment to hear the score of *Girl Crazy*. After Gershwin sight-read some of the tunes she was performing at the time, he hired her on the spot for $375 a week—about half of Danny Churchill's cab fare to Custerville and less than half the salary of her costar, the nineteen-year-old Ginger Rogers.

Merman's debut in Philadelphia in September and then on Broadway in October quickly became the stuff of theater legend. "I Got Rhythm" was her second song in the show. She had already won the audience over with her opening number—"Sam and Delilah," but the frenzy that greeted "I Got Rhythm" was something else entirely. In her autobiography, Merman describes this famous moment in theater history:

> As I went into the second chorus of "I Got Rhythm," I held a note for 16 bars while the orchestra played the melodic line—a big tooty thing—against the note I was holding. By the time I'd held that note for four bars the audience was applauding. They applauded through the whole chorus and I did several encores. It seemed to do something to them. Not because it was sweet or beautiful, but because it was exciting.[14]

So what is it that made this song so exciting? Surely some of the answer has to do with Ira Gershwin's remarkable lyrics. Though we have grown accustomed to this kind of casual, vernacular speech as the basic vocabulary of the classic Broadway musical, comparing Ira's words to operetta—the Sigmund Romberg/Rida Johnson Young, "Will You Remember (Sweetheart)" from their popular *Maytime*—immediately makes us realize how striking Gershwin's lyrics were at the time. The lyrics to Romberg's chorus are:

> *Sweet-heart, sweet-heart, sweet-heart*
> *Will you love me ever?*

Will you remember this day,
When we were happy in May,
My dearest one?
Sweet-heart, sweet-heart, sweet-heart,
Though our paths may sever,
To life's last faint ember
Will you remember Spring-time, Love-time, May?

These lyrics come from another time and place—Europe at the turn of the century. They speak an elegant, civilized, nostalgic, Old World language of sweet-hearts, paths that sever, and life's last faint ember, filled with cozy, traditional rhymes like "day-May" and "sever-ember" and, most precious of all, "Springtime-Love-time." *Maytime*'s voice is ultimately a borrowed one—Rida Johnson Young imitating and translating the language of European operetta into American English. In a sense these lyrics represent everything that America had been rebelling against since the colonies first rejected English rule. Comparing Young's lyric, "Sweet-heart, sweet-heart, sweet-heart, / Though our paths may sever, / To life's last faint ember / Will you remember Spring-time, Love-time, May?" with Ira's "I got rhythm / I got music / I got my man / Who could ask for anything more?" immediately gives us a sense of the fresh American voice that Ira's lyrics brought into the world of the Broadway musical, a voice too energetic and fast-paced to bother with European contractions like "I've." (It's not "*I've got* rhythm, but "*I got* rhythm.") A vernacular voice that speaks in contemporary, straight-to-the-point slang: not "I *have* my *love*," but "I got my man." A voice that finally is ours, not Europe's. A voice that is American.

The writer, philanthropist, and cofounder of the New York City Ballet, Lincoln Kirstein, beautifully summed up Ira's overall style as a lyricist:

Without condescension or parody, Ira created a new prosody, a new means for lyric-writing which incorporated the season's slang, reference to local events, echoes of the vernacular rhythms of ordinary speech in a frame of casual, thrown-away elegance which was never false, insistent or self-conscious.[15]

Ira's role in helping to create a new American voice for lyricists was more than matched by George's role in creating a new American voice for composers. Irving Berlin links the essence of this new American voice to the changes in technology at the heart of the modern era:

> All the old rhythm is gone, and in its place is heard the hum of an engine, the whirr of wheels, the explosion of an exhaust. The leisurely songs that men hummed to the clatter of horses' hooves do not fit this new rhythm. The new age demands new music for new action.[16]

No one wrote the kind of music that captured this new world of whirring wheels, exploding exhaust, and humming engines better than George Gershwin. In his songs, "all the old rhythm is gone," and Romberg's operetta world of clattering horses' hooves has been replaced by the rhythm and music that the new age demanded. *Girl Crazy* might be set in Custerville, Arizona, but its words and music come directly from contemporary, Machine Age New York City.

One of the absolutely essential ingredients for any great popular-music songwriter is the ability to create character and mood in an instant. A standard Broadway song has to tell a complete story in 32 measures, so clarity and economy are absolutely essential. The essence of "I Got Rhythm" lies in its first 2 measures. A song that repeats the lyric, "Who could ask for anything more?" four times would ordinarily be called, "Who Could Ask for Anything More?" The decision to call this song "I Got Rhythm" is a stroke of genius, since the song is defined by the fact that its main idea has a highly distinctive rhythm that dominates the entire song. The opening 8 measures are shown in Example 3.1.

This one phrase goes to the heart of Gershwin's voice, so let's examine it closely beginning with its rhythm and melody. To really grasp what makes Gershwin's rhythm so new, let's build up this key opening rhythm in three steps beginning with a version of, "I got rhythm, I got music" that has neither rhythm nor music. In this version (Ex. 3.2, Step 1), I have kept all of Gershwin's notes and simply changed the rhythm to all half notes, squarely on the beat. In Step 2, I give the phrase a little music and a little rhythm by beginning a beat later, syncopating it. Now it's almost Gershwin. In both of these versions, each note of "I," "got," and "rhy-" lasts four, square, eighth-note beats. In Gershwin's version (Step 3), however, these words last only three, irregular, eighth-note beats. That's what makes the syncopated phrase unusual, jazzy, and new, turning it into a phrase that's got rhythm.

Example 3.1 "I Got Rhythm"

Example 3.2 "I Got Rhythm," Steps 1–3

Furthermore, this syncopated, four-note rhythm ("I got rhy-thm") is actually the key to the entire song. Gershwin uses the same rhythm for "I got music," as well as "I got my man." If he were a terrible composer, he might have finished the phrase squarely, using a rhythm like Example 3.3.

Instead, we get the musical equivalent of a punch line—the only new rhythm in the phrase for the lyric, "Who could ask for anything more?"

But it is not only rhythm that makes these opening 8 measures so new and so striking. The notes of the melody complement its rhythm in an amazing way. As we saw in Example 3.1, the melody begins with four ascending notes on "I got rhythm"—C–D–F–G—followed by the same four notes backward on "I got music"—G–F–D–C. Then the original four notes repeat on "I got my man"—C–D–F–G. And then, after using noth-

Example 3.3 "I Got Rhythm," Kapilow version

ing but the same four notes forward and backward and the same rhythm for the first three lines of text, the melody that concludes the phrase, like the rhythm, is brand new. It has a different melodic shape, using eight notes instead of four, as well as two new pitches—A and B♭—with the B♭, the highest note of the phrase on the word "who," kicking off the punch line.

In addition to the phrase's jazz-influenced rhythm, and riff-like melody, what makes it new, modern, and American is its jazz-influenced harmony. Gershwin's ear for harmony went far beyond most songwriters of the time, and the hours he spent listening to the era's great jazz pianists in Harlem nightclubs heavily influenced his harmonic style. In "Jazz Is the Voice of the American Soul," a 1926 article for *Theatre Magazine*, Gershwin described the voice of that soul as "jazz developed out of ragtime, jazz that is the plantation song improved and transferred into finer, bigger harmonies,"[17] and those "finer, bigger harmonies" will play a major role in the voice of this song. For example, each chord in the right hand underneath the words "I got rhythm" has three notes (Ex. 3.4A). He could easily have continued with three-note chords in the next measure (Ex. 3.4B). But instead, each chord adds an extra, fourth note, giving the harmony incredible richness (Ex. 3.4C). He could then have resolved the first chord in the fourth measure immediately (Ex. 3.4D). But instead, he delays the resolution, building tension (Ex. 3.4E). And instead of staying with bright major chords for "I got my man who" (Ex. 3.4F), Gershwin substitutes a bluesy minor chord on the word "who" (Ex. 3.4G).

Example 3.4A "I Got Rhythm," Gershwin version

Example 3.4B "I Got Rhythm," Kapilow version

Example 3.4C "I Got Rhythm," Gershwin version

Example 3.4D "I Got Rhythm," Kapilow version

Example 3.4E "I Got Rhythm," Gershwin version

Example 3.4F "I Got Rhythm," Kapilow version

Example 3.4G "I Got Rhythm," Gershwin version

Example 3.4H "I Got Rhythm"

This one "bluesy" minor chord hints at a crucial, often-misunderstood emotional aspect of this song. On the surface, it initially sounds like the optimistic, joyful song of a woman who has it all—rhythm, music, daisies in green pastures, starlight, sweet dreams, and most important, *her man*. But in fact, Kate's husband Slick is constantly flirting with other women, and in her second-act number, "Boy! What Love Has Done to Me!" she expresses the real truth of their relationship: "My life he's wrecking, bet you could find him now / Out somewhere necking somebody else's frau." Kate is anything but sure of the fact that she's "got her man." In fact, right before she sings "I Got Rhythm" in Act I, she catches Slick flirting with some girls, and in "I Got Rhythm" she is actually trying to convince herself, as much as anyone else, that she has her man and that she's got it all. That one minor chord is her moment of doubt. She's wondering, "Maybe I'm not enough?" The major-key ending of the phrase (Ex. 3.4H) answers her question. It sounds upbeat, resolved. All doubt is gone. "Who could ask for anything more?"

Since the end of the war, America had been searching for an authentic, homegrown voice that would reflect the new reality of postwar American life. A voice that would say no to the European-style operettas of Rudolf Friml and Sigmund Romberg. A voice that would answer the question metaphorically posed by the famous 1924 Aeolian Hall concert during which *Rhapsody in Blue* had its premiere—"What is American Music?"* The opening phrase of "I Got Rhythm," like *Rhapsody in Blue*, is a perfect example of Gershwin's answer. American music, it proclaims, is sophisticated, focused, vernacular, dynamic, fast-paced, and above all it "has rhythm." It swings. For Gershwin, the operetta's days of leisurely waltzes are over. "I Got Rhythm" might not be authentic jazz, but it authentically captured the new energy and spirit of the times.

---

* The actual title of the "educational concert" was "An Experiment in Modern Music," and it was designed to demonstrate the development of jazz.

Example 3.5 "I Got Rhythm," B section

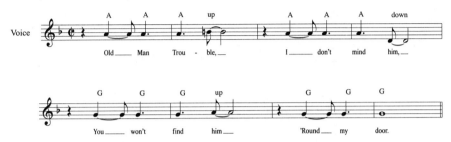

In a standard 32-bar Broadway song, the opening 8-bar idea—called A—repeats three times (AABA) and makes up 75 percent of the song, so this opening phrase has to contain the essence of the song and the essence of the singer's character. In "I Got Rhythm," the distinctive rhythm of the A section is actually at the heart of the B section as well (Ex. 3.5).

The two sections use the same rhythm. "I got rhythm, I got music, I got my man," follows the same pattern as "Old Man Trouble, I don't mind him, You won't find him." Though completely different in shape from the A section, the melodic idea of the B section is equally clear. Four notes of which the first three are the same. First it goes up. "Old Man Trouble" (A–A–A *up*). Balanced by, "I don't mind him" (A–A–A *down*). The whole combination then starts to repeat a step lower: "You won't find him" (G–G–G *up*). An exact copy would finish as in Example 3.6 (G–G–G *down*).

But once again, we get a punch line. Not G–G–G–C, but simply G–G–G for "'Round my door." The punch line in the opening phrase ("Who could ask for anything more?") added notes—the four-note idea became eight—while the punch line in the B section ("'Round my door") subtracts notes—the four-note idea becomes three. Utterly clear, focused, and unified.

Example 3.6 "I Got Rhythm," Kapilow version

Example 3.7A "I Got Rhythm,"
Kapilow version

Example 3.7B "I Got Rhythm,"
Gershwin version

Example 3.7C "I Got Rhythm,"
Kapilow version

Example 3.7D "I Got Rhythm,"
Gershwin version

Example 3.7E "I Got Rhythm,"
Gershwin version

Example 3.7F "I Got Rhythm,"
Kapilow version

Example 3.7G "I Got Rhythm," Gershwin version

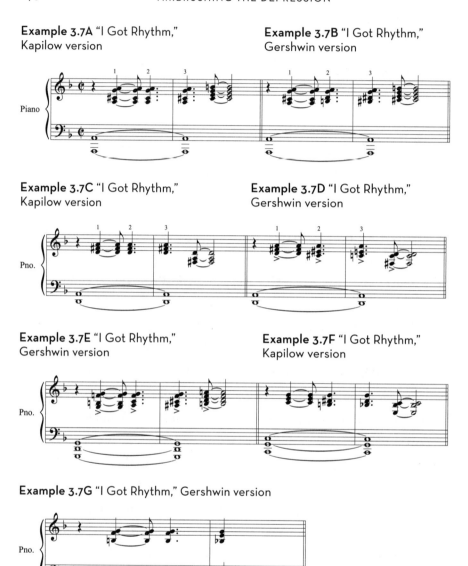

But what really gives the B section its voice is the jazz-influenced harmony. Since each unit of melody begins with three repeated notes, Gershwin could simply have repeated the same chord three times, as in Example 3.7A. Instead, each melody note gets a different chord, with the lower two notes in the right hand sliding *upward* chromatically—a technique copied directly from the Harlem pianists who influenced Gershwin's voice (Ex. 3.7B). He could have used three repeated chords for "I don't mind him" as well (Ex. 3.7C). But instead the harmony slithers *downward*, again with a different chord for each melody note (Ex. 3.7D). The harmony, like the melody, then begins to repeat lower for "You won't find him" (Ex. 3.7E), but instead of copying the pattern to finish like Example 3.7F, a surprising bass note kicks off the punch line (Ex. 3.7G)

One of the glories of a standardized form like the sonnet, haiku, or 32-bar Broadway song form is that the slightest variation gets noticed, and the ending of "I Got Rhythm" doesn't disappoint. If Gershwin had simply copied the A section for the third time to finish the piece—the standard form—the final section would have lasted 8 measures and finished like in Example 3.8.

But instead, Gershwin adds 2 extra measures to the section, allowing Frisco Kate to say the last line twice. The first time she's asking a question: "Who could ask for anything more?" The second time she's exclaim-

Example 3.8 "I Got Rhythm" final section, Kapilow version

ing a fact. "Who could ask for anything more!" Instead of the standard 8 + 8 + 8 + **8**, 32-bar form, Gershwin gives us 8 + 8 + 8 + **10**, with the extra 2 measures to convince her and us that she really has got it all. In the not-as-simple-as-it-seems world of *Girl Crazy*, and in the surely-not-simple world of the 1930s, the answer to the question "Who could ask for anything more?" had no easy answers.

As the decade progressed and the Depression deepened, the question "Who could ask for anything more?" and its corollary, "From whom?" became one of the country's central concerns. When *Girl Crazy* opened

Example 3.9 "I Got Rhythm" final section, Gershwin version in October 1930, both Hoover and most of the country saw the downturn in the economy as something temporary, similar to recessions of the past. But by the time Franklin Delano Roosevelt took office in March 1933, it was clear that something far more extreme was taking place. With nearly 25 percent of the workforce unemployed, millions of people were asking for more, and for the first time the federal government was taking on the responsibility of answering their pleas on an unprecedented scale. Hoover and past presidents had believed that the government should stay out of the business of regulating the economy, thereby leaving the poor, the unemployed, and the elderly without meaningful safety nets. Roosevelt, however, believed it was the government's job to provide more to people for whom music, rhythm, daisies, starlight, and sweet dreams were not enough. In the imaginary town of Custerville, people might not have to worry about mortgages, rent, food, clothing, and jobs, but in the real world of the 1930s, Old Man Trouble was a ubiquitous presence at most people's doors.

Even someone as rich and famous as Gershwin could not remain unaffected by the alarming changes in the world around him. As the decade progressed, a new seriousness would enter his work on three satirical musicals written with George S. Kaufman—*Strike Up the Band, Of Thee I Sing*, and *Let 'Em Eat Cake*—and most significantly his unique folk opera, *Porgy and Bess*. This work would take the issues of appropriation and voice raised by his "whitening" of jazz in works like *Rhapsody in Blue* and songs like "I Got Rhythm" to new and more controversial levels. In a classic story of American reinvention, the son of Jewish immigrants would join a white southern author to invent the voice of a southern black community in a work that would ultimately become the quintessential American opera. Had Gershwin replaced jazz as "the voice of the American soul?" The answer would clearly depend on which American you asked, but there was no doubt that America had found a unique, distinctive voice. A voice of synthesis, integration, and appropriation. A voice forged in the melting pot of America. A voice drawn from many sources, but finally a voice that was indisputably our own.

4

Segregation and Opportunity in Harlem

Harold Arlen's "Stormy Weather"

Like George Gershwin, Harold Arlen became famous overnight thanks to the success of a single song. In February 1930, almost exactly ten years after Gershwin struck gold with Al Jolson's recording of "Swanee," Ruth Etting's performance of "Get Happy" in Ruth Selwyn's *Nine-Fifteen Revue* launched Arlen's career in equally meteoric fashion. The show premiered on Broadway on February 11, only eight months before *Girl Crazy*, and though it closed in less than a week, in that short time "Get Happy" became, in Arlen's modest words, a "noisy song." By February 19, Ted Wallace and his Campus Boys had already recorded the piece, and two more recordings by other orchestras would follow that same year. Benny Goodman later recorded an enormously popular version in 1936. But despite the success of "Get Happy" and many of his other songs, Arlen's fame would ultimately be of an entirely different kind than Gershwin's.

Ed Jablonski, Harold Arlen's biographer, tells a story that goes to the heart of his perplexing, contradictory career.

One day Arlen took a taxi across town in Manhattan. As he stepped into the cab, he heard the driver whistling "Stormy Weather." Arlen asked him if he knew who wrote that song.

"Sure," the driver said. "Irving Berlin."

"Wrong," Arlen answered, "but I'll give you two more guesses."

When the driver couldn't come up with another name, Arlen prompted him: "Richard Rodgers?"

The driver admitted that was the name he was thinking of, but he knew it was wrong.

"Cole Porter?" Arlen offered.

"That's it!" the driver exclaimed.

"Wrong again," Arlen told him. "I wrote the song."

Embarrassed, the driver asked, "Who are you?"

"Harold Arlen," he replied.

The driver turned around in his seat and asked, "Who?"

Arlen would go on to say that the four words that summed up his entire career were, "You wrote that too?"[1] "Over the Rainbow," "Get Happy," "Stormy Weather," "That Old Black Magic," "I've Got the World on a String," "Blues in the Night," "Come Rain or Come Shine," "The Man That Got Away," "Ac-Cent-Tchu-Ate the Positive." Everyone knows the songs, but almost no one knows the composer.

Harold Arlen was born Hyman Arluck, in Buffalo, New York in 1905.* Like Irving Berlin and Al Jolson, Arlen was the son of a cantor, and like Berlin, Jolson, and Gershwin, he Americanized his name as soon as he was able in order to remove any trace of his immigrant, Jewish past. (Arlen was an invented combination of the last names of his parents—Arluck and Orlen.)[2] Given his later attraction to black performers and what Duke

---

* Arlen felt oppressed by the Buffalo he grew up in and later said, "To commit suicide in Buffalo would be redundant."

Ellington called "the Negro musical idiom," it is interesting to note that the Arlucks rented the upstairs of their two-family home to a black family—Anderson and Minnie Arthur and their three children. The neighborhood was largely Jewish, but there were a significant number of African American and German American families as well and supposedly little racial tension between the groups. Arlen and the Arthur children not only were constant playmates, but they all attended the same school, Bennett Park #32, which was the first school in Buffalo to be integrated. Arlen's father gave Minnie a mezuzah, which she kept on her door throughout her life, and her grandson claimed that the friendship between the families "made Arlen feel at home among African Americans and with their music."[3]

Arlen was not only comfortable with their music; he immersed himself in it through the dance band recordings he brought home and, to the horror of his father, played incessantly on the family's phonograph. His father's recordings of synagogue music competed with Hyman's recordings of the Original Dixieland Jazz Band, Bessie Smith, Fletcher Henderson, and James P. Johnson. Singing in his father's synagogue choir mixed with the hours he spent listening to local dance bands to create an unusually rich musical background that he would draw on throughout his career. Though it might seem like the worlds of the synagogue and the local dance hall would have nothing in common, Arlen would later say, "I was jazz crazy. I don't know how the hell to explain it—except I hear in jazz and in gospel my father singing. He was one of the greatest improvisers I've ever heard."[4]

In spite of his parents' hopes for him to go to college and take up a legitimate profession, like Gershwin, Arlen dropped out of high school. He quickly became the pianist, vocalist, and arranger for several bands with such great names as the Snappy Trio and the Buffalodians. After touring with the latter to Cleveland and Pittsburgh, the band, like so many aspiring musicians in the 1920s, eventually made its way to New York City. There, after Americanizing his name, Arlen landed a small singing part in a Vincent Youmans musical, *Great Day*.

During rehearsal one day, the dance accompanist got sick, and Arlen offered to fill in. Pianists used to play a standard pickup, a 2-measure vamp to cue in the dancers and lead into the music—the equivalent of counting off "5, 6, 7, 8." Bored with playing the same pickup over and over again, he started to fool around with it. Will Marion Cook, a composition student of Antonín Dvořák, was at the rehearsal and encouraged Arlen to develop his improvisation into a song. Harry Warren, the composer of the first hugely successful film musical, *42nd Street*, suggested he work with the lyricist Ted Koehler to add words. Together, Koehler and Arlen turned the little vamp into the song "Get Happy," and when the publisher Al Piantadosi heard it, he offered Arlen his first contract as a songwriter for $50 a week.[5] Arlen's career was launched at the age of twenty-five. Or so he thought.

Unfortunately, Arlen signed his publishing contract on July 31, 1929, only months before the stock market crash and the beginning of the Depression—a challenging time for a young songwriter to make his mark on Broadway. Broadway theaters were closing and productions declined, and though many composers went to Hollywood looking for new opportunities, Arlen went north—or slightly north of Broadway—to the legendary Cotton Club on 142nd Street and Lenox Avenue in Harlem.

One of the reasons for the Cotton Club's enormous success was its ability to circumvent Prohibition, which by law was supposed to keep the country dry beginning in 1920.* The club opened in 1923 and was essentially run from jail by the white bootlegger and gangster Owney Madden, whose #1 beer was one of the establishment's key attractions. Though the clientele was all white, the performers were all black (with their own separate entrance), and the elegant, expensive club with its stylish plan-

---

* "Stormy Weather" debuted at the Cotton Club on April 6, 1933, eight months before the ratification of the 21st Amendment, which ended Prohibition on December 5, 1933.

tation environment was a chic meeting place for celebrities throughout the 1920s and '30s. Fletcher Henderson's big band was the first to play at the club, and Duke Ellington's legendary engagement there from 1927 to 1931 aired nationwide weekly on radio WHN, bringing his music not only to white audiences in New York but to audiences around the country.

The rich, elegantly dressed clientele came uptown to see an up-tempo, Broadway-style revue featuring beautiful, scantily dressed women. The female performers had to be light-skinned blacks, and the dancers had to be at least five feet six inches tall and under twenty-one years old.[6] Lyrics and comic sketches were filled with double entendres and salacious innuendo. The club had a large dance floor, dining areas, and a stage that could fit the band, the show's stars, vocalists, comedians, and dancers. The club was advertised as "The Aristocrat of Harlem," and Maurice Chevalier, the famous French cabaret singer, actor, and entertainer, called it "the most sophisticated café in New York."[7] Though many people today look back at the racial segregation of the club and its demeaning depiction of its black employees as exotic, sensual savages in a fantasy plantation atmosphere as blatantly racist, perpetuating humiliating stereotypes that reached back to the days of the minstrel shows; the club, and the world of musical theater in general, did, in spite of it all, offer employment to large numbers of black artists and musicians in a time of extraordinary economic crisis, providing one of the few avenues of social mobility in the first decades of the twentieth century.

The club also created writing opportunities for white composers and lyricists like Arlen and Koehler. The two worked on five different shows there between 1930 and 1934, writing "Stormy Weather" for their penultimate show, the *Cotton Club Parade of 1933*.* Nearly all of the songs in these Cotton Club shows were written for particular performers, and the match between "Stormy Weather" and its first singer, the great Ethel

---

* The club's heyday was during Prohibition from 1923 to 1933. The Harlem version closed in 1935, one year after Arlen and Koehler's last show at the club and the end of Prohibition. The club reopened briefly in the Theater District from 1936 to 1940.

Waters, was a perfect one on multiple levels.* In addition to being a superb singer, she had a special connection to the song's story. Her marriage to her second husband, Eddie Matthews, had ended badly, and the lyrics of "Stormy Weather"—"Don't know why / There's no sun up in the sky / Stormy Weather / Since my man and I ain't together / Keeps rainin' all the time"—perfectly matched her mood. She later wrote in her autobiography:

> When I got out there in the middle of the Cotton Club floor, I was telling things I couldn't frame in words. I was singing the story of my misery and confusion, of the misunderstandings in my life I couldn't straighten out, the story of wrongs and outrages done to me by people I had loved and trusted. . . . If there's anything I owe Eddie Matthews, it's that he enabled me to do one hell of a job on the song "Stormy Weather."[8]

Waters's performance represents an extraordinary moment in the history of America finding its voice. Though she may have been performing in a segregated, racist club—a club she could not even enter as a customer—when she sang "Stormy Weather," she was stepping outside of conventional black stereotypes. She was no longer simply taking on one of the standard roles to which black women had previously been consigned—that of a Jezebel (a lewd, lower-class, sexually promiscuous woman), a Mammy (a house servant dedicated to serving her white family and their children), or any of the other minstrel-show caricatures that continued to represent blacks as ignorant, lazy, and superstitious. Instead, she was speaking directly from

---

* The song was originally intended to be sung by Cab Calloway, but when he abruptly left the Cotton Club, his band was replaced by Duke Ellington's. Ellington's band had no singer for the song, so Ethel Waters was brought in. Arlen and Koehler met with her and adapted the song to suit her. Though Waters was the first singer to perform the song in its public Cotton Club debut on April 6, 1933, a recording by the Leo Reisman orchestra featuring a vocal by Arlen himself was recorded on February 28, and the recording's popularity helped build anticipation for the song's Cotton Club premiere. Arlen's wonderfully spontaneous vocal embellishments of his own melody on the Reisman recording are a superb demonstration of his instinctive feel for jazz.

her heart, directly from her pain, to a white audience as an equal. As a person, not a type.

Waters, a child of rape, had first been married at age thirteen; Eddie Matthews was her second divorce. In 1914, the total number of divorces in America reached 100,000 for the first time. In 1929, 205,000 couples divorced *in a single year*.[9] Waters was one of the new, liberated women who symbolized the disintegration of the traditional family that the Roaring Twenties seemed to represent to many conservative Americans. Yet through a white man's music, she was singing her story, breaking down decades of stereotypes to humanize her race to the club's white audiences and, through her recording of "Stormy Weather," to America as a whole. She would soon become the single highest-paid performer on Broadway, an astonishing feat, given the times.[10] It is hard to imagine there being any other field in America in 1933, at the height of the Depression, in which the highest-paid employee was a black person. But what made this moment so significant was not just that a black woman was being treated as an artist and an equal, but that the very music she was singing—Arlen's music—was itself deeply influenced by the music and speech of black Americans.

The connection between Arlen's music and black American music has always been apparent to performers as well as commentators. In his classic 1972 book, *American Popular Song*, Alec Wilder points out that Arlen's music, more than any of the other major songwriters of the time, grew directly out of American jazz. Johnny Mercer, one of Arlen's greatest collaborators, said in a television interview with Walter Cronkite that Arlen "plunged himself into the heartbeat of the popular music of his youth, the dance band. . . . He had that crazy jazz going. . . . George's [Gershwin] jazz was mechanical compared to Harold's." Pointing to his stomach, Mercer said, "Harold's was right from in there." And Ethel Waters made it personal when she said that she considered him to be "the Negro-est white man I know."[11] Arlen's music was not only deeply influenced by black American music, it was also eloquently served by some of the greatest black singers of the time. Not just Ethel Waters, but also Pearl Bailey, Diahann Carroll, and Lena Horne, as well as the bands of Cab Calloway and Duke Ellington.

Arlen was able to combine the improvisatory feel of his father's cantorial embellishments that he heard singing in the synagogue choir as a child with the wail of the blues and the jazz-influenced harmonies of 1920s and '30s dance bands to create some of the most affecting and uniquely personal torch songs in the history of American popular music. The all-black musical environment of the Cotton Club, as well as the late-night New York City clubs where Arlen received an informal conservatory degree listening to the city's great African American jazz musicians, turned out to be the perfect incubator for the development of Arlen's style. At the Cotton Club, he was immersed in the world of African American jazz on a daily basis. The club's bands were among the finest in America, and working with Cab Calloway, Jimmie Lunceford, and Duke Ellington's groups as well as some of Harlem's finest singers enormously influenced Arlen's music. Perhaps because of his early friendship with the Arthurs in Buffalo, his relationship with the black employees at the club was extraordinarily warm. The musicians in Calloway's and Ellington's bands admired Arlen's playing and compositions, and the free exchange between Arlen and the club's musicians contributed significantly to his developing style. When a new dance craze came on the scene, he saw it demonstrated at the club, and it became part of his musical vocabulary. Dancers like Bill "Bojangles" Robinson and the Nicholas Brothers as well as singers like Leitha Hill, Adelaide Hall, and Ethel Waters were all part of the rich musical environment that the club provided, and this unique environment helped to shape Arlen's approach to songwriting in ways that would last throughout his career.

Torch songs are about failing in love and the misery that failure brings. To carry a torch for someone means to be deeply in love without any hope of that love being returned. These songs were vehicles for the expression of a composer and performer's deepest personal feelings. They are gut-wrenching, heart-on-the-sleeve songs, and "Stormy Weather" is a classic example.* Like so many of Arlen's works, "Stormy Weather" was built out of a short sketch, or a "jot," as he called them. They were musical fragments, a few notes to a couple measures in length. He wrote them down whenever he had a musical idea and found a place for them later. To get a sense of what made this jot and opening phrase so special, here is an ordinary version of the opening phrase (Ex. 4.1) that we can compare with Arlen's (Ex. 4.2), note by note and jot by jot.

Example 4.1 "Stormy Weather," Kapilow version

Example 4.2 "Stormy Weather," Arlen version

---

* Though Arlen never spoke about his own feelings when writing the song, it is possible that the "stormy weather" in his own relationship with Anya Tarenda, the beautiful model he would eventually marry in 1937, in some sense fueled the song. Arlen met Anya in 1932, and the fact that she was Gentile and he was Jewish caused immense difficulty with both of their parents. Though this is pure speculation, it is possible that the difficulties in his own relationship with Anya gave him an emotional insight and personal understanding that helped inspire the song.

My version has absolutely no pain or longing in either the vocal part or the piano part, whereas Arlen's genius begins with the very first note. His original jot was nothing but the opening of the vocal line: G#–A–C. Only his first note is different from mine (G# instead of A), but that one dissonant, chromatic note—a half step between the first and second notes instead of my repeated notes—makes all the difference. That dissonance— Arlen's blues note—is the pain of someone who has lost their love, someone for whom "there's no sun up in the sky." (Fascinatingly, the original lyric was the far-less desolate "clouds are dark up in the sky.") In the hands of a great vocalist like Ethel Waters, that painful, dissonant, opening half step instantly creates the mood of the entire song.

My version continues with a boring melody that repeats the rhythm of the first three notes ("Don't know why") on the next three notes ("there's no sun"). Arlen instead repeats his first three notes (G#–A–C) but with a quicker rhythm on an offbeat, conveying urgency and angst and giving the melody a spontaneous, improvised feeling. My version finishes the thought by using only notes in the key of the song, creating a nice, pain-free, greeting-card, singsong melody on "sun up in the sky, Stormy Weather." But in typical Arlen fashion, he writes a chromatic melody instead, a melody more instrumental than vocal (chromatic scales are difficult to sing but easy to play on instruments) that offers a great singer an opportunity to convey heartache with the little chromatic scale on "in the sky."

What follows is classic Arlen: an octave leap that you find over and over again in his music, almost like a personal signature. Instead of my conventional, small leap down on "Stormy Weather," he has the singer jump down to the pain-filled, low register of the voice, down to the solar plexus, where grief is actually felt.

What really makes Arlen's music so expressive here is his extraordinary use of blues notes, which goes far beyond what we saw from Kern in "Can't Help Lovin' Dat Man." An ordinary version of "keeps rainin' all the time" with an ordinary melody and ordinary chords—with no dissonance, no "rain" and no "pain"—would sound like Example 4.3. It's Arlen's blues note in the vocal part on "all" (Ex. 4.4), a note emphasized both by its syncopation and length, and the jazz-inflected harmony in the piano underneath it,* plus the return of the opening blues note on "the" that gives the phrase its power—a poignancy borrowed from the wail of the southern blues.

When Gershwin heard "Stormy Weather," he said, "You know you didn't repeat a phrase in the first eight bars?"[12] Arlen replied that he never gave it a thought. He always claimed he simply wrote what he felt and what pleased him, extending a phrase till he thought it was done and extending a song until he had finished saying what he had to say. That quality has a great deal to do

Example 4.3 "Stormy Weather," Kapilow version

Example 4.4 "Stormy Weather," Arlen version

---

* For musicians: C♭9♯5.

with what makes not only "Stormy Weather" but so many of his other songs unique. Though Arlen rarely spoke about the technical aspects of composition, he suggested that his melodic style might have been influenced by his father's cantorial singing. "He improvised wonderful melodies to fit the texts that had no music, and that's undoubtedly where my sense of melody comes from.[13] Instead of writing phrases built out of repetitions of catchy fragments like "I Got Rhythm," Arlen, perhaps more than any other popular songwriter of the time, wrote in what's called through-composed style, in which a musical idea develops and expands freely, without inner repetition. And though "Stormy Weather" appears to begin like any other 32-bar Broadway song—that is, with an 8-bar phrase—the opening phrase is irregularly divided, starting with a 3-measure idea instead of a 2-measure ("Don't know why there's no / sun up in the sky, stormy / weather.") A 2-measure idea follows ("Since my man and I ain't to- / gether."), and then another 3-measure idea ("keeps rainin all the / time"/ turnaround bar).* The result is an 8-measure phrase divided not in typical 4 + 4 fashion but instead 3 + 2 + 3, and with no repetition of ideas within the phrase.

Arlen's willingness to allow a musical idea to expand freely and to extend a phrase until he felt it was done gives his music a spontaneous feel, which affects not only the measure-by-measure flow of "Stormy Weather" but also its overall structure. If Arlen were following standard 32-bar song form, he would have repeated the 8-measure A section with new lyrics and ended like Example 4.5.

But the singer is so weary, so filled with pain, so unable to get her "poor self together" that she can't finish the A section and move on to the B section. In her weariness, she spontaneously repeats the phrase, "so weary all the time," making the phrase 10 bars instead of 8—an extension that caused enormous problems for bandleaders, who were used to popular music constructed exclusively in 8-bar phrases (Ex. 4.6).

---

* A turnaround bar is a measure at the end of a section whose principal function is to circle back seamlessly to the starting point. A turnaround bar "turns the phrase around."

Example 4.5 "Stormy Weather," Kapilow version

Example 4.6 "Stormy Weather," Arlen version

The B section is a release from the painful, chromatic writing of the opening two A sections. It has an almost gospel-like feel, as Arlen simply alternates back and forth between two basic chords (B♭ and F major) for 6 measures with a simple, driving, quarter-note rhythmic beat in the accompaniment. At the same time, the vocal line repeats a single measure at the beginning of each 2-bar group (the melody of measures 1, 3, and 5 of Ex. 4.7

Example 4.7 "Stormy Weather"

are identical) with only the final two notes of each group changing. Measure 2 ends with A–F on "met me." Measure 4 ends lower, sitting in the rocking chair, so to speak—D–C on "get me." Measure 6 ends higher, up in the region of "the Lord above" on B♭–A for "let me," which leads to the quasi-religious climax on C for "walk." The gospel/blues-style repetition of a lead measure (measures 1, 3, 5, and 7) and the back-and-forth harmony (B♭–F, B♭–F) release the listener from the through-composed A sections with no repetition and constantly changing harmony and push the song to its

Example 4.8 "Stormy Weather," Kapilow version

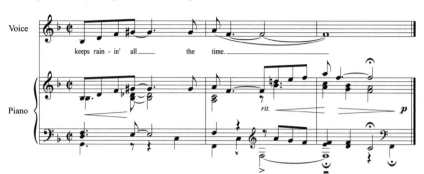

climax on the highest note of the B section, followed by its only new melodic fragment—the punch line of the phrase ("walk in the sun once more").*

In a standard 32-bar Broadway song, the opening 8-bar A section returns. If Arlen had followed this formula, "Stormy Weather" would end like Example 4.8.

But instead, Arlen has to finish what he's saying. After repeating the 10-bar A section, he adds a powerful interlude (Arlen's term marked in the score), which not only dissolves the standard form but also raises the emotional intensity of the song to an almost unbearable level. The interlude begins with a dark, minor-key painting of what it feels like to walk around "heavy hearted and sad" (Ex. 4.9).

Removing the blues notes in the next phrase, "Night comes around and I'm still feelin' bad" (Ex. 4.10A), shows how essential these notes were to Arlen's expressive vocabulary. Without them, the phrase is almost cheerful. No one is "feelin' bad" at all. Arlen's blues notes on "comes" and "feel" (Ex. 4.10B) bring the singer's pain and misery to life. The pitch of the vocal line then starts to rise higher as the expression becomes more intense and passionate.

---

* Koehler's attention to detail in the song's lyrics is extraordinary. He changed "When he went away the blues *came* and met me" to the far more specific, "When he went away the blues *walked in* and met me," and "All I do is *hope* the Lord above will let me," to "All I do is *pray* the Lord above will let me."

Example 4.9 "Stormy Weather," interlude

Example 4.10A "Stormy Weather," Kapilow version

Example 4.10B "Stormy Weather," Arlen version

Once again, Arlen's blues notes on "pour" and "hope" (Ex. 4.11) make the image of "Rain pourin' down, blindin' ev'ry hope I had" excruciatingly, exquisitely painful. The vocal line's fast notes onomatopoetically represent the rain's "pitterin' patterin' beatin' an' splatterin,'" and the wailing E♭ on "drives me mad" concludes the phrase and leads to the

Example 4.11 "Stormy Weather"

song's climax. Suddenly we get the highest note of the entire song—the F on "love"—and a huge, trademark-Arlen octave leap. All rhythmic motion in the accompaniment stops, and the phrase is as close to a wail of pain as music gets. These four "loves," shouted above dissonant harmony, are stabs in the heart. This extraordinary moment—the emotional core of the song—is followed by a stunning fragment of utterly naked, blues-like speech: "this misery is just too much for me."

It's a heartrending representation of despair and psychological break-down. This gut-wrenching climax, welding the emotional catharsis and expressive vocabulary of the blues to Arlen's distinctive musical language is electrifying, and when the song goes on to repeat its A section one last time, the bare, emotional honesty of the interlude changes how we hear the music from earlier. "Can't go on, ev'ry thing I had is gone" now has a new aura of desolation as the singer tries to move forward in an emotional world that "keeps rainin' all the time."

橶

"Stormy Weather" premiered at the Cotton Club on April 6, 1933, only a month after Franklin Delano Roosevelt took office as president and began his historic first 100 days. The Depression was at its height, and the unemployment in some cities almost defied belief. By 1933 nearly 90 percent of Lowell, Massachusetts, was jobless.[14] Farm prices had fallen by 60 percent and industrial production by more than half since 1929.[15] The banking system was in complete disarray, and the country was in a state of panic. While Arlen and Kohler were putting the finishing touches on *The Cotton Club Parade of 1933*, FDR was just beginning his quest to pull the country out of the Depression—to "wage a war against the emergency"—through bold legislation like the Emergency Banking Act, the National Industrial Recovery Act, the Agricultural Adjustment Act, and the Tennessee Valley Authority Act.

Greek tragedies provide catharsis by projecting a culture's sufferings onto a given individual, thereby allowing these sufferings to be experienced intensely and artistically by proxy from a safe personal distance. Though "Stormy Weather" is certainly a classic torch song about one woman's misery, it also describes the larger Depression-era world, a world where "there's no sun up in the sky," where "life is bare" with "gloom and mis'ry ev'rywhere." Where "ev'ry thing I had is gone," and it "keeps rainin' all the time." Somehow this song expresses one woman's deeply personal story while simultaneously standing for the struggle of the culture at large, providing, if only for a moment, some sense of catharsis.

But whatever the song's artistic relationship to the world outside the Cotton Club, there can be no doubt about its impact for the people inside. Though it is easy to look back and criticize the Cotton Club's whites-only admission policy, as well as the racist stereotypes its atmosphere and shows perpetuated, the club offered work and wages to black performers at a time when black unemployment massively exceeded the already staggering figures of the time. (Some estimates put the figure for blacks as high as 50 percent nationwide.) And in a time when blacks earned approximately 30 percent less than whites,[16] the club paid its performers extremely well, thanks to the exorbitant prices the club charged its customers.

The club and its revues, however, did much more than simply offer employment in the midst of the Depression, it also helped launch important careers. Bands like Fletcher Henderson's and Duke Ellington's—the house band from 1927 to 1931—were given unprecedented national exposure through weekly radio broadcasts, as well as a laboratory in which to develop their craft. Lena Horne got her first professional job at the club as a sixteen-year-old chorus girl, and a wide range of other performers like Dorothy Dandridge, Adelaide Hall, Florence Mills, Sammy Davis Jr., the Nicholas Brothers, and jazz greats Coleman Hawkins, Cab Calloway, and Don Redman all had their careers launched or aided by the club.

At a time of limited possibilities, the Cotton Club, racist though it may have been, provided desperately needed opportunities not only for black performers like Ethel Waters but also for a white composer like Harold Arlen. And it not only exposed white audience members and radio listeners to black culture at a time when such opportunities were rare, it exposed Arlen to black culture in ways that helped shape the language and expression of his own music.* Arlen may have fled north from a Depression-battered Broadway to the imaginary southern plantation setting of the Cotton Club for purely economic reasons, but his immersion in the club's black world and his absorption of the music he heard there were key factors in his creation of an artistic style that in many ways brought the black and white worlds that were so forcefully segregated at the club together in his own music. The world of the thirties may still have been a largely segregated one, but Arlen, the "Negro-est white man" Ethel Waters ever knew, looked past these differences and instead saw only possibility, finding, as did so many other white American composers of the time, a rich source of inspiration in the black musical world that would become a major component of Arlen's—and America's—voice.

---

* White audiences outside New York City also got a chance to see an original Harlem revue when the entire *Cotton Club Parade of 1933*, now renamed the *Stormy Weather Revue*, went on tour for the first time in the club's history with Adelaide Hall headlining the company in major cities throughout the country.

5

Appropriation or Inspiration?

George Gershwin's "Summertime"

In 1892, six years before George Gershwin was born, the Czech composer Antonín Dvořák came to America to lead the recently formed National Conservatory of Music in New York City. Unable to resist an offer of as much money for a single year as director as he had previously earned in his entire lifetime as a composer, Dvořák spent three years in America, during which time he produced some of his greatest music, including the *New World Symphony*, the *Cello Concerto*, and the *American String Quartet*. He became fascinated with American indigenous music—in particular the music of the American Indians and African American spirituals. Legend has it that Dvořák heard Harry Burleigh, a young black composer at the Conservatory who worked as a handyman to help pay his tuition, singing spirituals while cleaning the Conservatory's halls. Dvořák asked Burleigh to sing for him. The two grew close, and Burleigh would later say, "I sang our Negro songs for him very often, and before he wrote his own themes, he filled himself with the spirit of the old spirituals."[1] Though Dvořák was adamant that no actual spirituals ever appeared directly in his music, he clearly absorbed their directness of expression, and perhaps the overriding message of his three-year stay, articulated in the press and in interviews, was his belief that America needed to create a school of composition based on its indigenous folk music.

> The future music of this country must be founded upon what are called the Negro melodies. This must be the real foundation of any serious and original school of composition to be developed in the United States. . . . These beautiful and varied themes are the product of the soil. They are American. . . . These are the folk songs of America and your composers must turn to them. All the great musicians have borrowed from the songs of the common people. Only in this way can a musician express the true sentiment of his people. He gets into touch with the common humanity of his country.[2]

Dvořák was not the only one who was deeply moved by the spirituals he heard Burleigh sing. In 1917, Burleigh published his arrangement of "Deep River," and its enormous success inspired the publication of nearly a dozen more spirituals that same year.* Settings of spirituals began to appear for vocal soloists of every range, as well as for mixed chorus, men's chorus, and women's chorus. Countless books of spirituals were published during the 1920s, with James Weldon Johnson's *Books of American Negro Spirituals* being the most famous, and black choirs like the Fisk Jubilee Singers performed spirituals in concerts for white audiences, as did black male solo singers including Paul Robeson and Jules Bledsoe. Radio programs regularly featured vocal quartets and choral groups from black colleges. Spirituals

---

* Burleigh, who studied with Rubin Goldmark, later Gershwin's teacher, had a remarkable career bridging the black and white musical worlds. He was the first African American composer who was acclaimed for both his adaptations of spirituals as well as his art songs. He was also a superb singer and became the only African American soloist at St. George's Episcopal Church of New York—a position he held for over fifty years—as well as the first African American soloist at Temple Emanu-El in New York. In addition, he was a founding member of ASCAP and in 1941 was given a seat on its board of directors.

could be heard on Broadway as interludes in serious musical revues. Concluding a vocal recital with a set of them became almost standard.

Though nearly all of these arrangements were considerably "artified"—harmonized and arranged using classical techniques—at a time when white composers were freely appropriating black music for their own purposes, spirituals gave black singers, choirs, and arrangers an opportunity to transmit black music and culture on their own terms. They gave African Americans a place in white concert halls and a chance to perform for white audiences. This widespread exposure to spirituals had a major influence on what white people in general and two white artists in particular—DuBose Heyward and George Gershwin—thought of as an authentic, black musical sound.

It is striking to see how naturally Gershwin's folk opera, *Porgy and Bess*, grew out of Dvořák's idea of an American music founded on its indigenous black music. As early as 1920, Gershwin talked about wanting to write "operettas that represent the life and spirit of this country."[3] By 1925, a year after *Rhapsody in Blue* and still ten years before the premiere of *Porgy and Bess*, this general impulse had become a more specific desire to write an opera for African American singers because "[b]lacks sing beautifully. They are always singing; they have it in their blood."[4] A year later, during the summer of 1926, Gershwin read DuBose Heyward's immensely popular 1925 novel, *Porgy*, supposedly in a single mesmerized sitting,* and the desire became concrete: to turn Heyward's novel into the first American "folk opera."

Though Gershwin's vision of an opera based on Heyward's novel might have coalesced in a single afternoon in 1926, it would take nine difficult years for that vision to become a reality. Gershwin immediately approached Heyward about turning the novel into an opera, but

---

* Though this story initially sounded to me like another Gershwin invention, it actually turns out to be quite plausible. The novel is in fact reasonably short, and like Gershwin, I also read it in approximately three hours in a single, mesmerized sitting.

at the time Heyward and his wife, the playwright Dorothy Hartzell Kuhns, were busy turning *Porgy* into a play that would be produced by the Theatre Guild. The stage version was as successful as the novel, and it launched the career of its innovative Armenian director, Rouben Mamoulian, who would ultimately direct Gershwin's *Porgy and Bess* as well. After the play opened, Gershwin and Heyward met in Atlantic City to discuss a collaboration, but Gershwin felt he needed more time and study to prepare himself to write an opera. These preparations involved composing an enormous amount of "classical music" between *Rhapsody in Blue* in 1924 and *Porgy and Bess* in 1935, including the *Concerto in F* (1925), *An American in Paris* (1928), the *Second Rhapsody* (1932), the *Cuban Overture* (1932), and *Variations on "I Got Rhythm"* (1933–34). When the Metropolitan Opera finally got around to commissioning an opera from Gershwin in 1929, he chose to adapt Szymon Ansky's *The Dybbuk* rather than *Porgy*, but after several years, *The Dybbuk* project fell through because of problems acquiring the rights. At the same time, a plan for Al Jolson to star in a Jerome Kern/Oscar Hammerstein version of *Porgy* had also fallen apart.

Finally, by the fall of 1933, with the economic pressures of the Depression weighing heavily on Heyward, he struck a deal with Gershwin. Heyward would write the libretto, and Heyward and Ira Gershwin would collaborate on the lyrics. Ira took charge of the up-tempo, Broadway-style numbers, Heyward wrote the more lyrical ones, and the two polished everything together. Though Otto Kahn offered Gershwin a $5,000 bonus if he produced the work at the Met, Gershwin declined, claiming that he "felt that for the Met to acquire an all-Negro cast to be available six to eight performances a season, was not too practical a project."[5] Instead, they decided to produce the project on Broadway with the Theatre Guild, the same group who had produced the play *Porgy* in 1927. Gershwin began sketching the work in February 1934, completed the score eleven months later, and then spent nine months orchestrating the mammoth work in time for its Boston premiere on September 30, 1935. (Its Broadway premiere would follow on October 10, 1935.)*

The work was controversial from the moment it opened, and that controversy continues unabated today. In Ellen Noonan's 2012 book *The Strange Career of Porgy and Bess: Race, Culture, and America's Most Famous Opera*, she examines "the opera's long history of invention and reinvention as a barometer of twentieth-century American expectations about race, culture, and the struggle for equality."[6] Given the complexity of the racial, cultural, and musical issues surrounding the work both in its time and ours, we would do well to keep Santayana in mind: "We must welcome the future remembering that soon it will be the past and *we must respect the past remembering that once it was all that was humanly possible*"[7] [emphasis mine].

No work in this book raises issues of white appropriation of black culture more profoundly than *Porgy and Bess*. Who owns the cultural heritage of black Americans? Who has the right to tell their stories, and what constitutes an authentic telling of those stories? These questions are at the heart of both the underlying controversy surrounding *Porgy and Bess* and its ongoing cultural importance, and to begin to come to terms with them requires an understanding of DuBose Heyward, what he and Gershwin were trying to accomplish, the opera's place and meaning in the cultural context of the time, and what relationship the fictional world of Catfish Row had to do with the real world of Cabbage Row, the Charleston, South Carolina, neighborhood on which it was based.

Heyward came from a prominent Charleston family with an ancestor, Thomas Heyward, who signed the Declaration of Independence. But by

---

* In classic Broadway fashion, the piece was barely finished in time. Though rehearsals had started in New York City in July, Gershwin did not finish most of the orchestration until mid-August 1935 and only completed the final passages on September 2, just in time for the Boston premiere. The debate over whether the work is an opera or a Broadway show may never be resolved, but in terms of its timeline, out-of-town tryout, and last-minute orchestration, it was certainly handled by Gershwin like a Broadway show.

the time DuBose was born in 1885, the family had fallen into poverty, and the situation deteriorated further when a mill accident killed Heyward's father, when DuBose was two. After a childhood that included, according to his wife, "long happy summers on his aunt's plantation, where his only playmates were Negro children," Heyward was forced to leave school at the age of fourteen, and several of the jobs he took to help support his family brought him into contact with the many members of the black community he would later fictionalize in *Porgy*. He worked as a collector of burial insurance payments in the black neighborhoods of Charleston, possibly inspiring the undertaker scene in *Porgy and Bess*. During summers, he supervised the black workers on his aunt's plantation, where he learned to speak "Gullah like a Gullah."[8] (Gullah was the African dialect spoken by Gullah slaves and their descendants living in Charleston, and the dialect that Heyward tried to approximate throughout *Porgy and Bess* as the language of Catfish Row.) His work as a cotton checker and timekeeper for a steamship line, and his daily experiences with Charleston's black stevedores on the city's wharves were clearly the basis for his portrayal of the powerful Crown in *Porgy and Bess*.

While still young, Heyward was afflicted with several serious illnesses, including polio, typhoid, and pleurisy, and it seems hard to believe that there was no connection between his own physical weakness and the fact that he was drawn to the story of Samuel Smalls, who inspired *Porgy*—the story of "a cripple . . . familiar to King Street with his goat and cart,"[9] who was held on a charge of aggravated assault for his attempt to shoot Maggie Barnes. What captured Heyward's imagination was the fact that a crippled, peanut-cake vendor like Smalls, whose only mode of transportation was an upside-down soapbox pulled by a goat, was somehow also capable of the kind of "passion, hate, and despair" that his crime revealed. Psychologically speaking, the novel's improbable, climactic encounter during which the crippled Porgy somehow manages to kill the enormously powerful Crown seems to be a kind of wish fulfillment that the sickly Heyward could accomplish only in the realm of fiction.

One of the major influences on Heyward's conception of Charleston's black community was his mother Janie Screven Heyward, a folklorist interested in the black Gullah culture of coastal South Carolina and Georgia. A great deal of the paternalism toward blacks evident in *Porgy* and so much of DuBose's work can already be found in his mother's 1912 pamphlet, *Songs of the Charleston Darkey*, which talks nostalgically about the "loving sympathy, loyalty, and spirit of mutual kindness" that existed "between the old-time Darkey and his Master."[10] It is only a short step from this pamphlet to DuBose's description of the "Golden Age" when Porgy lived, during which, "instead of the elaborate and terrifying process of organized philanthropy," a beggar's plea for help "produced the simple reactions of a generous movement of the hand, and the gift of a coin."[11] The great southern historian C. Vann Woodward remarked that "[o]ne of the most significant inventions of the New South was the Old South."[12] Heyward believed that the urbanization of the New South was destroying an Edenic, innocent, preindustrial Old South filled with the warm black-white relationships his mother had described "between the old-time Darkey and his Master." Like his mother, DuBose believed that a certain type of Negro was disappearing. One that was more primitive, in touch with his basic humanity and instinctual drives, and unspoiled by the fetters of civilization. In his description of the grand parade of "The Sons and Daughters of Repent Ye Saith the Lord" in *Porgy*, Heyward waxes poetic:

> Out of its fetters of civilization this people had risen, suddenly amazingly. Exotic as the Congo, and still able to abandon themselves utterly to the wild joy of fantastic play, they had taken the reticent, old Anglo-Saxon town and stamped their mood swiftly and indelibly into its heart. Then they passed, leaving behind them a wistful envy among those who had watched them go,—those whom the ages had rendered old and wise.[13]

There is no doubt that Heyward thought of himself as someone who had been "rendered old and wise" and viewed the "wild joy" and "fantastic play" of the Charleston Negroes with "wistful envy." Yet in spite of his unrealistic view of Charleston's black community, Heyward's Catfish Row cannot be easily dismissed as pure fiction, nor can Heyward himself be dismissed as completely ignorant of Charleston reality. The novel is not, as Heywood Broun of the *New York World* feared, "another of those condescending books about fine old black mammies and such like."[14] There are many details that, living in close proximity to Charleston's black community, Heyward clearly got right. According to Ellen Noonan, the stevedores, fishermen, street vendors, and domestic workers that populated Catfish Row accurately reflected the kinds of jobs available to the black people of Charleston. Heyward's descriptions of the fisherman in the "mosquito fleet" also seem to be quite authentic—the result of repeated viewings on his part—as were the novel's descriptions of the mixture of Christianity, African beliefs, and superstitions that composed the Gullah religion. The way the residents of Catfish Row turned inward and became mute, blank ciphers in the presence of white authority figures in the novel was also, according to contemporary accounts, an accurate reflection of Charleston realities. Cabbage Row, the model for Catfish Row in *Porgy and Bess*, was a decaying tenement that had once been a grand house during colonial times, and it was not far from Heyward's Charleston home. Though Heyward might have had an aristocratic white man's incomplete, elitist view of the lives of Charleston's black community, he had clearly experienced a lifetime of actual interactions with that community, and his novel shows that he felt a great deal of sympathy and compassion for its inhabitants.

Gershwin's knowledge of and experience with this community, however, was completely different. In an attempt to get a firsthand sense of the world he was turning into music (unlike in "Swanee," where he felt no such need), Gershwin made two visits to Charleston.* Before his first short visit in December 1933 and January 1934, he told Heyward that he "would like to see the town and hear some spirituals and perhaps go to a colored cafe or two if there are any."[15] Heyward guided him through the city's local black musical scene, and Gershwin was particularly struck by the pushcart vendors shouting out their wares, and by the "primitiveness" of several of the church services he attended—one of which included a woman singing a spiritual that began, "Oh Dr. Jesus." Heyward, who had spent a lifetime becoming familiar with these black folk traditions, told Gershwin, "You really haven't scratched the surface of this native material yet."[16]

Gershwin returned for about five weeks beginning in mid-June 1934 to spend time near Heyward's summer home on Folly Island, off the coast of Charleston. There, he went to recitals and church services and heard a white group from the Society for the Preservation of Spirituals (a group that Heyward had been involved with since its formation in 1922) perform "sperrituals," as well as performances by black singers from neighboring communities. According to Heyward, "James Island, with its large population of primitive Gullah Negroes, lay adjacent and furnished us with a laboratory in which to test our theories, as well as an inexhaustible source of folk material."[17]

As with so much of Gershwin's life, legends have grown up around this visit, some passed down by Heyward and some by Gershwin, and though it is almost impossible to know how to separate fact from fiction, biographer Howard Pollack recounts the two most frequently told anecdotes. According to Heyward, "one night at a Negro meeting on a remote sea-island, George started 'shouting' with them, and eventually to their huge delight stole the show from their champion 'shouter.'" Building on the story, Gershwin said

---

* I have drawn the basic facts of these visits from Howard Pollack's Gershwin biography. His book has a more extensive description of these visits for interested readers.

that at the end of the evening an elderly man congratulated him and said, "By God, you can sure beat out them rhythms, boy. I'm over seventy years old and I ain't never seen no po' little white man take off and fly like you. You could be my own son."[18] Implicit in the story is the idea that though Gershwin might have been an outsider geographically and racially, he was so sympathetic musically and personally that within a few hours he was able to absorb and speak the musical language of Charleston's African American community like a native, ultimately giving *Porgy and Bess* an authenticity of expression it might otherwise never have had.

The second story Pollack recounts has to do with a meeting of black Holy Rollers that Gershwin and Heyward attended in Hendersonville before Gershwin returned to New York. According to Heyward, just before entering the meeting, Gershwin

> caught my arm and held me. The sound that had arrested him was one to which, through long familiarity, I attached no special importance. But now, listening to it with him, and noticing his excitement, I began to catch its extraordinary quality. It consisted of perhaps a dozen voices raised in loud rhythmic prayer. The odd thing about it was that while each had started at a different time, upon a different theme, they formed a clearly defined rhythmic pattern, and that this, with the actual words lost, and the inevitable pounding of the rhythm, produced an effect almost terrifying in its primitive intensity.[19]

The section of *Porgy and Bess*'s storm scene "with six different prayers sung simultaneously" was Gershwin's self-acknowledged attempt to re-create the effect he first heard in Hendersonville, translated into his own musical language with his own self-created rhythmic prayers, forming his own clearly defined rhythmic pattern and creating his own terrifying effect of primitive intensity.

This phrase—"his own"—is central to understanding Gershwin's achievement in *Porgy and Bess*, as well as the controversy and misunderstanding that has surrounded the work since its inception. Reviews of the original 1935 Broadway production were polarized, and critical reactions to the work have continued to be divided. Though several of the most hostile opening-night reviews have received disproportionate prominence over the years, in general the reviews of the first production were positive, with most critics loving the piece. They not only considered it Gershwin's greatest work, but also the greatest American opera to date. Arthur Pollock of the *Brooklyn Daily Eagle* wrote, "This is the sort of thing that Pulitzer Prizes are not good enough for," and a Boston reviewer said that the work not only managed to "transfuse vital, black blood into the somewhat hardened arteries of conventional opera," but that it was finally an opera "about Americans, for Americans, and by Americans sympathetically and completely understood" written in English "whose every word [Americans] are able to follow, and whose comical twists come to them directly in their own tongue."[20]

Aside from the ultimately pointless debates over whether the work was an opera or a work of musical theater, and the discussions of the merits of the work's recitatives, perhaps the most significant and most intense divides occurred (and continue to occur) over the work's representation of the black experience, and the extent to which Gershwin was simply another white musician in a long line of white musicians stretching back to the days of minstrelsy, unconscionably appropriating black musical and cultural resources for his own purposes. Interestingly enough, opinions on this topic from black and white commentators do not divide in a simple and obvious way. Floyd Calvin, an important black journalist for the *Pittsburgh Courier* and a host of the first black radio show, *The Courier Hour*, applauded *Porgy and Bess* as well as four other Broadway productions in the mid-1930s that starred African Americans, saying confidently, "At last the old 'Blackface' stereotype has been broken. White people now pay to see Negroes be themselves, and rate them on the faithful interpretation of character rather than on the faithful portrayal of preconceived prejudiced notions."[21]

The importance of Gershwin's radical insistence that all productions of *Porgy and Bess* be performed by all-black casts (the original production employed 70 black singers) created and has continued to create substantial performing opportunities for generations of black performers, and the significance of Gershwin's bold casting decision was commented on extensively at the time. When the *Chicago Defender*, one of the two most important black newspapers in the country (the other being the *Pittsburgh Courier*), heard about the Kern-Hammerstein version of *Porgy* that was in the works before Gershwin took over the project, the paper reacted with horror, calling the idea of Al Jolson, the "white mammy singer" playing Porgy, "an obscene suggestion" that would be "a bombshell to the lovers of Race talent in the theater." Running throughout the reaction to the work in the black press was a relief that Gershwin's all-black casting and the critical praise the cast received had finally put an end to the legacy of blackface minstrelsy on Broadway that was personified by Al Jolson.

Yet while many in the black press applauded Heyward and Gershwin's opera as moving past the "clowning, playing the banjo, dancing and comic rolling of the eyes [that had been] the accepted repertoire of colored actors"[22] in favor of a more nuanced, dignified, and humane representation of African Americans, not all black critics agreed. A reviewer for the *Amsterdam News*, one of the country's oldest African American newspapers, thought that *Porgy and Bess* did "harm to the advance of the Negro. He [Gershwin] continues to be shackled by what the whites think Negroes are like."[23] Later, Harold Cruse, the author of *The Crisis of the Negro Intellectual,* went further, stating that "*Porgy and Bess* belongs in a museum and no self-respecting African American should want to see it, or be seen in it."[24] But the most blistering indictment of the opera came from one of America's most distinguished white music critics, the composer Virgil

Thomson. After famously declaring that "Gershwin does not even know what an opera is," Thomson went on to attack any pretensions to authenticity that the opera might presume to have, saying that it was "fake folklore" and "has about the same relation to Negro life as it is really lived and sung as have *Swanee River* and *Mighty lak' a rose*." Finally, he questioned Gershwin's basic right to even tackle the subject at all: "Folk-lore subjects recounted by an outsider are only valid as long as the folk in question is unable to speak for itself which is certainly not true of the American Negro in 1935."[25]

The ability of black Americans to "speak for themselves" was in fact a major cultural issue of the time. The Great Migration that brought more than a million African Americans to northern cities between 1910 and 1930 helped lead to the Harlem Renaissance of the 1920s and '30s—the movement of writers and artists that celebrated black expression culturally, socially, and artistically. The critic Alain Locke summed up its essence when he said that through art "Negro life is seizing its first chances for group expression and self-determination."[26] Harlem Renaissance writers like Langston Hughes, W. E. B. Du Bois, Zora Neale Hurston, and Countee Cullen were expressing their experience of "Negro life as it is really lived," which in Virgil Thomson's mind invalidated Gershwin's work. Interestingly enough, it was the distinguished black composer, arranger, and critic Francis Hall Johnson who answered Thomson's critique by saying the Gershwin was "as free to write about Negroes in his own way as any other composer to write about anything else."[27] Wherever one stands on the issue, Thomson's criticism raises important questions about cultural appropriation and the American voice that are at the heart of the development of American popular music. Does an outsider like Gershwin have the right to portray the world of African Americans? What constitutes being an outsider? Is it simply the color of one's skin? If only an African American can accurately write about or portray an African American character, can only a woman write about or portray a female character? Is race more or less fundamental than gender? Is the reach of an artist's imagination limited to his personal profile—his own race and gender?*

These are complex questions, and different moments in history generate different answers. Given our heightened sensitivity to the painful, ongoing story of race in America, answers to these questions in the segregated, pre–Civil Rights movement, Depression-era world of 1935 will inevitably be different from answers in a twenty-first-century world in which, though massive racial issues and tensions remain to be solved, we now celebrate the musical *Hamilton*, in which nonwhite actors portray America's Founding Fathers. Yet without coming to any definitive answers, let us keep these questions in mind, and see if Dvořák, Gershwin, and critic W. J. Henderson can offer us a perspective from which to hear *Porgy and Bess*'s most famous number, "Summertime," in a new way.

Though Dvořák, like Gershwin, heard and studied Negro spirituals, they never appeared directly in his music. He absorbed their clarity of expression, and their simplicity of resources, economy of vocabulary, and rhythmic life are everywhere in the *New World Symphony* and the *American String Quartet*. But only in spirit. This was exactly how he approached the folk music of his own country. His *Slavonic Dances*, the work that first brought him fame, were an attempt to capture the spirit of the folk dances of his native Bohemia—as well as those of Slovakia, Moravia, Silesia, Serbia, Poland, and Ukraine—through idealized compositions rather than transcriptions or arrangements of actual folk material. Unlike Brahms's *Hungarian Dances* (the inspiration for Dvořák's *Slavonic Dances*), which were settings of actual

---

* Today, at a different moment in America's racial history, the movement in the world of the theater is in precisely the opposite direction. Currently, color-blind casting, in which black actors can freely portray white characters and vice versa—in which the musical *Hamilton* can cast America's Founding Fathers with black actors—is considered to be the most progressive approach. Color-blind casting is an attempt to create, at least on the stage, a postracial reality, in which we are not defined by race or color. A reality in which we are human beings first, and ethnic and racial beings second.

folk melodies, Dvořák filtered these folk-dance forms through his own compositional language, creating an effortless fusion of the serious and the popular that was uniquely his own. His country's folk songs and dances were the foundation of the *Slavonic Dances*—the songs of the common people that represented the common humanity of his country.

Gershwin followed this same approach. Though *Porgy and Bess* references many different kinds of black popular and folk music with an emphasis on Negro spirituals, in the end Gershwin filtered this source material through his own musical language to produce an utterly original work of art. Gershwin told the *New York Times* in 1935 that, though he had decided early in the process to make his recitatives "as close to the Negro inflection in speech as possible," he would write his own spirituals and folk songs rather than use preexisting material, saying, "I wanted the music to be all of one piece."[28] Gershwin even insisted on inventing his own street cries for the street vendors, rather than simply transcribing the ones he heard during his visits to Charleston.

W. J. Henderson understood Gershwin's achievement clearly. Writing in the *New York Sun*, he said that *Porgy and Bess* "is not grand opera; it is not folk opera; it is not pure Negro; but it is Gershwin talking to the crowd in his own way. And that is a very persuasive way."[29] But what was Gershwin's way? How did Gershwin filter the black music he heard and saw in Charleston and on Folly Island into the music of "Summertime," perhaps the most famous number from *Porgy and Bess*?

"Summertime" was the first number that Gershwin worked on when he began sketching in December 1933. The lyrics were written exclusively by Heyward, and no less an authority than Stephen Sondheim believes that "DuBose Heyward has gone largely unrecognized as the author of the finest set of lyrics in the history of the American musical theater—namely, those of *Porgy and Bess*. I admire his theater songs for their deeply felt poetic style and their insight into character. It's a pity he didn't write any others. His work is sung, but he is unsung."[30]

In Heyward's novel, there are two fundamentally different vocabularies of expression. There is the highly literate speech of the omniscient narrator—in some sense a stand-in for Heyward himself—describing the world and actions of the story, and then there is the dialogue of the Catfish Row inhabitants, expressed in transcribed Gullah dialect: "Yo' bes sabe yo' talk for dem damn dice. Dice ain't gots no patience wid 'oman!" (Notice the similarities here to the imitation-black lyrics we saw in "Can't Help Lovin' Dat Man" and "Stormy Weather.") Some critics found the clash between the highly intellectual, philosophical tone of the narrator and the Gullah dialect of the Catfish Row dialogue problematic, but the omniscient narrator allowed Heyward to express the poetry and humanity of the novel's characters in his own language. With no omniscient narrator available for the play or the opera, Heyward was forced to channel all of the poetry of the story into the dialect of the Catfish Row inhabitants. That Heyward was able to capture the heartbreak, poignancy, joy, passion, and intensity of the story solely within this vocabulary is remarkable, and the exquisite lyrics of "Summertime" are a superb example of his achievement. Looking at the famous opening line, "Summertime an' the livin' is easy," Sondheim points out the care with which Heyward chose even a simple word like "and":

> That "and" is worth a great deal of attention. I would write "Summertime when" but that "and" sets up a tone, a whole poetic tone, not to mention a whole kind of diction that is going to be used in the play; an informal, uneducated diction and a stream of consciousness, as in many of the songs like "My Man's Gone Now." It's the exact right word, and that word is worth its weight in gold. "Summertime when the livin' is easy" is a boring line compared to "Summertime and." The choices of "ands" [and] "buts" become almost traumatic as you are writing a lyric—or should, anyway—because each one weighs so much.[31]

Sondheim points out how Heyward's opening immediately sets a poetic tone and style of diction for the piece, as well as a feeling for the unhurried pace and languor of summertime in Catfish Row, and Gershwin achieves a similar effect musically. Because "Summertime" has taken on a life outside the opera as an independent piece, where it is usually performed with a simple 2- or 4-bar introduction, we rarely hear the extraordinary transition Gershwin wrote that leads not only into the song, but into the entire world of Catfish Row.

The opera itself begins on a summer evening in the fictitious black tenement community. After a brief orchestral introduction, the libretto sets the scene: "Evening, Catfish Row is quiet. Jasbo Brown is at the piano, playing a low-down blues while half a dozen couples dance in a slow, almost hypnotic rhythm." The orchestra gradually joins Jasbo's unaccompanied piano playing and builds to a climax on the highly energetic, obsessive, rhythmic figure that has dominated the opera so far (marked "x" in Ex. 5.1). Finally, the music's pulsing rhythm stops, and unison strings try to find a key to settle down in measures 5–6. After 2 measures, Gershwin underscores the frantic strings with a chord that starts to give the figure some focus. The chord then drops out right at the moment in the score when Gershwin marks, "Lights come up on another group on stage in the center of which Clara, a young mother and wife of a fisherman named Jake, sits with her baby in her arms, rocking it back and forth." The unison strings play the figure from measure 5, but now it begins to define a key, outlining a dissonant, unstable chord (a diminished triad F–D–B)—first up high in measure 9 and then an octave lower in measure 11.

Then, after the rhythmic and dynamic intensity of the opening scene has finally ebbed and a key center has begun to emerge, a single, extraordinary note transitions us into the world of Catfish Row. Having heard the circular figure F–D–F–E–D–B–D–E in measure 9 resolve to F♮ in measure 10, we expect it to resolve the same way in measure 12. But instead, Gershwin

Example 5.1 "Summertime"

magically replaces the F (measure 10) with an F♯ (measure 12). To make sure the moment is not missed, he marks *espressivo* and *ritardando* (slow down) in the score, shifts the orchestration from strings to winds, and sits on the F♯ for two-and-a-half beats while we catch our breath. That F♯ is the world of Catfish Row. It is its foundation, and as soon as Gershwin establishes it, a single clarinet arpeggio cascades down atmospherically, introducing every note that will be used by the voice in the song (B–C♯–D–E–F♯–[G]–A, the

Example 5.1 "Summertime" (continued)

natural minor scale, minus the G), leading to the two crucial notes that make up the world of the song's accompaniment: G♯ and A♯ (measure 14).

If we think of the F♯—the long note that holds in the bass for these 4 measures of introduction (measures 13–17)—as the foundation of Catfish Row, then the G♯ and A♯ that lazily alternate back and forth above, depict Clara rocking her baby back and forth. G♯—rock left, A♯—rock right. G♯—rock left, A♯—rock right. Then, in a simple yet utterly effective theatrical moment, the rocking slows to half speed as the G♯ and A♯ quarter notes become G♯ and A♯ half notes, while the delicate echo of bells fills the extra musical space. One of the essential ingredients for any great popular-music songwriter is the ability to create character and mood in an instant. This slowing down of Clara's rocking music creates the languid, intense heat of summertime in Catfish Row with only three notes and a simple alternating figure that cross fades beautifully into the song's opening vocal melody.

If, as W. J. Henderson said, *Porgy and Bess* is Gershwin talking to the crowd in his own way, we are now in a position to see what Gershwin's "way" was all about. The key to his theatrical and musical magic lies in the accompaniment. Having built up the overall texture in the orchestra from unison strings to three notes (F♯, G♯, A♯), Gershwin finally gives us complete harmony: full, four-note chords that sound lush after the sparse texture of the transition. Two rocking *chords* now alternate (measures 18–20), exactly like the two rocking *notes* of the introduction. The way these two chords move back and forth comes right out of the world of Negro spirituals, and if I were to remove one note from each chord as in Example 5.2, the result could be the harmony that opens one of the spirituals from Clarence Cameron White's *Forty Negro Spirituals* in Gershwin's library.

What makes the opening uniquely Gershwin is the one note that he adds to each chord. They not only enrich the harmony, they are in fact the "rocking notes" from our introduction—G♯ (added to the first chord) and A♯ (added to the second)! The way that Gershwin first introduces these notes one at a time and then seamlessly makes them part of the song's harmony is a perfect example of the kind of craft that Gershwin brought to his source material to make it his own.

Once the song begins, Clara's vocal line is filled with the same kind of subtlety as the accompaniment.* Gershwin could easily have gone

Example 5.2 "Summertime," Kapilow version

---

* Some commentators have tried to claim that this opening vocal phrase and the song are drawn from either the spiritual "Sometimes I Feel Like a Motherless Child" or the South-Russian Yiddish lullaby "Pipipipipee," but these kinds of tiny melodic similarities are musically insignificant, and purely coincidental. Gershwin's connection to spirituals is a connection of feeling, not quotation.

rhythmically from "time" to "an'" without pause, as in Example 5.3A. But the long note on "time" (like the slowing down of the rocking to half speed in the introduction) instantly specifies the song's languid mood as summertime in Catfish Row. Nothing is rushed or hurried. We have all the time in the world. Just two chords rocking back and forth and an exquisitely long, stretched-out note on "time." The rhythm of "an' the livin' is easy" comes out of this same, languorous, southern world. My version (Ex 5.3A) also uses "straight," square eighth notes on "an' the livin' is easy" for Gershwin's dotted-note version (Ex. 5.3B); like so much of the blues and jazz-oriented music of the period, it is meant

Example 5.3A "Summertime," Kapilow version

Example 5.3B "Summertime," Gershwin version

to be "swung"—with "an' the livin' is" sung as triplets.* This kind of swing rhythm—in which traditional eighth-note rhythms are relaxed in performance to become jazzier, looser, triplets

—is basic to nearly all of the black musical idioms of the period. It is in a sense analogous to the way southern speech takes northern English, blurs its contours, and slows its speed. If eighth and sixteenth-note rhythms grow out of a precise, rational, Enlightenment world—a world of science and grids— swing rhythms grow out of southern plantation heat, where speech is softened to a humid drawl. A world where "and the living is" takes too much effort to enunciate and gets replaced by "an' the livin' is," and classical music's strict eighth notes are replaced by jazz and blues's swung eighth notes.

As the opening phrase continues, more elements of Gershwin's approach become clear, and once again the rich accompaniment is crucial. After lazily alternating two chords per measure in measures 18–20, one extra chord in measure 21 (see Ex. 5.4) gently nudges the phrase forward, and though the next 2 measures harmonically are all essentially a single E-minor^7 chord,† the exquisite chromatic decorations that Gershwin adds in measure 22, and the passing notes in measure 23 (see bracketed notes in Ex. 5.4) make the music his own.

---

* Also notice how beautifully the two long notes on "easy," after the swing rhythms on "an' the livin' is," bring the "easiness" of summertime in Catfish Row to life. Had Gershwin used two quarter notes instead of half notes on "easy," the word would have had no impact whatsoever, and the magical atmosphere would have dissolved.

† With the song's opening 4 bars basically a B-minor chord, these first 6 bars, like a spiritual or southern blues, are essentially the beginning of a standard 12-bar blues progression—4 bars of I, 2 bars of IV— though the continuation alters the traditional pattern. It has the feel of the blues, but filtered through Gershwin's voice.

Example 5.4 "Summertime"

Example 5.5 "Summertime," Kapilow version

However, it is really measures 24 and 25 that show Gershwin's "way," and comparing these 2 measures with my more standard version (Ex. 5.5) illustrates Gershwin's relationship to his black musical sources. First of all, Gershwin's overall handling of the restricted pitch material of the song's vocal line is remarkable. There is not a single note outside the song's key in the entire voice part, and Clara, as is appropriate in a simple lullaby, uses only six different notes in the whole song, all within a single F♯–F♯ octave: B, C♯, D, E, F♯, and A. Of these six notes, the C♯ and A each appear only once per verse (C♯ on "high" and A on "hush"), so that the vast majority of the song's vocal line uses only four notes—B, D, E and F♯. Because of this, the arrival of C♯ on the word "high"—its only appearance in the song, on the longest note so far—is striking.

This opening phrase is a superb example of how Gershwin invented a black American voice for Clara that draws on the world of the blues and spirituals for its harmony, rhythm, and expression, as well as on the simplicity of a lullaby for its limited, six-note vocal range. Yet he uses this material in his own, utterly original way, filtering it through his formidable, "white" compositional technique. As the voice holds its C♯ for six long beats in measures 24 and 25, attention shifts to the remarkable fill in the accompaniment—a tiny, four-note figure ("y" on Ex. 5.4) consisting of a leap up to a descending, three-note chromatic scale (F♯–F–E) with a wonderful "blues note" on F instead of my "correct" F♯. This leads to a spectacularly expressive E♮ in the melody that clashes with the E♯ underneath to make a bluesy, modern, Gershwin chord that existed nowhere in Charleston—a wonderfully crunchy chord theorists call a "split-third" chord. The little four-note idea ("y") repeats three times—twice in the right hand, once in the left hand—each time beginning with a larger leap (first a fourth, then a fifth, then a sixth) but always keeping the same expressive, three-note chromatic scale at the end, conveying all the warmth that Clara feels toward her baby in Gershwin's own blues-derived language. Comparing the last two chords of measure 25 in my version with Gershwin's, you'll see the same care Sondheim pointed out in describing Heyward's attention to a single word ("Summertime when" versus "Summertime and"). For Gershwin, the distinction is a single note. Each chord in my version is only one note different from Gershwin's version (an E in my first chord versus Gershwin's D♯, and a C♯ in the bass in my second chord versus Gershwin's C♮), but it's that simple difference that turns a Charleston spiritual into a Gershwin spiritual.

Though the musical details of the song are subtle and complex, as befits a lullaby, the basic structure is remarkably simple. The opening 8-bar phrase (call it "A") ends by extending the little chromatic scale in measure 25 (D♯–D–C♯) by two notes (C♮ and B) to return smoothly to the opening phrase in measure 26. Gershwin repeats the first 3 measures of the A section, but then the final 5 magical bars of the phrase change everything, demonstrating how he transformed the black spirituals he heard in Charleston into his own musical language. Instead of continuing to alternate back and forth between his two rocking chords, a poignant, whole-tone scale floats up evocatively in a solo English horn,* and as the beautifully dissonant A♯ in the melody holds, the bass

---

* I have always felt that this orchestration is, in some way, a reference in feeling to the English horn solo from Wagner's *Tristan and Isolde*. (Gershwin often said that Wagner and Bizet's *Carmen* were his biggest operatic influences in *Porgy and Bess*.) The way the A♯ in measure 29 is suspended to become part of a beautifully dissonant chord (E7♯4) before resolving to a more normal dominant chord—the actual chord the famous "Tristan chord" resolves to in Wagner's opera—and the overall feeling seems Tristanesque to me. In addition to Gershwin's general admiration for Wagner, when Heyward and Gershwin decided to name the opera *Porgy and Bess* as opposed to *Porgy* to avoid confusion with Heyward's novel and play, Heyward said the title was in perfect keeping with other great operatic pairings like *Romeo and Juliet* and *Tristan and Isolde*.

changes to a major chord,* altering the entire direction of the phrase and preparing for its heartfelt conclusion.

Many of Heyward's lyrics in *Porgy and Bess* are drawn from fragments of the 1927 play's script, and in the play, Clara sings two lines of the southern, folk spiritual/lullaby "All My Trials," itself said to be based on an old Bahamian lullaby: "Hush, li'l baby, don' yo' cry. Fadder an' mudder born to die." The fragment of the spiritual that Clara sings in the play depicts resignation in the face of mortality, as no matter what happens on earth, "All my trials Lord, soon be over." Heyward's lyrics in "Summertime," however, are far more hopeful. Clara tells her baby that "the livin' is easy," her "daddy's rich" and her "ma is good-lookin'," and that one morning she's "goin' to rise up singing," spread her wings and "take the sky"—an optimistic, courageous belief for a poor black woman living in the tenement world of Catfish Row. Instead of quoting both lines from his play, Heyward uses only the first line, completely altering the fatalistic tone of the original to simply: "Hush, little baby, don' yo' cry."

Gershwin's setting of this phrase is a masterpiece of subtlety. The vocal line still uses only six notes, and two of them appear only once (see Ex. 5.4). On the word "hush," the A makes its lone appearance in the voice accompanied by a radiant D-major chord, and the combination of the new note and the major-key harmony gives the moment a glowing freshness that leads to the remarkable cadence that ends the phrase. To make the vocal line expressive, Gershwin takes two gestures from the world of spirituals and the blues, asking the singer to slide between two notes on "don'" and then insert a quick, decorative, sobbing grace note on "cry."

But it is the harmony of this final cadence in the accompaniment that ultimately makes the moment so spectacular. Instead of a standard cadence, Gershwin substitutes an unexpected, heart-stopping chord under "yo'" in measure 31, and when this beautiful chord resolves to the home chord of the

---

* For musicians, an E7 chord with the beautiful A♯ as a ♯4 decoration.

piece on "cry" (B minor), there is an enormous sense of release. This is the first pure home (or tonic) chord in the entire song without any embellishments. And as the vocal line holds "cry" for 2 measures, instead of simply having the accompaniment play the "an' the livin' is easy" melody twice starting on an E (as in Ex. 5.6) to match the harmony, Gershwin has the flute play the first fragment starting on an A, making it subtly dissonant to the harmony underneath until the second fragment starts "correctly" on an E and resolves the phrase to lead to the song's second verse (Ex. 5.4, mm. 32–33).

Amazingly, other than a brief 4-measure coda at the end, these two 8-measure phrases are essentially the complete song. The second verse of "Summertime" has a soaring lyric that imagines the expansive future of Clara's child once she "spreads her wings and takes the sky," but the vocal line and accompaniment are essentially repetitions of the first verse. The only musical change is the addition of the chorus—which in this work represents the entire Catfish Row community—backing Clara up with wordless harmony, but though this does not affect the overall musical structure of the piece, it is significant dramatically. In the tight-knit community of Catfish Row, the children are everyone's responsibility. Clara's lullaby becomes the community's lullaby, and as it will turn out when Clara dies later in the opera's hurricane, it will be the community that the chorus represents who will ultimately be responsible for Clara's child.

Example 5.6 "Summertime," Kapilow version

Once Clara finishes the second verse of "Summertime," a brief coda ends the song, and once again, subtle changes are what make Gershwin's version so superb. At heart, the coda is a simple, circular progression called a sequence of fifths, where the bass line moves by the interval of a fifth, repeating the pattern over and over, each time one note lower or higher. Here, after arriving on the home chord of B, the circle of fifths begins on an E in the left hand (Ex. 5.7, m. 1) then moves by fifth: E–A, D–G, C–F♯, and back to B, where it began. Gershwin arranges the choral voicing so that the sopranos descend expressively for 4 measures in a single, long, chromatic scale—G♯–G–F♯–F–E–D♯–D. This is lovely but relatively standard. What is anything but standard, however, are the subtle changes Gershwin makes to the second chord in each measure.

In the standard version shown in Example 5.8, the first chord of each measure is identical to Gershwin's (E major, D major, C major) and the

Example 5.7 "Summertime" coda

second chord in each measure is traditional.* Listening closely to the poetic, deeply moving chords that Gershwin substitutes for each second chord in Example 5.7 brings us to the heart of what he brought to his source material, and how, like Dvořák, he absorbed the spirit of his folk material yet ultimately made it his own.†

It is interesting that Gershwin chose to begin working on the opera by writing "Summertime" first. Opening an enormous work like *Porgy and Bess* with what is essentially an introspective soliloquy, as well as choosing to find his way into the world of Catfish Row through a single individual's voice, shows Gershwin's desire to move beyond stereotypes and create a world of real individuals. A world that sadly includes violence and death. In spite of Clara's reassurance to her child that "there's a-nothin' can harm you / With Daddy and Mammy standin' by," at the end of the opera, both she and Jake will be killed by a hurricane. It's the chorus—the widowed Serena and the rest of the community—who will be responsible for helping the poor, orphaned child to spread her wings and "take the sky." The opera's tragic dimension is already implicit in this exquisitely moving, opening lullaby.

Example 5.8 "Summertime" coda, Kapilow version

---

* For musicians, a dominant-7th chord: A7, G7, F♯7.

† I have included the few measures at the end of the song that transition into the next scene (Ex. 5.7, mm. 5–10) to show how effortlessly Gershwin is able to transition out of the folklike, lullaby-world of "Summertime" into the complex, dissonant, "modern" music that follows. Gershwin simply places the song's "an' the livin' is easy" fragment in increasingly more dissonant, "modern" harmonic settings and within four measures the lights have come up on a completely different world—the world of the crap game—and a completely different musical universe.

In spite of largely positive reviews, the 1935 Broadway production of *Porgy and Bess* was not a financial success. Though the show ran in New York for 127 performances, it had a huge cast and a huge orchestra, and Gershwin, who, along with Heyward, cut their royalties to help the production continue, never recouped his own investment. The tour that followed also lost money. Stung by the production's commercial failure, George went off to Hollywood where he assured producers who were nervous that an opera composer like Gershwin might "only do highbrow songs" that he was out to write hits.[32] And in the brief time remaining to him, that is exactly what he did, writing major hits for two great Fred Astaire films: *Shall We Dance*—which included "Slap That Bass," "They All Laughed," "Let's Call the Whole Thing Off," and "They Can't Take That Away from Me"—and *Damsel in Distress*, featuring "A Foggy Day" and "Nice Work If You Can Get It." Shortly after the release of *Shall We Dance* on May 7, 1937, Gershwin began experiencing a series of coordination problems, headaches, hallucinations, and blackouts, and was finally diagnosed with a brain tumor. After an unsuccessful emergency operation, Gershwin died at the age of thirty-eight. The writer John O'Hara spoke for the entire, shocked musical community when he said, "George Gershwin died on July 11, 1937, but I don't have to believe it if I don't want to."[33]

Five years after Gershwin's death, Cheryl Crawford, who had been an assistant stage manager for the original *Porgy and Bess* production in 1935, revived the work, eliminating most of the sung recitatives, considerably shortening the piece, reorchestrating a great deal of the score, and using a much smaller orchestra. The 1942 version, which far more closely resembled a traditional Broadway show, was a commercial success and in many ways began the work's rehabilitation as popular entertainment. However, it was the 1952 version that restored a great deal of the music and recitatives cut by Crawford and starred Leontyne Price, William Warfield, and Cab Calloway in a full-scale, worldwide tour that helped turn the work into what it has been ever since—the "Great American Opera" and Gershwin's greatest achievement.

The nature of that achievement and who it represented has remained a source of controversy ever since, and each generation has seen the work through the prism of its own time. Was *Porgy and Bess* simply the work of another white borrower that did "harm to the advance of the Negro"? Or was it a major step forward in its attempt to depict "Negro life as it is really lived" and bring a previously invisible black world into mainstream American theater? Though these questions may never be fully answered, one thing is clear: the work expanded Broadway's conception of what was possible in the musical theater, and the so-called "Broadway operas" of Leonard Bernstein, Kurt Weill, Marc Blitzstein, and Gian Carlo Menotti owe an enormous debt to *Porgy and Bess*. Deeply embedded in the work is the belief that African American expression in its many shapes and forms is a vital, central component of America's musical voice. Dvořák had insisted that the future music of America "must be founded upon what are called the Negro melodies," and in ways he could never have imagined, Gershwin, in *Porgy and Bess*, took him at his word. In America's mythic melting pot tradition, two Russian Jews from the Lower East Side, a white southern aristocrat from Charleston, and an Armenian director collaborated to create an extraordinary portrait of a largely unknown black southern community in an invented yet utterly self-confident American voice. It was a bold vision not only of what the theater could be but of what America could be as well, and the legacy of both the work and its vision continues to this day.

6

Immigration and the American Voice

Irving Berlin's "Cheek to Cheek"

When Alexander II, the great Russian reformer who freed the serfs, was assassinated on March 13, 1881, his son Alexander III ascended to the throne, and it quickly became clear that his repressive regime would have an enormous impact on every aspect of Russian society. What was not nearly as clear was that his regime would also play a major role in the history of the Broadway musical, as well as the life of Irving Berlin, whose career was launched by a song about a very different Alexander: "Alexander's Ragtime Band."

During his reign as emperor from 1855 to 1881, Alexander II enacted a historic program of domestic reforms designed to bring Russia into the modern world. Though his emancipation of the serfs in 1861 is the decision for which he is most famous, he also reorganized the country's entire judicial system, abolished capital punishment, promoted local self-government, supported the universities, terminated some of the privileges of the nobility, and permitted a kind of freedom of the press and of public opinion completely unprecedented in Russian history. Unlike his father, Nicholas I, who brutally tried to Russianize the country's Jewish population, Alexander II adopted a far more liberal approach. He got rid of the hated cantonist schools, where Jewish minors as young as eight years old were sent for military training often after being forcibly separated from their parents, and he allowed Jews to attend high schools and universities.[1] Though nearly all Jews were still forced to live within a geographical area in Russia called the Pale of Settlement, certain classes of Jews deemed helpful to the country's economic and political future—scholars, university graduates, and selected merchants and artisans, for example—were permitted to settle outside the Pale in other parts of Russia.[2] In spite of the extremely difficult situation for those who lived within the Pale, most Russian Jews still considered Alexander II to be a benevolent czar who liberated them from the despotic rule of his father.

This was decidedly not the case with Alexander II's son, who did everything possible to undo his father's work. On the very day he was assassinated, Alexander II was about to announce the creation of commissions that could have led to Russia's first constitution; one of Alexander III's first official acts was to immediately cancel the new law. Rather than turning toward the West like his father, he became fanatically devoted to returning Russia to its sacred traditions and national identity, eerily foreshadowing Russia under Vladimir Putin. In order to combat the radicalism that had led to his father's assassination, Alexander III reinstituted autocratic rule, increased censorship of the press, and heightened police oppression. Liberal ideology was seen as a threat to monarchical authority, and the Jews became a scapegoat linked in the public's mind with Alexander II's assassination.

Government-organized pogroms throughout southern Russia began almost immediately after the assassination in 1881, and in May 1882 the notorious May Laws were enacted to regulate the activities of the Jews. Though these regulations were supposed to be temporary, they in fact remained in place for twenty-five years and became even more oppressive through frequent revisions.[3] Konstantin Pobedonostsev, one of the tutors and closest advisors of Alexander III and the chief administrative officer of the Russian Orthodox Church, succinctly expressed the essence of the new emperor's attitude toward the Jews when he said it was his hope that "one-third of the Jews will convert, one-third will die, and one-third will flee the country."[4] For better or worse, Pobedonostsev's third wish was largely granted as the repression generated by the May Laws and their subsequent revisions led to mass emigration. Between 1881 and 1914, the period between Alexander III's ascension and the beginning of World War I, more than 2 million Jews left Russia.[5] Among the many who found their way to America were Asa Yoelson (Al Jolson) in 1891, and Leah, Moses, and the seven Beilin children, including five-year-old Israel, in 1893.

The number of immigrants flooding into America by the early twentieth century was simply astonishing. The first major wave came between 1815 and 1865 and was initially dominated by the Irish fleeing famine,[6] followed by almost 5 million Germans. The California Gold Rush lured Asian immigrants, and by the 1850s, approximately 25,000 Chinese had come to make their fortunes,[7] generating the first nativist resistance in the form of the anti-immigrant Know Nothing party. The Civil War and the economic depression that followed temporarily slowed immigration, but another major wave between 1880 and 1920 brought more than 20 million newcomers to America, now largely from central, eastern, and southern Europe—Italians, Jews, Hungarians, and Poles.[8] Ellis Island was opened off the coast of Manhattan in 1892 as the federal government struggled to deal with the staggering numbers fleeing Europe, and the flood of immigrants reached its climax in 1907, when in a single year approximately 1.3 million people were admitted into the United States.[9] This extraordinary period ended dramatically with World War I and the restrictive laws that followed. In 1914, 1.2 million immigrants entered the country, but in the following year, the number dropped to 315,700.[10] In 1917, the U.S. government enacted legislation requiring all immigrants over the age of sixteen to pass a literacy test, and the Immigration Acts of 1921 and 1924 set quotas limiting both the total numbers of immigrants and the percentages for each nationality, reducing immigration to 165,000 in 1924, less than 20 percent of the pre–World War I average.[11]

No single American city was affected more by immigration at the time than New York City, and no single group more than the Jews. As conditions in Russia and eastern Europe grew worse, Jewish immigration increased exponentially.[12] The Jewish population in New York City in 1870 was approximately 80,000, but by 1915 it had grown to 1.4 million, or almost 28 percent of the city's total population.* Like the Beilins, almost half of them settled on the Lower East Side.[13] The world they found there was one of almost unimaginable poverty and squalor. In July 1893, two months before the Beilins arrived, the *New York Times* wrote, "This neighborhood [the Lower East Side], peopled almost entirely by the people who claim to have been driven from Poland and Russia, is the eyesore of New York and perhaps the filthiest place on the western continent. It is impossible for a Christian to live there because he will be driven out either by blows or the dirt and stench."[14]

The Beilins, whose name was Americanized to Baline at Ellis Island, moved into a squalid basement apartment on Monroe Street. It consisted of three tiny, windowless rooms in which Leah, Moses, and their children not only slept and ate, but also worked.[15] Though Moses was a cantor (like Harold Arlen's, Al Jolson's, and Kurt Weill's fathers), he first found work in the kosher meat markets, but he also led a choir in the local synagogue where his son Israel sang—the closest the child ever came to any kind of musical training.

Everyone in the family worked—his daughters wrapped cigars and did beadwork, his elder son worked in a sweatshop, and Israel sold newspapers

---

* Since the government census did not ask for religious affiliations at the time, all of these figures are necessarily estimates.

after school. When Moses died in 1901, leaving his wife who spoke no English to care for all of their children, the thirteen-year-old Israel was forced to quit school to support his family. Soon afterward, for reasons that biographers seem unable to agree on—either to ease the financial burden on the family or out of shame at contributing so little—Israel left home to live on the streets of the Bowery. He slept in flop houses and earned the 10 cents a night it cost for a cot by showing up at a bar, singing, and grabbing up the change drunken patrons dropped on the floor. Though this was a horrific existence for a thirteen-year-old runaway, seeing the reaction of inebriated customers to the various songs he sang in the Bowery saloons—which songs generated a reaction and money, and which songs did not—made Israel acutely sensitive to the average man's tastes. His survival literally depended on it.

After two years of busking and living on the streets, Israel eventually found a job as a singing waiter at a Bowery saloon called the Pelham Café, run by a dark-skinned Russian Jew known as "Nigger Mike." For seven dollars a week, Israel, or Izzy as he was known at the time, worked from eight in the evening until six in the morning, but before and after work, he often sat down at a piano in the back room and supposedly picked out popular tunes using only the black keys. But it wasn't his piano playing that made him so successful, it was his singing, in particular his parodies of popular songs. It was his words, not his music, that started him—humbly at first—on his road to fame.

He worked at the Pelham Café for three years, until by chance a competing saloon, Callahan's, began to draw customers away with "My Mariucci Take a Steamboat," a song written by Callahan's pianist and waiter that patrons were clamoring to hear. Nigger Mike demanded that Izzy and M. "Nick" Nicholson, the Pelham's pianist, come up with a song of their own, and though neither of them knew how to notate music, with the help of an unidentified young violinist—the first of a long line of musical secretaries for Berlin—they produced "Marie from Sunny Italy." The song was not only Israel's first, it was also the song that gave him his name. When it was accepted by Jos. W. Stern & Co. for publication, a typographical error on the cover read "Words by I. *Berlin*." Though his sisters had almost immediately changed their first names from Sifre to Sophie, Rebecca to Ruth, and Chasse to Gussie, Israel had simply become Izzy. But Izzy seemed too informal and undignified to put on the title page of a published song, so the initial I. had to suffice as a temporary solution. No biographer seems able to pinpoint the exact moment when Israel became Irving, but the typographical error that changed Ellis Island's Baline to Berlin stuck, and at the age of nineteen, in 1907, Israel Beilin, a street bum from Russia with almost no education, no musical training, and Yiddish as a first language, became I. Berlin, a published lyricist with a new American name.*

Nearly all of the Jewish songwriters and lyricists who dominated the world of musical theater in the 1920s and '30s chose to Americanize their ethnic names. Israel Beilin became Irving Berlin, Hyman Arluck became Harold Arlen, Isidore Hochberg became "Yip" Harburg, and Jacob and Israel Gershowitz/Gershwine became George and Ira Gershwin. But leaving their names behind was only the beginning. Though there was a vital Yiddish theater on the Lower East Side, most of the major Jewish songwriters and lyricists chose instead to write for Broadway in a voice that was almost completely free of any trace of their Jewish heritage. This desire to assimilate and create an American identity rather than an ethnic one was, of course, not limited to Jews. Because of the continual influx of immigrants into the United States throughout its brief history, by 1914 one out of every three Americans was either an immigrant or the child of an immigrant.[16] And though immigrants dominated places like New York City—even

---

* Since all of Berlin's published music from 1909 on used the name Irving Berlin, he must have taken on Irving sometime between 1907 and 1909, between the ages of nineteen and twenty-one.

establishing their own neighborhoods, like Little Italy and Chinatown—the overwhelming impulse, particularly among the children of immigrants, was toward assimilation. If they had made a concerted effort to retain their ethnic languages and traditions, New York City and the voice of the Broadway musical might have been very different, but with the exception of institutions like the Yiddish Theatre and foreign-language newspapers, children of immigrants like Berlin largely did everything they could to distance themselves from their foreign-born pasts. One of the mysteries of Irving Berlin's adolescence is the fact that he seemed to sever contact with his family for the entire duration of his Bowery years, even though he lived and worked only a few blocks from their home. Like so many first-generation immigrants, Berlin was desperately trying to make his own way, and his family's Old Country language and customs represented everything he was trying to escape. Like America, he needed to invent himself from scratch, free of an encumbering past, and the New York City melting pot was a perfect place for his and America's new voice to emerge.

Though Jewish songwriters, lyricists, directors, producers, theater owners, and sheet music publishers dominated Broadway during its formative years, the reasons for this are often examined only superficially. No one has come up with a more succinct explanation than Minnie Marx, the mother of the Marx Brothers, who said, "Where else can people who don't know anything make so much money?" As the story of Irving Berlin demonstrates, the combined effects of poverty, almost complete lack of education, and systemic discrimination left Jews, as well as blacks who faced similar challenges, with very few options. Berlin was never going to be a concert pianist, classical composer, doctor, lawyer, or any of a thousand other professions whose doors were closed to a Jew with his background. However, American popular culture—and the Broadway theater in particular—had its doors wide open to talent of any kind, no matter where it came from. Berlin was able to work his way up from the Pelham Café to a slightly higher-class singing-waiter job at Kelly's—an establishment closer to the 28th Street

Tin Pan Alley music publishers*—where someone who heard his singing commissioned him to write a song called "Dorando."† The song was good enough to interest the Tin Pan Alley publisher Ted Snyder, and when a second song, "Sadie Salome, Go Home," based on Richard Strauss's scandalous opera *Salome,* sold 300,000 copies of sheet music, Snyder offered Berlin a job as a staff lyricist, finally ending Berlin's days as a singing waiter at the age of twenty-one. Several successful Tin Pan Alley songs further enhanced his reputation, and Berlin took the next step on a path to Broadway by interpolating songs into Broadway shows, including two songs into Ziegfeld's *Follies of 1910.* The following year, Berlin wrote what *Variety* called "The Song of the Decade": "Alexander's Ragtime Band." Its phenomenal success launched Berlin's career into the stratosphere virtually overnight.

One of the remarkable things about the Broadway musical during these formative years was the way a distinctively American voice was largely generated not by traditional Americans but by recently arrived immigrants who wiped their ethnic pasts clean and discovered a country and a genre that were far less encumbered by centuries-old traditions than their European homelands and cultures. Compared to Europe, America was still in its infancy. In 1914, most communities in the country as a whole were less than a hundred years old,

---

* Tin Pan Alley was the name of the block on 28th Street between 5th Avenue and Broadway in New York City that was the home of the major publishers of American popular music between the 1880s and 1920s. Supposedly the name came from the writer Monroe Rosenfeld who thought the noise of so many pianos being pounded in the publisher's cubicles sounded like people pounding on tin pans. Though Tin Pan Alley was an actual place, it has come to be used in a more general way as a term encompassing the entire era and its style of popular song.

† Though the Broadway musical of the 1920s and '30s would try to develop a voice that was larger than any particular nationality or ethnic group, the Tin Pan Alley songs of the first two decades of the twentieth century were fully aware of the reality of New York's multiple ethnicities, and publisher's catalogues were filled with songs that appealed in dialect and topic directly to Italian, Irish, German, and Jewish ethnic groups. Both "Marie from Sunny Italy" and "Dorando," which tells the story of an Italian American barber who loses his life's savings betting on an Italian marathoner in the 1908 Olympics, are two of the many Tin Pan Alley songs designed to speak directly to the Italian community, and there are similar examples directed toward Irish and German groups as well.

and even the first settlements, like Jamestown, were only a little more than three hundred years old. More important, the country did not have the kind of engrained, indigenous culture that Europe had. America's concept of itself was fluid and continually changing as each new wave of immigrants added their ingredients to the mix. What it meant to be American, as opposed to French, German, or Italian, had not crystallized in America the same way national identities had crystallized in Europe, and when technological innovation accelerated in the opening years of the twentieth century, the opportunity arose to invent a distinctively American voice in art, literature, dance, and music, and the newly arrived immigrants jumped at the chance.

Three years after the staggering success of "Alexander's Ragtime Band," Irving Berlin got the opportunity to compose his first musical for Broadway, *Watch Your Step*, advertised as the "Syncopated Musical Show *Made in America*." After the opening, one reviewer wrote, "Berlin is now a part of America,"[17] and though this may not have been the critic's intention, the comment has a prescient double meaning. Having made it to Broadway all the way from his humble beginnings in Russia and the squalid poverty of the Lower East Side, Berlin was definitely now a part of America in the sense of being a successful member of society. But, perhaps more important, his syncopated voice was itself part of America—that is, part of America's voice. The earlier kinds of popular songs that had depicted an Edenic, pastoral world that believed in God, virtue, chastity, and Puritan morality were simply no longer relevant to the modern world of automobiles, engines, and exhaust explosions that defined the new America of the teens and twenties, and it was Berlin who would be at the center of finding the new music and new rhythm that this new age demanded.

Perhaps because of his hardscrabble beginnings, Berlin more than any of the other great songwriters of his time was attuned to the tastes and sentiments of the ordinary man. As he put it, "My ambition is to reach the heart of the average American, not the highbrow nor the lowbrow but that vast intermediate crew which is the real soul of the country. The highbrow is likely to be superficial, over trained, supersensitive. The lowbrow is warped, subnormal. My public is the real people."[18] Berlin was quite clear about the ingredients required for a songwriter to reach "the real people," and he compiled them into a list of "Nine Rules for Writing Popular Songs," published in an interview for *American Magazine* in 1920.

1. The melody must be within the average voice of the average singer.
2. The title must be planted throughout the song via use of repetition.
3. The idea and lyric must be appropriate for both sexes . . . so that both will want to sing it.
4. The song should contain 'heart interest' (pathos) even for a comic song.
5. The song must be original . . . success is not accomplished . . . by imitating the hit song of the moment.
6. Your lyric must deal with ideas, objects or emotions known to everyone.
7. The lyric must be euphonious: simple and pleasing to the ear.
8. Your song must be perfectly simple.
9. The songwriter must look upon his work as a business.[19]

Though "the songwriter must look upon his work as a business" was the final item on Berlin's list, it actually is a subliminal component of all the other entries. Every item speaks directly to Berlin's desire to make his songs reach the widest possible audience through catchy titles, frequent repetition, average voice ranges performable both by men and women, universal emotions and topics, and simple lyrics and forms. For Berlin, songwriting was most definitely a business, a business at which he proved to be remarkably adept. Since his very survival from the age of thirteen had depended on his ability to promote himself, he was anything but shy about publicizing his work. The advertisements for his songs on the back of sheet music read, "Irving Berlin, The Song Genius of the world says: This song surpasses all my previous efforts. I can safely say—this is the best song I ever wrote [insert name of latest song]."[20]

He became involved in the publication of his songs as well, first partnering with Ted Snyder's firm—now reorganized officially as Waterson, Berlin & Snyder—and then, at the time of his first Broadway show in 1914, venturing on his own to form Irving Berlin Inc.* To protect the royalties of his new company, that same year he went a step further and became a founding member of the American Society of Composers, Authors and Publishers (ASCAP), the new performing rights organization, and to guarantee absolute control over the presentation of his works, he partnered with Sam H. Harris in 1921 to build his own Music Box Theatre. Though the theater would ultimately house musicals other than Berlin's, for its first four years, it presented only Berlin's own *Music Box Revues.* As he was now the owner of the theater as well as the producer and composer of all of its shows, he was able to exert complete control over every aspect of production, from the choice of directors, performers, conductors, and orchestrators, to the smallest detail of sets and costumes. Given the extreme hardships and precariousness of his formative years, it is not surprising that Berlin did everything he could to exert complete control over the financial side of his business, and he remained fiercely protective of his copyrights throughout his career, even calling the Shubert Organization to check on the box office receipts of his theater, and in particular *White Christmas,* during the final years of his life.

A great deal of Berlin's success as a composer and a businessman had to do with his remarkable ability to sense the mood of the country at any given moment. "Alexander's Ragtime Band" capitalized on the period's obsession with dancing, and whenever a new dance craze arose, Berlin wrote an

---

* The firm of Waterson, Berlin & Snyder was allowed to keep Berlin's name when he left, and during World War I, while he was away in the Army, they handled his copyrights for him.

appropriate song. When the Grizzly Bear dance hit the Staten Island ferry-boats, Berlin responded with "The Grizzly Bear." A Hawaiian dance craze prompted "That Hula Hula." Realizing the ephemeral nature of each new dance, Berlin wisely wrote the all-encompassing, "Everybody's Doing It Now," which allowed "it" to refer to whatever dance was the current fad at the time.

Berlin's songs reflected America's preoccupations. Like dancing, the country's ethnic diversity was a topic known to everyone, and Berlin cleverly wrote songs directed at every possible immigrant group, with "Abie Sings an Irish Song" for the Irish, "Yiddisha Eyes" for the Jews, "Sweet Italian Love" for the Italians, "Oh, How That German Could Love" for the Germans, and some wonderful songs that managed to combine ethnic appeal with the craze for ragtime, like "Yiddle on Your Fiddle Play Some Ragtime" and the fabulous, dialect title, "Sweet Marie, Make a Rag-a-Time-a-Dance with Me." Songs tied to holidays that could become perennial sellers, like "Easter Parade," "White Christmas," "I've Got Plenty to Be Thankful For," and the generic "Happy Holiday" were a particular Berlin specialty, and as songwriter Sammy Cahn once put it, referring to Berlin, "Somebody once said you couldn't have a holiday without his permission."[21]

Berlin's connection with the public reached perhaps its deepest level during the two world wars. He was intensely patriotic, and as soon as America entered World War I, he wrote "Let's All Be Americans Now," as well as "For Your Country and My Country," a song whose second verse has a particularly powerful emotional resonance given Berlin's immigrant background.

> *America has opened up her heart*
> *To ev'ry nationality…*
> *It makes no diff'rence now from where you came*
> *We are all the same.*

Writing these songs was only the beginning of Berlin's patriotism. When he was drafted in 1917 and stationed at Camp Upton in Yaphank, Long Island, he composed and produced an all-soldier revue entitled *Yip! Yip! Yaphank!* which featured his own legendary performance of "Oh, How I Hate to Get Up in the Morning." The show was an enormous hit in New York, where it extended its planned weeklong run at the Century Theatre to thirty-two performances and earned the Army $83,000.* His patriotic involvement in World War II was even greater. *This Is the Army*, his sequel to *Yip! Yip! Yaphank*, recycled a song cut from the earlier show—"God Bless America"—and in a patriotic gesture, Berlin assigned all royalties from the song to the God Bless America Fund, to be redistributed to the Boy Scouts and Girl Scouts of the United States.

After World War I, Berlin himself became one of the country's most talked-about topics when he added the final chapter to his rags-to-riches story by marrying the socially prominent heiress Ellin Mackay, daughter of Clarence Hungerford Mackay, the head of the Postal Telegraph Cable Company.† Ellin's father vehemently opposed the match from the moment the couple first met in 1925, and their relationship played out in the tabloids, juicy detail by juicy detail, like the plot of a 1920s Broadway musical. Mackay whisked his daughter off to Europe to get her away from Berlin, and Berlin wrote songs to her—"Remember" and "Always"—which the publicity surrounding their affair helped turn into hits. When she finally returned to New York, they were married in spite of her father's threat to disown her, and Berlin gave her the song "Always" and its royalties in perpetuity as a wedding gift. Continuing to turn his private life into song,

---

* Dollar amounts vary in different sources. Berlin's biographer Edward Jablonski gives $83,000 as the figure, but Berlin's *New York Times* obituary places it at $150,000. Whatever the exact figure, the show was a hit critically, financially, and patriotically.

† This was actually Berlin's second marriage. His first marriage in 1912 to Dorothy Goetz ended tragically when she died of typhoid fever six months into the marriage, and Berlin waited thirteen years before becoming involved with his second wife, Ellin.

Berlin wrote "Blue Skies" in 1926 for the birth of his first daughter, and its insertion into *The Jazz Singer*—supposedly the first talking film—helped turn this intimately personal song into an enormous hit.

The success of *The Jazz Singer* and the distressing realities of Broadway during the Depression ultimately led Berlin to join nearly all of his fellow songwriters in Hollywood during the 1930s. Even though his 1933 show, *As Thousands Cheer*, had been a hit on Broadway, only three of the four-teen stage musicals produced that year were real successes. The same year, however, had seen the phenomenal run of the film musical *Flying Down to Rio*—the film that brought Fred Astaire and Ginger Rogers to everyone's attention and inaugurated their legendary, ten-film partnership. (The year had also seen the inauguration of Franklin Delano Roosevelt and the appointment of Adolf Hitler as chancellor of Germany, but no one at the time was truly aware of the implications these two events would have on history.) Other than a few films like *Flying Down to Rio*, *42nd Street*, and *King Kong*, 1933 was largely a financial disaster for Hollywood, but New Deal activity toward the end of the year had led to a slight uptick in the economy, and 1934 saw Hollywood turn back toward profitability. Buoyed by the success of *As Thousands Cheer* and aware of the finan-cial turnaround in Hollywood, Berlin negotiated a remarkable deal in November 1934, in which he would be paid $75,000 plus 10 percent of the film's gross after earnings of $1,250,000 for an Astaire–Rogers picture called *Top Hat*.*

Certain songs will be forever connected with certain performers, and in the same way everyone thinks of Judy Garland's performance of "Over the Rainbow," "Cheek to Cheek" will always be associated with Fred Astaire. In addition to the scrupulous attention he paid to composers' notes and rhythms, there was something about Astaire that made everyone want to

---

* Initially Berlin had asked for a fee of $100,000 for the film but compromised to $75,000 plus 10 percent of the gross described above. When the film went on to earn over $3 million, Berlin ended up with more than double the fee he had initially asked for (Jablonski, *Irving Berlin: American Troubadour*, 168).

write for him, and he seemed to bring out the best in nearly everyone who did. "Cheek to Cheek" is one of Irving Berlin's most experimental songs and also, perhaps thanks to Astaire, one of his most elegant. Astaire said that in choreographing the number, he "arranged a romantic flowing type of dance, and took special pains to try for *extra-smooth smoothness,*" and in a way, that is a perfect description of the quality that best defines the song: extra-smooth smoothness.

In *Top Hat,* "Cheek to Cheek" takes place at a nightclub as part of an ongoing case of mistaken identities. Astaire, playing an American dancer in London named Jerry Travers, falls in love with Ginger Rogers (Dale Tremont), who mistakenly thinks Astaire is married to her best friend. Though Rogers gradually falls in love with Astaire, she does so against her will, and the tension between her growing feelings for him and her guilt over being attracted to a man she thinks is married to her best friend is a crucial plot element in the film. After leaving Astaire behind in London and escaping to Italy, the two meet up again in an impossibly elegant hotel nightclub in Venice (somewhere unimaginably distant from "Nigger Mike's" Pelham Café where Berlin began his career). The club's dance band plays "Cheek to Cheek" throughout the scene, insinuating the number into the audience's subconscious and turning the dialogue into a kind of voiceover, setting the scene and filling the role of a typical Broadway song's verse or introduction. The song itself begins directly with the chorus—"Heaven, I'm in heaven"—coming straight out of Astaire's spoken words.

Whether the words or the music come first, in a great song it is the combination that counts. Music and lyrics cease their independent existence and become part of a new, inseparable unit. It makes no sense to look at the lyric "Heaven, I'm in heaven" without also examining the music underneath. If I were to keep all of Berlin's notes and words and

Example 6.1 "Cheek to Cheek," Kapilow version

simply change the rhythm, as in Example 6.1, the opening would become utterly banal.

By beginning with a two-note sigh and then simply stretching the second note of "Heaven," Berlin makes the word luxuriantly long. Floating above the accompaniment's lilting rhythm, it's almost as if time has stopped. The note seems to last forever, and it actually gives Astaire time to look upward to the heavens as it holds. The first 4 measures instantly transport us out of the Depression into Astaire's and *Top Hat*'s elegant nightclub world (see Ex. 6.2). An incredible way to begin a song.

What comes next is a superb example of the inextricability of words and music in a great song, as well as the masterful way Berlin builds a memorable musical idea. The vocal melody starts with two notes—A–G—on the word "heaven." He then adds two more words and two more notes—E–F–A–G—for *I'm in* heaven." These four notes then become "and my

Example 6.2 "Cheek to Cheek," Berlin version

Example 6.3 "Cheek to Cheek"

heart beats"—E–F–A–G (Ex. 6.3). He then takes the last two of those notes—the "heart beats" notes, A–G—and moves them up in sequence higher and higher to become "so that" (B–A), "I can" (C–B), "hardly" (D–C), resolving on "speak" (E). This shortened fragment rising higher and higher perfectly captures the way Astaire's heart beats so fast that he can hardly speak, with the vocal line on "hardly speak" at the edge of his vocal range where he can, in fact, hardly speak!

But this is a world of elegance, charm, white ties, top hats, and tails, so the opening phrase's outburst of emotion is quickly stifled, as Berlin's melody moves back down the scale musically into a more comfortable vocal range, balancing the phrase's emotion-filled ascent and smoothly bringing things back under control (Ex. 6.4). The piano chords follow the lyric as they seek stability under the vocal line's "seek." The bass line descends

Example 6.4 "Cheek to Cheek"

chromatically, B–B♭–A, below dissonant harmony, with the direction clarified only when the bass has arrived on A.

What follows as a kind of punch line for the phrase is the most surprising moment in the entire song—a moment that is rarely performed as Berlin wrote it. Up to this point, every rhythm in the vocal line has been regular and even; there are no syncopations of any kind. Each note is either a single-beat quarter note or a held note, and Berlin could easily have continued this way and finished the phrase, as in Example 6.5, with more of the same.

Instead, Berlin writes an almost-impossible-to-perform, complex rhythm that is syncopated on every beat, literally putting you on the dance floor dancing cheek to cheek (Ex. 6.6).

As in a standard AABA Broadway song, the music of A repeats with new words, followed by a contrasting B section (Ex. 6.7). However, in this

Example 6.5 "Cheek to Cheek," Kapilow version

Example 6.6 "Cheek to Cheek," Berlin version

Example 6.7 "Cheek to Cheek," B section

case the B section's music and lyrics are far more perfunctory, and that is precisely the point. All the things that the B section's lyrics mention—climbing a mountain and reaching the highest peak, going fishing in a river or a creek—are far less interesting to a cosmopolitan dancer like Astaire than dancing cheek to cheek, so Berlin writes a simple musical idea that fulfills his rules for a successful song with a catchy tune, in an average voice range, singable by a man or woman, that repeats.

This is the moment where the song becomes experimental for Berlin. Though each section has been double the normal length, with 16-bar instead of 8-bar units, up to this moment it has still followed the standard Broadway form. Now, instead of returning to A one final time, Berlin adds a completely new section—call it C (Ex. 6.8). Once again, there is a perfect fusion of music and lyrics, as the new section allows us to see a completely different side to Astaire's character. The music switches to a minor key and is filled with passionate intensity, as if Astaire's emotions can no longer be held in check. As the song's form opens up, so does Astaire's character.

Finally, one simple word and note—the word "to" on a D—are the difference between ordinary and great. The C section opens with an impassioned "Dance with me. I want my arms about you." The music's address is direct and fervent in a tone completely absent from the song to this point. The four notes of "arms about you" (E♭–G♭–G♭–G♭) are copied lower for "charm about you" (D–F–F–F), and still lower for "carry me thru" (C–E–E–E). Having completed his third rhyme, he could easily have returned to the opening ("Heaven, I'm in heaven"), but instead he adds an extra word and an extra note, making a beautiful, fourth inner rhyme—"Carry me *thru to*"—seamlessly eliding the return to the A section, as Astaire would say, with "an extra-smooth smoothness."

"Cheek to Cheek" is extraordinary in and of itself, but watching and listening to it in *Top Hat* while keeping in mind Berlin's biography and the film's social and cultural context adds another layer of meaning to the

Example 6.8 "Cheek to Cheek," C section

experience. The harrowing story of the Berlin family's escape from persecution in Russia, a story shared by so many other Jewish immigrants, seems almost impossible to believe.* Their arduous trek of some 1,500 miles by train, cart, and foot to Antwerp was followed by a nauseating, inhuman eleven-day crossing of the Atlantic on the *Rhynland* only to ultimately land them in the utter poverty of New York's Lower East Side. Given the astonishing difficulties of Berlin's runaway, Bowery childhood years, it seems

---

* Edward Jablonski's biography of Berlin describes the journey in considerable detail.

incredible that he could have survived to adulthood at all. Watching Astaire in his white tie and tails and Rogers in her luxurious gown in the elegant nightclub setting of "Cheek to Cheek," gliding across the dance floor without a care in the world, oblivious to the Depression, it is startling to realize that not only had Irving Berlin, without education or musical training, somehow transcended all the obstacles life threw his way in order to write this song, but that he himself actually now lived in the world portrayed on the screen. What for millions of Americans was an escapist fantasy to be savored as a momentary respite from their Depression-era existence had become Irving Berlin's reality.

In spite of his enormous success and wealth, Berlin somehow never lost touch with mainstream America. He lived to the astonishing age of 101, and when he died, tributes came from everywhere. One of the most perceptive was an earlier evaluation of his work written by Jerome Kern that was quoted on the occasion. Kern said:

> The average citizen was perfectly epitomized in Irving Berlin's music. Both the typical Yankee and a Berlin tune had humor, originality, pace and popularity; both were wide-awake, and both, sometimes, a little loud—but what might unsympathetically be mistaken for brass, was really gold. Berlin doesn't attempt to stuff the public's ears with pseudo-original ultra-modernism, but he honestly absorbs the vibrations emanating from the people, manners and life of this time, and in turn gives these impressions back to the world,—simplified, clarified, and glorified. Irving Berlin has no place *in* American music. He is American music.[22]

For Israel Beilin from a small village in Russia, to Irving Berlin and the embodiment of American music, no more astonishing transformation could have been imagined. Arriving in the United States as an impoverished immigrant and coming of age in the second and third decades of the century, he listened to America as an outsider and helped to invent its voice. At a moment in time when the "swellelegant" lifestyle portrayed by Astaire and Rogers in *Top Hat* seemed to be a pure escapist fantasy available nowhere but on the silver screen, Berlin was actually living that lifestyle offscreen. He had become the living embodiment of the iconic, rags-to-riches American dream. At Berlin's hundredth birthday party in Carnegie Hall, Walter Cronkite summed up Berlin's achievement beautifully when he said, "Irving Berlin helped write the story of this country by capturing the best of who we are and the dreams that shape our lives." As George Gershwin might have said, "Who could ask for anything more?"

7

How the Other Half Lived

Cole Porter's "Begin the Beguine"

On March 4, 1933, Franklin Delano Roosevelt took office at one of the most troubled moments in American history. Unemployment had reached somewhere between 14 and 16 million, or approximately a quarter of the nation's workforce.[1] More than a million Americans were homeless, and the entire banking system had collapsed. Since the 1929 crash, approximately 9,000 banks had failed.[2] The situation for farmers, which had been dire even during the general prosperity of the 1920s, reached disastrous proportions. Between 1929 and 1933, food prices fell by more than 50 percent. During the same period, approximately 60,000 farmers lost their land to foreclosure, and in 1933 the pace accelerated to nearly 20,000 foreclosures a month.[3] The situation was no better in other areas of the economy. By 1932, the overall income from manufacturing had fallen to 56 percent of what it was in 1929.[4] International trade, largely in response to the disastrous Smoot-Hawley Tariff Act, also fell massively, from $9 billion to $3 billion.[5] The stunning economic gains of the 1920s had been almost completely erased in a matter of months.

Roosevelt gave hope to a panicked America with a flood of new legislation introduced during his remarkable first one hundred days as president. Fifteen major bills reshaped nearly every facet of the economy, from banking and agriculture to industry and social welfare. In his "war against the emergency," Roosevelt vastly expanded the role of government in people's lives while demanding and receiving broad executive power "as great as the power that would be given me if we were in fact invaded by a foreign foe."[6] He ultimately used those powers—with the help of his "brain trust" of Ivy League advisors—to experiment with some of the boldest and most radical government programs in the country's history. Summing up his pragmatic philosophy, he said, "Take a method and try it. If it fails admit it frankly and try another. But above all try something."[7]

Roosevelt expressed his commitment to solving the nation's problems during his many radio "fireside chats," reassuring his audience that there was light at the end of the tunnel. But by the fall of 1935, that light was barely visible. In spite of all his efforts, unemployment was still over 20 percent. Even those who had jobs suffered, as many were working only a few days a week and factories were often paying workers only half of what they had previously earned. With almost no unemployment insurance or welfare available, many people, including the middle class, went hungry—a shocking fact for a nation that believed hard work and frugality were all that was necessary for a secure future. Even nature itself seemed to have turned her back on America. From 1930 to 1936, nearly every state suffered from drought, but the Great Plains was hit the hardest. Western Kansas and eastern Colorado experienced dust storms in 1931 and 1932, and due to the complete lack of soil conservation measures, by the spring of 1934 enormous black dust clouds of loosened topsoil swept through the region. On April 14, 1935, one of the worst dust storms in the history of the United States, later known as "Black Sunday," struck the already-decimated West, destroying farms and devastating infrastructure. Hopeless farmers abandoned their ravaged farmlands and fled westward to California, a journey memorialized later in the decade by John Steinbeck in *The Grapes of Wrath*.

The news from abroad only added to the nightmare at home. In 1935, in defiance of the Treaty of Versailles, Hitler publicly and brazenly began to rearm Germany. At the annual Nuremburg party rally that year, he announced the so-called "Nuremburg laws," which stripped Jews of their civil rights and forbade marriage and sex between Jews and Germans. To make matters worse, Italy invaded Ethiopia eighteen days later. The weak and ineffective League of Nations was dealt a staggering blow, as it had been unable to stop the attack or effectively respond to it in any way.

Amazingly, in spite of (or because of) the alarming international situation and the collapse of the domestic economy, the entertainment industry—particularly the movie business—remained one of the few vibrant areas of American life. Ten days after Mussolini invaded Ethiopia, George Gershwin's *Porgy and Bess* and Cole Porter's *Jubilee* opened on Broadway. Though only two days separated their opening nights, the world those shows represented could not have been more different. Even without retrospect, the circumstances surrounding the creation of the musical *Jubilee* seem scarcely believable; placed in the context of worldwide crisis, the story takes on an almost surreal quality.

Jubilee was a collaboration between Cole Porter, who wrote the music and lyrics, and Moss Hart (no relation to Lorenz Hart of Rodgers and Hart fame) who wrote the book. In the middle of the Depression, on January 12, 1935, Porter and Hart began a four-and-a-half-month luxury cruise around the world on the Cunard liner *Franconia* so they could write the show on board. In order to re-create on the high seas the extravagant lifestyle Porter had become accustomed to on land, he not only brought along his wife Linda and a retinue of friends, but also two maids, a valet, twenty-seven suitcases, and purportedly six cases of champagne. The *New York Herald Tribune* reported the news of the trip stating that "When Messrs. Porter and Hart return to New York, they expect to have on paper a complete score and book for a new show." To accomplish the task, Porter established a working routine on board that sounds like something out of a Fred Astaire movie. Each day would begin with a luxurious breakfast on deck, and a visit to the barber. (It's easy to imagine a witty, barbershop tap-dance sequence for Astaire.) In between dips in the pool, Porter would work on the show in his bathing suit, and then, after an equally lavish lunch retire for a well-earned nap. Afternoons included a daily session in the gym, and cocktails and dinner were formal affairs. Evenings would conclude with a de rigueur game of backgammon and then off to bed by ten.[8] While unemployed workers sold apples on street corners and struggled to find food to eat back home, Porter and Hart traveled to Jamaica, Honolulu, Tahiti, Samoa, the Fiji Islands, New Zealand, Australia, Bali, Mombasa, Zanzibar, Madagascar, India, Africa, and South America on their air-conditioned ship with sun deck, indoor and outdoor swimming pools, and sumptuous cuisine.

As I mentioned earlier, if you were to listen to many of the famous theater songs from the 1930s without knowing anything about history, you would have no idea that the Depression ever happened. Rather than dealing directly with reality, most musicals chose instead to offer an escape. But creating an imaginary world filled with rich, elegantly dressed people with champagne glasses and ivory cigarette holders dancing beneath crystal chandeliers in a Broadway musical was one thing. Actually living that life on a daily basis in the middle of the Depression was something else entirely, yet amazingly enough, that was exactly what Cole Porter did.

Porter had been groomed for a life of luxury since early childhood. Unlike so many of the great Broadway composers of the 1920s and '30s, Porter did not grow up penniless and Jewish on the streets of New York but instead came from a rich Baptist family in Peru, Indiana—a town not widely known as an incubator for great theater composers.* His grand-

---

* See William McBrien, *Cole Porter: A Biography* (HarperCollins, 1998) for the basic Porter biographical details.

father was one of the richest men in the state. Porter's mother, Kate, groomed him for success from an early age, changing his birth date from 1891 to 1893 so he would seem even more of a child prodigy. He played both piano and violin from the age of six, and Kate offered financial support to orchestras in exchange for guarantees that they would invite Cole to perform violin solos. Some claimed that she even bribed critics to influence their reviews.

In order to become the lawyer his grandfather wished him to be, Porter was sent east to go to school. He first attended the Worcester Academy, where he studied with Dr. Abercrombie, a music teacher who greatly influenced Porter's lifelong ideas about the connection between words and music in songs. (Later in his career, Porter would often quote Dr. Abercrombie: "Words and music must be so inseparably wedded to each other that they are like one.") After graduating as the class valedictorian, he went to Yale, where he not only composed several full-scale musicals and soloed with the Yale Glee Club, but also wrote what would become the school's most enduring football song with the first of his witty, literate lyrics: "Bull Dog, Bull Dog, Bow wow wow, Eli Yale."

After Yale, he spent one miserable year at Harvard Law School, dropped out, took two courses at the graduate school of liberal arts—one in music appreciation and one in basic harmony—and then left for Broadway. Unfortunately, his first full production, *See America First,* was a flop, closing after two weeks in 1916. One reviewer called the show the "worst musical comedy in town" and advised, "Don't see *America First*."[9] Unable to handle this kind of rejection after a lifetime of pampering and success, he banished himself to Europe, where he lived off his inheritance and later the money of his fabulously wealthy wife, the socialite Linda Lee Thomas, for most of the 1920s. He finally got up the courage to return to America in 1928 and reintroduced himself to Broadway with the musical *Paris*, featuring "Let's Do it (Let's Fall in Love)." It was an enormous hit, and he never turned back. He ultimately composed over 800 songs for 26 Broadway shows and 18 Hollywood films and lived a society life of staggering success, wealth, and luxury until his death in 1964.

Porter's biography is a reminder that even in the midst of the country's worst economic downturn, there were still extraordinarily wealthy people. However, beneath the glittering surface of Porter's life, there was a shadow side the public knew little about. Though he was married for thirty-four years to a woman once described as the most beautiful in the world, it was a marriage of convenience. Porter, like Lorenz Hart and so many others in the theater community at the time, was a closeted homosexual involved in countless infatuations and affairs with men throughout his life, even after a tragic riding accident in 1937 (four months after Gershwin's death) and thirty operations left him crippled and in pain until his death nearly thirty years later.

To fully understand Porter, as well as the many other gay men in the theater community at the time, it is important to realize that homosexuality was not only shunned socially in the 1930s; it was also illegal. New York laws forbade homosexuals from gathering in state-licensed public places, and bars, restaurants, and cabarets were often shut down if they tolerated a gay presence. A 1923 law made it illegal for a man to invite another man to have sex, and plainclothes policemen were sent into gay bars to proposition customers and arrest them if they responded.

Even mentioning homosexuality in a public forum became nearly impossible. The Hollywood production code of the 1930s forbade the representation of gay characters or the mention of homosexuality on screen, and a 1927 state law similarly prohibited the representation or discussion of homosexuality on the stage. Though the theater community was more accepting of homosexuality than the general public, homosexuals had to continually deal with the fear of arrest, loss of work, public shaming, and destroyed reputations.[10]

The innuendo, sexuality, and titillation that made Porter's lyrics so popular grew out of a personal subtext that, once understood, gives many of his songs a completely different meaning. The tension between his socially perfect public persona and his socially unacceptable private life—not to mention the difficulties it caused for his marriage—were not topics Porter talked about, but their effects can be felt in many of his most famous songs, including "Begin the Beguine," the hit number from *Jubilee*.

If *Porgy and Bess* was Gershwin's attempt to tell a serious story about some of the most downtrodden people in America, *Jubilee*, considered to be one of the great theatrical events of the 1930s, had absolutely nothing serious whatsoever on its mind. The story and title were inspired by the English royal family's Silver Jubilee celebrating King George V's 25th anniversary on the throne. The lighter-than-air plot focuses on the royal family of a fictional European country (suspiciously similar to England) who have been warned of an impending revolution. They use the threat to abandon their royal duties and instead pursue their own private agendas, which primarily consist of romantic entanglements with commoners who are satirical versions of contemporary celebrities. The King becomes interested in Eva Standing—a thinly disguised version of the famous party hostess Elsa Maxwell. The Queen falls for Charles Rausmiller—a thinly disguised version of the swimmer-turned-actor Johnny Weissmuller. The Prince pursues the cabaret singer Karen O'Kane, and the Princess is wooed by Eric Dare—a thinly disguised version of the playwright Noel Coward.

Though the show purports to take place in a fictional world, both the book and Porter's lyrics are filled with references to topical events, society celebrities, and inside jokes that come straight out of Porter's upper-class milieu. Almost every line of "A Picture of Me Without You," for example, depends on an intimate knowledge and familiarity with elite personalities like the opera singer Lily Pons, the wealthy railroad executive Harold Vanderbilt, and even Father Harkness from Porter's alma mater, Yale. And only those who had been to the kind of parties Porter attended—or who had at least read about them in the society pages—and knew about Gershwin's reputation for hogging the piano at every party he attended, would appreciate the hostess in *Jubilee* singing that her next party " 'Twill be new in every way; / Gershwin's promised not to play."

At the end of the show, it turns out that the supposed revolution that set the entire plot in motion was in fact a hoax, and the royal family is returned to power. When they return to the palace with their new friends in tow, however, they bring with them the valuable life lessons they learned from their time among the common people. This of course, from Porter's point of view, represents a kind of reverse fantasy as inconceivable as the show's farcical premise, as Porter had absolutely no place in his high-society world for any of the commoners found in *Jubilee*. Whatever life lessons they may have had to teach the upper-crust royals would certainly not have interested Porter in any way. The humorist Robert Benchley remarked that Cole Porter's lyrics were really written "with an eye to pleasing perhaps eighteen people,"[11] and those eighteen people all came from the same circles Porter did, summered in the same exotic locations, wined, dined, and ate at the same extravagant restaurants, and understood every reference in his ultrasophisticated lyrics. Though almost none of the theatergoing public was part of this circle, their desire to get a glimpse of it onstage—to participate, if only vicariously, in a world they could never inhabit*—helped make Porter one of the most successful songwriters of the era.

As frothy, insubstantial, and escapist as *Jubilee* was,† many of the songs did grow directly out of Porter's actual experiences and travels. "Begin the Beguine" is a wonderful example of how Porter filtered these

---

* Not unlike the attraction of today's celebrity reality shows.

† Though this is perhaps taking a silly plot too seriously, the idea at the heart of the show—of the royals facing an impending revolution, abdicating their responsibilities to pursue their own private, romantic agendas—might be seen as a lighthearted, humorous description of Porter and his own class's actions during the 1930s. By 1935, in the midst of the Depression, revolution was a real possibility. Yet in spite of the troubling economic and political realities of the country as a whole, Porter continued to pursue his own private agendas, seemingly oblivious to the dire situation around him.

experiences into a song that became one of the decade's hits. When asked where the title came from, Porter described living in Paris around 1925 and going

to see the Black Martiniquois . . . do their native dance called The Beguine. . . . I was very much taken by the rhythm of the dance, the rhythm was practically that of the already popular rumba but much faster. The moment I saw it I thought of BEGIN THE BEGUINE as a good title for a song and put it away in a notebook, adding a memorandum as to its rhythm and tempo. . . . About ten years later . . . while going around the world [during his cruise with Hart] we stopped at an island in the Lesser Sunda Islands, to the west of New Guinea. . . . A native dance was stated [sic] for us, the first bars of which was to become my song. I looked through my note-book, and found again, after ten years, my old title BEGIN THE BEGUINE. For some reason the melody that I heard and the phrase that I had written down seemed to marry. I developed the whole song from that."[12]

Like Kern and Gershwin, Porter was comfortable with appropriating whatever music he happened to hear, whatever the source, without the slightest concern for authenticity. Hearing a touring troupe from Martinique performing their native dance in Paris (surely a homogenized version for tourists), Porter heard its rhythm through his own lens as a faster version of the rhumba. It was enough to inspire a title, and when he heard actual natives perform in the Lesser Sunda Islands ten years later, he took the first bars he heard, merged them with the earlier title, and turned the combination into the core idea for "Begin the Beguine" (Ex. 7.1). Clearly it was the beguine rhythm that attracted Porter to the dance in both instances, and that sensual rhythm dominates the entire song, though it is not at all clear that any of the dancers Porter saw in the

Example 7.1 "Begin the Beguine"

Lesser Sunda Islands would recognize Porter's rhythm as their own. Nor would he have cared.

Unwilling to have a verse delay the arrival of the song's key rhythm, "Begin the Beguine" opens directly with the chorus, and one of the keys to the sensuous feel of this song is the way the vocal line floats on top of the beguine accompaniment rhythm. Porter could easily have had the voice and the accompaniment combine in square, matching rhythms, as in Example 7.2A. But instead Porter's triplet on "When they begin" hovers alluringly above the piano, and rather than simply repeating the same triplet rhythm on "the beguine," a graceful syncopation ends the fragment with a lovely dissonance in the piano part (Ex. 7.2B).

Example 7.2A "Begin the Beguine," Kapilow version

Example 7.2B "Begin the Beguine," Porter version

The memory of the magical night Karen O'Kane, the cabaret singer, had shared with the Prince comes back gradually. It begins with restraint with the four notes B♭–C–D–**F** on the words "When they begin" (Ex. 7.1). The emotion rises one note higher for "It brings back the sound" by raising the final note to a G (B♭–C–D–**G**). At the same time, the bass line develops gradually. It repeats the same pattern six times before finally changing on measure 7 on the word "tender." Porter invokes the image of "music so tender" by giving the piano accompaniment a sweet duet (in thirds) right underneath those words.

The memory and music have begun to stir Karen's emotions. As we saw, the first fragment rose up to an F, the second fragment to a G. Now as the memory of their night together becomes even more present on "it brings back a night," the fragment is pitched a step higher and leaps not a third, not a fourth, but a sixth to a C—the highest note of the entire phrase and the song so far (C–D–E♭–**C**). As Porter learned from Dr. Abercrombie at Worcester Academy, words and music must be inseparably wedded, and harmony is what brings these words to life and makes the difference in the following phrase between ordinary and great.

My version (Ex. 7.3A) puts an ordinary chord underneath "splendor"— a chord that has no splendor whatsoever—and then, as the music turns quiet and reflective to end the phrase, I've written an equally ordinary chord under "memory." My version deprives Karen's memory of all its emotional power. Porter's surprising chord under "splendor" with its active accompaniment (Ex. 7.1, m. 11), however, brings the word to life, and the way his version delays resolution at the end of the phrase with an exquisite chord under the last two syllables of "memory" (Ex. 7.3B) is heartrending. The music hangs on to dissonance as Karen hangs on to her memory.

This opening A section is actually double the length of a normal Broadway song—16 measures instead of 8. In typical songbook fashion, the sec-

Example 7.3A "Begin the Beguine," Kapilow version

Example 7.3B "Begin the Beguine," Porter version

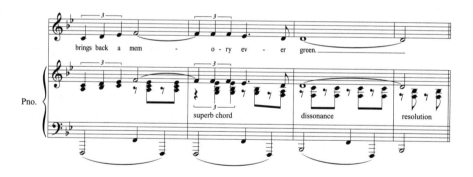

ond verse repeats the music of the extended A section (with a slightly higher climax note in the voice on "palms"—now a D instead of a C) as the memory becomes more and more vivid.

I'm with you once more, under the stars.
And down by the shore, an orchestra's playing*
And even the palms seem to be swaying
When they begin the beguine.

The second verse alters its final measure to end lower vocally (on a B♭ instead of a D) and resolves the opening section of the song (Ex. 7.4, mm. 2–3), at which point the piece becomes truly unique with one of the most unusual forms in the entire American Songbook repertoire. To begin

Example 7.4 "Begin the Beguine"

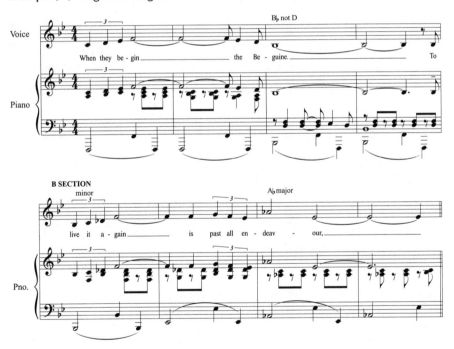

---

* Incredibly enough, this image accurately reflects Porter's own lifestyle in which an orchestra might well be playing on the beach. In 1926 while summering in Venice, Porter converted a huge barge into a floating dance hall and brought in an African American band from London to play jazz on the boat. The great Russian impresario Serge Diaghilev (and evidently many Venetians as well) complained that Porter's "Negroes" were "teaching the 'Charleston' on the Lido Beach!" (McBrien, p. 107).

the B section, Porter takes the song's opening gesture, "When they begin" (B♭–C–**D**–F, Ex. 7.1), and shifts it into a minor key for "To live it again" (B♭–C–**D♭**–F, Ex. 7.4). This causes the piece to shift key (briefly to A♭ major) on "past all endeavor," and then true Porter magic takes over.

He continues as if to copy the 4 measures of "To live it again is past all endeavor" a step lower for the lyric "Except when that tune clutches my heart." An exact copy would sound like Example 7.5A.

But the tune has to "clutch our hearts," so instead he leaps higher with an exquisite major-seventh chord underneath "heart" (G♭-major-seventh chord, Ex. 7.5B). This superb leap and deeply expressive harmony as we change keys for the second time in 4 measures—highly unusual in a popular song—conveys a Karen increasingly caught up in the emotion the memory has conjured. As that emotion becomes more intense, the register of the vocal line begins to rise for "there we are swearing to love forever," until finally she brings herself back under control, sadly remembering their promise "never, never to part."

Like the two double-length A sections, this B section is also 16 bars, not 8, and when Porter returns to the music of the A section, we assume he will finish this double-length but still fundamentally standard AABA Broadway form with one more verse of A. And in fact, all of the music of the opening A section does return but with so many wonderful alterations in the vocal line that the composer and critic Alec Wilder in his classic book *American Popular Song* exclaimed that even after hearing the song hundreds of times, he was still unable to sing, whistle, or play it from start to finish without the printed sheet music. Then, instead of ending the song at measure 67 as expected, Porter adds 44 more measures and an entirely new C section to this already-extended AABA song (Ex. 7.6).

It is important to realize that the extended length of this song has nothing to do with experimentation for its own sake, and everything to do with the emotion and narrative of the song. Porter adds an entirely new

Example 7.5A "Begin the Beguine," Kapilow version

Example 7.5B "Begin the Beguine," Porter version

Example 7.6 "Begin the Beguine," C section

section of music because it will take Karen that much time to extinguish the emotion her memory has brought to life. Thinking of the lyrics of the song in the context of all of the transient couplings in Porter's own life gives an even greater sadness and poignancy to the lines, "What moments divine, what rapture serene. Till clouds came along to disperse the joys

Example 7.6 "Begin the Beguine," C section (*continued*)

we had tasted. And now when I hear people curse the chance that was wasted, I know but too well, what they mean."

The song, however, does not end with resignation. Karen is unable to repress the intensity of desire conjured up by her memories, and the voice leaps into a high register for her urgent plea, "So don't let them begin the

Example 7.6 "Begin the Beguine," C section (*continued*)

beguine. Let the love that was once a fire remain an ember." The urgency
with which she tries to get rid of this painful memory—to tamp down the
emotion and turn a fire back into an ember—is beautifully captured by the
way her voice descends in pitch throughout the section. D is the highest

Example 7.6 "Begin the Beguine," C section (*continued*)

note of the song,* and for five and a half measures (Ex. 7.6, mm. 69–74) she urgently sings almost nothing but high D's. On "let the love that was once a fire remain an ember," the pitch of the vocal line begins to fall—to become an ember—descending from the high D down to an F (mm. 76–77). As the ember becomes a "dead desire," the pitch goes even lower, now down to a low D (mm. 80–81).

But the memory refuses to die, and the song refuses to end. In a superb melding of music and lyrics, the phrase that began this section, "*So don't let them* begin the beguine," now becomes "*Oh yes let them* begin the beguine." Finally, in the grip of the past, she says yes to the memory.

---

* There is one higher note—an E♭—in measure 91, but it is merely a decoration. D is the climactic note vocally and it represents the highest pitch of emotion in the song.

She acknowledges it with all of the pain it entails, and the whole C section repeats (m. 86).

Having said yes to the past, her former love can now actually appear in the song. She has conjured his presence so vividly that he can actually speak in her imagination.

Oh yes let them begin the beguine, make them play.
Till the stars that were there before return above you.
Till you whisper to me once more, "Darling, I love you."

These last words, the actual words of her lover, bring her into another realm—to "the heaven we're in"—and amazingly add yet another 16 measures to the song. Suddenly time seems to stand still. The same melodic fragment (labeled x) repeats languidly three times (mm. 98–103), each with a different harmony underneath, finally resolving as in verse two to a low B♭ in the vocal line, as if to end the song.

Yet the song still refuses to end! The melodic fragment (x) repeats one more time and sustains its final note for twelve and a half seemingly endless beats, giving both Karen and the audience time to think about the song's emotional journey. The subtle flicker of pain in the G♭ that colors the accompaniment in measure 108 beautifully conveys the mixture of joy and pain the memory has brought up. Finally, the vocal line floats up to end the song on a high B♭, not the low B♭ that has ended so many of the previous sections. It's not a high note of triumph, but of acceptance of the past, earned by traveling the emotional journey of the song.

Porter was always pushing sexual boundaries in his work and challenging the censors' concept of what was permissible in a Broadway song, much as his own homosexuality challenged society's concept of what was permissible in a life. The autobiographical penultimate line of "Begin the Beguine" was originally, "And we suddenly know the sweetness of sin," which Porter ultimately changed to the far more conventional, "And we suddenly know what heaven we're in." Exchanging the honest, forthright, brazen expression of "sweetness of sin" for the more respectable, socially acceptable "heaven we're in" was a trade-off that Porter chose to make throughout his life, and the strength of the sinful emotions that he was forced to repress publicly shows up in the intensity, titillation, and edginess of many of his most heartfelt lyrics. When Karen sings, "And now when I hear people curse the chance that was wasted / I know but too well what they mean," it was not only Karen but Porter himself who knew too well what they meant. He too had spent nights "swearing to love forever and promising never, never to part" only to see those promises dissolve in the light of day. In the kind of letter that Porter would replicate over and over again to many of his lovers throughout his life, he writes to the Russian poet Boris Kochno, "When will I find you again? There are not enough letters . . . I miss you so much that I am falling apart and if this continues—this utter silence—I don't dare think what I could do. Oh, Boris, write me and tell me that you love me as much as I love you."[13]

The extraordinary pressure of leading the kind of double life that the times and Porter's social circle seemed to require was unbearable for many gay men. Larry Hart escaped into alcohol, which ultimately ended his partnership with Richard Rodgers and eventually contributed to his death at the age of forty-eight. But Porter, thanks to his extraordinary wealth and self-discipline somehow managed to keep his hyperactive private life private and his upper-class society life free from scandal. That glamorous life was never more on public display than on the nights of his Broadway premieres, and the Depression did nothing to dampen their glitter. The radio commentator Mary McBride, describing the opening night of *Jubilee*, said, "not since 1929 [and the stock market crash] had there been such a convocation of ermine, mink, Russian sable, diamond dog collars and star sapphires as was brought forth by the opening night of *Jubilee*."[14] Porter designed a diamond and aquamarine necklace for his wife Linda to wear to the event, and as was her custom she bought Cole an elegant cigarette case. The extravagantly dressed, upper-crust crowd included princes, dukes, theatrical royalty, and high-society A-listers. For the dispirited, Depression-era onlookers lining the sidewalks to get a glimpse of how the other half lived, the opening-night event, like the actual show itself, was an irresistible, escapist fantasy. The onlookers might never meet the royals who inhabited the plot of *Jubilee*, or wear the furs and jewels of the crowd that attended the premiere, but for a few moments in the theater—if they could afford a ticket once the show had opened—or on the sidewalks on opening night, they could forget the grim reality of the seemingly never-ending Depression and find happiness in Porter's fantasy world.

ARTIE SHAW AND "BEGIN THE BEGUINE"

As the popularity of theater songs became more and more dependent on versions arranged and recorded by bandleaders, it was often these arrangements—which were frequently quite different from the original—that became known by the general public. In 1938, the bandleader Artie Shaw recorded a swing version of "Begin the Beguine" that sold 6.5 million copies and continues to sell today. Some people think it may be the single most popular recording ever made, and it became not only Shaw's signature tune but also a kind of albatross around his neck, as audiences demanded that he play the tune night after night, year after year. Shaw made the original recording for Bluebird records, and initially the executives were completely uninterested. They thought it was too long and, like Alec Wilder, too difficult to remember. It was recorded almost as an afterthought as the B-side of "Indian Love Call," but quickly became enormously popular, skyrocketing Shaw and his band to worldwide fame.

What is particularly interesting about this is the relationship between Shaw's recorded version and Porter's original. In spite of the way words and music are "inseparably wedded to each other" in the song, Porter's words played no part in the recording's success: Shaw's recording was purely instrumental. Not only did Shaw remove Porter's lyrics, he changed the fundamental rhythm of the song as well. When Shaw first asked Jerry Gray to arrange the tune for the band, Gray stuck to the beguine rhythm—the rhythm that runs throughout Porter's song and gives it its title. But Shaw didn't think the song worked that way, and in his own words, Shaw changed Porter's "Latin beat to a swing time." With Porter's words and fundamental rhythm gone, all that was left was the song's basic melody and harmony. Most of this remains intact, though there is some light, jazzy swing decoration and improvisation in the solo and ensemble choruses, as well as an occasional alteration of the harmony. Perhaps the biggest overall difference in the two versions is the way Shaw has turned the song into smooth, elegant, refined, swing-era dance music with no hint of the intense emotion that is at the heart of the original. Like so many dance band recordings of Broadway songs, the arrangement is a completely different piece of music, serving a completely different function, producing a completely different emotional response.

Porter was evidently quite happy with Shaw's version (unlike Jerome Kern, who tried to forbid all dance band arrangements of his songs), and in some ways it is easy to see why. Shaw's arrangement fits in perfectly with the surface of Porter's upscale, society world. No one sweats when the band plays the tune in the 1938 short film, "Artie Shaw and His Orchestra." The band—all white except for the bass player—is impeccably dressed and plays with smooth precision and controlled emotion. Nothing excessive or vulgar is permitted to intrude. It is, in a sense, the surface of Porter's music and life without the underlying passion, pain, and intensity that give his music its depth and emotion.

Once the specifics of Porter's song had been removed, it became possible to superimpose many different interpretations on the piece. During World War II, Shaw performed extensively for the troops overseas, and to

these soldiers the tune became a source of nostalgia for the Saturday evening dances and girlfriends they had left behind. Yet it had an entirely
different meaning for the president of Minolta, Sam Kusumoto, who said.
"The culture shock that followed Japan's surrender to the Allies changed the
Japanese completely. . . . The first music we heard was 'Begin the Beguine'
by Artie Shaw's band. If you talk to Japanese of my generation and mention 'Begin the Beguine,' everybody will rise and smile because that song
represented a new era for the Japanese."[15] From a song about a particular woman confronting a painful memory, to a source of nostalgia for the
home front during World War II, to a symbol of a new era for the Japanese,
Porter's song had traveled back to the part of the world that had originally
inspired it. A title suggested in Paris had joined with a melody inspired by
an Indonesian dance to become a hit Broadway tune as well as the symbol
of the new Japan. A song written "with an eye to pleasing perhaps eighteen people," in the midst of the worst Depression America had ever faced
had become perhaps its most successful export. How the other half lived—
Porter's reality—had become America's soundtrack for the world.

8

Love in New York

Richard Rodgers's "I Wish I Were in Love Again"

One of the most remarkable aspects of Richard Rodgers's career was his loyalty to the two lyricists who helped define it—Lorenz (Larry) Hart and Oscar Hammerstein II. In an era when songwriters tended to change writing partners frequently (in 1929–30 alone, "Yip" Harburg wrote songs with ten different composers), Rodgers collaborated exclusively with Hart from 1919 until Hart's collapse and death at the age of forty-eight in 1943, and then with Oscar Hammerstein II from 1943 until Hammerstein's death in 1960. Conventional wisdom has largely accepted the view that the enormous changes in Rodgers's musical style were the direct result of this switch. As Robert Gottlieb put it succinctly in *The Atlantic*, "It's as inconceivable that Larry Hart could have written 'Oh, What a Beautiful Mornin'' as it is that Hammerstein could have written 'Zip.'"[1] Although there is no doubt that the vast differences in Hart's and Hammerstein's aesthetics played a key role in the very different kinds of music Rodgers wrote with each collaborator, the complete shift in style cannot be simply explained by the differing worldviews of his two lyricists. It was equally a result of the social, political, economic, and cultural currents in the music industry specifically and the country as a whole.

At first glance, the similarities in the backgrounds of Rodgers, Hart, and Hammerstein seem more striking than their differences. Hart and Rodgers were Jewish, and though Hammerstein was technically Episcopalian (Judaism is matrilineal, and Hammerstein's mother was the daughter of Scottish and English parents), his famous grandfather, Oscar Hammerstein I, and his father were both Jewish. Unlike Berlin, Gershwin, and so many other songwriters and lyricists who came from the tenement world of New York's Lower East Side, Rodgers, Hart, and Hammerstein II all came from well-to-do families and grew up blocks apart in the same elegant, Harlem neighborhood near Mount Morris Park—an area that by 1900 had become the second-largest Jewish settlement in New York.[2]

Rodgers's attitude toward the family's Judaism is revealing. Though many scholars of the Great American Songbook have remarked on the overwhelming dominance of Jewish songwriters, lyricists, theater owners, and music publishers, what is equally remarkable is how assimilated and "un-Jewish" nearly all of them tried—consciously or unconsciously— to become. Rodgers chose to begin his autobiography, *Musical Stages*, with a striking description of his great-grandmother's Jewish Orthodox funeral. Included were beautiful details about the elevator that carried her coffin—the operator tugging on a cable running through the car— and the use of ice as a substitute for embalming, which was forbidden by Jewish law. The event clearly made a deep impression on the young Rodgers, but then he writes, "This hurried ritual was the end of orthodox Judaism in our family. The next step was known as Reform, and even this faded after the bar mitzvah of my brother and me as a gesture to my grandfather on my mother's side. From that time on, my parents, my brother and I were Jewish for socioethnic reasons rather than because of any deep religious conviction."[3] This is the last mention of religion in his entire autobiography. No entry for "Judaism" or "religion" appears in the book's index, and Rodgers's story proceeds without any further reference to his Jewish heritage.

The overwhelming impulse among children of immigrants was toward assimilation, which usually began with the Americanization of their ethnic names. Rogazinsky became Abraham, sometimes shortened to Abrams, and then finally Rodgers in 1892. The Rodgers and Hart biopic, *Words and Music* (1948), takes the process of assimilation to its logical conclusion by casting the bland Tom Drake as a Richard Rodgers with no perceivable religion or ethnicity of any kind. However, though neither Hart, nor Rodgers, nor Hammerstein II connected in any significant ways to their religious backgrounds, they did follow social and ethnic paths similar to those of other children of well-off immigrant Jews. All three went to Jewish summer camps that offered significant first experiences in musical theater, and later to Columbia University (less well-off Jews like Ira Gershwin and "Yip" Harburg tended to go to City College), where they worked on various Columbia University Varsity Shows.*

Rodgers knew by the age of fifteen that he wanted musical theater to be his life's profession. That year, his brother, a student at Columbia, took him to the spring Varsity Show, *Home, James*, where he met Oscar Hammerstein II, who had written most of the libretto. (Hart appeared in the show as well, playing Mary Pickford in a curly blond wig.)[4] Though Rodgers had no interest in academics, he immediately decided to attend Columbia for the sole purpose of writing a Varsity Show. He enrolled in the fall of 1919, two years behind his brother, and that spring was introduced to Larry Hart. Hart was twenty-three at the time—Rodgers was only sixteen—and had already finished two years at Columbia's School of Journalism, but their connection was immediate, and Hart would play a

---

* The Columbia Varsity Show is a full-length, original musical that satirizes campus life put on each year by Columbia University students. It began as a fund-raiser for varsity athletics in 1892, and many famous theatrical personalities got their start working on these shows.

major role in helping to shape the young Rodgers's ideas about songwriting and musical theater.

◌◌

The influence parents have on their children often shows up in surprising ways. Rodgers seemed to have inherited his mother's hypochondria, whereas Hart's fascination with literary erudition was in striking opposition to his father's larger-than-life coarseness and vulgarity. No biographer seems to be able to pin down exactly what Max Hart did for a living, but he evidently was some kind of a combination businessman, Tammany Hall fixer, con man, founder of companies, and quite possibly a crook. In spite of wide swings financially, there was often enough money in the house for servants, cars, a chauffeur, and parties with a Bohemian crowd. Dorothy Hart, Larry's sister-in-law, describes the horrifying neighborhood scandal after Hart's father, irritated by the sound of the famous Cantor Rosenblatt (the same cantor who appeared in *The Jazz Singer*) practicing his chants outside to escape the summer heat, poured a bucket of water on his head.[5] Other neighbors claimed that he frequently urinated out his dining room window when he was too lazy to go to the bathroom.[6] In an almost complete rejection of his father's crudeness, Larry belonged to literary societies and edited the school papers at Columbia Grammar School and DeWitt Clinton High School, and when Rodgers first met him, he was translating German plays for the Shubert organization. The two hit it off immediately and began working together in what would turn out to be a nearly quarter-of-a-century collaboration.

If, as the saying goes, "practice makes perfect," there is no better example of this than the early struggles of Rodgers and Hart. They began writing songs together in the spring of 1919, and they had their first song interpolated into a Broadway show in August of that year, when Rodgers was only seventeen years old—a song called "Any Old Place with You" in Lew Fields's *A Lonely Romeo*. The following spring they wrote their first complete score, *You'd Be Surprised*, for an Akron club show,* as well as the score for the 1920 Columbia Varsity Show. Their good fortune appeared to continue when Fields, impressed by *You'd Be Surprised*, asked them to write an entire Broadway show, *Poor Little Ritz Girl*. *Variety*'s front page read, "17-YEAR-OLD COMPOSER / Richard E. Rodgers Writer of Field's New Numbers."[7] However, after finishing the score, they left the production for the summer only to discover when they returned that the show had been completely rewritten in their absence. Fields had gotten nervous and hired the more-experienced composer Sigmund Romberg without consulting Rodgers or Hart, and almost none of their work remained. It was one of the most humiliating experiences of their young careers, but many more would follow.

After writing another Akron Club show and a second Varsity Show for Columbia, Rodgers decided he had gotten what he needed from academia, and in 1921 he left Columbia to go to the Institute of Musical Art (now the Juilliard School). The practical experience Rodgers had gained from working on multiple shows was invaluable, but the training in composition and theory that he received at Juilliard gave him a technical foundation that went far beyond that of nearly all his fellow songwriters. Still, in spite of his training and the team's early successes, Rodgers and Hart would not make it back to Broadway until 1925. At the very moment a bitter, dejected, twenty-three-year-old Rodgers was about to give up on theater altogether and take a $50-a-week job selling diapers, he received a call from the prestigious Theatre Guild asking if he would write the score for a revue to be called the *Garrick Gaieties* (named after the Garrick Theatre, where the Guild staged its productions). By the time the Theatre Guild called, Rodgers and Hart had already written the scores to thirty

---

* The Akron Club was a New York social-athletic group that began raising money for charity with entertainment evenings in 1914. In 1917, at the age of fifteen, Rodgers had written music for a revue called *One Minute Please*, staged at the Plaza Hotel in order to raise money for the *New York Sun*'s Tobacco Fund, which provided cigarettes for soldiers (Hyland, p. 13).

amateur musicals; they were finally ready. The show was a huge success, and it launched their careers.

∾

Although the Founding Fathers of the Broadway musical were all born within a twenty-year span (1885–1905), Rodgers really represented the musical's second wave of creativity, a wave inspired by the pathbreaking achievements of Kern and Berlin, who had grown up in a very different musical environment. The world of operetta and ragtime that once had such a powerful influence on the earlier composers' music was not the principal influence on Rodgers and Hart. Their music was first and foremost the music of the Roaring Twenties: fast-paced, upbeat, witty, self-aware, literate, and, most important, New York–centered. It could not be more appropriate that their breakthrough hit from the *Garrick Gaieties* was an ode to the city that was their music's hometown, "Manhattan."*

New York was the center of the literary and theatrical universe in the twenties. Books, plays, and musicals were first and foremost designed to appeal to sophisticated New York audiences, and Hart's lyrics perfectly captured the urbane, self-referential, effortlessly virtuosic voice that defined the era, first for New Yorkers and then by extension for the rest of the country. Though the scintillating lyrics of these musicals have almost come to define Broadway's Golden Age, it is important to recognize that their New York focus was both new and short-lived. In the first two decades of the century, most Broadway operettas were set in Europe, Asia, or some equivalently exotic locale, while early musical comedies were likely to take place somewhere in rural, small-town America. It wasn't until the 1920s that Manhattan became the default setting for musicals in the scores of Gershwin, Porter, and Rodgers, and once the

---

* Though it had actually been written three years earlier in 1922 for an unproduced show called *Winkletown*.

focus had shifted to New York, Rodgers and Hart embodied the voice of that time and place perfectly.[8]

The team's productivity in the second half of the 1920s was simply astounding. Between 1925 and 1930, they collaborated on a mind-boggling seventeen shows, including such hits as *The Girl Friend, Peggy-Ann, One Dam Thing After Another,* and *A Connecticut Yankee.* In 1926 alone, they had three shows running simultaneously, and out of the seventeen shows they wrote in those years, only three were failures. But once the Depression hit, everything changed.

When the funding for Broadway musicals dried up in the 1930s, Rodgers and Hart, like nearly all of the major songwriters of the period, went to Hollywood. As Rodgers put it in his autobiography, "Nobody *had* to go to the theatre. In the world of entertainment, it cost a great deal less to see a movie or a vaudeville show—and it cost nothing at all to stay home and listen to the radio. With the market continuing to slide at a rapid pace, we couldn't help but worry that our world was in danger of being destroyed."[9] And destroyed, at least temporarily, it was. *America's Sweetheart* in 1931 marked the end of their astonishing first phase on Broadway, and though they had initially planned to go to Hollywood for only three months, they would not return to Broadway with a new show until 1935.

Nearly all of the major Broadway songwriters and lyricists struggled to adapt to the Hollywood studio system, but perhaps no team was more unsuccessful than Rodgers and Hart. After a promising outing with the film *Love Me Tonight* in 1932, they accomplished almost nothing in 1933—perhaps the nadir of the Depression for both the country and Rodgers and Hart. As Rodgers put it bluntly, "And that was the way Rodgers and Hart spent the year 1933: one score for a film that wasn't made; one score, mostly unused, for a film no one can recall; one song for Goldwyn; one song for Selznick."[10] Though their difficulties in dealing with the studio system were surely at the heart of the problem, the very New York–centric qualities that had made Rodgers and Hart so successful on Broadway were a drawback

in the world of Hollywood, which had to reach a much wider, less sophisti-
cated, recently developing national audience. It was surely no surprise that
Irving Berlin, who had the most populist voice of all of the New York songwriters, would also be the most successful of the Hollywood transplants.
But as debilitating and artistically barren as the Hollywood experience was
for Rodgers, with a new wife and child to support and no prospects on
Broadway, he had little choice but to accept the studio's weekly paycheck.
However, when he happened to see a column written by the widely syn-
dicated New York writer O. O. McIntyre that read, "Whatever happened
to Rodgers and Hart?"[11] he was jolted into action and decided to return to
Broadway, whatever the risks involved.

As astonishing as the team's burst of productivity in the late twenties
had been, in some ways their achievements from 1935 to 1942 were even
more remarkable. Two years into Roosevelt's presidency, the Depression
refused to ease, and the New York landscape they came back to was bleak.
Nationwide, unemployment hovered around 20 percent, while on Broadway only half of the theaters were in use and less than half of the actors were
employed. To attract ticket buyers, prices had to be substantially reduced,
which meant lower royalties and salaries for composers and performers.
In spite of an almost universal tightening of belts, Rodgers and Hart hit
Broadway in 1935 with *Jumbo*, a spectacular, enormously expensive, circus-
themed show produced by the flamboyant Billy Rose. They turned the
5,000-seat Hippodrome Theatre into a circus tent and featured a huge cast
that included acrobats, animal acts, a live elephant, and Jimmy Durante.
The critical response was ecstatic, and an extraordinary five-year run of hit
shows followed. Between 1935 and 1938, they wrote five incredibly successful shows: *Jumbo* (1935), *On Your Toes* (1936), *Babes in Arms* (1937), *I'd
Rather Be Right* (1937), and *I Married an Angel* (1938). They were featured
on the cover of *Time* magazine in September 1938,[12] and their amazing run
then continued with *The Boys from Syracuse* (1938), *Too Many Girls* (1939),
Higher and Higher (1940—their only flop), *Pal Joey* (1940), and their last

new musical, *By Jupiter* (1942), completed at Doctors Hospital, where Hart had been sent to dry out from "acute and chronic alcoholism."

From 1935 to 1942 they collaborated on ten shows, and all but one had been either a smash hit or a solid success, but even more remarkable than the quantity and quality of these shows was how different they were from each other. *On Your Toes,* with its famous ballet, "Slaughter on Tenth Avenue," brought classical dance into the world of the Broadway musical with brilliant choreography by George Balanchine. *Babes in Arms* utilized a book written by Rodgers and Hart themselves and attempted to create a hit musical with only young, unknown actors. *I'd Rather Be Right* was a bold attempt to create the first satirical musical about a sitting president, while the *Boys from Syracuse* turned Shakespeare into musical comedy ten years before Cole Porter's *Kiss Me, Kate.* Perhaps most radically, *Pal Joey* was a bold, bitter, cynical, startlingly realistic show about a thoroughly unlikable, amoral antihero. Perhaps it was the pent-up creativity generated by years of frustration in Hollywood that fueled this outburst of creativity, or simply the realization that the formulas of the 1920s musicals had become clichéd by the second half of the 1930s; but whatever its source, their desire to create something fresh and new made these shows (as opposed to their individual songs) the most extraordinary in all of their years of collaboration.

Throughout his career, Rodgers would continually refer to his fear of repeating himself, and for a songwriter and lyricist there was no more dangerous topic than the one that inevitably reared its head in every musical: love. As Rodgers put it, "One [problem] every songwriter must face over and over again, is how to say 'I love you' in a way that makes the song different from any other romantic ballad ever written."[13] Interestingly enough, as Ben Yagoda points out in *The B-Side*, his insightful book on the history of American popular song, though love became the quintessential topic for popular songs (and continues to be in today's pop songs as well), this fixation was actually a post–World War I phenomenon. Early Tin Pan Alley songs tended to focus on topical events or fads. The craze for bicycles, for example, prompted songs like "A Bicycle Built for Two," and the fascination with baseball brought "Take Me Out to the Ball Game." Ethnic diversity was also a popular topic, and Berlin, like so many other songwriters, wrote Tin Pan Alley songs directed at individual immigrant groups—"Abie Sings an Irish Song" for the Irish and "Yiddisha Eyes" for the Jews. World War I, of course, spawned an enormous number of songs dealing with the war itself, with George M. Cohan's "Over There" becoming its signature, but as radio and recordings helped create a truly national market for songwriters in the 1920s and '30s, love became the central topic for popular songs not least because it was a universal theme that could resonate with everyone regardless of race, color, nationality, or income level. Also, given the puritanical morality of the country in the opening years of the twentieth century, songs were one of the few places where the topic of love could actually be mentioned. Parts of the body and sentiments that were taboo nearly everywhere else found their way into song lyrics, but not without significant resistance from censors, ministers, and moralists. The discomfort that love songs created can be seen as late as 1934, when composer Kenneth S. Clark complained that popular songs were "[a]ll too often ultra-sentimental, the almost unvarying theme being love—particularly the unrequited or unsatisfied love of the 'torch' song. Who is going to take any pleasure in singing such songs ten years from now!"[14]

In spite of the moral resistance to songs about love in some quarters, as well as the dangers of boredom and cliché that its ubiquity created, once love became the default theme of popular song, every songwriter was forced to continually define and redefine themselves through their particular approach to the subject. Like religious paintings for artists in the medieval world, or history paintings in the eighteenth century, love songs in the Broadway world of the twenties and thirties became the principal arena in which songwriters had to prove themselves, and no team was more adept at creating fresh approaches to this potentially hackneyed topic than Rodgers and Hart.

It is not surprising that Hart would have a fresh, irreverent, somewhat cynical approach to love given the complex nature of his own sexuality. Like so many closeted individuals during this era, Hart was extremely discreet about his relationships, and by all accounts he was terrified that his mother Frieda, a traditional German woman whom he still lived with, would discover his secret. In spite of his homosexuality, he pursued a number of women throughout his life and even proposed marriage more than once (though always unsuccessfully). Knowing how harmful it would have been to Hart to have his sexuality aired publicly, Rodgers stood loyally by his partner and defended his reputation throughout Hart's lifetime, only acknowledging the truth after Hart's death.[15] Given Hart's anything-but-straightforward sexuality, it is not surprising that he approached the topic of love from a different angle, and no song better illustrates the brilliant results than one of the hits from *Babes in Arms*, "I Wish I Were in Love Again."

According to Rodgers, the idea for *Babes in Arms* literally arose from a walk in the park.

> Sometime during the summer of 1936, while Larry and I were strolling through Central Park, we noticed a bunch of children in a playground who were making up their own games and rules. We began talking about kids and what might happen if they were suddenly given adult responsibilities, such as finding ways to earn a living. One way might be to put on a big benefit show that would turn out to be a hit. And that's the way *Babes in Arms* was born.[16]

It is interesting to see how determined Rodgers and Hart were to create something outside of the formulas that were everywhere in 1930s musicals. In 1936, the same year they wrote *Babes in Arms*, Rodgers agreed to a commission from the bandleader Paul Whiteman to write a narrative concert piece for soloist and symphony orchestra called *All Points West*. Though the piece was not successful in any way, it was a clear attempt, as Rodgers put it, to "expand the scope of our writing," and everything about *Babes in Arms* grew out of a similar ambition. After trying their hand at writing the book for *On Your Toes*—they ultimately turned the job over to George Abbott— they were determined to write the book for *Babes in Arms* without outside help. And in a clear desire to break away from the ubiquitous pattern of star-driven musicals, they boldly decided to write a show that would be cast exclusively with new, young talent that had yet to be discovered by the general public. This absence of stars, along with a low-budget production concept that did away with fancy sets and costumes, made the show incredibly cheap to produce, and it was easy for Rodgers and Hart to find backers even in the middle of the Depression.

Though all of these choices signaled a willingness on Rodgers and Hart's part to move in new directions and break new ground, it cannot be said that the story they ultimately came up with was brilliant, fresh, or innovative. The simple plot centers around a group of teenagers in Seaport, Long Island, who get left behind when their vaudevillian parents go off on tour. In order to save themselves from being sent to the work farm by the local sheriff, the teenagers decide to "put on a show"—one of the hoariest clichés in the musical-theater repertoire. Though the book Rodgers and Hart came up with was anything but original (and, by the middle of the second act, anything but coherent), there was at least an attempt to include material in the story that reflected contemporary concerns in an interesting way. One of the show's subplots deals with a potential backer—a rich, racist, southerner named Lee Calhoun who refuses to put up money for the kids' show if it includes two black dancers, Ivor and Irving de Quincy. Communism, Nietzsche, capitalism, feminism, free speech, aviation, and the Depression all make an appearance in the script, and though its overall tone is lighter than air, there is at least a hint of real satire hidden beneath the silly antics of a traditional musical-comedy plot.

When Rodgers was asked why he wanted to write *All Points West*, the symphonic score he composed the same year as *Babes in Arms*, he said:

> We wanted to do something with more freedom. We wanted to escape the conventions that hedge in the musical-comedy song. For one thing, you're supposed to work in your title in the first eight bars and then to repeat it at the end. If you're bursting with independence, you might add a few bars here or take away a few bars there, but the form is almost inflexible. Also we got pretty tired of writing about nothing but love.[17]

Though they might have gotten tired of writing about "nothing but love," in *Babes in Arms* there is certainly no evidence of that fatigue in the brilliant first-act number "I Wish I Were in Love Again." One of the ways they avoided compositional fatigue and the seemingly inevitable clichés of the genre was by replacing a traditional love song with what is essentially an antilove song. Like Sondheim's "Being Alive" thirty years later, Hart's lyrics, rather than praising love poetically, instead complain about all of the painful, horrible things that love can bring while concluding that, in spite of it all, "I wish I were in love again." In the show, the song is sung by Dolores and Gus—originally Grace McDonald and Rolly Pickert—"ex"-boyfriend and girlfriend, who are obviously still attracted to each other and sing this duet as a form of flirting.

As we have seen over and over again, every popular song depends on its opening idea. If a song is successful, it's the idea that you walk out of the theater whistling. In a standard AABA Broadway song, the opening idea repeats three times, and if the number is a major song in the show, you are likely to hear it repeated in the overture, as a reprise, and underneath the cast bows at the end of the show. It is hard to imagine a more perfect marriage of words and music or a more perfect example of the art of Rodgers and Hart than this opening phrase. Though this 8-measure idea will repeat

Example 8.1 "I Wish I Were in Love Again"

three times within the song itself, it is actually the repetition of a tiny, three-note motive—a simple scale, F♯–G–A (labeled "x" in Ex. 8.1)—within the idea itself that makes the phrase so catchy and memorable.

You first hear the motive on "sleepless nights," then on "daily fights," and Rodgers could easily have repeated it twice more with a slight change of words, as in Example 8.2. But instead of an exact repetition, Rodgers decorates the idea with faster notes, which perfectly represents the "quick toboggan," and then copies this version for "I miss the kisses and I miss the bites." We have now heard that tiny, three-note idea repeat six times, setting us up for the perfect musical punch line—a completely new rhythm, new

Example 8.2 "I Wish I Were in Love Again," Kapilow version

notes, and a new shape to end the musical sentence. The only nonrhyme in the phrase: the title line, "I wish I were in love again."

The reason all of this repetition sounds so right goes to the heart of Rodgers and Hart's perfect marriage of words and music. The song is ultimately a witty laundry list of all the terrible things that love creates. Not its poetic qualities, as in so many Broadway songs, but its darker side. Hart's lyric essentially says, "Love is this, this, and this." Since this is musical comedy, all of the items of course rhyme—"nights, fights, heights, bites"—and they're all paired to the same melody. (In fact, after the initial upbeat in the voice, the vocal line uses only three notes, F♯–G–A, until the punch line, with the limited melodic interest allowing the listener to focus on the clever words.)

Since this song is a classic, 32-bar, AABA Broadway song, the second 8 bars, musically speaking, are a repeat of the first 8, but, as we will see, Rodgers makes one crucial change in the final bar. In a traditional AABA song like this one, the burden in the first A section, in a sense, falls most heavily on the composer. He has to immediately establish the song's hook, the musical idea that grabs the listener and defines the world of the song. But in the second and third repeats of A (A**BA**), the burden shifts to the lyricist, whose new words have to reenergize and deepen the meaning of the melody as it repeats, and this is where Hart was a true master. The lyrics of the second A section are even wittier than the first:

> *The broken dates,*
> *The endless waits,*
> *The lovely loving and the hateful hates,*
> *The conversation with the flying plates—*
> *I wish I were in love again!*

Following up the brilliant, almost-poetic lyric, "the lovely loving and the hateful hates," with the active, physical image of "the conversation with the flying plates" is a great example of the kind of sophistication and verbal virtuosity that Hart brought to the world of the 1930s musical, and Rodgers's music offers the perfect support for Hart's incomparable lyrics. Vocally speaking, this second A section is an exact repeat of the first A section until its final four notes—the repeat of the title line, "I wish I were in love again." For its first iteration, Rodgers had the vocal line leap *down* in resignation to three repeated D's—the lowest note in the phrase (Ex. 8.3A). But the second time, Rodgers has the vocal line leap *up* brightly with excitement to three repeated B's—the highest note of the song so far—giving the title words a whole different feel and giving the piece the energy to continue the narrative and move on to the B section (Ex. 8.3B).

This one higher note opens up a whole new side of Gus's character and a whole new section of music. Form is character. In this new section, instead

Example 8.3A "I Wish I Were in Love Again"

Example 8.3B "I Wish I Were in Love Again"

Example 8.4 "I Wish I Were in Love Again"

of repeating the ascending scale, F♯–G–A, that represented the fights, the sleepless nights, and the pain of being in love, its opposite, a descending scale, B–A–G (labeled "y" in Ex. 8.4) that represents the joy of life-out-of-love repeats over and over again.

The song's simplicity is extraordinary here, and the greatness of Rodgers and Hart can be summed up in a sense by a single note accompanying a single word—the word "but." After describing the supposed joys of *not* being in love—no more pain, no more strain, and sanity—still, Gus says, he'd "rather be gaga!" Love may be torture, but in the end, it's what we all want. How does Rodgers emphasize the word "but"? He first states the B section's three-note idea, B–A–G, on "No more pain," then repeats it on "No more strain," does it a third time on "Now I'm sane," and then adds one extra note for the word "but"—not B–A–G, but B–A–G–**C**—and that C is the highest note of the entire chorus, perfectly pointing up and emphasizing

Example 8.5 "I Wish I Were in Love Again," final verse

the song's key word. (Also notice the way the accompaniment then stops completely to bring out the punch line, "I would rather be gaga!")

In the hands of lesser artists, this AABA song would end with a repeat of the opening 8 measures and a final set of lyrics copying the opening section's rhyme scheme; however, both the words and music are subtly but spectacularly different. Looking at Hart's lyrics, the first two A sections each rhyme four words followed by the unrhymed title line, "I wish I were in love again." But the final verse (Ex. 8.5) resolves the song and Gus and Dolores's relationship in quintessential musical-comedy fashion by rhyming *everything*. "Fur, cur," and "her" not only rhyme with each other but also with "I wish I *were* in love again," creating a subtle inner rhyme that makes for a perfect ending.

The music beautifully supports this. As you can see in Example 8.6, the first 6 measures come back unchanged, but the small changes in the final 2 measures are superb. The whole song ultimately turns on the three subtly

Example 8.6A "I Wish I Were in Love Again"

Example 8.6B "I Wish I Were in Love Again"

Example 8.6C "I Wish I Were in Love Again"

different versions of "I wish I were in love again," shown in Examples 8.6A, 8.6B, and 8.6C.

The first version leaps *down* dejectedly. The second version leaps *up* with excitement. To provide a definitive ending to the piece, the final version lengthens the notes on "love a-" to half notes with "love" on a C—the highest note of the chorus—and for the first time the song resolves the phrase to a G—the home or tonic note of the song—saved for the final note to make a satisfying ending. Music and words are in complete harmony. The perfect ending to a perfect song. The essence of Rodgers and Hart.

In spite of a now-famous notice in *Variety* that said "no nudity, no show girls, no plush or gold plate may mean no sale,"[18] *Babes in Arms*, after initially almost collapsing at the box office, ran for 289 performances. It was turned into a film in 1939 starring MGM's young and upcoming stars Mickey Rooney and Judy Garland, but as with so many Hollywood versions of Broadway shows, the original score was almost completely destroyed. The only songs that were retained in the film were "Babes in Arms" and "Where or When," and at least four other composers contributed to the hodgepodge of a score. In the 1948 biopic *Words and Music*, Rooney and Garland joined together to sing a version of "I Wish I Were in Love Again" that perhaps made up for its exclusion from the *Babes in Arms* film.

But by that time, the Rodgers and Hart partnership had ended and Hart had been dead for five years, done in at the age of forty-eight by his longtime alcoholism and dissolute lifestyle, a condition that made their stunning run of successful shows from 1935 to 1942 all the more incredible. Hart would often go on alcoholic binges for days during rehearsals, leaving Rodgers to rewrite and edit lyrics on his own. To finish the score to *By Jupiter*, Rodgers had to check himself into the hospital where Hart was trying yet again to dry out and get Steinway to install a piano. Given the difficulties of getting Hart to work, or even locating him at all, it seems almost inconceivable that he managed to produce the lyrics for twenty-six Broadway shows with Rodgers, but it is a testament both to Rodgers's infinite patience and Hart's astonishing ability to produce impeccable material under intense pressure that they were able to create a canonic repertoire of superb songs that continue to survive in the hands of gifted performers. Long after Hart's death,

Irving Berlin offered an insightful observation about Hart's lyrics and their connection to Rodgers's music:

> You can't divorce those lyrics from Rodgers' melodies. They're not just lyrics, they're songs. If Larry had just written those lyrics . . . and just printed them, they'd mean nothing. And if you just took the Rodgers melodies, as fine as they are, and just played them as orchestral numbers, they would last four hours. You see they are *songs*.[19]

Taking this a step further, it is largely Rodgers and Hart's *songs*, not their *shows* that have survived. On occasion, *Babes in Arms, Pal Joey*, and *On Your Toes* have been revived, but it is principally through the countless recordings and performances of multiple generations of singers and instrumentalists that their work has endured. Though it is easy to attribute the survival of the Rodgers and Hart songs as opposed to the shows of Rodgers and Hammerstein to the difference between Hart and Hammerstein, it is also a result of the two collaborations occurring at different moments in the history of both the country as a whole and the Broadway musical as a genre.

Rodgers first discussed the possibility of ending his relationship with Hart in a private conversation with Hammerstein in September 1941. Three months later, the Japanese attacked Pearl Harbor, and by the time Hammerstein and Rodgers began working together in 1942, the world had become an unimaginably different place. Americans had topics other than love and New York on their minds. Rodgers and Hammerstein found their collective voice and developed a new concept for the Broadway musical as the madness of World War II descended upon them. The chaotic events unfolding in America and around the globe shaped the theatrical worlds that Rodgers and Hammerstein would create onstage in the groundbreaking musicals *Oklahoma!* and *Carousel*, and it was this new American and global reality as much as his new partner that would change Rodgers's music forever.

9

The Impact of Recorded Sound

Jerome Kern's "All the Things You Are"

The invention of the phonograph in 1877—actually a long string of inventions, developments, adaptations, and improvements—was arguably the single most important event in the history of twentieth-century music. It transformed every aspect of the composer-performer-listener relationship, and the impact of recorded sound on the composition of music has been as revolutionary as the development of notation. For the very first time in history, a recording could take something that had always been ephemeral—a musical performance—and turn it into something permanent: a physical commodity capable of reaching previously unthinkable numbers of listeners. The use of recorded sound—first in phonograph records, then radio, and then sound films—not only changed the way music reached the public and the way composers, performers, producers, and publishers were paid, it also changed the actual content of the music songwriters wrote for the theater, while reshaping the place of music in American homes, and the entire economic structure of the music industry. Recording technology was crucial to our national musical identity and, in conjunction with radio and the movies, the development of a shared American voice created by a newly formed and ever-expanding mass media.

Before the invention of recorded sound, there were two primary ways that a popular song could reach the public: either through live performance (a minstrel, burlesque, or vaudeville show; or a revue, operetta, or musical), or through the sale of sheet music. During the Victorian era, nearly every middle-class or lower-middle-class family with social aspirations had a piano in the parlor around which they gathered in the evenings to sing the latest popular songs. Before phonographs replaced pianos as the most common "musical instrument" in people's homes, sheet music sales for popular songs were often in the hundreds of thousands, and many songs sold more than a million copies. A single hit could make a composer rich. Charles K. Harris's "After the Ball" (1891) was the first to sell more than a million copies of sheet music, selling over 2 million in 1892 alone and more than 5 million total.[1] (It was in fact the song's enormous popularity that inspired Kern to interpolate it into *Show Boat* when he needed a song that would instantly conjure up the world of the 1890s for his 1927 audience.) "You're a Grand Old Flag" from George M. Cohan's 1906 show *George Washington Jr.* was the first song written specifically for a musical to sell over a million copies of sheet music, and the phenomenal success of "Alexander's Ragtime Band," which sold 200,000 copies of the sheet music overnight and a million copies within three months of its publication in September 1911, launched Irving Berlin's career.[2]

However, by 1920, the shift in importance from sheet music to recordings can be seen by looking at the numbers for George Gershwin's hit "Swanee." The song made almost no impact as part of the *Capitol Revue*, but after Al Jolson heard it at a party, he inserted it into one of his shows, and within a month he had already recorded it for Columbia Records. It "penetrated the four corners of the earth," as Gershwin put it, selling a million copies of sheet music and, even more important, over 2 million records, making it the single biggest hit of Gershwin's career.[3]

These kinds of sales figures only hint at the seismic shift resulting from the rise of the record industry. When the principal market for Tin Pan Alley's popular songs was the huge number of families with pianos at home, writers published songs that unskilled amateurs could play and sing: songs with small vocal ranges and easily singable melodies accompanied by simple piano parts that invariably included the melody. Tying a song to a popular fad also helped sales; "Bicycle Built for Two" (1892) was written in response to the popularity of bicycling in the 1880s and '90s, while "Take Me Out to the Ball Game" (1908) took advantage of the enormous interest in baseball at the turn of the century. These early songs were a mirror—a kind of social history in song—of the tastes, fashions, morals, and current events of the times, and the abilities of songwriters and publishers to tap into popular taste turned the sheet music industry into a big business.

Before recordings transformed the industry's economic model, the only real profit in writing shows, other than tickets sales, came from the sale of sheet music. Featuring a song like Kern's "They Didn't Believe Me" in *The Girl from Utah* (1914) was the best way to encourage an audience member to buy the sheet music—almost always sold in the lobby of the theater or around the corner in a local music store—and sing it at home. Consequently, sheet music publishers did everything in their power to convince performers to sing their songs in their shows. They hired song pluggers like the young George Gershwin, Jerome Kern, and Irving Berlin to play and sing the company's latest songs for performers who would come to the cacophonous Tin Pan Alley publishing houses looking for new material.

For many young songwriters, working as a song plugger or boomer—a singer hired to stand up during the intermission of a show and sing a publisher's songs from the balcony—not only provided an entry into the music business, it served as a kind of unofficial training ground where they could soak up the forms, techniques, and languages of the songwriters of the day. The goal of the entire industry, from pluggers and boomers to publishers and theater owners,* was to create hits, songs that would catch the public's fancy. Songs that hopefully millions of people would buy, put on their pianos at home, and sing at night. (Kern, realizing the key role publishers played in a composer's success, was deeply involved in the sheet music business, not only in terms of his own songs but in his role as vice president of the music publisher T. B. Harms—the company that had first hired him as a composer.) The new medium of the recording, however, fundamentally altered the entire relationship of a song to its creators, performers, publishers, and public.

For a song to come to life, it needs an intermediary—a performer—to translate the songwriter's notes into sound. Before the advent of recordings, the only way to do this was through a live performance. The entire musical culture of the world before recordings was an active, participatory one. Of the more than 2 million people in 1892 who bought the sheet music to "After the Ball," probably only a few thousand actually heard the song performed as an interpolation in the Percy Gaunt/Charles Hoyt hit musical comedy *A Trip to Chinatown*. Still, millions of people learned the song, internalized it, and made it their own by singing it with their families and friends.

The arrival of recorded sound marked the beginning of a profound shift from an active musical culture to a passive one, from music as a participatory activity to music as a spectator sport. In fact, early advertisements tried to spin this shift in a positive way, telling consumers that recordings would free them from having to buy a piano and spend years practicing. (This turned out to be prophetic, as recordings led to a huge decline in piano sales.) They "might not play like Rachmaninoff," as one ad put it, but through the magic of recordings they could now "experience his playing at

---

* Theater owners got a percentage of sheet music sales from songs in their shows, so generating hits was in their interest as well.

home." A similar shift from an active to a passive culture occurred with the enormous rise of spectator sports in the 1920s. Though an ordinary American "might not play baseball like Babe Ruth," they might follow his exploits in the newspapers that now featured regular sports sections, or, once radio entered the picture, listen to his games live.

The implications of this shift for the musical lives of performers were enormous. With the help of sheet music, a songwriter like Kern, Gershwin, or Berlin had always been at least theoretically able to have his songs reach an unlimited public without an intervening performer, as long as a distributor could make the sheet music physically available and the purchaser could read notation. Once a composer wrote down a song, it had a permanent, reproducible, transportable existence, and it could come to life anywhere in the world without the composer needing to be present. This was not the case for performers. Their art was impermanent, ephemeral, of the moment. Before recordings, performers could only reach people who were physically present, one live performance at a time. Without amplification, that number rarely exceeded 2,000 people per performance. (When the New Amsterdam Theatre was built in 1902–1903, it was the largest theater in New York, with a seating capacity of 1,702.)[4] The performer's reach was limited geographically as well. Though Broadway shows did tour, and there was a national circuit for vaudeville, New York City was the center of the theatrical world, and it was far more difficult for a performer who needed to be seen in person to generate a nationwide reputation than it was for a songwriter.

Recordings changed all that, and they did so at a remarkably fast pace. Edison invented the phonograph in 1877, initially recording sound acoustically on cylinders. Ten years later, Emile Berliner invented a way to store the sound on flat disks that revolved on a turntable—a solution that by the 1910s became the industry standard. Edison's Columbia Gramophone Company would ultimately turn into Columbia Records, while Berliner's Victor Talking Machine Company would become RCA Records.

Interestingly enough, these early inventions were not aimed at the entertainment market but rather at businesses as a way of capturing speech for lawyers or court reporters. The focus was on using the machines as a kind of mechanical stenographer to record dictation, not play back music.[5] It wasn't until coin-operated phonographs caught on in arcades that the industry began to shift its focus toward entertainment and a relatively inexpensive machine that could play back music.

Commercial recording really began to heat up around the turn of the century, and since no one knew yet what would sell, the first recordings included a wide range of repertoire, from popular songs to marches and dances of various kinds. In an attempt to attract a middle-class audience, Victor promoted classical recordings, boldly hiring the young opera singer Enrico Caruso—whose ten European records made in a Milan hotel room in 1902 had become best sellers—to record in America for a staggeringly high fee as early as 1904. The more than 250 recordings he made for the Victor Talking Machine Company and then RCA Victor between 1904 and 1920 not only earned him and the company millions of dollars but helped turn him into an international celebrity of a kind unknown before the era of recorded sound. Suddenly a performer's art—like a songwriter's art—could reach anyone, anywhere.

Once Caruso led the way, others followed. Not only classical singers like Adelina Patti, but also vaudeville stars like Sophie Tucker and George M. Cohan. By 1920, when Jolson's recording of "Swanee" took the world by storm, over 150 companies were making records or record players.[6] Collectively these companies produced over 100 million records, and millions of homes had phonographs in their living rooms. The technology generated new revenue streams for songwriters and performers alike and created a national audience for both, but the industry's rapid growth drastically undercut sheet music sales in the late 1910s, and by the end of the 1920s when records were selling in the millions, any song that sold 100,000 copies of sheet music was considered to be an enormous hit. Publishers' profits plummeted, and the next wave of technology—radio and talking pictures—combined with the Depression to produce a knockout punch from which the industry never truly recovered.

೧౧

The history of the record industry in the 1930s is deeply intertwined with the history of radio and the movies, and the complex relationship among the three profoundly affected the Broadway songwriters of the era. Like recordings, radio began with individual inventors at the end of the nineteenth century—principally Guglielmo Marconi,* Reginald Fessenden, and Nikola Tesla—experimenting with the possibilities of electromagnetic waves. Also like the record industry, radio initially did not focus on entertainment. Early radio pioneers instead concentrated on the shipping industry and navies, both of which used the technology as a substitute for the telegraph to communicate via Morse code at sea. During World War I, the potential of radio for spying became clear, and for security reasons the U.S. Navy acquired control of all of the wireless technology in America.[7] Once the war ended, however, commercial radio exploded.

In November 1920, the Westinghouse Broadcasting Company inaugurated the first radio station in America—KDKA in Pittsburgh—with a broadcast of the 1920 presidential election results. By 1921, the number of stations had grown to 5, but by 1923 there were 556. On the consumer side, the growth was equally explosive. By 1922, 3 million homes had radios, and sales of radio sets and parts reached $60 million a year. Seven years later, 40 percent of Americans had radios in their homes, and

---

* Marconi successfully transmitted and received his first radio signal in Italy in 1895. By 1899 he had sent a signal across the English Channel and by 1902 across the Atlantic from England to Newfoundland. Fessenden was the first person to transmit voice and music instead of the dots and dashes of Morse code, and in 1906 he broadcast music and speech in Massachusetts that could be heard all the way to the West Indies. Tesla demonstrated the first primitive radio as early as 1893 and was ultimately given the patent for the first radio transmitter when the Supreme Court overturned Marconi's patent in 1943.

sales had reached $842 million a year—a staggering increase of 1,400 percent.[8] In 1926, only six years after KDKA's first broadcast, the National Broadcasting Company (NBC) was formed, linking individual stations throughout the country to create the first national broadcasting network. By the time Lindbergh made his historic flight across the Atlantic in 1927, 50 stations in 24 states were able to cover the celebrations heard by a radio audience of 30 million people, and Lindbergh became the first national, radio-generated celebrity.

The role of radio as a creator of a shared national identity cannot be overstated. Perhaps no one recognized its potential to unify a nation's voice more than Adolf Hitler. To make sure his state-controlled propaganda and National Socialist worldview reached every German, he subsidized the purchase of radios, and under Hitler there were more radios in German homes than in any other country in Europe. In America, politicians gradually discovered radio's unique ability to reach the masses. Although Calvin Coolidge aired his 1925 inaugural address on the radio, it was Franklin Delano Roosevelt's mastery of the medium in his immensely popular fireside chats that truly revealed radio's ability to create a personal relationship between a president and his country. In the same way that the microphone allowed a new kind of intimacy between singer and audience, replacing Ethel Merman's belting with Rudy Vallee's crooning, radio allowed FDR's casual speech to replace the pre-microphone style of shouting that politicians once had to use to be heard.

More quickly than politicians, advertisers realized the medium could be an effective way to reach a national audience. In the early days of radio, no one knew how to pay for it. At first it seemed like it might be financed through the sale of radio equipment, but that proved insufficient. Eventually commercial advertising became the primary financing tool, beginning with simple corporate sponsorships of programs like Feen-A-Mint laxative's sponsorship of George Gershwin's radio program. Once sponsors overcame their initial reluctance to aggressively advertise individual products, advertising revenues took off. In 1927 advertisers spent only about $4 million, but in 1937 they spent approximately $145 million.[9]

What politicians and advertisers capitalized on was radio's unique ability to create, for the first time in history, a national audience for a real-time event. Whether it was a sporting event like the World Series, a political speech, news of Hitler invading Poland, or an episode of the wildly popular radio serials *Amos 'n' Andy* and *The Lone Ranger*, approximately 40 million people—almost a third of the country's population—heard it at the same time.

Though radio offered remarkable opportunities for politicians and advertisers, its impact on the music industry in general and Broadway composers in particular was even greater. On the one hand, the medium's benefits to popular songwriters like Gershwin, Rodgers, Berlin, Kern, and Porter were obvious. Radio stations had a lot of airtime to fill, and approximately three-fourths of that time was filled with music. Though jazz gradually became more prominent on radio in the 1930s, giving many Americans their first chance to hear black music and black performers, and classical music was surprisingly popular, radio stations mostly played Tin Pan Alley and Broadway songs. In 1927, five of the top ten songs on the radio were from Broadway shows, and two others were written by Broadway songwriters. In 1928, Kern's "Ol' Man River" was number 4 and "Bill" was number 24. As radio became a mass medium in the 1930s, disc jockeys—the term that replaced the earlier "radio jockey"—gave songwriters the previously unimaginable ability to plug their songs nationally and, like politicians and advertisers, reach millions of listeners in an instant. And, most important for Depression-era listeners, radio—unlike recordings—was free.

The fact that it was free, while a boon for the country's economically challenged listeners, proved disastrous to the theater and record industry. Largely due to the rise of radio, the record industry declined by almost 50 percent in the first few years of the 1920s, and when the Depression hit, most record companies collapsed. Edison's phonograph division went bankrupt in 1929, RCA bought Victor soon afterward, and the Columbia

Broadcasting System bought Columbia. Though small numbers of records continued to be sold during the 1930s by fewer and fewer labels, the very same radio stations that had largely been responsible for the industry's decline became one of its major purchasers. Stations still had to buy the recordings they needed to fill their airtime, but listeners no longer were willing to purchase the recordings they could now hear for free on the radio,* so radio became the principal forum for introducing new recordings.

For a song to come to life, it needs a performer, an interpreter. Even with a Broadway show, where the composer is present at every stage of the creative process, the song's original version, usually written for piano and voice,† is first interpreted by an orchestrator, who arranges it for instruments. The song is then further interpreted by the vocalist in the show. Some performers, like Fred Astaire, were famous for adhering scrupulously to what the composer wrote, while others took far more liberties. Judy Garland, for example, scarcely sings a single rhythm of "Over the Rainbow" as Arlen wrote it. Songwriters cared in varying degrees about fidelity to their scores, but they almost always gave tacit approval to the version presented to the public. Once a show opened, a song would go into print, reaching the

---

* Jukebox owners also became a major purchaser of records. Jukeboxes had already become popular by the middle of the 1920s in restaurants and bars, as they were not only capable of providing music for people to listen to but also to dance to without having to invest in hiring a band. But in the thirties, their popularity increased massively with 25,000 sold in 1933 and 300,000 in 1939. Since at any given time jukeboxes held only fifty or sixty of the most popular records of the moment, they were also a powerful force in creating a unified, shared national culture.

† The entire concept of an original version of a Broadway song is itself complex. For the purposes of this book and in nearly all discussions of the American Songbook, the printed sheet music of a song is considered to be its original version, yet in many cases, this version was created by a publisher, an arranger, or an assistant, not the composer himself. In the case of Irving Berlin, who could not notate or read music, all of his original versions were either transcribed or arranged by a musical secretary. In addition, the song's actual original version—the orchestrated version heard in the show—was itself an arrangement made by the orchestrator, not the composer. Like other commentators I am treating the published sheet music as the song, but it is important to realize that in actuality the concept is far more fluid than in classical music.

public either through dance band arrangements or sheet music performed at home. However legendary a particular performance of a song might have been, before the era of recordings it would almost never have been heard by anyone more than once. The song existed, in a sense, above and beyond any particular performance or arrangement of it.

Once recordings and radio entered the picture, all of this changed. Almost no one heard Gershwin's original version of "Swanee" in the *Demi-Tasse Revue,* but once Jolson sold over 2 million copies of his recording, for all practical purposes, *his version became the song.* (His later re-recordings and performances in the movies further cemented his version in the public's mind.) It wasn't simply that Jolson's performance was powerful. For the first time in history, his recording allowed people to hear him sing it the same way *over and over again.* Similarly, Cole Porter's show, *Jubilee,* ran on Broadway for 169 performances, allowing perhaps 100,000 people to hear June Knight's original version of "Begin the Beguine," but millions of people bought Artie Shaw's recording of the song, learning every nuance with repeated listening. Shaw's arrangement became the song, as did his and Tommy Dorsey's arrangements of "All the Things You Are." Unlike earlier days when the public knew a song primarily by its composer—Stephen Foster's "Jeannie with the Light Brown Hair" or "Camptown Races"—they now knew Artie Shaw's "Begin the Beguine," Judy Garland's "Over the Rainbow," Frank Sinatra's "New York, New York," and Madonna's "Like a Virgin." Though performers had always been a key component of the composer-performer-listener relationship, once records and radio entered the picture, the performer became vastly more important, and in the case of Broadway songs, another largely unnoticed and unheralded contributor was added to the mix—the arranger.

In the 1930s, nearly all the Broadway songs that became popular did so through recordings and radio performances of dance bands like those of Artie Shaw, Glenn Miller, Tommy Dorsey, Benny Goodman, Count Basie, Woody Herman, and Duke Ellington. Because a large number of bands were playing the same popular songs, an incredible emphasis was put on the originality of each group's arrangement. Since Artie Shaw's recording of "All the Things You Are" had a woman, Helen Forrest, as vocalist, Tommy Dorsey's recording, which reached No. 1 on the Billboard charts, used a male vocalist, Jack Leonard.

Dance band arrangements altered Broadway songs in other important ways as well. In the 1920s, nearly all Broadway songs began with an introductory verse. Like the recitatives that generally preceded arias in an opera, the verses in Broadway songs generally set the scene for the song to follow. Like recitatives, Broadway verses were often in freer, more improvisatory rhythm and frequently set up the chorus in interesting and ingenious ways. However, due to the limitations of how much music could fit on a 78 rpm record, and their lack of "danceability," nearly all dance band versions eliminated these verses entirely, leaving the public to hear a Broadway song without its verse, without its words, and often with a completely different tempo, feel, and character. The narrative component of a Broadway song in which great songwriters managed to tell complete stories in 32 measures was abandoned; a song became nothing more than the melody of its chorus (and sometimes just its harmony) in whatever arrangement seemed most suited to relaxed listening and dancing.

Different songwriters felt differently about these dance band arrangements, but Jerome Kern, perhaps more than any other Broadway songwriter, left no doubt about his feelings on the subject, and his attitude reveals his profoundly traditional mind-set and his resistance to the changes the "modern world" of jazz, radio, and recordings was imposing on the musical theater:

> None of our music now reaches the public as we wrote it except in the theatre. It is so distorted by jazz orchestras as to be almost unrecognizable. A composer should be able to protect his score just as an author does his

manuscripts. No author would permit pirated editions of his work in which his phraseology and punctuation were changed thereby giving to his work a meaning entirely different from what he intended. . . . The public, through the cabaret and radio broadcasting, is not getting genuine music, only a fraudulent imitation.[10]

Kern's distaste for the dance band arrangements that were flooding the market was so extreme that he actually tried to prohibit any songs from his 1924 musical *Sitting Pretty* from being recorded or performed outside of the show. In some ways, it was not surprising that out of all of the songwriters of the 1920s and '30s, it would be Kern whose reaction would be the most intense. His music never lost a kind of European gentility and elegance that was part of the cultured, upper-class, German-Jewish world he grew up in, and the brasher, hard-edged sound of Gershwin, Berlin, and Rodgers and Hart was far more suited to the world of jazz and dance band arrangements than Kern's romantic, lyrical voice. Though he composed a number of successful musicals in the twenties, including *Sally* (1920), *Stepping Stones* (1923), *Sunny* (1925), *Show Boat* (1927), and *Sweet Adeline* (1929), neither his personality nor his music truly fit comfortably within the world of the Roaring Twenties. There was a retrospective feeling to many of his songs that made them seem old-fashioned when compared to the work of his contemporaries, and in a way, it is not surprising that he was a passionate collector of antique books.* However, though his songs might not have been at the cutting edge of New York sensibilities, they turned out to be a perfect match for Hollywood. The audience for his films was less sophisticated, urban, and up-to-the-minute than a Broadway audience, and he had a remarkably successful movie career, earning five Academy Award nominations and two wins for Best Song.

---

* He acquired a world-class collection, which he sold for $1.75 million in 1929, but he lost almost all of it shortly after in the stock market crash.

He was also paid staggeringly well. But, like so many songwriters in Hollywood at the time, he longed to return to the more creatively rewarding environment of Broadway, and in 1939 he collaborated one more time with Hammerstein on what would turn out to be Kern's last Broadway musical, *Very Warm for May*. Sadly, the show was a complete flop, closing after only 59 performances, but it did yield a song that many consider to be the finest of all Kern's songs, a song that would inspire more of the jazz arrangements that Kern despised than any of his other works: "All the Things You Are."

The original context for this song has been largely forgotten along with the rest of the show, and given the convoluted, barely comprehensible plot of the book, that is not necessarily a bad thing. When the show begins, May's father, William Graham, has gotten himself into debt with some unsavory criminals. They threaten to do harm to his daughter if he doesn't go along with their plans, so May hides herself away in a summer stock theater company led by a flamboyant artistic director named Ogden Quiler. The company is located on property owned by an eccentric Connecticut matron named Winnie Spofford, who has two children with theatrical ambitions. "All the Things You Are" is sung as part of a play the troupe is presenting, and though the entire ensemble ultimately becomes part of the scene, it is fundamentally written for a bizarre quartet. In the script Ogden explains to the rest of the cast:

> In this scene the two lovers are too shy to express their real feelings, so this duet is sung by their heart voices. . . . People in love don't sing into each other's faces, do they? They look at each in silence, don't they? But somebody's got to sing, so. . . . This gentleman plays the voice of my heart. He sings what I feel. This lady plays the voice of the girl's heart. This song expresses our emotions as we look at each other in silence.[11]

In this strange, artificial staging, Ogden, playing the role of Adam Standish in the play-within-a play, and Winnie's daughter Liz, playing the role of Hester, have two other cast members—Charles and Carroll—singing Ogden and Liz's "heart voices." Somehow, in spite of this contrived setting, the music that ultimately pours forth from them, twice-removed from reality, is as captivatingly romantic and as moving as any theater song ever written.

Though none of the dance band or jazz versions that made this song so popular include it, "All the Things You Are" begins with a 16-bar verse (Ex. 9.1 shows the first half) that completely transforms the way we hear the opening of the chorus.* The verse not only begins in a different key, it's in a

Example 9.1 "All the Things You Are," opening verse

---

* Two different versions of this verse were published. The original show version had the same melody but was 16 bars longer, was written for the whole quartet, and began with the lyric "Never can be at ease when I meet him. . . ." I have used the far more familiar version that has become standard and begins with "Time and again I've longed for adventure."

completely different expressive world. The tone is lighthearted and conversational. Each 2-bar group begins with three repeated D's, followed by a leap and a phrase that circles up and back to that note. Each successive 2-bar group leaps one note higher, and the gradually rising phrases perfectly capture the way the singer's "heart beats the faster," leading to the excited question, "What did I long for? I never really knew," as the orchestra responds with sliding, chromatic harmonies that sound appropriately quizzical.

Kern then moves as if to repeat the music of the first 8 measures, but "touching your hand" changes everything. Instead of copying the first phrase as in Example 9.2, the touch of a hand causes the music to descend lower, into a darker and more expressive minor key—the first foreshadowing of the kind of emotion the chorus will ultimately contain.

As the song's lyrics become more direct and honest—"All that I want in all of this world is you"—the verse seems to end in the key where it began: G major. But the verse's final measure instead modulates so that the chorus begins unexpectedly in F minor (Ex. 9.3). This subtle shift, absent from all the dance band and jazz versions, is not just a musical event—it's a psychological one.

What comes next is perhaps Kern's greatest chorus, one that is so complex that Kern worried it was too sophisticated to ever become popular.[12] At its harmonic heart is a circle of fifths similar to the one we encountered in Gershwin's "Summertime." This pattern is perhaps even more fundamental

Example 9.2 "All the Things You Are," Kapilow version

Example 9.3 "All the Things You Are"

Example 9.4 "All the Things You Are," circle of fifths

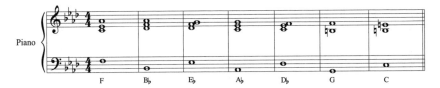

to the song than the melody above it, and ironically for Kern, who hated jazz versions of his music, it is this harmonic pattern that jazz musicians like Charlie Parker, Dizzy Gillespie, Bill Evans, Dave Brubeck, and Miles Davis latched onto in their versions of the song. The chorus outlined in Example 9.4 begins with the bass moving by a fifth from F down to Bb, followed one step lower by an Eb moving down to Ab, then again from Db to G, finishing on C.*

Though many popular songs use this progression ("Autumn Leaves," for example), what makes Kern's version so beautiful are the chords he puts above the bass line, chords drenched in warmth and heartrending dissonances.† While the accompaniment traces its circle-of-fifths harmonies, the vocal line follows the sequence melodically, with one essential note per measure (Ab, Db, G, C, F, B, E—always a third above the bass). Several things make this melody poignantly expressive as opposed to rigidly mechanical. The first note of the chorus—on "you"—lasts for an entire measure and sounds full of yearning because of its contrast with the rhythmically active, conversational verse that preceded it. The emotion that swells on this sustained note is so powerful that it generates the poignant leap on "are" (Ab to Db) that becomes the melodic idea of the vocal line (see Ex. 9.5). Though the pattern continues with the same leap copied sequentially on "springtime" (G to C),

---

* If we were to continue the pattern purely by fifths (that is, F–Bb–Eb–Ab–Db–Gb–Cb[B]–E–A–D–G–C–F, we would ultimately return to the chord where the progression started. Because it would take twelve steps to complete the full cycle, frequently one step is altered—here Db–Gb becomes Db–G—to shorten the process.

† For musicians, minor and major 7th and 9th chords.

Example 9.5 "All the Things You Are"

and "winter" (F to B), what makes Kern's version so elegant is the way these two echoing leaps never occur on the downbeat, instead floating gracefully between the first and second beats of the measure (Ex. 9.3, mm. 10 and 12).

In a standard 32-bar Broadway song, the music of these opening bars would be repeated a second time to begin the second A section. But instead, in a lovely touch, Kern unexpectedly repeats the music in a new, lower key meant to depict "the breathless hush of evening" (see Ex. 9.6).

Example 9.6 "All the Things You Are"

The B section—the only completely new music in the song—is as exquisite as the A section, and as is so often the case, details are the difference between good and great. In Example 9.7 I have changed three melody notes (marked with asterisks) in the phrase "You are the angel glow that lights a star": on the first syllable of "angel" and on "that lights."

It's the dissonances that Kern uses on these three notes instead that makes the section so moving, and these lovely details are also copied when the phrase repeats lower on, "the dearest things I know, are what you are" (see Ex. 9.8).*

The moment the opening A section returns is, harmonically speaking, the most glorious moment in the entire song. The B section ends (Ex. 9.8) in E major—a key quite remote from the rest of the song. Kern then has the voice hold the same note for 3 measures (G♯ = A♭), while the harmony underneath takes a wonderfully surprising route back to the chorus's opening chord (Ex. 9.9).† Though we are back where we started, the arrival of this opening music now sounds fresh and new.

Kern could easily have finished the song with a simple repeat of the opening music, but he has one final surprise up his sleeve. Example 9.9,

Example 9.7 "All the Things You Are," Kapilow version

---

* Harmonically, the B section works with sequences of fifths as well, as the bass now moves from A–D–G, then F♯–B–E.

† For musicians, changing from an E-major chord, to an A♭ augmented triad, and then the opening F-minor chord with the G♯/A♭ in the voice as a common tone throughout.

Example 9.8 "All the Things You Are," Kern version

Example 9.9 "All the Things You Are," Kapilow version

following the standard Broadway 32-bar form, concludes with music I have copied from the opening section of the chorus on the words, "and someday I will know that you're mine." But instead, the yearning of a single word— "someday"—changes the entire ending (Ex. 9.10). Though his beloved may be "the promised kiss of springtime" and "the angel glow that lights a star," she is not yet his. He sings, "*Someday* my happy arms will hold you," and

Example 9.10 "All the Things You Are," Kern version

all the yearning for that "someday" is captured by this moment where the music changes. Two long notes and a huge leap to the highest note of the entire chorus on "someday" (Ex. 9.10, mm. 5–6) are accompanied by a heartbreaking, darkly colored yearning chord.* There is an operetta-like feel to the lyricism and the lush lyrics here, and the new music that is added to finish the phrase—"I'll know that moment divine,† when all the things you are, are mine"—pushes to a final cadence that beautifully reflects the straddling of the worlds of operetta and Broadway that was always a part of Kern's musical language.

The final cadence is one of the most remarkable in the American Songbook. The last chord of the song—A♭ major—is the first and only time the unadorned home chord appears. Only at this final, imagined moment—"that moment divine," when she is finally his—can the song's harmony conclusively resolve. The lyrics have yearned for this moment of resolution the same way the music has yearned for it harmonically. But what note does the singer end on? The sheet music lists two possible alternatives—a high A♭ or a low A♭—and which note is chosen is much more than a simple matter of taste. Not surprisingly, Artie Shaw's 1939 recording that turns the piece into cool, sophisticated, swing dance music has Helen Forrest taking the lower note (a low F in her key—even lower than the printed low A♭), making the ending inward, reflective, and intimate. John McGlinn's re-creation of the original version for full orchestra and chorus, however, builds toward a huge, operatic climax with Rebecca Luker soaring up even higher than the printed A♭ to a high B♭ (the actual high note sung in the original show's key) fully revealing the operetta roots of Kern's style and acting as a kind of inspired time machine bringing us back to a long-vanished past.

---

* Wagner's Tristan chord. A half-diminished 7th chord once the piercingly dissonant E♭ resolves to D♭.

† Hammerstein claims to have always regretted his inability to find a better word than the clichéd "divine," to use here, but said he was unable to find a more original word to rhyme with the final "mine." Somehow to me the word "divine" harks back to an earlier operetta-like aesthetic that matches the music perfectly.

Which note is the right note? Which Kern is the real one? What is important here is to realize that choosing to end high or low is not just a choice of note, but of a world. Once the jazz recordings that Kern detested loosened up the rhythm and feel of the song and inserted new melodies above the song's harmonic framework, we leave the world of operetta behind and high notes no longer make sense. Those high notes were part of an aesthetic world that recordings, radio, and jazz had largely left behind. Yet the same recordings that ruptured Kern's delicate mixture of classical, operetta, and Broadway sensibilities helped his music to reach millions of listeners as each new generation of performers translates his music into languages he could never have imagined. Recordings, dance bands, and the radio might have been anathema to Kern, and he might have despised the way they transformed his music, but they are in fact the key to his legacy.

And not only *his* legacy, but the entire legacy of the American Songbook. Though each generation of classical music performers also finds new ways to interpret the genre's canonical works, classical pieces from the past are fundamentally passed down intact. A pianist playing Beethoven's *Appassionata* sonata today will play the same notes and rhythms that Beethoven wrote more than two hundred years earlier. Varieties of interpretation largely have to do with matters of tempo, character, touch, and phrasing. However, as Kern so vehemently pointed out, this is not at all the case with the American Songbook. Its repertoire has survived by being perpetually reinvented in precisely the ways Kern objected to. The versions of "All the Things You Are" recorded by artists as diverse as Ella Fitzgerald, John Coltrane, Bill Evans, Frank Sinatra, Charlie Parker, and Keith Jarrett transform Kern's song in imaginative ways that diverge so far from the original that midway through—with improvised melodies, advanced substitute chords, and no lyrics—Kern might not have even recognized his own song. But it is precisely the freedom to take these canonical works—these "standards"—and continually reinterpret them in the multiplicity of musical languages that have evolved over time that has kept the repertoire alive. Though Kern might have despised the new world ushered in by jazz, recordings and radio, without their help his music would not have become part of America's voice and part of our legacy. For that, we—if not he—can only be grateful.

10

America Goes to the Movies

Harold Arlen's "Over the Rainbow"

We tend to think of the twenty-first century as a time when new technologies make older ones obsolete at dizzying speed, but the pace of invention in the 1920s and '30s makes contemporary innovation seem slow by comparison. The first significant experiments with capturing movement on camera took place in the 1890s. Early moving pictures, like those of the Lumière brothers in France, were nothing more than that—pictures that moved. Compilations of short, fifteen-to-thirty-second scenes captured ordinary events like people playing cards, watering gardens, or arriving on a train. Too primitive to be called movies by today's standards, moving pictures seemed so realistic that an early film of a train pulling into a station caused viewers to flee in panic, thinking the train had actually entered the theater.

In America, Thomas Edison premiered his first attempt at film using a Kinetoscope in 1894. Like the Lumière brothers, Edison's early films were nothing more than short moving pictures without any plot—a scene in a barbershop, the famous strongman Eugen Sandow flexing his muscles, men boxing, blacksmiths pounding an anvil, Edison's assistant Fred Ott taking a pinch of snuff and sneezing—but by the first decade of the 1900s, several companies like the Selig Polyscope Company, the Edison Company, and the Gaumont and Pathé companies were starting to make films with actual stories, like *The Great Train Robbery* (1903). The invention of the nickelodeon around 1905 gave people the chance to view these short five- to six-minute shows for only a nickel and helped increase awareness of the new medium, and from this point on, the industry took off. Though most early films in America were produced near New York, in 1910, D. W. Griffith shot the first film entirely in Hollywood, *In Old California,*[1] and within a single decade, Hollywood and its film studios would become the worldwide face of American cinema.

The speed and enthusiasm with which America took to film is almost impossible to overstate. The first feature-length, multi-reel film wasn't produced until 1906 in Australia,[2] and actors didn't even receive on-screen credit for their roles until about 1910, but by 1923, 15,000 silent-movie theaters were selling an average of 50 million tickets a week[3] in an America with a population of almost 112 million.[4] In a short time, the movie business had become one of the ten largest industries in America, with over $1.5 billion of invested capital, and movie stars like Charlie Chaplin and Rudolph Valentino had become the celebrity fascination of the nation.

The 1920s saw the rise of the Hollywood studio system, which managed to release up to eight hundred films a year. Many were short, single-reel films, but full-length features started to become popular as well. In the space of just a few years, silent films became the most successful form of entertainment in American history, yet at the very height of their popularity, the industry began to experiment with techniques that would quickly make them obsolete.

Capturing movement on film was the industry's first challenge. As soon as they'd mastered that, inventors and filmmakers began to think about adding sound. As early as 1921, D. W. Griffith experimented with an early sound-on-disc process in a film called *Dream Street,* which included a sequence where Griffith spoke directly to the audience, as well as a scene with singing. Either because the quality was so poor or because no other theaters had the Photokinema sound system required to show it, the film made little impact and closed shortly. Two years later, Lee de Forest tried another system, Phonofilm, which synchronized sound and dialogue, but once again neither the sound nor the content were exciting enough to compete with the sophisticated silent films of the time.[5]

Unimpressed by these early attempts and on the verge of bankruptcy, Warner Bros. decided to invest in a new technology, the Vitaphone sound-on-disc system. The Vitaphone system placed the film's soundtrack on phonograph records separate from the film itself. To synchronize the sound, the turntable was physically connected to the projector while the film was being shown.[6] In 1926 and 1927, Warner Bros. experimented with the Vitaphone using five films that synchronized music and sound effects but had no speaking or singing. These five films gave the studio sufficient experience and confidence with the technology to lay the groundwork for the landmark 1927 film that saved the Warner Bros. studio and changed movies forever—*The Jazz Singer* starring Al Jolson.

Though *The Jazz Singer* is almost always described as the first "talkie"—the milestone film that introduced sound and singing into movies—in truth it was neither the first film with sound, the first film with speech, nor the first film with singing. Like Warner Bros.' previous Vitaphone releases, *The Jazz Singer* featured a synchronized musical score that accompanied the action. It mixed classical music (Tchaikovsky, Sibelius, and Bruch), traditional Hebrew music, themes for individual characters, and popular songs. The picture actually had very little talking and was in many ways an awkward mixture of a silent film and a sound film.* Most of the movie consists of music accompanying action without speech. For the first fifteen minutes of the movie, no one utters a single word or sings a single note.

---

* Jolson spoke in only two scenes: 60 words in the first scene and 294 in the second.

Printed intertitles convey important dialogue and explanations of what was happening in the plot.* For most of its eighty-nine minutes, *The Jazz Singer* is, for all practical purposes, a silent movie.

About fifteen minutes into the film, we literally get to watch the future of cinema spring into being before our eyes. Synchronized musical accompaniments had become common in silent films by 1927, and as the scene transitions to Jolson dining in a cabaret, background music jauntily introduces the moment. Sound effects had also been heard in some recent silent films, and various background noises in the cabaret are audible on the soundtrack. When the cabaret owner invites Jolson to sing a song, just as in other contemporary silent films, we do not hear him speak. We merely see his lips move as an intertitle conveys the information: "Jack Robin will sing 'Dirty hands, Dirty face.' They say he's good—we shall see." We hear some applause as Jolson walks up to sing—again the kinds of sound effects heard in the most advanced silent films of the era. The orchestra holds the final chord of the song's introduction, Jolson steps into the spotlight, and after a split-second pause separating cinema's past from its future, he begins to sing in real time: "Wonderful pals are always hard to find." A single line that would ultimately change the course of an entire industry.

During the course of the movie, Jolson sings the Hebrew "Kol Nidre" as well as six popular songs, including Irving Berlin's "Blue Skies," "Toot, Toot, Tootsie! (Goo' Bye!)," and Jolson's signature song, "My Mammy," in blackface to end the movie. Though most of the critical writing about the film has rightly focused on the way its vocal numbers opened the door for the deluge of film musicals that would follow, in some ways what was equally important in convincing producers of the viability of the new medium was

---

* The film tells the story of Jakie Rabinowitz (Al Jolson), the son of a devout Jewish cantor, who defies his father's wishes, changes his name, and runs away from home in order to become a jazz singer—Jack Robin. It is interesting how the movie's plot parallels Harold Arlen's story. He too was the son of a cantor, left home, changed his name, entered the show business world, and got involved with a non-Jewish woman, the starlet Anya Taranda, who became his wife, much like Jack Robin gets involved with a non-Jewish actress named Mary Dale.

what I believe was the film's most extraordinary moment—a brief scene that had no singing in it at all.

A little more than thirty-five minutes into the film, Jolson sings "Blue Skies" to his mother. After the song is over, Jolson has what was, if you believe contemporary accounts, a completely improvised conversation with his mother. The scene is so natural, spontaneous, and charming that it showed in little over a minute the Vitaphone's enormous potential for a new kind of realism and naturalism on the screen.

The effect of *The Jazz Singer* on audiences and the movie industry was astounding. The film was among the biggest box office hits of 1927. With an approximate budget of $422,000, the picture earned about $3.5 million in profits, turning Warner Bros. into the hottest studio in the country. Watching *The Jazz Singer* today, with its primitive technology, over-the-top sentimentality, and maudlin histrionics, it can be hard to understand the overwhelming response it generated, but Doris Warner, who attended the premiere, claimed that during the improvised dialogue scene between Jolson and his mother, "the audience became hysterical." In one of the most prescient reviews ever penned, Robert Sherwood of *Life* magazine said that the scene was "fraught with tremendous significance. . . . I for one suddenly realized that the end of the silent drama is in sight."[7]

Theater professionals in the audience at the premiere saw the same thing as Sherwood. Samuel Goldwyn's wife Frances attended the opening, and as the applause swelled and the houselights came on, she looked around at all of the celebrities in the crowd. What she saw was "terror in all their faces," as if they knew that "the game they had been playing for years was finally over."[8] Though some saw the writing on the wall, many in the industry were in denial, calling the picture's success a fluke and claiming that sound films were nothing more than a passing fad. One of the main reasons *The Jazz Singer* did not earn more than it did was the fact that few theaters were equipped with the technology to show it. But the enormous public response encouraged Warner Bros. to produce more Vitaphone films and outfit theaters nationwide with its sound system. By the time the studio released its next Al Jolson feature, *The Singing Fool*, the following year, a nationwide network of theaters equipped with the new technology was in place, and the film, which cost approximately $388,000 to make, was able to earn a profit of $5.9 million worldwide.[9]

Like the release of the first iPhone, the overwhelming public response to the Vitaphone caught the industry by surprise. Studios were totally unprepared to meet the demand for the new talking films. Performers and producers scrambled to react to the new reality and its unsettling implications. Vaudeville stars quickly realized that audiences would choose to see one of the new, exciting, cheap talkies rather than one of their more expensive live shows, and they began to film their acts for Vitaphone. This actually hastened the end of vaudeville, as it was far cheaper to see vaudeville stars perform on film than it was to see them in person, and there was certainly no reason to pay money to see inferior vaudeville performers live once the best ones could be seen on film. As the vaudeville audience became a movie audience, vaudeville theaters became movie theaters, and theater owners had to invest in expensive new sound equipment to keep up with the demand for talkies.

Silent film actors were also affected. Having never spoken on camera and spending years performing with the exaggerated body language that silent films required, they suddenly had to adapt to a naturalistic acting style where emotion is generated by speech instead of gesture. Movie studios had to reinvent themselves as well. They not only needed new facilities to produce sound pictures, new actors to perform in them, and new directors who understood the new technology, they also desperately needed new content. Executives went on buying sprees, grabbing up existing plays and songs by the handful while offering huge sums of money to any composer on Broadway who might be able to write for the screen.

❧

Two years after the release of *The Jazz Singer*, the silent film—the most popular form of entertainment ever created—was dead. At the same time, vaudeville, which had been the dominant form of live entertainment in America for at least a half a century, vanished in less than four years. The enthusiasm for sound pictures swept through the country, driving attendance at the movies to levels that would never again be reached. The number of moviegoers doubled in three years, from approximately 50 million in 1926—the year before *The Jazz Singer*—to approximately 100 million by 1930.[10]

As in the early days of video games and the internet, demand for the new product was so strong that quality was almost beside the point. After the success of *The Jazz Singer* and *The Singing Fool*, film studios churned out musicals at an extraordinary rate, releasing more than 50 in 1929 alone and some 150 films with music in the early years of talkies. Studios flooded the market with so many low-quality musicals that audiences quickly tired of them, and anxious theater owners were forced to post signs informing potential viewers that the movie they were showing was *not* a musical. The studios finally caught on to the problem, and after releasing almost 100 musicals in 1930, they released only 11 in 1931.[11]

These production cutbacks were not simply a response to the early glut of musicals but also to the Great Depression. Many smaller studios were forced to close, and even the major ones barely scraped by. By 1933, despite reducing their prices and offering merchandise giveaways, double features, and popcorn and candy, a third of the movie theaters in the country were forced to close their doors.[12] Though the industry would never recapture its earlier levels of attendance, movies were still remarkably successful during the 1930s as their darkened theaters, glamorous stars, and happy endings provided an inexpensive form of escape that grew more necessary as the Depression dragged on.

The financial challenges the movie industry faced were even greater on Broadway. With ticket prices far higher than at the movies, theaters had difficulty luring audiences. Investors grew scarce, and fewer and fewer productions made it to the stage. As a result, nearly every major Broadway songwriter and lyricist spent a significant portion of the 1930s working for Hollywood studios. Rodgers and Hart, Jerome Kern, Oscar Hammerstein, Irving Berlin, Vincent Youmans, Buddy DeSylva, Cole Porter, Harold Arlen, Yip Harburg, George and Ira Gershwin, and many others went back and forth from New York to Hollywood, though rarely with happy results. Writing for the movies was nothing like writing for Broadway, where composers were kings, crucial to shows and at the heart of every stage of the creative process, from conception to rehearsals to production. In Hollywood, despite their huge salaries, composers were treated as minor contributors. A composer would be hired to write a certain number of songs, often at an enormous fee (in 1933, Vincent Youmans was paid $8,000 for four songs), but their work might be thrown out or altered in any way the studio wanted. Even when an existing show was transferred to Hollywood, there was no guarantee its songs would not be replaced by the work of other composers. Once a song was turned in to the studio, the composer's job was done, and the next time he would hear his work would be in a theater after the film opened—if he was lucky.

The challenges that Hollywood presented were psychological as well as creative. Composers like Gershwin, Rodgers, Berlin, Porter, and Arlen were stars in New York. But in Hollywood, they were treated like hired help. As Johnny Mercer, one of Arlen's lyricists, put it bluntly, "Hollywood was impressed with songwriters for a minute and a half. Then the producers decided that songwriters didn't add any money to the box office."[13] And that was that.

❧

But things change, and after the glut of poor-quality film musicals produced in the wake of *The Jazz Singer* came the Golden Age of the Hollywood musical. In 1933, Busby Berkeley collaborated with composer Harry Warren (another renamed immigrant—originally Salvatore Guaragna) on the phenomenally successful *42nd Street*, which combined dance and music in startling new ways. What was crucial about Berkeley's work was the way he developed a voice for the film musical that was uniquely suited to both medium and audience. In the same way the voice of the early Broadway musical borrowed from Europe, the voice of the early Hollywood musical borrowed from New York. But Berkeley saw the film musical as something more than a staged production transferred to the screen. He used camera angles that provided views that no spectator could have ever experienced from the audience, and he often shot scenes from above, turning his armies of chorus girls into precise geometric formations. He created opulent visual fantasies that burst the conventions of stage musicals, inspiring other directors to devise a visual vocabulary appropriate to the new medium.

As the film musical became more cinematic, Broadway songwriters found it increasingly difficult to adapt their work to the new medium. The two forms had very different audiences. Though some New York theaters dropped ticket prices as low as 25 cents in an attempt to keep customers, the people who attended Broadway shows were still relatively wealthy and educated, with sophisticated, New York–centric musical tastes. Major studio films, however, had to appeal to a much wider, less wealthy, less sophisticated, national audience that wasn't really interested in New York topics, humor, and tone. In the 1920s, a play, book, or film was designed first and foremost to please Manhattanites, with the assumption that if it succeeded there its success would eventually radiate out to the rest of the country. But with the rise of Hollywood, New York began to lose its role as the nation's arbiter of taste, and nothing showed this westward shift in cultural values more clearly than the Hollywood production rules known as the Hays Code.

Named after Will Hays, the president of the Motion Pictures Producers and Distributors of America from 1922 to 1945, the code defined what was permissible in films. Initially adopted in 1930, it only began to be strictly enforced in 1934. (Astonishingly, it remained in place until 1968.) Many of its provisions seem unbelievable today, and reading them is a powerful reminder of the conservative climate that dominated the country for much of the twentieth century.

The code was divided into two parts: a statement of General Principles and a seemingly endless list of Particular Applications, often referred to as the "Don'ts" and the "Be Carefuls." The code's three general principles were:

1. No picture shall be produced that will lower the moral standards of those who see it. Hence the sympathy of the audience should never be thrown to the side of crime, wrongdoing, evil or sin.
2. Correct standards of life, subject only to the requirements of drama and entertainment, shall be presented.
3. Law, natural or human, shall not be ridiculed, nor shall sympathy be created for its violation.

The long, detailed list of applications were grouped into twelve different categories: Crimes Against the Law, Sex, Vulgarity, Obscenity, Profanity, Costume, Dances, Religion, Locations, National Feelings, Titles, and Repellent Subjects. The section governing Crimes Against the Law required that no film show a crime in a way that will "throw sympathy with the crime or inspire others with a desire for imitation." No actual methods of "theft, robbery, safe-cracking, and dynamiting of trains, smuggling, or arson" can be shown in a film, and "revenge in modern times shall not be justified." As might be expected, the section on Sex contains the most restrictions, including an overall injunction that "the sanctity of the institution of marriage and the home shall be upheld," and specific prohibitions on depicting adultery, "excessive and lustful kissing, lustful embraces, suggestive postures and gesture, sex perversion, and miscegenation (sex relationships between the white and black races)." "Sex hygiene and venereal diseases are not subjects for motion pictures," and "Obscenity in word, gesture, reference, song, joke, or by suggestion is forbidden," as is "nudity in fact or in silhouette," or "indecent or undue exposure." Even "Dances which emphasize indecent movements are to be regarded as obscene," and "Pointed profanity (this includes the words, God, Lord, Jesus, Christ—unless used reverently—Hell, S.O.B., damn, Gawd), or every other profane or vulgar expression however used, is forbidden." (This is why Rhett Butler's famous line in *Gone with the Wind*—"Frankly, my dear, I don't give a damn"—caused such an uproar.) A sentence that goes to the heart of the Code's entire purpose, declared, "Entertainment can be a character either HELPFUL or HARMFUL [capitals are in the original code] to the human race. . . . Correct entertainment raises the whole standard of a nation. Wrong entertainment lowers the whole living conditions and moral ideals of a race."

For Roaring Twenties composers like Cole Porter, who had been pushing the envelope of what was morally permissible on Broadway, it was hard to find an article in the Hays Code that in some show or song he had not already broken. Moving from the permissive world of Broadway to the puritanical world of Hollywood required considerable adaptive skills on the part of songwriters, and though the composer of five racy Cotton Club shows might seem ill-suited to the restrictive world of film, Harold Arlen would collaborate with Yip Harburg on one of the most successful Hollywood films of all time. A film that by its very nature would fit smoothly into the world of the Hays Code. The quintessential family film: MGM's *The Wizard of Oz*.

By the time Arlen and Harburg became part of the *Wizard of Oz* team, they both had considerable experience with Hollywood, and none of that experience had been particularly unusual or rewarding. Busby Berkeley's extraordinary 1933 trifecta of hits—*42nd Street*, *Footlight Parade*, and *Golddiggers*

of 1933—had revived interest in the film musical, and Arlen was one of the many composers hired to fill the renewed demand. For his first picture, *Let's Fall in Love* (1933), Arlen wrote five songs: two were discarded, two remained in the film, and one was turned into background music.[14] This was a much better result than most. When Rodgers and Hart's musical *On Your Toes* was turned into a film in 1939, all that survived from the original score were a few songs that had become underscoring.

The Wizard of Oz, however, was one of the few film musicals of the 1930s in which the music, lyrics, dances, and book were fully integrated into the final film. Though ten screenwriters wrote multiple versions of the script and four directors at different times worked on portions of the film, all of the songs and lyrics were Arlen's and Harburg's. The two were involved with the production from the outset thanks to the influence of Arthur Freed. Though technically only an assistant to producer Mervyn Leroy, Freed made most of the musical decisions for the film, and it was Freed who hired Arlen and Harburg in May 1938 on a fourteen-week contract for $25,000.* At the time, the script was still in its earliest stages, and the only hired actor was the sixteen-year-old Judy Garland. Film musicals were normally star-driven, and the composer's job was to tailor the songs to fit each star's particular personality and talents. But *The Wizard of Oz* offered Arlen and Harburg the rare opportunity to write music and shape the story before stars even entered the picture.

They began with what they called "the lemon-drop songs"—the lighter material like "Ding Dong! The Witch Is Dead" and "We're Off to See the Wizard"—but though these songs came relatively quickly, they struggled with the ballad that would define Dorothy's character and become the film's signature song. "I felt we needed something with a sweep, a melody with a broad, long line," Arlen said. "Time was getting short, I was getting

---

* All of these basic facts about the production of the film are drawn from Aljean Harmetz's classic behind-the-scenes book, *The Making of the Wizard of Oz*.

anxious. My feeling was that picture songs need to be lush, and picture songs are hard to write."[15] Though stories about the inspiration for famous songs tend to be polished over years and years of retellings, according to Arlen, the song came to him out of the blue while he was driving with his wife to a movie at Grauman's Chinese Theater. He immediately stopped the car across from Schwab's drugstore and jotted down the melody. "It was as if the Lord said, 'Well, here it is, now stop worrying about it!'"

But the song almost didn't make it past Harburg. When he first heard Arlen play it, Harburg thought the song was too old and symphonic for Dorothy's character. Ira Gershwin, however, liked it so much he helped convince Harburg, and the song became part of the score. Or so they thought. The studio executives, unfortunately, didn't want it. They thought it slowed down the opening of the picture, was too difficult to sing, and wouldn't sell sheet music or get played on the radio. After the first sneak preview, the studio head, Louis B. Mayer, cut the song for the next preview, at which point an enraged Arthur Freed essentially said, "Either the song stays or I go." "Over the Rainbow" was inserted back into the film, the audience loved it, and the rest, as they say, is history. But what is it that makes this iconic song so great?

In an interview for Aljean Harmetz's book *The Making of the Wizard of Oz*, Harburg described his creative process for the opening of the song:

The book had said Kansas was an arid place where not even flowers grew. The only colorful thing Dorothy saw, occasionally, would be the rainbow. I thought that the rainbow could be a bridge from one place to another. A rainbow gave us a visual reason for going to a new land and a reason for changing to color. "Over the Rainbow Is Where I Want To Be" was my title, the title I gave Harold. A title has to ring a bell, has to blow a couple of Roman candles off. But he gave me a tune with those first two notes. I tried *I'll go over the rainbow, Someday over the rainbow*. I had difficulty coming to the idea of *Somewhere*. For a while I thought I would just leave those first two notes out. It was a long time before I came to *Somewhere over the rainbow*.[16]

Interestingly enough, the "bridge from one place to another" that Harburg refers to is already set up beautifully before the song even begins. After Dorothy tries to tell her aunt and uncle about the unfortunate incident between the town spinster Miss Gulch and Dorothy's dog Toto, an annoyed Aunt Em tells Dorothy to "find yourself a place where you won't get into any trouble." Though Aunt Em is simply referring to an actual, physical place on the farm where Dorothy won't get into trouble, as Dorothy reflects on this, she turns the real into the metaphorical, saying to Toto, "Some place where there isn't any trouble. Do you suppose there is such a place, Toto? There must be. It's not a place you can get to by a boat, or a train. It's far, far away. Behind the moon, beyond the rain." This little scene elegantly creates a "bridge from one place to another"—from the reality of Dorothy's Kansas farm to the world of her imagination, a world that comes to life with the first two notes of "Over the Rainbow."

In a musical language utterly different from the through-composed, non-repetitive style of "Stormy Weather," "Over the Rainbow" has only two melodic ideas in its famous opening (Ex. 10.1). The first I will call "leap," and the second "circle-and-yearn." The full-octave leap on "somewhere" is enormous for the opening of a popular song. It's a leap between two different parts of the voice—and between two different worlds. The first note is low, almost in chest voice. It's Dorothy's troubled reality—Kansas, aridity, no flowers, the black and white of the opening of the film. The second note is higher, lighter, and more ethereal. It's "over the rainbow," Oz, the place she wants to escape to. The other melodic idea occurs in the second measure, on "over the rainbow." It begins on a B, circles back to a B, and then yearns upward to a C. These gestures—leap and circle and yearn—are the two key musical ideas of the song.

There are three leaps in the opening phrase. The first one, on "some-where," is the largest—a full octave (C–C). The leap on "way up" is smaller—a major sixth (C–A)—and the final leap on "there's a" is both lower and

Example 10.1 "Over the Rainbow," opening

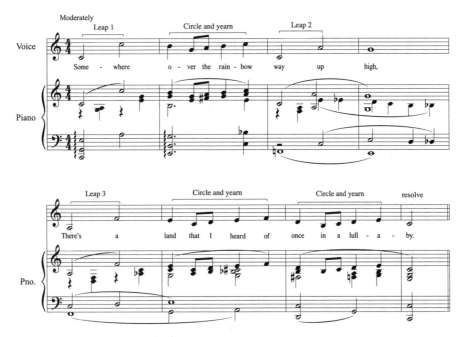

smaller—a minor sixth (A–F). Like these vocal leaps, Dorothy's dreams are poignantly contracting within these opening 8 measures.

Harburg called "Over the Rainbow" a "song of yearning," and the harmony underneath these three leaps shows us how much yearning Dorothy feels. Arlen could easily have written bright, cheery chords underneath "way up high," as in Example 10.2A, but it's the yearning in the harmony that makes the leap so poignant (Ex. 10.2B). Similarly, the last chord of "there's a" could have been simple, like my version in Example 10.2C. But Arlen's final chord* in Example 10.2D is much darker.

The phrase finishes with two circle-and-yearns—one on "land that I heard of" (**E**–C–D–**E**–F) followed by the same idea lower (**D**–B–C–**D**–E) on "once in a lulla-," with a resolution on "-by" (Ex. 10.1). Though these

---

* For musicians, a half-diminished 7th chord.

Example 10.2A "Over the Rainbow,"
Kapilow version

Example 10.2B "Over the Rainbow,"
Arlen version

Example 10.2C "Over the Rainbow,"
Kapilow version

Example 10.2D "Over the Rainbow,"
Arlen version

opening 8 measures could not sound more spontaneous, they are actually carefully and ingeniously composed. Remembering our opening leap from Kansas to Oz—from low C to high C—Arlen essentially takes us from Oz back to Kansas with a subtly decorated scale, C–B–A–G–F–E–D–C (Ex. 10.3). Dorothy yearns for Oz, but at the end of this first A section, she is still stuck in Kansas, on low C.

The music of the A section then repeats with new lyrics ("Somewhere over the rainbow / skies are blue / and the dreams that you dare to / dream really do come true"), but at the end of this second A section ("dreams really do come true"), we are again stuck in Kansas, on low C.

According to Harburg, the song's B section came from a tune Arlen used to whistle whenever his dog Pan ran away—E–G–E–G–E—which became the central notes of "someday I'll wish upon a star" (Ex. 10.4).*

---

* Like so many anecdotes about famous theater songs, Harburg's story about Arlen's inspiration for the B section coming from his whistle is his version. Arlen claimed that the melody was inspired by a simple children's piano piece.

Example 10.3 "Over the Rainbow," descending scale

Example 10.4 "Over the Rainbow," opening of B section

The phrase begins to repeat for "where troubles melt like lemon drops" (Ex. 10.5). Arlen could have continued the pattern, resulting in the bland and monotonous Example 10.6.

Example 10.5 "Over the Rainbow," B section

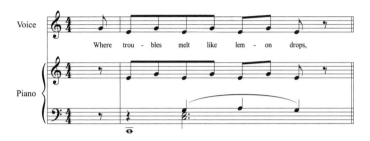

Example 10.6 "Over the Rainbow," B section, Kapilow version

But he doesn't. Instead, swept up in the vision of an imaginary world far from Miss Gulch and Kansas, Dorothy's melody reaches higher, "away above the chimney tops," to the highest note of the song on "find me" (Ex. 10.7).

Following AABA form, the song returns to the opening music a third time, and if this were a standard song, Arlen would finish exactly as he finished the first two A sections on "Why then, oh why can't I?" But this would end the song with Dorothy still on low C, still stuck in Kansas, and

Example 10.7 "Over the Rainbow," B section, Arlen version

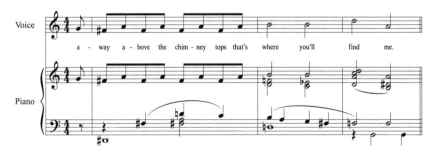

Example 10.8 "Over the Rainbow," B section, orchestral interlude

there would be no transformation. Instead, Arlen decided to bring back the music of the B section in the orchestra alone. Harburg once said, "Words make you think thoughts. Music makes you feel a feeling. But a song makes you feel a thought,"[17] and as the orchestra plays the music of the B section, we can actually feel Dorothy's thoughts (Ex. 10.8).

The voice enters on "If happy little bluebirds fly" exactly as in the B section. If Arlen had continued as before, the music would sound like Example 10.9.

Once again, Arlen subverts our expectations (Ex. 10.10). This time, Arlen alters the melody so that it rises beautifully one last time, completing its stepwise ascension to Oz—to high C (F–G–A–B–C). Over the course

Example 10.9 "Over the Rainbow," Kapilow version

Example 10.10 "Over the Rainbow," Arlen version

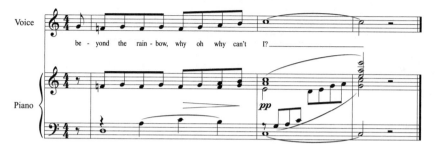

of this magical song, Dorothy has traveled across a rainbow bridge: from low C to high C, from Kansas to Oz, from reality to fantasy. Her transformation is complete.

Though *The Wizard of Oz* has become one of the best-known films of all time, initially it was only a moderate success. It fared well during its opening weeks, but reviews were mixed, and most of the audience consisted of children who paid lower ticket prices. Though the film grossed a little over $3 million on a budget of $2.7 million, with the cost of advertising, prints, and distribution added in, the studio lost nearly a million dollars on the film's initial release.*[18] It's difficult to know the extent to which world events affected the picture's first run, but it's important to recognize that *The Wizard of Oz* was released on August 15, 1939, a week before Hitler and Stalin signed the Nazi-Soviet Non-Aggression Pact and seventeen days before the Nazis invaded Poland, beginning World War II. Though MGM's head, Louis Mayer, believed that movies shouldn't be a reflection of real life but rather an entertaining escape from it, domestic and international realities added a layer of meaning both to "Over the Rainbow" and *The Wizard of Oz*, as the desire to escape from reality—whether it be the Depression

---

* The film was nominated for six Academy awards, and though it lost to *Gone with the Wind* for the Best Picture award, "Over the Rainbow" won the award for Best Original Song. Within two days of the film's New York premiere, "Over the Rainbow" had already found its way on the Hit Parade chart, and it remained on the chart for an unprecedented fifteen weeks with seven weeks at No. 1.

and the Dustbowl or a continent on the precipice of another world war—to a Technicolor world where "troubles melt like lemon drops" had never seemed more urgent or more meaningful.

In the same way that the technology of the movies gave new life to the Broadway musical, the advent of a still newer technology—television—gave new life to *The Wizard of Oz*. In 1956, CBS went to MGM Studios to see if they would be willing to lease *Gone with the Wind*, throwing in a request for *The Wizard of Oz* almost as an afterthought. MGM said no to *Gone with the Wind* but were willing to consider *The Wizard of Oz*. Though no one at CBS thought there would be an audience for more than two or three showings, they negotiated a deal for two broadcasts at $225,000 each—a huge fee at the time—and an additional deal for seven more showings at $150,000 per broadcast, included largely as insurance.[19] What neither CBS or MGM ever anticipated was that the film would become more popular each time it was shown until it finally became an American institution. By the 1970s, the picture and its characters were cultural touchstones, and by the time she died in 1969, Judy Garland had become as iconic as the film. In 2000, the Recording Industry Association of America picked "Over the Rainbow" as the song of the century, and the 2005 Yip Harburg commemorative postage stamp featured the opening lyric from "Over the Rainbow," both indicators of the song's enormous cultural reach.

Though the iconic status of *The Wizard of Oz* and "Over the Rainbow" are perhaps extreme examples, they are reflective of one of the most important trends of the 1930s—the development of a shared national culture. Before the 1920s and '30s, America's voice was largely a compilation of diverse regional voices. Country and western music, jazz, and the blues each grew up and flourished in different parts of the country, and cultural activities were locally defined. However, new technologies like the automobile, records, radio, and films made it possible for the first time for a single message to reach the entire American population at once. Music became a national commodity. Local spectators were replaced by a mass national

audience. People listened to the same music, heard the same radio programs, read the same news, followed the same sporting events, and saw the
same movies. A participatory culture became a spectator culture, and the
end result was the creation of a common set of cultural references; a common, national voice that became the American voice.

Given its uniquely powerful combination of story, picture, and sound,
and its extraordinarily large audience, Hollywood played a central role in
this standardization of culture and the projection of that culture to the rest
of the world. Even today, for many people in remote parts of the globe, Hollywood films and the America they represent *are* America. Yet what those
films largely represented in the 1930s was not what America was but rather
a fantasy of what it wished it could be. Like the Kansas of the opening of
The Wizard of Oz, America was trapped in the black-and-white reality of
the Depression, desperate to find an escape "over the rainbow"—even if
only for ninety minutes in a darkened theater—to a happier, trouble-free,
Technicolor world without breadlines, Hoovervilles, or unemployment.

It might at first seem that the Technicolor, alternate universes that *The
Wizard of Oz* and so many of these Depression-era musicals inhabited were
simply escapist fantasies unconnected to the gritty reality that existed outside
the theater in 1930s America. Yet often the more difficult and untenable the
reality, the more powerful the desire to escape. Yearning, as Harburg said,
is what "Over the Rainbow" is ultimately all about—the yearning to leave
our own personal Kansas behind in order to travel to whatever we imagine
our own Oz might be. In the end, we are not only who we are but also who
we wish we could be. We are our hopes, dreams, and fantasies as well as our
realities, and it is those hopes, dreams, and yearnings that Arlen captured.
For Dorothy, for an America exhausted by the Depression yet united by the
hope of something better, and ultimately for all of us who continue to yearn
for that place "where there isn't any trouble . . . far, far away."

11

World War II and the Integrated Musical

Richard Rodgers's "If I Loved You"

On May 17, 1942, the *New York Times* interviewed Irving Berlin about the new wartime show he was writing for the Armed Forces called *This Is the Army*. In discussing the influence of history on music, he remarked: "It needed a French Revolution to make a 'Marseillaise' and the bombardment of Fort McHenry to give voice to 'The Star-Spangled Banner.' . . . Songs make history. History makes songs." Berlin's shrewd observation helps explain the unprecedented success of the two wartime works that kicked off the Rodgers and Hammerstein partnership: *Oklahoma!* (1943) and *Carousel* (1945). Though the greatness of the two shows is undeniable, the electrifying effect they had on the American public is inseparable from the moment in time when they were created. But to understand the multi-layered historical context of these two works, it is first necessary to understand their role in the development both of Richard Rodgers as a composer and the Broadway musical as an art form.

In June 1942, Larry Hart, in a state of near total physical collapse, turned down Rodgers's request to collaborate on transforming Lynn Riggs's play *Green Grow the Lilacs* into a musical. Hart insisted that he needed to go to Mexico for a vacation, but Rodgers, who had dealt with Hart's unreliability for years, knew that the trip was simply an excuse to drink. He'd had enough, and he tearfully ended their twenty-three-year partnership less than a month after the opening of *By Jupiter,* their last show together—ironically their most successful in terms of the box office.* One might expect the ending of one of the singular composer-lyricist relationships in musical-theater history—and the only partnership of Rodgers's professional career up to that point—to be followed by a period of pause and reflection, but Rodgers was not the type to allow himself that kind of break. A month after Rodgers's split from Hart, the *New York Times* erroneously announced the pair's upcoming production of a musical version of *Green Grow the Lilacs,* when in fact, Rodgers had already partnered with Oscar Hammerstein II on the project that would become *Oklahoma!,* inaugurating a seventeen-year collaboration that would end only with Hammerstein's death in 1960.

Like a butterfly shedding its chrysalis, the Rodgers of *By Jupiter* and the twenty-five other musicals he wrote with Hart was left behind. In a matter of weeks, a new Rodgers emerged with a strikingly different musical voice, attributed by most critics and biographers to the radical change in the new collaborators' creative process. In his work with Hart, Rodgers almost always wrote the music first. This was partly a matter of necessity, as Hart could rarely be found or, if found, made to work. For anything to get done, Rodgers had to give Hart an instrumental version of a song to write lyrics for—something Hart often did at an astonishing pace. Hammerstein, however, preferred to write his lyrics first and then hand them to Rodgers to turn into music. And since Hammerstein, unlike Hart, also wrote the books for his musicals, he had an inordinately large role in determining the shape of the shows he and Rodgers worked on together.

---

* After the split over *Oklahoma!,* Rodgers did collaborate with Hart on a revival of *A Connecticut Yankee* from May to October of 1943, but *By Jupiter* was their last complete show together. The revival of *A Connecticut Yankee* opened on November 15, 1943. Hart arrived at the premiere inebriated, was escorted out, disappeared, and was found drunk, sitting in the gutter sopping wet at 3 a.m. He was taken to the hospital with pneumonia on November 19 and died on November 22.

It is hard to imagine two lyricists with more fundamentally different aesthetics than Hart and Hammerstein, and the fact that Rodgers collaborated so successfully with both is remarkable. The profound disparities between them were already apparent when they were both in their twenties and met Rodgers at Columbia.* "Any Old Place with You," interpolated into Lew Fields's *A Lonely Romeo* may have been Rodgers and Hart's first professional song written together as a team, but the lyrics are already quintessentially Hart. Lines like, "In dreamy Portugal, I'm goin' to court you gal" and rhymes like "hell for ya" and "Philadelphia" have the kind of fresh, self-aware playfulness that would become a Hart signature. Though written in 1919, Hart's words already breathe the air of the Roaring Twenties. They're sophisticated, irreverent, New York–centric (in equating hell with Philadelphia), American, vernacular, energetic, and self-consciously verbal.

Hammerstein's work from the same time comes from a completely different world. Before Rodgers and Hart became a full-time team, Hammerstein actually wrote a few songs with Rodgers. One year after "Any Old Place with You," Hammerstein's lyrics for "There's Always Room for One More" began:

> *My heart is an airy castle*
> *Filled with girls I adore.*
> *My brain is a cloud of memories*
> *Of peaches galore.*

This comes straight out of the world of operetta. A world filled with "clouds of memories" where hearts are "airy castles." ("Of peaches galore" is just terrible and can't be blamed on operetta.) Though the lyric is clearly meant to be funny—in spite of all of the girls filling the airy castle of his heart, the punch line claims that there's always room for one more—its gentle humor

---

* Hart and Hammerstein were both born in 1895.

is operetta-like, turn-of-the-century, and old-fashioned, producing a smile at best. In comparison to Hart's wit, it's weak, feeble, and already behind the times. Hart's humor crackles with the energy and vitality of the present, the new—a feeling his lyrics would retain throughout his life. Hammerstein's lyrical sensibility comes from an older world that would remain a part of his aesthetic for the next forty years.

❧

The two shows that nearly all musical-theater historians choose as the watershed works in the history of Broadway were both written by Hammerstein: *Show Boat* (1927) and *Oklahoma!* (1943). For many scholars, the latter marks the beginning of the so-called "integrated musical," though definitions of the term differ widely. Shortly after *Oklahoma!* opened, Hammerstein said that the songs in an integrated show "must help tell our story and delineate characters, supplementing the dialogue and seeming to be, as much as possible, a continuation of dialogue."[1] Several years later, he talked about the integrated musical as one that merged words and music into a "single expression."

> It is not so much a method as a state of mind, or rather a state for two minds, an attitude of unity. Musical plays, then, are not "books" written by an author with songs later inserted by a composer and a lyric writer.[2]

Rodgers took the definition even further, describing the integrated musical as one in which every element of the production—not only words and music, but sets, costumes, choreography, and orchestrations as well—are united in service of the show's narrative.

> When a show works perfectly, it's because all the individual parts complement each other and fit together. No single element overshadows any other. In a great musical, the orchestrations sound the way the

costumes look. That's what made *Oklahoma!* work. All the components dovetailed. There was nothing extraneous or foreign, nothing that pushed itself into the spotlight yelling "look at me!" It was a work created by many that gave the impression of having been created by one.[3]

Out of these general observations, the *Oxford Handbook of the American Musical* sums up five key principles at the heart of the integrated musical:

1. The songs advance the plot.
2. The songs flow directly from the dialogue.
3. The songs express the characters who sing them.
4. The dances advance the plot and enhance the dramatic meaning of the songs that precede them.
5. The orchestra, through accompaniment and underscoring, parallels, complements, or advances the action.[4]

Though all of this may be true of *Oklahoma!*, *Carousel*, and the musicals that followed in their wake, none of these features were really new. As Rodgers himself said humbly, "Everyone suddenly became 'integration'-conscious, as if the idea of welding together song, story and dance had never been thought of before."[5] But of course the idea had been thought of long ago. It can be traced back almost a hundred years to Wagner's concept of the "Gesamtkunstwerk"—the totality of the work of art—in which all aspects of an opera would combine to make the whole. In his essays on the topic—*The Artwork of the Future* (1849) and *Opera and Drama* (1852)—Wagner traces the concept of integration as far back as Greek antiquity, a time, according to him, when word, music, and dance existed in perfect harmony. Even leaving classical music antecedents behind, the idea of an integrated musical with an intimate connection between book and score surely existed in the nineteenth-century works of Gilbert and Sullivan, and it was the basis of Jerome Kern's Princess Theatre musicals as well.

Kern summed up the key principle behind these landmark musicals in 1917, essentially giving a definition of the integrated musical twenty-six years before *Oklahoma!*

> It is my opinion that the musical numbers should carry on the action of the play and should be representative of the personalities of the characters who sing them. . . . Songs must be suited to the action and mood of the play.[6]

Ten years later, Kern would collaborate with Hammerstein on *Show Boat*—surely an example of an integrated musical long before *Oklahoma!*—and a year later, in 1928, Rodgers himself consciously experimented with integration in a radical way in the musical *Chee-Chee*. He explicitly described the process:

> To avoid the eternal problem of the story coming to a halt as the songs take over, we decided to use a number of short pieces of from four to sixteen bars each, with no more than six songs of traditional form and length in the entire score. In this way the music would be an essential part of the structure of the story rather than an appendage to the action. The concept was so unusual, in fact, that we even called attention to it with the following notice in the program:

> NOTE: the musical numbers, some of them very short, are so interwoven with the story that it would be confusing for the audience to peruse a complete list.[7]

What set *Oklahoma!* and *Carousel* apart from the works that were modeled on their achievements was the thoroughness of their integration. It was no longer simply the words and music that were organically connected, but the costumes, orchestrations, sets, and choreography as well, and the self-consciousness with which this ideal was applied. For example, the striking way *Oklahoma!* began immediately set a tone for the rest of the musical. Instead of a traditional medley overture followed by a conventional, fast-paced dance number with chorus girls, *Oklahoma!* opened in a radically unpretentious way. Without an overture, the curtain rises on Aunt Eller, an old lady, churning butter on a bare stage as Curly begins to sing "Oh, What a Beautiful Mornin'" a cappella from the wings. This boldly simple, direct opening is completely integrated into the show's overall concept and instantly establishes its mood. The dancing in the show worked similarly. Agnes de Mille's choreography for "Laurey Makes Up Her Mind" does much more than simply extend a number and add entertainment value. It conveys aspects of Laurey's unspoken thoughts—in particular her fear that Jud will murder Curly—that her words and songs could not bring to life. The choreography is thoroughly integrated into the overall dramatic arc and purpose of the entire production.

Critics were immediately aware of the integration at *Oklahoma!*'s first performance. In the opening-night review in the *New York Times*, Lewis Nichols wrote, "Mr. Rodgers's scores never lack grace, but seldom have they been so well integrated for *Oklahoma!*"[8] And John Martin, the dance critic of the *Times*, applauded de Mille's ballet for the way "it is so integrated with the production as a whole that it actually carries forward the plot and justifies the most tenuous psychological point of the play, namely, why Laurey, who is obviously in love with Curly, finds herself unable to resist going to the dance with the repugnant Jud."[9] Though a great deal of critical energy has been spent debating whether *Oklahoma!* was the first integrated musical, that debate misses the key point. The integration in the two Rodgers and Hammerstein wartime musicals was actually a reflection of something deeper and more profound having to do with a new seriousness these two shows brought to the form itself, a seriousness that was a result of developments in the world of Broadway, as well as in the larger political, social, cultural world of which it was a part.

In many ways, the development of the Broadway musical in the teens and twenties was similar to the start-up culture of the 1990s and 2000s. The modern musical was being invented at an astonishing pace with successes and failures alternating in rapid succession. New shows sprouted everywhere, as they were relatively inexpensive to put on (unless you were Florenz Ziegfeld) and didn't require significant runs to recoup their investment. A show that lasted for two hundred performances was considered a hit, and composers frequently wrote multiple musicals in a single season. By the 1920s a vibrant Broadway theater district had approximately 80 theaters presenting more than 200 productions a year, of which about 45 were new musicals. Like much pop music today, these shows were fundamentally designed for short-term consumption rather than long-term artistic achievement. The musical was finding its voice, seeing what did and didn't work, while changing and adapting to an America whose self-image it was helping to invent.

The goal of the musical, first and foremost, was entertainment and commercial success. Even in the 1917 interview in which Kern articulated his initial views on what would later be called the integrated musical, he says:

> Plausibility and reason apply to musical plays as to dramas and comedies, and the sooner librettists and composers appreciate this fact the sooner will come recognition and—royalties.[10]

Recognition and *royalties*. Esteem and artistic achievement were fine, but a successful show that entertains and brings in audiences—*that* was the ultimate goal. The reason composers should write shows with plausible plots and believable characters, according to Kern, is not because they are in-and-of-themselves better, but because audiences will find them more entertaining. Today, we have been so thoroughly indoctrinated in the post–Rodgers-Hammerstein world of the integrated musical that it can be difficult to realize there is nothing inherently better about integrated musicals than nonintegrated musicals. Revues, like the *Ziegfeld Follies*, that presented sequences of great performers in first-rate, stand-alone songs that may or may not have been linked were just as popular in the 1920s and '30s as so-called book musicals.

Oklahoma! and *Carousel* have been celebrated for supposedly ushering in not only the era of the integrated musical but also of the musical play, a term invented to describe the new, more serious kind of works that Rodgers and Hammerstein were creating. Industries tend to traverse similar life cycles, passing from emerging, to growing, maturing, and then declining. Business writer Jason Van Bergen points out, "It takes only a single company or small group of companies to jump-start an entire industry,"[11] and composers like George M. Cohan and Victor Herbert in the first decade of the twentieth century—as well as Berlin, Kern, and Ziegfeld in the second decade—essentially jump-started the Broadway musical. But its emergence, growth, and maturation did not occur as a purely artistic phenomenon. It was deeply influenced by the emergence, growth, and maturation of the nation as a whole. The 1920s saw a new America suddenly emerge from World War I as a major player on the international stage, with a booming economy fueled by the advent of the radio, advertising, automobile, and commercial aviation industries. The Broadway musical kept pace with each new fad, developing a voice that was distinctly American, syncopated, vernacular, and New York–centric. As a result of the dissemination of its songs through radio, recordings, dance bands, and—by the end of the decade—talking films, Broadway's voice was quickly becoming a national one.

Though occasionally an extraordinary musical like *Show Boat* came along, by and large the purpose of musicals in the 1920s was entertainment. Almost none of the decades' shows had any serious artistic pretensions. This was musical *comedy*, not high art—here one day, gone the next—and its transience was a perfect match for the decade's sensibility. Even after the

Depression hit, musicals continued to portray a Roaring Twenties world, but now an intense escapism fueled the onstage fantasies audiences desperately sought as a refuge from the grim realities outside the theater. Though most musical comedies in the early 1930s barely acknowledged the real world, as the decade progressed and the Depression refused to end, musicals began aspiring to more than sheer entertainment. In addition to the premiere of the Rodgers-Hart musical comedy *Babes in Arms*, the year 1937 also saw premieres of the George S. Kaufman/Moss Hart political satire *I'd Rather Be Right*, Marc Blitzstein's *The Cradle Will Rock* (temporarily shut down by the WPA because of its controversial nature), and the satirical revue *Pins and Needles*, backed by the International Ladies' Garment Workers' Union and focusing on the lives of laborers in a rapidly changing society. As the country was changing, so was the Broadway musical, and the positive reaction to these three productions showed there was an audience for a musical with something more on its mind than pure comic entertainment.

The way that industries emerge, grow, and mature in response to external economic events is in many ways similar to the way individuals and nations emerge, grow, and mature in response to outside forces. A new America emerged after World War I practically bursting with adolescent energy, vitality, and optimism. During the boom years of the 1920s, the country developed an almost childlike self-confidence and enthusiasm, as if it believed its remarkable growth and prosperity would never end. After the stock market crash of 1929 brought America to its knees both economically and psychologically, the nation began the slow process of maturation. Like a child who leaves home and is forced to deal with hardship and failure for the first time, America grew up. Through FDR's New Deal, the country began taking responsibility for others—the poor, unemployed, elderly, and disenfranchised. Whatever one's opinion of FDR's presidency, or the long-term results of any individual law, agency, or policy, the clear legacy of the New Deal was the belief that the government bore some responsibility for the welfare of its people.

If the 1930s began with the aftermath of the stock market crash and the Depression that followed, it ended with the emergence of Hitler, fascism, and the prospect of yet another world war; however, with rare exceptions, musicals of the 1930s were no more likely to reflect international realities than they were domestic ones. Hitler's *Anschluss* with Austria, the occupation of the Sudetenland, Chamberlain's appeasement at Munich, and *Kristallnacht* all took place in 1938, the same year *The Boys from Syracuse* opened on Broadway, but there's no evidence of these events in Rodgers and Hart's witty rewrite of Shakespeare's *Comedy of Errors*, nor does the Nazi invasion of Poland and Britain or France's subsequent declaration of war with Germany in September 1939 show up in Rodgers and Hart's silly, college-football musical, *Too Many Girls*, which opened the following month on Broadway. But by the time Rodgers ended his partnership with Hart and began working on *Oklahoma!* in June 1942, the Japanese had attacked Pearl Harbor, the United States had entered the war, and the first American forces had arrived in Europe. When *Carousel* opened on Broadway on April 19, 1945, Germany's unconditional surrender was only weeks away, and over 60 million people had been killed in the world's deadliest military conflict. Somehow, during this horrific period of time, there was still room on Broadway stages and in Hollywood films for laughter and comedy, but something changed with the terrifying prospect of a postnuclear world opened up by the atomic bombs dropped on Japan in August of that year. During the first forty-five years of the century, America had *emerged* onto the world stage as a superpower, *grown*, and in difficult ways *matured*, and this painful process added a depth of seriousness and gravitas to the country that affected nearly every aspect of American life, including the Broadway musical.

The impact of real-world events on the arts in general and musical theater in particular can be surprising and indirect. One of the most striking artistic responses to the unimaginable horrors of World War II was a retreat into a kind of mythical, imagined American past. A simpler, rural, communal past (epitomized by the extraordinary appeal of Berlin's "White Christmas") that was largely invented out of thin air. A past that would serve to remind Americans of their Edenic roots and national character in the midst of a horrific war. A past that might provide hope for a bright future that seemed increasingly inconceivable with each new casualty report. As Rodgers put it when describing the appeal of *Oklahoma!*, "People said to themselves, in effect, 'If this is what our country looked and sounded like at the turn of the century, perhaps once the war is over we can again return to this kind of buoyant, optimistic life.'"[12]

American composer Aaron Copland responded to this impulse by inventing an imaginary Old West in his two cowboy ballets, *Billy the Kid* (1938) and *Rodeo* (1942). Like Kern and Hammerstein who invented the world of *Show Boat* without ever seeing the Mississippi River, Copland—a Brooklyn Jew—invented what would become the quintessential sound of the American West without any actual contact with it whatsoever. In fact, while writing the music for *Billy the Kid*, Copland insisted that people not tell him too much about the real man because he thought it would get in the way of the one he was inventing. Two years after *Rodeo*, he created an equally idyllic, equally imaginary Shaker world as a retreat from World War II in his classic 1944 ballet, *Appalachian Spring*.

It should come as no surprise that Copland's key collaborator on *Rodeo* would become Rodgers and Hammerstein's partner in the creation of the cowboy world of *Oklahoma!*—the choreographer Agnes de Mille. De Mille's extraordinary success may have come in part from her original desire to become an actress, as she was able to write choreography that was not simply entertaining to watch but was also deeply connected to the narrative demands of the shows she worked on. As gifted as de Mille was, her role in elevating the importance of choreography on Broadway was actually part of the increasing seriousness and sophistication of the musical as a whole. In 1936, seven years before *Oklahoma!*, George Balanchine had fought for his title on the Rodgers and Hart musical *On Your Toes* to be listed as "choreographer" rather than the usual designation, "ensembles staged by" or "dances by." This was not simply an argument over credits but rather a recognition of the central role his legendary ballet "Slaughter on Tenth Avenue" played in the show, as well as a recognition of how sophisticated and serious the role of dance on Broadway had become. Having an acclaimed classical choreographer like Balanchine create extended choreography for a musical was a mark of how the genre had matured, and Balanchine's work opened the door for choreographers like de Mille and Jerome Robbins to bring their imaginative theatrical concepts of dance to the increasingly sophisticated musical plays that, thanks to Rodgers and Hammerstein, were beginning to replace older, traditional musical comedies. Interestingly, the original sheet music for *Oklahoma!* billed the show as a musical comedy, but later versions referred to it as a "musical play"—a drama with music—and as with the use of the new term "choreographer," the change in title reflected far more than a simple semantic shift.

Without the increasing sophistication and artistic pretensions of the musical play, as well as the increasing seriousness of the world situation, it seems inconceivable that Rodgers and Hammerstein would have ever considered turning Ferenc Molnár's classic Hungarian play *Liliom* into the musical we now know as *Carousel*. It is hard to imagine, even today, a more unlikely candidate for a musical than Molnár's play. It first premiered in Budapest in 1909 and so baffled audiences that it was almost immediately withdrawn. Ten years later, it was revived there to tremendous acclaim, turning Molnár into a national hero. In the introduction to his English translation, Benjamin Glazer speculated that the tragedy of World War I had made the public more sensitive to the play's spiritual values. Whatever the reason, the success of the Budapest revival led to its translation and a Broadway staging of the play in 1921, produced by the very same Theatre Guild that four years later would commission Rodgers and Hart's Broadway debut, the

Garrick Gaieties. The Guild revived *Liliom* in 1940 in a production seen by both Rodgers and Hammerstein, and in January of 1944, a year after their enormous success producing *Oklahoma!,* Theresa Helburn and Lawrence Langner of the Theatre Guild proposed that Rodgers and Hammerstein do for *Liliom* what they had done the previous year for Lynn Riggs's *Green Grow the Lilacs*—turn it into a musical.

It is not at all surprising that Rodgers and Hammerstein's initial response to the Theatre Guild's proposal was an unqualified no. After the enormous success of *Oklahoma!,* movie mogul Sam Goldwyn suggested that the best thing for Rodgers and Hammerstein to do was "shoot yourselves," and turning *Liliom* into a musical would seem tantamount to doing just that. Nothing about the play suggests that it would make a good musical. The title itself, *Liliom,* is the Hungarian word for "lily" and the slang term for a "tough." The play takes place almost exclusively in the gritty underbelly of Budapest. The tone is European, almost unrelentingly bitter, and the lives of nearly all of the characters reek of desperation and poverty.

Liliom, a tough carousel barker and a reprehensible bully and womanizer, impetuously quits his job, lures Julie, an infatuated, poor maid, into a relationship, and in doing so causes her to lose her job. They move in together (they marry in the musical to make the relationship more palatable), living in the run-down home of Julie's aunt, and while Julie works, Liliom loafs all day and carouses all night. In spite of his wife's remarkable and completely unreasoning loyalty, Liliom beats her and is on the verge of leaving when Julie announces that she is pregnant. In a brief, rare moment of brightness, Liliom is excited by the possibility of becoming a father, and in a desperate attempt to find money to escape to a better life in America, he cooks up a scheme with his lowlife friend to rob Linzman, a Jewish cashier. (Hammerstein turns the cashier, Linzman, into the mill owner, Mr. Bascombe, erasing any trace of his Jewishness or of the play's ugly anti-Semitism from the musical.) The robbery attempt fails miserably, and rather than being caught by the police, Liliom kills himself, at which point the bleakly realistic play becomes a fantasy. Liliom is sent to a court in "the Beyond," where the Magistrate, seeing his lack of repentance, sentences him to sixteen years in the purifying fires (a kind of purgatory) with the understanding that once he has served his sentence he will have the opportunity to go back to earth and perform one good deed as a chance to change his eternal sentence from Hell to Heaven. Sixteen years later, he returns to earth with a chance to meet his daughter, Louise, and redeem himself, but he fails, slapping Louise's hand out of frustration when she refuses to take the star he has stolen from Heaven for her as a gift. The play ends with Louise asking her mother if it's possible to receive a slap that doesn't hurt at all, to which Julie answers yes as the curtain falls.

A play with that kind of plot does not immediately seem like prime material for a Broadway musical, and Rodgers and Hammerstein turned down the project not once but twice. Perhaps they ultimately changed their minds due to a sense of obligation to the Theatre Guild for producing *Oklahoma!*, or perhaps they were intrigued by the challenge of turning such an unlikely play—as far removed from *Oklahoma!* as could possibly be imagined—into a musical.[13] They could certainly not be accused of repeating themselves with a property like *Liliom*, but whatever the reason, once the Guild agreed to move the play's locale from Budapest to New England, the team signed on. It is interesting that two previous composers, Giacomo Puccini and Kurt Weill, had tried to obtain musical rights to the play but had been turned down by Molnár. Given the material of the play, a tragic opera by Puccini or a theatrical adaptation along the lines of Weill's *Threepenny Opera* seem far more appropriate than a sunny Broadway musical, set on the New England coast, with a "real nice Clambake" and a happy ending. But not only did Molnár grant the rights to Rodgers and Hammerstein over Puccini and Weill, he claimed to be delighted by their treatment, and in particular with their completely altered, happy ending. Given the play's unrelentingly harsh and bitter nature, Rodgers put the problem they faced in the simplest possible terms: "What kind of music to write and where should it go? How do you sing *Liliom*?"[14]

Surprisingly enough, the collaborators found the answer in Molnár's original words. As they searched through the text they "suddenly . . . got the notion for a soliloquy in which, at the end of the first act, the leading character would reveal his varied emotions about impending fatherhood. That broke the ice. Once we could visualize the man singing, we felt that all the other problems would fall into place."[15] One of the most striking things about *Carousel* is how remarkably faithful to the outline and text of Molnár's play it manages to be while somehow, through the addition of music, completely altering its tone. Perhaps the best example of this is the show's great love duet, "If I Loved You." Hammerstein found the key to writing the song in Molnár's original dialogue:

> **LILIOM:** But you wouldn't dare to marry any one like me, would you?
> **JULIE:** I know that . . . that . . . if I loved any one . . . it wouldn't make any
>   difference to me what he . . . even if I died for it.
> **LILIOM:** But you wouldn't marry a rough guy like me—that is . . . eh . . .
>   if you loved me—
> **JULIE:** Yes, I would . . . if I loved you, Mr. Liliom.[16]

It's the awkwardness and hesitancy with which the two characters express their feelings that Hammerstein captured in the duet (now with Liliom renamed Billy), drawing out the thrice-repeated phrase "if I loved you" as the song's title.

> *If I loved you,*
> *Time and again I would try to say*
> *All I'd want you to know.*
> *If I loved you,*
> *Words wouldn't come in an easy way—*
> *'Round in circles I'd go!*

These words mark the beginning of the song's refrain. The way this refrain is interwoven into a scene that blends dialogue, underscoring, and song illustrates perfectly what Hammerstein meant when he said that the songs in an integrated show had to supplement the dialogue and seem to be a continuation of that dialogue. Before the duet begins, a policeman who sees the couple together tries to warn Julie to stay away from a "low-down scalawag" like Billy. She refuses to listen to his scathing indictment of Billy's character, and once the policeman has finally left the couple alone, an entire scene unfolds that ultimately leads to "If I Loved You." It begins with Billy speaking, not singing. In an acknowledgment of the policeman's warning, he says to Julie, "Say, tell me somethin'—ain't you scared of me?" To connect this moment with what has come before, the underscoring to Billy's words is music we have already heard, sung earlier by Julie's friend Carrie ("You're a Queer One, Julie Jordan'). Billy then asks Julie her name, and when she replies, "Julie Jordan," the underscoring smoothly becomes Billy singing Carrie's earlier music. This is neither a traditional reprise nor even a traditional song, but simply three lines of singing that heighten the expression of the dialogue. It is, however, an extremely effective theatrical moment. Repeating Carrie's music and words shows us that it's not only Carrie who senses Julie's uniqueness (she truly is "a queer one") but Billy as well. The scene then flows seamlessly back and forth between spoken words with musical underscoring, fragments of sung dialogue, and passages in which three or four lines of dialogue are grouped together into almost-songs until finally Billy asks, "Suppose I was to say to you that I'd marry you?" Underneath this question and the remaining spoken dialogue, Rodgers has the orchestra develop the "You're a Queer One, Julie Jordan" melody, adding ever warmer and richer harmony to each version to underline the scene's shifting emotional situation. The orchestral underscoring shows us what Billy and Julie feel for each other before they themselves are aware of it, intensifying the sentiment of the scene so that the move into continuous singing feels completely natural.

Once the actual introduction to "If I Loved You" finally begins, it too is smoothly integrated into the overall scene. The awkwardness with which Liliom and Julie try to express their feelings in Molnár's original text is not only beautifully captured by Hammerstein's hesitant libretto but also by the way Rodgers shifts back and forth between dialogue, accompanied dialogue, sung dialogue, and almost-song. Both the lyrics and the music gradually approach full expression, finally flowering in the refrain, "If I loved you."

Right before the song's verse begins, Billy asks, "How do you know what you'd do if you loved me? Or how you'd feel—or anything?" To which Julie replies, "I know how I—how it'd be—if I loved you." As she begins to paint the scene for Billy, the vamp that starts in the orchestra is really spinning music—a musical depiction of Julie weaving at her loom in the mill. It's the same spinning music we heard earlier in the scene accompanying Carrie's affectionate chastising of Julie for her being distracted—for gazing "absent-minded at the roof." The return of this music again functions not like a typical reprise but rather to subtly advance the plot: we realize that the reason Julie's been so preoccupied at work is because she's in love with Billy.

The partnership between music and text in this introduction could not be more superb. The orchestral vamp introduces the section's basic accompaniment, and the first line of text, "When I worked in the mill, weavin' at the loom, I'd gaze absent-minded at the roof" clarifies the meaning of the orchestral accompaniment as spinning ("weavin'") music (Ex. 11.1). But as Julie describes the way her shuttle would get tangled in the threads, the spinning music changes in measure 17 and becomes dissonant,* perfectly depicting her annoyance at the tangled shuttle. Then, right on the titular words "If I loved you," the music modulates to a different key (from G

---

* For musicians, notice the clash between A#/B♭ in the left hand and A♮ in the right hand, as well as the tritone D#–A clash between left and right hands on the third note of the new pattern.

major to E♭ major). The words come from a different emotional place for Julie, made musical through a surprising shift in harmony. After a pause for spoken dialogue, a fragment of what would be called *arioso* in opera—something between recitative and aria—sets the line "But somehow I ken see, Jest exackly how I'd be." The tempo changes and the vocal line becomes more melodic as her voice, like her heart, begins to sing. One last key change (to D♭ major) takes her to yet another emotional plane, where she can finally express the feelings the scene has been building to. After all the hesitation, fragmented melodies, and key changes, there's a palpable sense of release

Example 11.1 "If I Loved You," opening

Example 11.1 "If I Loved You," opening (*continued*)

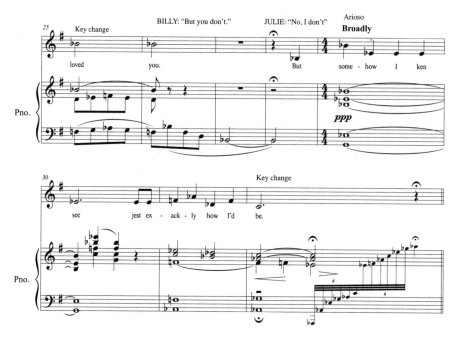

when the refrain begins and Julie truly starts to sing. Nothing has prepared us for the song's passionate lyricism, and Rodgers uses every musical means at his disposal to make the moment emotionally revealing.

Melody, harmony, and rhythm all combine to bring Julie's unique combination of fragility and desire to life. Though the opening phrase sounds effortlessly natural and spontaneous, Rodgers's technique is extremely subtle. Altering a single note, rhythm, or harmony destroys its magic. In Example 11.2A, I have slightly changed the rhythm, melody, and harmony of the song's second measure, placing two even half notes on "loved you," conventional A♭s in the melody, and a traditional, textbook chord underneath. In Example 11.2B, I changed the vocal line back to Rodgers's rhythm, which gives "loved you" a much greater urgency, but in Example 11.2C, Rodgers's complete version, the melody rises one step higher (to a B♭, not an A♭) with a poignant, heart-tugging, dissonant harmony underneath, beautifully capturing Julie's anything-but-ordinary feelings for Billy.

Example 11.2A "If I Loved You," Kapilow version

Example 11.2B "If I Loved You," Kapilow version

Example 11.2C "If I Loved You," Rodgers version

One of the key ways Rodgers depicts Julie's hesitancy and awkwardness is through rhythm. Keeping all of Rodgers's notes and chords but making the rhythm more regular (Ex. 11.3A) turns "Time and again I would try to say" into a matter-of-fact declaration, whereas Rodgers's sustained notes followed by quicker triplets perfectly conveys her sense of longing and hesitancy (Ex. 11.3B).

Rodgers's melodies are beautifully constructed. The vocal line for "All I'd want you" (E♭–G♭–C–C) copies the opening melody of "If I loved you"

Example 11.3A "If I Loved You," Kapilow version

Example 11.3B "If I Loved You," Rodgers version

(D♭–F–B♭–B♭) one step higher, and then adds two repeated, shy notes for the two extra words, "to know" (Ex. 11.4).*

"Know" marks the end of the song's opening 8-measure A section, and as in a standard Broadway song, this music repeats for "If I loved you / Words wouldn't come in an easy way." What follows is a superb example of the power of a single note. If Rodgers had copied the opening phrase exactly, the second phrase would have ended as in Example 11.5 (E♭–G♭–C–C–D♭–A♭).

Rodgers instead changes only one note in the vocal line—the last note—from an A♭ to a D♭, and that one higher note sweeps us into the B section, perfectly capturing the way Julie herself is swept up in the fantasy she is inhabiting (Ex. 11.6).

---

* Also notice that as the voice holds "know," the orchestra works with the melodic fragment (x) originally heard in the voice on "Time and again I would."

Example 11.4 "If I Loved You"

Example 11.5 "If I Loved You," Kapilow version

Example 11.6 "If I Loved You," B section

By this point in his career, Rodgers was an absolute master at creating subtle emotion and narrative sweep within the confines of a 32-bar Broadway song, and every compositional choice he makes is emotionally telling. As the "If I Loved You" fantasy becomes more real for Julie, the music of the B section becomes more openhearted and emotionally honest. The B section begins with a dark minor chord underneath "Longin' to tell you" followed by a wonderfully unexpected, strange harmony to depict the lyric "afraid and shy" (see Ex. 11.6).* Then comes the kind of subtle harmonic stroke of which Rodgers was such a master. The three notes of "Longin' to" (Db–C–Bb) return for "I let my," but this time, as the song builds to its climax, Rodgers writes a radiant major chord underneath (Ex. 11.7A), leading to the final 2 measures of the B section, where Rodgers raises the repeated C's of "-fraid and shy" to Eb's for "pass me by" (Ex. 11.7B).

The ending of the song is a wonderful example of the kind of lyrical, emotional power Rodgers and Hammerstein were able to achieve in this landmark musical. Following the standard AABA form of a 32-bar Broadway song, the A section returns one last time, and the music for "Soon you'd leave me, / Off you would go in the mist of day, / Never, never" is an exact copy of the opening. However, what happens next ultimately turns on the

Example 11.7A "If I Loved You"

Example 11.7B "If I Loved You"

---

* For musicians, a tritone substitution. Instead of the expected Ab7 chord, a D7 chord.

three different endings of this phrase, with each successive ending representing a further opening of Julie's emotional world (Ex. 11.8A–C).

At the end of the first phrase, the melody jumps down to an A♭ (C–D♭–A♭) as Julie retreats, still not ready to fully express how she feels. At the end of the second phrase, the melody stays up high on a D♭ (C–D♭–**D♭**), with a surging chord underneath* as the vision of what it would be like if she loved him begins to take over. The final version leaps up to an F (C–D♭–F)—the highest note of the song so far. Having fully embraced her vision of a life with Billy, she is now in a completely different emotional place, and the thought of him leaving "in the mist of day" without her telling him how much she loved him overwhelms her.

This moment is followed by pure theatrical magic. Formally speaking, at this point Rodgers has completed the 32 bars of a standard Broadway song, but what Julie has finally brought herself to tell Billy (and what he

Example 11.8A "If I Loved You"

Example 11.8B "If I Loved You"

Example 11.8C "If I Loved You"

---

* For musicians, an F7/♯5. A dominant-7th chord with an augmented fifth.

will bring himself to tell her when he sings the same music in his half of the duet) takes her beyond the standard form and vocal range of the piece up to this point. In 4 extra measures, she adds the words necessary to finish her thought (Ex. 11.9). She finally admits the truth that it has taken her the entire scene to get to—"How I loved you"—causing her to rise to the highest note of the entire piece (G♭). She has discovered a new voice within herself that neither she nor Billy knew existed. But then, with heartbreaking poignancy, realizing that the fantasy has perhaps gone too far and pushed her into dangerous territory, the music stops and brings her back to reality (and a comfortable vocal range) with the crucial, face-saving word: "if." All of this is of course hypothetical. None of it is true, it's only "*if* I loved you."

Perhaps the most significant change Hammerstein made in reworking Molnár's original play had to do with the ending of the musical. In the original, an unrepentant Liliom slaps Louise when she rejects his gift of a star stolen from the Beyond. Louise asks her mother if it's possible to receive a slap that doesn't hurt at all, and Julie answers yes as the curtain falls. Hammerstein keeps Molnár's moment, but adds a completely invented final scene in which Billy stays to witness Louise's graduation day, tells Julie that he loved her, and encourages Louise to believe in the graduation speaker's words: that no matter what difficulties life brings your way, if you have hope

Example 11.9 "If I Loved You," ending

in your heart, there will be a golden sky at the end of the storm (the classic Hammerstein hymn, "You'll Never Walk Alone.")

Nothing terrified Rodgers and Hammerstein more than the thought that Molnár would despise their inspirational, sentimental ending, yet by all accounts, he adored it.[17] The song's tone of moral uplift and almost hymnlike religiosity is pure Hammerstein, and one can only imagine what Hart would have done with the same material had he still been alive. But audiences loved it, as they loved Rodgers's other wartime show, to a degree that no one had ever loved musicals before.

Their previous collaboration—*Oklahoma!*—ran for an unprecedented 2,212 performances on Broadway while the road company toured for ten and a half years. It became the first American musical to tour the world and was the first show to record an original cast album*—a mark of how seriously the Broadway musical was now being taken, as well as a recognition that a Rodgers and Hammerstein show was a complete entity, not simply a collection of independent, stand-alone songs.

Carousel, though enormously successful as well (it ran for 890 performances with an original cast recording, tours, and multiple revivals), was never quite as big a hit as *Oklahoma!*, perhaps because its material was so much darker. It was Rodgers's favorite of all his musicals, and Stephen Sondheim, applauding the way Rodgers and Hammerstein were able to apply their innovations from *Oklahoma!* to a far more serious setting, captured its significance brilliantly, saying, "*Oklahoma!* is about a picnic, *Carousel* is about life and death."[18] It is a mark of how much the Broadway musical had grown as an art form, as well as of the serious moment in America's history in which it was written. It is almost impossible not to read the words of "You'll Never Walk Alone" as a message beyond Louise and Julie to America itself. As a plea to Americans during World War II to keep their chins

---

* The first complete, commercial, U.S. recording with the original cast, chorus, orchestra, orchestrations, and conductor.

up and not to be afraid of the dark at one of the darkest moments in the history of civilization. As encouragement that at the end of the storm (which actually was only weeks away from the show's opening on April 19, 1945, in the form of V-E Day) there would be some kind of "golden sky" and "sweet silver song" to look forward to.

Rodgers and Hammerstein would go on to apply the principles of *Oklahoma!* and *Carousel* in three more staggeringly successful musicals—*South Pacific* (1949), *The King and I* (1951), and *The Sound of Music* (1959)—however, their fundamental breakthrough as a collaborative team came in their two wartime musicals. Many commentators have remarked on the fact that the music Rodgers wrote with Hammerstein—particularly beginning with *Carousel*—was darker, more serious, more somber, and more mature than the music he wrote with Hart, that the zest and animation of his earlier partnership was missing in his later work. Rodgers himself acknowledged this when he said that out of all of his musicals he was proudest of *Carousel* because "he felt it cut deeper and moved people more." Often critics attribute the shift primarily to Hammerstein's influence, as he not only began the collaborative process with his lyrics, but as book writer as well, creating the basic narrative, moral, and emotional voice for all of their shows.

Yet it was not solely the new collaboration that changed Rodgers, it was larger historical and cultural forces at well. Forces that changed Hammerstein as much as they changed Rodgers. There are certain moments when an artist, artwork, and genre are completely in sync with the spirit of the times, and in *Oklahoma!* and *Carousel*, Rodgers and Hammerstein's development as artists coincided perfectly with the increasing sophistication and maturation of the Broadway musical as a genre, and a wartime nostalgia for a simpler, pastoral, American past. A past that may have existed only in the collaborators' imaginations, but one that resonated deeply with the entire country at a profoundly unsettling moment in America's history. In the face of unprecedented death and destruction overseas, mothers who might never see their sons return home might find solace in *Liliom*'s "Beyond" after death. In contrast to a world gone mad, Rodgers and Hammerstein offered a world where right and wrong were clearly defined, where traditional American values still held sway. Their musical morality plays were serious and dealt with real social problems in a way that was new for Broadway, yet they still managed to move and entertain audiences. All while creating a template that would inspire future theater composers for years to come.

In a gesture of humility, Rodgers would nearly always deflect praise, saying his phenomenal success was purely a matter of luck. And in a way he was right. He was lucky he had found Hammerstein at the precise moment when his partnership with Hart had ended. Lucky that their two sensibilities played off each other so well, and that their working styles were so compatible. Lucky that their partnership began at a unique moment in American history when the country's needs perfectly matched the projects they chose to work on. Lucky that the Broadway musical had progressed to a stage where their new kind of work had become possible. As Seneca put it, "Luck is what happens when preparation meets opportunity," and Rodgers and Hammerstein had been preparing for this opportunity since they were teenagers. Songs may make history, and history may make songs, but in the end, Rodgers and Hammerstein made their own luck.

12

America Gets a Classical Voice

Leonard Bernstein's "I Can Cook Too"

Broadway's great songwriters each experienced World War II differently. Richard Rodgers, due to a crackdown, was unable to get a civilian commission in spite of passing the U.S. Army Air Forces physical exam,[1] but he supported the war effort through work for the Red Cross, the Writers' War Board, and the USO. Irving Berlin spent nearly every waking moment writing and then touring his all-soldier revue, *This Is the Army.* Leonard Bernstein, because of asthma he'd had since childhood, was physically unfit to be drafted,[*] and while nearly everyone his age was fighting overseas, he burst onto the music scene as a composer and a conductor at the age of twenty-five.[†]

---

[*] His *On the Town* collaborators Jerome Robbins and Adolph Green were also exempted from military service, Robbins because of his gay sexual orientation and Green for unspecified reasons. See Carol J. Oja's *Bernstein Meets Broadway: Collaborative Art in a Time of War* (Oxford University Press, 2014), 5.

[†] The basic facts of Bernstein's biography in this chapter are drawn from Humphrey Burton's *Leonard Bernstein* (Doubleday, 1994).

At the beginning of 1943 he was a relatively unknown assistant conductor with the New York Philharmonic.* On November 14 he made his now-legendary last-minute debut at Carnegie Hall substituting for the ailing Bruno Walter. Though this performance made him an overnight sensation as a conductor, the next year, 1944 saw him make an equally stunning debut as a composer with three major premieres—his First Symphony, *Jeremiah*, in January; the ballet *Fancy Free* in April; and his first musical, *On the Town*, in December. The critical response to all three premieres was as wildly enthusiastic as the response to his conducting debut with the Philharmonic. The Associated Press reviewer Jack O'Brien described the opening night of *On the Town* as one of the rare occasions when "a reviewer gets an opportunity to heave his hat into the stratosphere, send up rockets and in general start the sort of journalistic drooling over a musical comedy that puts an end to all adequate usage of superlatives."[2] The show was not only a critical success but a commercial one, grossing over $2 million on an initial production cost of only $150,000 during a run of 436 performances. Like the success of Rodgers and Hammerstein's two wartime musicals, *Oklahoma!* and *Carousel*, the overwhelming impact Bernstein made as a composer and a conductor in 1944 was intimately connected to the unique moment it occurred.

When America emerged from its isolation and stepped onto the world stage, it began searching for a voice that would reflect its way of life. During the 1920s and '30s, the Broadway musical freed itself from the influence of European operetta by focusing on subject matter and creating a style of speech that felt distinctly American, and with the help of Hollywood, film musicals exported that speech to the world at large. Ballet and classical music, however, remained largely European, and an American voice was virtually nonexistent in the field of symphonic conducting. Every major

*To be precise, in 1928 the New York Symphony and the New York Philharmonic merged to become the Philharmonic-Symphony Society of New York, conventionally referred to as the New York Philharmonic.

American orchestra was led by a European—a Toscanini or a Stokowski—and it seemed inconceivable that an American conductor would ever be seriously considered for such a post. When Bernstein made his debut with the Philharmonic, the frenzy surrounding the event did not arise simply because a young conductor had appeared out of nowhere and performed superbly, but because that conductor was *American*. Bernstein's performance did far more than introduce a star; it heralded the possibility of a cultural sea change for classical music in America—the possibility that an American might someday lead an American orchestra, breaking years of European hegemony and bringing an American voice to the podium.

That the same young American who had stunned the music world as a conductor in November 1943 would make an equally startling debut as a serious classical composer two months later only added to the frenzy. It was the middle of World War II, America was in desperate need of optimistic hero stories, and Bernstein's triumphs were just what the country needed. The fact that he was Jewish at the same moment Hitler was attempting to complete his "final solution" gave Bernstein's meteoric rise an even deeper resonance. If Kern and Berlin represented the first generation of Jewish American theater composers, and Rodgers and Arlen led a second generation, then Bernstein ushered in a third, this time with a completely different relationship to Judaism. For the Jewish songwriters of Berlin's and Rodgers's generations, assimilation was almost always the goal. They wanted to fit in, and not only was their music conspicuously absent of Jewish influence, their public behavior rarely acknowledged their heritage in any significant way.

Bernstein, however, was profoundly Jewish in both his life and music. To begin with, he kept his name, even after his mentor Serge Koussevitzky suggested he change it to Leonard S. Burns. Humphrey Burton's biography points out that Bernstein is actually the name of several towns and villages in Germany and Austria, and in these towns, the pronunciation is Bern-STINE. Leonard's parents, however, came from Jewish ghettos in northwestern Ukraine, where the pronunciation is Bern-STEEN,[3] but his father insisted on pronouncing the name in the mid-European style, the way the earlier immigrants did—Bern-STINE—and the children followed suit.

Retaining a Jewish name, however, was only the surface manifestation of Bernstein's deep connection to Judaism. He actually spoke Hebrew and briefly considered a career as a rabbi. He was also a major champion of the State of Israel and the Israel Philharmonic from its very inception, and he had significant connections with Brandeis University in the late 1940s and early '50s. And perhaps most significantly, he chose to introduce himself to the world as a composer with a Jewish symphony, *Jeremiah*—a bold statement at a time when Judaism was fighting the gravest threat in its history. The core of the work is its final section. After two instrumental movements, the third adds a mezzo-soprano singing a text from the book of Lamentations in which the Old Testament prophet Jeremiah mourns the way Jerusalem has been "ruined, pillaged, and dishonored after his desperate efforts to save it." Given what was happening in Europe at the time, the meaning of the symphony's final plea—"Wherefore dost Thou forget us forever, And forsake us so long time? Turn thou us unto Thee, O Lord" (Lamentations 5:20–21)—could not have been clearer, more poignant, or more conspicuously Jewish.

Jeremiah was only the first of many works he would compose that dealt with Jewish texts and topics. The "Bernstein" portion of his persona was that of an acknowledged Jew who wrote serious classical symphonies and conducted the core works of the European symphonic tradition, but he was also "Lenny" in a world of "maestros." A handsome, informal, chain-smoking American who could sit at the piano at parties and play jazz for hours, write a hit Broadway show and a ballet. To use the slang phrasing of *On the Town*, as a musician, Bernstein could "cook too."

Now, more than a quarter-century after his death, it is possible that we take Bernstein's unprecedented versatility and unabashed eclecticism for granted. Has there ever been another composer who wrote a serious, award-winning, classical symphony,* then three months later an adrenaline-filled, jazz-influenced ballet that received twenty-four curtain calls at its premiere, followed by a hit Broadway show? All within a single year? While at the same time becoming the most sought-after young conductor in America? By the age of twenty-six? One of the things that made Bernstein so unique was his remarkable ability to speak so many different musical languages with equal facility and first-order immediacy. He seemed as comfortable playing a boogie-woogie bass line at the piano as he did conducting a Mahler symphony, and there was not the slightest trace of condescension or slumming in any of his forays into popular music. Boundaries between genres of music seemed to dissolve in Bernstein's hands, and Duke Ellington's famous comment, "There are simply two kinds of music, good music and the other kind," [4] could easily have been uttered by Bernstein himself.

One of the keys to Bernstein's success in both *Fancy Free* and *On the Town* was finding collaborative partners with similarly eclectic sensibilities, and none of these partners was more important to Bernstein than Jerome Robbins, the choreographer for both works. The profound connection between Robbins and Bernstein was both personal and aesthetic. Not only were they identical in age (both were born in 1918) and the sons of immigrant Jewish fathers who initially disapproved of their career choices, but they both had an innate, genre-crossing sense that allowed them to draw fluidly from both highbrow and lowbrow culture in their work and feel as comfortable in the Broadway world as in the concert hall. And neither was straight.

In her extensively researched book *Bernstein Meets Broadway: Collaborative Art in a Time of War*, Carol Oja makes this a core premise of her understanding of both *Fancy Free* and *On the Town*—that both Robbins

---

* *Jeremiah* won the New York Music Critics Circle award in 1944 as the outstanding new classical work of the season.

and Bernstein were actively bisexual during this period. She proposes a bisexual reading of the ballet, with an overtly heterosexual main plot focusing on the sailors' attempts to win over the female dancers, as well as a homosexual subplot lurking just below the surface of the sailors' intense camaraderie. To make her case, Oja begins with a discussion of painter Paul Cadmus's *The Fleet's In!* which served as Robbins's inspiration for the ballet. The painting was at the center of a notorious scandal when it was first shown in 1934, and it became the focus of a volatile debate over censorship when it was withdrawn because of its extremely sexual nature. According to Lincoln Kirstein, director of the New York City Ballet and president of the School of American Ballet, the painting depicted a "strip of public land bordering the broad Hudson, [which] was then a fast and happy hunting ground for sailors on summer liberty with their casual pickups, male or female."[5] *The Fleet's In!* not only portrays flirtation between sailors and women, but also less overt, sexualized pairings between the sailors themselves. It is the painting's homosexual subtext that Oja feels is the key to the "double-gendered" message of the ballet.

Like Bernstein, Robbins had publicly visible relationships with women while pursuing intense affairs with men that he tried to keep secret. Oja reports that dancers from the original *Fancy Free* production believed that Robbins and Bernstein themselves had an affair while working on the score, but whatever happened between them, there can be no doubt that the focus of the ballet is as much on the relationship of the sailors to each other as it is on the sailors' relationship to the women they are trying to impress. In fact, one of the big differences between *On the Town* and *Fancy Free* is a marked shift in precisely this focus, as the women take center stage in the show as vivid, vibrant characters far more than they do in the ballet.

Beyond their shared Jewish heritage, New York background, and bisexual orientation, what was most important about the connection between Bernstein and Robbins was their shared eclectic, genre-crossing artistic sensibility. Robbins didn't begin studying dance until high school, and his training with Alys Bentley in modern dance was unusual in that she encouraged her students to improvise their own steps. Looking back, Robbins said, "What [she] gave me immediately was the absolute freedom to make up my own dances without inhibition or doubts," a freedom he would bring not only to the dances he created but to his entire career as well. After dropping out of New York University's chemistry program for financial reasons, he began studying ballet. Desperate for work during the Depression, he got an apprenticeship with Senya Gluck-Sandor's company while also studying Spanish and Asian dance. His new mentor's eclecticism was a perfect match for Robbins, as Gluck-Sandor had been ballet-trained, was an ardent devotee of modern dance, and also worked on Broadway, in burlesque, and in vaudeville.* Following Gluck-Sandor's approach, Robbins began his career in the chorus of Broadway shows like *Great Lady* in 1938 (one of several unsuccessful musicals Frederick Loewe wrote before teaming up with Alan Jay Lerner) and *Stars in Your Eyes* in 1939, while dancing and choreographing revues at Camp Tamiment, a progressive resort in the Poconos during the summers. The next year Robbins joined Ballet Theatre, a company formed as part of an attempt to find an American voice for ballet. By 1941 he was already starring in Agnes de Mille's production of *Three Virgins and a Devil*, and in 1942 he experienced perhaps his greatest triumph as a classical dancer in the role of Petrushka, which he was taught by its original choreographer, Michel Fokine. Desperate to find an outlet for his own choreography, he convinced Ballet Theatre to agree to a short ballet with a small cast. After considering several composers, Robbins finally found his ideal collaborator in Bernstein. Bernstein had never composed a ballet, Robbins had never choreographed one, and their budget was almost nonexistent, but they were united in what they wanted to achieve.

One thing that was clear to both Bernstein and Robbins was that though they were interested, like Aaron Copland and Agnes de Mille, in finding an American voice for ballet, they did not want to find that voice in

---

* The basic biographical information on Robbins is drawn from Amanda Vaill's 2001 article on Robbins in *The Scribner Encyclopedia of American Lives.*

the past—in a nostalgic retreat to the Wild West world of *Billy the Kid* and *Rodeo*—but in the present: in contemporary life as it was being lived every day on the streets of wartime New York City. *Fancy Free* was going to take place in the here and now in its music, choreography, sets, costumes, and story, and that aesthetic would be clear to the audience from the moment the ballet began. When the curtain rose at the majestic Metropolitan Opera House on April 18, 1944, the audience was shocked to see a bar that they could easily have gone to after the performance, and what they heard was even more surprising. Not a pretty orchestral overture, or even an orchestra at all. Not the serious, classical music of *Jeremiah*, but a jukebox playing the blues. A slow, down-home blues, "Big Stuff," that Bernstein had written (both music and lyrics) with Billie Holiday in mind.* In one fell swoop, Bernstein had accomplished what Gershwin had been unable to achieve ten years earlier with *Porgy and Bess*: he had brought a white man's version of African American music to the stage of the Metropolitan Opera House.

Even the idea of having the song play on a jukebox was an attempt to make the scene contemporary. Jukeboxes had become incredibly popular during the swing craze of the Depression. Dancing to a jukebox was inexpensive and could happen anywhere—in bars, restaurants, brothels, saloons, and social halls. By the middle of the 1940s when *Fancy Free* premiered, jukeboxes were an $80 million a year industry. Bernstein's slow blues playing while the bartender lazily beat time to the music instantly transformed the Metropolitan Opera House stage from a platform built for Puccini and Wagner operas into a Broadway bar with an atmosphere that Oja rightly compares to Edward Hopper's *Nighthawks* painting. Perhaps most important, it stated from the outset the crossover aesthetic that would fuel the entire ballet and, for that matter, Bernstein's entire career. Anything—choreographically or musically—would be fair game.

---

* Unfortunately, Holiday was too expensive to hire for such a shoestring production, but she did ultimately record the song in 1946. In a touching (and economical) decision, Bernstein had his sister Shirley record the song, and her recording was the one heard the night of the premiere.

One thing that is important to understand about the crossover nature of both the music and the choreography in *Fancy Free* is that neither Robbins nor Bernstein presented the popular elements in the piece in an unfiltered way. Like Gershwin choosing not to use actual Negro spirituals in *Porgy and Bess*, Bernstein and Robbins drew inspiration from popular sources but ultimately translated them through their own sophisticated musical and choreographic vocabularies. Their work was a take on popular sources, not the popular sources themselves. Though we only get to hear about thirty seconds of "Big Stuff" at the opening of *Fancy Free* before the sharp, rat-tat-tat rim shots of the snare drum interrupt the jukebox and the piece explodes into action; the song in its entirety is a sophisticated take on the blues.* It uses the same flattened notes, blues notes, grace notes, and lyrics, but it gradually incorporates advanced harmonies and modulations—clearly the work of a classical composer. Throughout the ballet, Bernstein brings a thoroughly developed, classical compositional technique to his popular, jazzy musical material.

Bernstein's score for *Fancy Free* is in many ways a collage. At different moments it touches on nearly every kind of popular music that existed at the time. It jumps back and forth between the blues, big-band jazz, solo jazz piano, cartoon music from animated films, and even Cuban-influenced rhumba rhythms, as well as classical music that could have come straight out of a Copland or Stravinsky ballet. Bernstein's ears were open to everything. He was able to reproduce any style he heard, and he embraced all of them with equal affection. It was almost impossible to know what kind of music or what instrumental sound would come next. Oja rightly compares the effect to someone continuously changing the dial on a radio, yet somehow the strength of Bernstein's personality allowed him to create a unified sound world for the ballet out of wildly disparate musical sources.

---

* The score actually indicates that the orchestra can interrupt the recording of "Big Stuff" at any point. How much of the song is heard is up to the conductor and choreographer, with thirty or forty seconds usually the duration.

Robbins found inspiration everywhere as well, often from popular sources that were as foreign to the stage of the Metropolitan Opera House as Bernstein's musical themes. The scenario for the ballet states that "the girls should wear actual street dresses," and the set "should represent a city street."[6] According to members of the company, Robbins would watch people dance at parties and create steps out of their movements. The actual social dances that were popular at the time—like the Lindy Hop, the Boogie-Woogie, and the Shorty George—became part of the ballet's core vocabulary, as did movements drawn from gymnastics, tap dance, and even cartoons. Robbins, like Bernstein, was ecumenical in spirit and responded viscerally to all contemporary source material, highbrow or lowbrow. The sailor's three solos—the Waltz Variation, the Danzon Variation, and the Galop Variation—are filled with sophisticated, virtuosic choreography. There's a witty pantomime of a rhumba with an imaginary partner and acrobatic splits out of a Nicholas Brothers tap-dance routine, while the mock battle between the sailors comes straight out of a slapstick vaudeville routine. Robbins's take on his source material allowed the audience to feel like the ballet had brought the world outside on 39th Street into the opera house and transformed it into something worthy of its new home. John Martin of the *New York Times* captured the ballet's unique blend of the serious and the popular when he wrote, "*Fancy Free* is utterly colloquial, but it would be a serious mistake to consider it for that reason as merely vaudeville highjinks." Though the piece might have employed what he called "jazz idioms" and the popular theater's sense of timing, it was "nevertheless an artistic entity and a modern ballet in the best sense of the phrase."[7]

The unique mixture of the serious and the popular in *Fancy Free* is a perfect metaphor for Bernstein's artistic ambitions throughout his *annus mirabilis,* and in many ways, throughout his entire artistic career. Two months after entering America's consciousness as a superstar conductor, the public was forced to change its perception of Bernstein when he was suddenly thrust into the spotlight as the composer of a classical, Jewish symphony. Though unusually young for two such high-profile debuts, there was at least a precedent in the classical music world for gifted composer-conductors. (The composer Gustav Mahler, for example, had been the music director at the New York Philharmonic from 1909 to 1911.) But there was no precedent for a serious composer-conductor to leave the classical world behind and create an eclectic, genre-crossing, jazz-influenced work like *Fancy Free*. Listening to the anguished, dissonant, Shostakovich-like string writing that opens *Jeremiah* next to the blues of "Big Stuff" that opened *Fancy Free* less than three months later, it is almost inconceivable that the two works could have been written by the same person. Though composers today tend to be less bound by musical genres, I can think of no contemporary composer or composer-conductor whose catalogue includes music as diverse and successful as *Jeremiah* and *Fancy Free*, not to mention works this diverse and successful written only months apart. And this was only the beginning.

Fancy Free, though striking in its eclectic use of musical genres and shocking as a follow-up to *Jeremiah,* at least retained some vestigial ties to the classical world. It was written for a classical ballet company, and its premiere took place at the Metropolitan Opera House—a bastion of classical music. Only eight months later, however, Bernstein left the classical world behind completely, as he boldly moved from the Metropolitan Opera to the Adelphi Theatre for his first Broadway musical, *On the Town*.

Today, Bernstein's straddling serious and popular music worlds is looked upon with much greater acceptance than it was during his lifetime. After attending the premiere of *On the Town* in Boston, Bernstein's mentor and the conductor of the Boston Symphony, Serge Koussevitzky, gave Bernstein a three-hour lecture, telling him he was wasting his time and talents on something as trivial and insignificant as a Broadway show, pleading with

him to focus on conducting instead. But Bernstein adored the collaboration involved in creating a Broadway musical, and *On the Town* not only
allowed Bernstein to continue working with his *Fancy Free* partners—
Jerome Robbins and the set designer Oliver Smith—but also to add two key
personalities to his creative team as well: Adolph Green and Betty Comden.

Bernstein had actually met Green, who was four years his senior, at
Camp Onota in the Berkshire Mountains during the summer of 1937. Like
Bernstein, Green was the son of Jewish immigrant parents, though his family
was not nearly as well off as Bernstein's.* The two immediately bonded over
Green's encyclopedic knowledge of films and classical music. Betty Comden
was also the child of first-generation, immigrant Jews, but unlike Bernstein,
she chose to change her name from Basya Cohen first to Betty Cohen, then
Betty Comden. She met Green at NYU, reconnected after college when they
were both looking for work, and along with Judy Tuvim (later Judy Holli-
day), John Frank, and Al Hammer formed a sketch-comedy group called the
Revuers in 1938. With the Village Vanguard venue as their base, the group
created satirical shows that the *New York Times* called the "wittiest sketches
in town."[8] Their popularity waxed and waned during the late 1930s, with
their sophisticated wit generating a group of intensely loyal fans, but they
never quite caught on with the general public enough to create secure, steady
employment, and the group finally disbanded in 1944. During the summer
of 1939, Bernstein, just graduated from Harvard and without steady work
himself, shared an apartment with Green and occasionally played piano for
the Revuers' sketches. Oja delves into the history and scripts of the Revuers,†
and it is clear from the excerpts she presents that their highbrow/lowbrow,
fast-paced, snappy dialogue filled with contemporary references became a
key element in the book and lyrics they wrote for *On the Town*. It is only

---

* Bernstein's father's firm—the Samuel Bernstein Hair Company—was the largest supplier of beauty parlor
goods in New England.

† See Chapter 2 of her book for an extensive discussion of the Revuers' material.

a small step from a Revuers sketch, with characters named Papa Rubato (a singing teacher) and Larynx Tonsil (his pupil), to *On the Town*, with characters named Brunhilde Esterhazy (mixing Wagner's Brunhilde and Haydn's patron Esterhazy), Claire de Loone (via Debussy), and John (Chip) Offenblock (a combination of Jacques Offenbach—highbrow—and "chip off the old block"—lowbrow).

When the *On the Town* creative team first assembled in June 1944, they discussed what their working process would look like and what kind of piece they ultimately wanted to produce. The enormous success of *Oklahoma!* the previous year hovers everywhere over the credo that Comden supposedly wrote on her legal pad. The show's approach centered on making sure "that the action should be integrated; that music and dance and book must be all of one piece and never stop telling the story, each number being part of the action; that nothing should be permitted that was 'cheap or crummy.'"[9]

The basic plot of *On the Town* is an expansion of *Fancy Free*, and the differences between the two are as interesting as their similarities.* Both tell the story of three sailors on a twenty-four-hour shore leave in New York City looking for female companionship. In the ballet, the sailors are the principal focus of the work both as individuals and in their relationship to each other. Though the women's roles are wonderful, they are clearly subordinate. In *On the Town,* however, this dynamic is reversed, and the women take center stage. The same three sailors, now given names—Chip, Gabey, and Ozzie (Adolph Green in the original production)—initially get sidetracked in their desire to meet girls when Gabey sees a poster of Miss Turnstiles on the subway. He becomes obsessed with the model Ivy Smith

---

* Robbins and Bernstein were adamant about the fact that, though the plots of the two shows were similar, not a single dance step or note of music from *Fancy Free* was used in *On the Town*. Although many critics have said that *On the Town* grew out of a suggestion from Oliver Smith, the set designer, to turn *Fancy Free* into a musical, Oja quotes conversations with Adolph Green and Betty Comden that explicitly deny this (p. 90 and endnote 27), with both of them claiming that many other ideas were discussed before they arrived at the notion of expanding the ballet's story of three sailors on a twenty-four-hour leave in New York City into a show.

and wants to meet her. (As part of the creative team's desire to make the show seem contemporary and realistic, the Miss Turnstiles campaign is a take on the popular "Miss Subways" beauty pageant that began in New York in 1941.) Chip and Ozzie offer to help Gabey track Ivy down, and in the course of the day, they meet up and pair off with Claire de Loone, a highbrow anthropologist (Betty Comden in the original production), and Brunhilde Esterhazy (Hildy), a sex-crazed taxi driver. They end up at several classic New York City locations, ranging from the highbrow— Carnegie Hall and the Museum of Natural History—to the lowbrow— Coney Island and a series of hot nightclubs like the Congacabana, modeled on actual clubs popular at the time. The highbrow girl of Gabey's dreams, Miss Turnstiles, turns out to be a lowbrow cooch dancer* in Coney Island trying to finance her singing lessons with Miss Dilly, an incompetent, alcoholic voice instructor. Though the locations, references, and look of the show are all meant to reflect up-to-date wartime New York City, the piece actually has the feel of a densely plotted, zany, 1930s screwball comedy infused with the fast-paced repartee, wit, and language of a Comden and Green Revuers sketch.

The escapist nature of many Depression-era screwball comedies and musicals arose from a desire to turn away from the harsh economic realities of life outside the theater. By 1944, changes in the outside world led to new kinds of anxieties, but the desire for escape was no less real. Soldiers were concerned less about money and more about surviving the most destructive war in human history, while Americans at home worried not only about their sons, brothers, and fathers fighting overseas but also about the survival of the American way of life. *On the Town*'s plot, framed by three sailor's twenty-four-hour leave, indirectly acknowledged the surface of this wartime reality, but its zany antics offered a welcome relief from that reality,

---

* A cooch dance was a suggestive, sinuous, quasi-oriental kind of dance that was often performed at carnivals or fairs. A cleaner predecessor of today's pole dancing.

allowing audiences to laugh at what was too terrible to contemplate in any other way.

Screwball comedies of the 1930s were filled with battles of the sexes, strong-willed women pitted against male characters whose masculinity is threatened (*Bringing Up Baby*, for example). Perhaps because of Betty Comden's involvement as a key member of the creative team, Ivy, Hildy, and Claire (the role Comden played in the Broadway production) are all strong characters, initiators of the action in ways that would have been unthinkable in *Fancy Free*. In many ways, the strength of the female leads in *On the Town* is a faithful reflection of the changes in the status of women brought about by World War II. With so many men away fighting overseas, women entered the workforce in unprecedented numbers, and this experience often led them to a new, stronger sense of self and a bolder belief in what they could accomplish. They could be riveters like Rosie, anthropologists like Claire, or taxi drivers like Hildy. (In fact, there were a considerable number of women cabdrivers in New York City during the war.) And in ways that would have been unthinkable even ten years earlier, they could initiate sex in the most blatantly aggressive manner possible—as long it was funny.

When we first meet Hildy—described in the script as a young, tough girl—she has fallen asleep in her taxi. In four quick sentences her boss, S. Uperman* (a silly, Revuers-style name), fires her for sleeping on the job and tells her that she has an hour to return her cab to the garage. She takes the news in stride and decides to make her one last fare a good one. She rejects the first potential passenger as "too small" (with the slightest hint of sexual innuendo), the second as "too big" (the innuendo becomes a little clearer), and when a girl tries to flag her down, Hildy shouts, "AND NO GIRLS!!"

---

* In yet another example of the creators' desire to make the show seem contemporary, the first appearance of Superman in DC Comics was in June 1938, and his popularity soared during the 1940s.

(The capital letters and exclamation points are in the script.) At just that moment she notices Chip poring over his guidebook, and her face lights up. Within seconds, she pulls him into the front seat of her cab, tells him to kiss her, and when he balks, she grabs him and initiates the kiss herself. Barely pausing for breath, she brazenly says, "Well let's go to my place." In spite of Chip's protestations, this leads to their first comic duet, "Come Up to My Place."

Sixteen years earlier, the censors rejected Cole Porter's song title "Let's Do It" as too risqué without the addition of the parenthetical "(Let's Fall in Love)." Yet here, in *On the Town*, mere moments after meeting Chip, Hildy is kissing him and telling him to come up to her place because she's young, free, and "highly attainable." Instead of the men on the prowl in *Fancy Free*, it is now the independent, strong-willed women who are prowling, and in Hildy's great, show-stopping number, "I Can Cook Too," the sexual explicitness reaches a level that might even have shocked Porter himself.

> Hildy has just dragged Chip up to her apartment and finally gotten rid of her roommate, Lucy Schmeeler, when she asks Chip, "Well, now what?"
>
> CHIP: We eat, huh?
>
> HILDY: Sure, we can do that first.
>
> CHIP: You claim you can cook.
>
> HILDY: That's often been considered one of my strongest points.
>
> CHIP: Yeah? What's the specialty of the house?
>
> HILDY: Me!!*

As she throws chicken into the frying pan and the music begins—the tempo marking, "Hot and Fast," is a perfect match for Hildy's personality—Hildy

---

* All lyrics are from the published script available in The New York Musicals of Comden & Green (Applause Books, 1997).

sings blatantly suggestive, double entendre lyrics. Somehow Bernstein, who had begun the year premiering his complex, classical setting of a biblical text, was finishing the year with a boogie-woogie setting of his own raunchy lyrics:

Oh, I can cook, too, on top of the rest,
My seafood's the best in the town.
And I can cook, too,
My fish can't be beat,
My sugar's the sweetest aroun'.

Bernstein, like Robbins, was completely open to the world around him and committed to bringing all that was vital and alive into the world of the show. As an award-winning symphonic composer, Bernstein brought a classical training and technique to the Broadway musical that went far beyond any of his contemporaries, but it is important to realize that Bernstein got as much as he gave. The world of the Broadway musical influenced and shaped Bernstein's music as much as he influenced and shaped the world of the Broadway musical. *On the Town* gave Bernstein the chance to explore the language and forms of the popular music that he loved. It gave him the chance to step outside the highbrow, tuxedo-and-tails world of classical music—and swing.

Like ragtime, blues, swing, and other early twentieth-century forms and styles of African American music, identifying the origins of boogie-woogie and distinguishing its lineage from the overlapping ancestries of other forms of jazz is almost impossible. An outgrowth of the blues, some writers trace the earliest forms of boogie-woogie to Texas in the 1870s, where the style was called "fast Western" to differentiate it from the slow blues of New Orleans. Legend has it that early boogie-woogie was played in logging camps by pianists who would travel from town to town by train, and that its distinctive left-hand rhythm grew out of the sound of the train wheels on the track. Other writers derive the term and the form from the word "boogie," which was another name for a house rent party.[10] House rent parties took place in poor, urban, black neighborhoods as a way of helping lower-class people pay their rent. For a small fee, neighbors would get together at a party to help a tenant pay his rent with the understanding that the party would ultimately be reciprocated. The two- or four-bit fee would get you a BYOB evening of boogie-woogie piano music played by a local celebrity, as well as some down-home southern cooking and neighborly company. Though boogie-woogie eventually became a small-group and big-band form, at heart it was piano-based, made famous by black pianists of the 1920s and '30s like Albert Ammons, Cripple Clarence Lofton, and Sugar Chile Robinson. Its distinctive 8-to-the-bar left-hand pattern can be seen as early as 1915 in the second chorus of Artie Matthews's "Weary Blues" and throughout Jimmy Blythe's "Chicago Stomp" in 1924, but Pine Top Smith's "Pinetop's Boogie Woogie" in 1928 was the first real, commercial, recorded boogie-woogie hit.

The 1930s and '40s were the heyday of boogie-woogie as both a dance and a style of music, and by the time of *On the Town* nearly every big band had one or two boogie-woogie numbers in their repertoire. Though the form may have grown up as the direct musical expression of poor black pianists, as was so often the case, it was white musicians that made the music commercially successful, often in significantly watered-down versions. The Andrews Sisters' "Boogie Woogie Bugle Boy" became enormously popular throughout World War II. Tommy Dorsey's band recorded an updated "Pinetop's Boogie Woogie," and in 1943, a year before *On the Town*, it became one of the biggest hits of the decade. Like so many before him, Dorsey took an indigenous black musical form, removed it from its original social and musical context, and made it commercially acceptable for mainstream America, laying the groundwork for Bernstein to continue the process in his own unique way in "I Can Cook Too."

Though Bernstein was classically trained, he also brought jazz credentials to his Broadway scores. During the winter of 1942–43, during what Bernstein would later call his bleak "Valley Forge" period, he was hired by the publisher Harms-Witmark to transcribe the solos of famous jazz musicians. (Mixed in with his sketches for *Fancy Free* is a page of music titled "7 Solos by Coleman Hawkins/Leonard Bernstein.")[11] He also worked as a staff arranger for the princely fee of $25 dollars a week. Though the job may not have been rewarding financially, it gave him invaluable experience and intimate knowledge of the popular music of the day.* In the evenings, he spent a good deal of time listening to great jazz pianists at nightclubs like the Café Society, where he was able to get a kind of postgraduate degree in boogie-woogie style from pianists like Pete Johnson and Albert Ammons. Bernstein had a phenomenal ear, tremendous keyboard facility, and a firsthand, insider's knowledge of jazz, and he put all of this together in "I Can Cook Too."

The song starts "hot and fast" with a thrilling, brassy 4-bar introduction (Ex. 12.1). One of the fascinating things about Bernstein's approach to the popular forms he works with in *On the Town* is the way he manages to take what he needs from his source material while using it for his own purposes. Many boogie-woogie pieces, to create contrast, begin with some kind of short introduction before the boogie-woogie bass line begins. "Pinetop's Boogie Woogie," for example, opens with slow tremolo chords that make the boogie-woogie rhythm that follows sound propulsive, but the brassy trade-offs of Bernstein's introduction bring Hildy's forceful character to life from the very first measure.

Boogie-woogie is an outgrowth of the blues, and nearly all boogie-woogie pieces follow the traditional 12-bar blues form we saw with Kern's

---

* Not wanting to be known for his work at Harms-Witmark, he published it under the name of Lenny Amber. According to Burton, the German noun *Bernstein* means "amber," which is a kind of resin that supposedly has magical properties.

Example 12.1 "I Can Cook Too," opening

Example 12.2 "I Can Cook Too," boogie-woogie bass line

"Can't Help Lovin' Dat Man." "I Can Cook Too," however, is a unique mixture of a Broadway song form and a boogie-woogie blues that fits no traditional mold. As you can see in Example 12.2, the piece has a classic, boogie-woogie bass line that uses the same three basic chords you would find in a 12-bar blues (G, C, D, or I, IV, V).* However, Bernstein shortens the pattern to 8 measures to fit the style of a traditional Broadway chorus, and the pauses in the boogie-woogie bass pattern in the fourth and eighth measures divide the phrase neatly in half—the kind of symmetrical division common to Broadway choruses but not the blues.

Above the bass line, the right hand adds syncopated chords straight out of a big-band arrangement, and big-band swing rhythm is at the heart of what makes this music "cook." If we remove the swing rhythm (see Ex. 12.3) and play the straight eighth notes that Bernstein would have found at the Philharmonic, the music falls flat.†

---

* For musicians, notice the up-to-date, idiomatic, harmonic additions to the basic blues chord here with added sixths added to the G chord, ninths and sixths added to the C chord, and ♯fifths added to the D chord.

† Though today, symphony orchestra musicians have gotten used to seeing straight notation and playing swing eighth notes, for many years it was extremely difficult for classical musicians to play these rhythms naturally. In fact, it was crossover musicians like Bernstein who brought this kind of music into the world of the symphony orchestra and eventually got those musicians comfortable playing jazz rhythms in the concert hall.

Example 12.3 "I Can Cook Too," Kapilow version

It's the swing rhythm, the syncopated, big-band chords, and the propulsive boogie-bass line that give the music its energy, but the opening 8-bar section as a whole—with a second 4 bars that repeat the first 4, changing only the last note—has the AABA shape customary to Broadway. Throughout the song—and the show as a whole—Bernstein uses popular source materials in his own inventive ways. If this were a typical 32-bar Broadway song like so many we have discussed, Bernstein would have followed this opening section with a repeat of its music with new lyrics, but that's not who Hildy is, nor is it what the fast-paced scene needs to progress theatrically. Instead, Bernstein immediately moves on to new music (a B section) and switches keys, with a new boogie-woogie bass pattern propelling the music forward (Ex. 12.4).

Bernstein continually takes us in unexpected directions. The first 2 measures of the section—"I'm a man's ideal of a perfect meal"—have a vocal line that *ascends* from F# to C# twice, balanced by 2 measures that *descend* to the lowest note of the chorus to wittily depict the lyric "Right *down* to the demitasse." He then starts to copy the 4 measures a step lower on "I'm a pot of joy for a hungry boy." If he had continued to copy, the phrase would have finished as in Example 12.5.

But instead, the boogie-woogie bass line stops, allowing us to focus on the punch line—a wonderful, double entendre, "Baby, I'm cooking with gas!" (Ex. 12.6).

Example 12.4 "I Can Cook Too," B section

Example 12.5 "I Can Cook Too," Kapilow version

Example 12.6 "I Can Cook Too," Bernstein version

Bernstein then returns to the opening idea as if to repeat and finish the song in classic ABA fashion (not the more standard AABA form, but still a familiar one). If he had followed expectations and copied the opening music, the phrase would have sounded like Example 12.7.

But instead, Bernstein changes direction once again and in the third measure leads to a brand new, applause-generating finale that, instead of ending, surprisingly leads to a transition and a key change (Ex. 12.8).

Example 12.7 "I Can Cook Too," Kapilow version

Example 12.8 "I Can Cook Too," Bernstein version

As I've mentioned, it was standard for a Broadway song to begin with a verse or introduction, often in free, conversational rhythms, setting the scene for the chorus that followed—the Broadway equivalent to the recitatives that generally preceded arias in opera. But Bernstein wanted this number to begin with a bang, and in order to achieve a momentary respite from the action midway through the scene, he puts the verse in the middle of the song instead of at the beginning. It now acts as a kind of interlude, giving us a break from all the "heat" (Ex. 12.9).

Everywhere you look, you find Bernstein's mastery of Broadway techniques. The interlude has a simple, 2-bar vocal idea ("Some girls make

Example 12.9 "I Can Cook Too," interlude verse

magazine covers") essentially repeated three times for maximum "getta-bility." Two quick jazz chords after the phrase "Some girls make wonder-ful lovers" make the lovers musically sexy, followed by yet another subtle change of key.

Bernstein was familiar with all styles of jazz, and hints of stride piano* start to show up in the accompaniment as the conversational verse repeats in a new key, giving it an entirely different character (Ex. 12.10).

The chorus then repeats with brand-new accompaniments until the earlier ending finally gets to finish the song and generate the applause that this unique, hybrid number has never failed to elicit since Nancy Walker's electrifying first performance. Bernstein's original cast recording gives an indelible

---

* A kind of jazz piano style in which the right hand plays the melody while the left hand virtuosically jumps back and forth between a single bass note and a chord more than an octave higher.

Example 12.10 "I Can Cook Too"

sense of the sheer energy, orchestral brilliance, vitality, and overwhelming talent that Bernstein brought to the Broadway musical. His performance of "I Can Cook Too" is faster and hotter than almost any subsequent performance, and the band plays with a stunning mixture of precision and swing. In addition to the high-octane verve of the performance, there is a sense of Bernstein letting go—of freeing himself from the restraints of the classical world—that drives the recording. No one had brought his level of pure intensity, complete technical command as both a composer and a conductor, as well as utter facility with all the popular-musical styles of the day to the world of Broadway before. Bernstein, the young classical maestro could indeed "cook too."

⤬

Bernstein, Robbins, Comden, and Green were determined to create a voice for *On the Town* that reflected the here and now of 1944, and for Bernstein that meant including an unprecedented range of musical styles. Though a thorough consideration of the entire score of the show is beyond the scope of this book, the music is all over the map, drawing from serious and popular-music sources such as Gilbert and Sullivan, opera buffa, boogie-woogie, big-band swing, as well as complex ballet music that director George Abbott jokingly referred to as "that Prokofiev stuff." However, the world of 1944 is reflected not only in the show's plot, choreography, and music but also in terms of its approach to casting and hiring. Carol Oja documents the numerous ways the show's hiring practices quietly challenged the segregationist attitudes of the time, beginning with the bold decision to hire the half-Asian Sona Osato for the role of Ivy Smith. At that same moment, her father was one of more than 110,000 Japanese Americans detained at internment camps in the United States. Though Osato's mother was European American, Osato was unmistakably Japanese in appearance, and the decision to cast her as Miss Turnstiles, described in the script as an "All-American girl," at a time when America was fighting a bitter war against the Japanese, was remarkable. This unprecedented approach to casting, however, went far beyond the hiring of Osata. According to Oja, the show was the first on Broadway to hire a mixed-race dance chorus in which both black and white dancers performed together in nonstereotyped roles and physically touched each other. And midway through the show's run, the black violinist and conductor Everett Lee was hired, making him one of the first African Americans to conduct an all-white orchestra on Broadway. In its casting and hiring, *On the Town* offered a prospective vision of what that world might look like in the future.

But that future for Bernstein would be put on hold for a considerable length of time. After the opening of *On the Town*, Bernstein's performing career took off, and composition was forced to take a back seat to one of the busiest and most extraordinary conducting careers in history. In 1953, nine years after *On the Town,* he would return to Broadway, again with Comden and Green, for *Wonderful Town*, which won five Tony Awards (including Best Musical) and ran for 559 performances. Both of these musicals show Bernstein to be a brilliant adapter of existing styles; however, *West Side Story*, written another four years later, would take these earlier achievements to a whole new level. Bernstein would synthesize the achievements of his two earlier musicals, fuse them with the lessons he learned from *Trouble in Tahiti* and *Candide*, and finally create a fully formed American voice for the Broadway musical. A voice that both grew out of a unique historical moment in time yet also transcended that moment to express something timeless and universal through a retelling of Shakespeare's tragic romance, *Romeo and Juliet.*

Though *West Side Story* found universality in an updating of the past, *On the Town* found its energy by completely focusing on the present. In fact, one of the main reasons the show did not run longer on Broadway was that by the fall of 1945, with the war ended, the entire atmosphere in America had changed. Soldiers were no longer being sent overseas, unsure if they would survive. The frantic energy of sailors desperately searching for perhaps one last love, under the extraordinary time pressure of a brief shore leave felt incredibly real to audiences when the show opened in December of 1944, but it no longer resonated in the same way after V-E Day and V-J Day. In "Some Other Time," one of the show's most moving numbers and one of the few that acknowledges the peril the show's joyful sailors actually faced, the line "Where has the time all gone to? Haven't done half the things we want to," had an emotional power precisely because young sailors might never live to do all the things they wanted to. "Some other time" might in fact never come for sailors like Gabey, Chip, and Ozzie, and this realization is what gave the song so much poignancy when the show first opened. However, only a year later, with the soldiers back home and America trying desperately to find some kind of normalcy in the post-Hiroshima nuclear age, the antics of Bernstein's young sailors already felt somewhat dated.

One of the instinctive human reactions in a time of massive uncertainty and danger like World War II is to block out the past and future (like Bernstein's sailors and the wartime audience) and focus entirely on the fragile, present moment, as nothing else can seem quite real. Yet one of the dangers of any artwork completely immersed in a particular moment in time is that in the future, once that context has vanished, the work can become merely a period piece. The greatest art somehow manages to both be of its and for all time, and the enormous success of the recent revival of *On the Town* shows that it continues to find meaning and relevance for audiences more than a half a century later. But whatever future generations may find in *On the Town*, it surely is a remarkably revealing document about America, Bernstein, and the Broadway musical in 1944. The form had matured sufficiently to induce an extraordinarily gifted, classical musician in the first flush of celebrity to leave the concert hall and opera house behind in order to write a Broadway show. It had also matured enough to have room for Bernstein's "Prokofiev stuff." For the first time, Americans like Bernstein and Robbins could not only dance classical ballets like *Petrushka* and conduct Mahler symphonies, they could take what they needed from the world of classical ballet and music and freely mix it with American vernacular idioms to create an original, American voice. A voice that could speak directly to Americans in the concert hall, the opera house, and on a Broadway stage. And for the first time, the country had reached a point where a Jew could do all this without having to change his name. It was the beginning of a new era for Bernstein, and a new era for America. They had both come a long way, and they were both just getting started.

13

Will the Real Annie Oakley
Please Stand Up?

Irving Berlin's "I Got the Sun in the Morning"

To audiences listening to *Annie Get Your Gun* some eighty years after its premiere in August 1946, Annie Oakley might seem to be a quaint figure of folklore or myth, an American icon like Paul Bunyan. But she was, of course, not only a real person, but a person whom Irving Berlin could have, at least in theory, seen perform.* In 1911, at the same time that "Alexander's Ragtime Band" was launching Berlin's career, Oakley had just come out of semiretirement to begin two intensive years of touring with young Buffalo Bill's Wild West show. Seven years later, while Berlin was supporting the war effort with his World War I revue, *Yip! Yip! Yaphank!*, Annie was doing shooting exhibitions and instructional sessions at Army camps around the country. Born in 1860, she was twenty-eight years older than Berlin and lived until 1926, when Berlin was thirty-eight years old. When he was writing his first Broadway scores, she was still one of the most famous women

---

* None of my research has turned up any actual meetings, and I am not suggesting that any actually occurred as Berlin would surely have mentioned it, only that it would have been possible chronologically and geographically. Though it is almost certain that Berlin never saw it, Thomas Edison did record a short clip of Annie shooting in one of his earliest films in 1894, and it is still viewable today on YouTube.

in America. Herbert Fields, coauthor of the book for *Annie Get Your Gun* with his sister Dorothy, was twenty-nine years old when Annie died, so he too must have been aware of the flesh-and-blood woman at the heart of his greatest theatrical triumph. Yet the facts of her life were ultimately no more important to Berlin and the Fieldses than the reality of the riverboat world of the Mississippi was to Kern and Hammerstein, the southern world of "Swanee" to Gershwin and Caesar, or Billy the Kid to Copland. They all invented imaginative versions of America, and their powerful, instinctive sense of what that America needed to be was far too strong to let something as unimportant and inconsequential as reality get in the way.

Before we judge too harshly the liberties that Berlin and the Fieldses took with the stories of Buffalo Bill, Frank Butler, and Annie Oakley, it is important to realize that the facts of the show's three superstar heroes were themselves the product of the same kind of invention and mythmaking. This blurring of the line between fact and fiction and between reality and entertainment has been (and continues to be) central to the creation of the story we call America since George Washington first chopped down the cherry tree.

To untangle the mythmaking at the heart of *Annie Get Your Gun*, it would seem logical to start simply with the biography of the show's heroine, Annie Oakley, but uncovering even her actual name or date of birth is anything but simple. Like Beethoven's father and Cole Porter's mother, Annie altered her birth date to serve her own PR needs. She was in fact born on August 13, 1860, but when Buffalo Bill hired the fifteen-year-old shooter named Lillian Smith for the 1886 season of his Wild West show, Annie chopped six years off her own age, a claim she reiterated throughout her career.* The place of her birth, Darke County, Ohio, is clear, but researchers have uncovered multiple versions of her birth name including Phoebe Ann Moses, or Mosey, or Mozee, as well as multiple stories about where the

---

* In fact, she continued the lie till the very end, and there is no birth date on her tombstone.

name Oakley originated. Some say it came from her paternal grandmother, others say it came from the neighborhood in Cincinnati where she and Frank Butler temporarily lived. Still others say it was the name of a man who paid her train fare at a crucial moment in her early years.

What *is* clear is that she had a horrific childhood that unsurprisingly had no place in an Irving Berlin musical. Her parents, Susan and Jacob Moses, were Quakers—seemingly an odd background for a woman who made her living with a gun. She was the sixth of seven children and was left destitute at the age of six when her father died of pneumonia.* The family was so poor that one of Annie's sisters was given away to another family to raise. Supposedly, Annie shot her first bird when she was only six years old and her first squirrel when she was eight, but different stories and legends have grown up around both of these events.

At the age of ten, Annie was sent to the Infirmary, a local poor farm, before being leased to a farmer and his wife who needed help. Though she never revealed the details of her time there, referring to the husband and wife simply as "The Wolves," she was overworked, starved, and physically abused. At one point, the wife put Annie out in the cold during a blizzard, and the husband only saved her life because he was unwilling to lose his slave. Finally, when she was twelve, she ran away and went back to the Infirmary, which was now run by a much nicer couple named the Edingtons. There she was taught to read (only in *Annie Get Your Gun* was she illiterate), as well as to knit, an activity that became a lifelong hobby that would sustain her through the countless hours of down time when touring with Buffalo Bill. When she was fifteen, she returned home to her mother, who was now remarried, at which point her story, at least in its broad outlines, gets picked up by *Annie Get Your Gun*.

---

* I have drawn the basic biographical facts, in dispute as they are, from Shirl Kasper's exhaustively researched biography, *Annie Oakley* (University of Oklahoma Press, 1992), and Larry McMurtry's wildly entertaining biography of Oakley and Buffalo Bill, *The Colonel and Little Missie: Buffalo Bill, Annie Oakley, and the Beginnings of Superstardom in America* (Simon & Schuster, 2005).

Seeing what elements of Annie's story the Fieldses retained and what they invented, as well as what elements of Annie's story were itself an invention, reveals much about the historical moment in which she lived, the moment when the musical was created, as well as the time in which we now live. It is clear that changing attitudes about women have shaped multiple stories of Annie. What is particularly interesting about the relationship between *Annie Get Your Gun* and Annie's actual life (insofar as that can be definitively ascertained) is that the musical does at many points faithfully intersect with Annie's story largely because that story was already the stuff of myth. When Annie returned home to her mother, she began to support the family by shooting small game, which she sold to local grocers. (This element of her story is more or less picked up in the musical.) Because she was such a spectacular shot, the animals she killed were not torn up, and the quality of the cleanly killed meat made it easy to sell. She became well known throughout the county for her marksmanship, and though the key event that launches the musical—her shooting contest with Frank Butler—seems like the kind of contrived event that could only take place on Broadway, it did actually occur. Or so it seems. Nearly every detail of the famous contest and Annie and Frank's courtship and marriage that followed—their origin story, so to speak, and the key generator of the musical's plot—has been contested.

Shooting contests were quite common at the time, and like Paul Newman's pool shark in *The Hustler*, sharpshooters traveled from town to town, contest to contest. In the most commonly told version of the Butler/Oakley shooting contest, the traveling Irish sharpshooter Frank Butler* comes to town, takes a hundred-dollar side bet on the match (approximately $2,000 today), and is shocked when his challenger turns out to be a tiny

---

* In the musical, Frank Butler is the handsome, womanizing star of Buffalo Bill's Wild West show, and when Annie wins the shooting contest she is immediately invited to join Buffalo Bill's show. In fact, Frank was not part of the show at all, and it would be several years before Annie joined Buffalo Bill, after a failed first audition and the retirement of the show's longtime shooter Captain Bogardus.

fifteen-year-old girl. (Annie was in fact only five feet tall and weighed about a hundred pounds.) Nearly every version of the story has a different numerical scoring of the contest. Some have Annie hitting 23 pigeons to Frank's 21, most have the score at 24 to 23, but what is most in dispute is when this all took place and what happened afterward, and here is where the musical veers most wildly from reality in revealing ways.

Annie's autobiography claimed that the shooting event took place in 1875 and that she and Frank were married a year later on August 23, 1876. This would make Annie fifteen at the time of the contest and sixteen at the time of their marriage, with Frank being twenty-three and twenty-four years old, respectively. Frank Butler, however, claimed the shooting match took place six years later in 1881* and the wedding in 1882. Biographer Shirl Kasper explains the six-year discrepancy by Annie's altered birth date and points to a Canadian marriage certificate from Windsor, Ontario, dated June 20, 1882, that Annie gave to her niece to keep for posterity should her marriage ever be questioned.† Whether Annie was fifteen or twenty-one when the contest occurred, all accounts agree that Butler was taken with the young sharpshooter and married her a year later, proving that, although Irving Berlin declared "You can't get a man with a gun," that's precisely what Annie did. This is where feminism, history, myth, and the imagination take over—and reality and *Annie Get Your Gun* part ways.

After Frank and Annie married, he continued touring for a few years with his partner John Graham in a shooting act billed as Graham & Butler: America's Own Rifle Team and Champion All Around Shots. Meanwhile,

---

* This later date would make the attraction a more "normal one" between a 21- and a 29-year-old as opposed to a 15- and a 23-year-old. Even granting that 16-year-old brides were far from uncommon in that period, there is certainly a different dynamic between a 15-year-old girl and a 23-year-old man, and a 21-year-old woman and a 29-year-old man.

† Both McMurtry and Kasper also point out the possibility that the confusion as to the marriage date might be connected to difficulties Frank had in divorcing his first wife and a need to delay the marriage to Annie until the first divorce came through.

Annie was sent east, purportedly to attend a Catholic school.* Eventually she joined Frank on tour and supposedly took over for Graham one day when he got ill. Her debut was nothing short of spectacular. According to Butler, he instantly realized her superiority, later saying, "From that day to this, I have not competed with her in public shooting. . . . She outclassed me."[1] She would go on to dazzle audiences on the vaudeville circuit, and once she joined Buffalo Bill's legendary show in 1885, wowed audiences in Europe as well, shooting a cigarette from the mouth of the German Kaiser Wilhelm II, impressing Queen Victoria, and becoming America's first female superstar.

Her nonstop touring with Buffalo Bill from 1885 through 1901 was filled with success after success as Annie's legend grew to mythic proportions. When she was presented to the Prince of Wales and Princess Alexandra in England after a command performance for the prime minister, Annie—supposedly to the horror of everyone assembled—shook hands with the Princess first, breaking centuries of diplomatic protocol, saying, "I'm an American and in America ladies come first."[2] The Queen called her "a very clever little girl," and she scored a triumph at London's famed Wimbledon sporting club when she shot a mechanical deer racing along a track. The legendary Indian chief Sitting Bull was so impressed with her shooting that he adopted her and gave her the nickname Watanya Cicilla, or "Little Sure Shot." (This became the basis for "I'm an Indian Too" in *Annie Get Your Gun*.)

By all accounts, her act was nothing short of astonishing. She could shoot with either hand at incredible speed and fire pistols simultaneously in both hands. She could smash balls while holding her shotgun upside down, over her head, or even while lying on her back across a chair. She would throw a glass ball in the air, pick up her gun, fire it, hit the ball before it landed, then

---

* Though if Annie and Frank were truly married in 1882, Annie would have been twenty-two years old and unlikely to attend a Catholic school.

throw a second ball into the air and spin around 180 degrees before shooting that one too. One of her most famous tricks was mirror shooting, where she turned her back to the audience and shot at her target using a handheld mirror. She could shoot the corks off bottles, split cards on their edges, and snuff out candles, and she somehow managed to accomplish these traditionally male sharpshooting feats while still retaining her femininity. She was a perfectionist about her outfits and careful about the impression she created. She never wore anything revealing, and as Shirl Kasper put it, "She was a contradiction when it came to a woman's role. While she was comfortable wielding a gun and living in a masculine world, and while in later years she would be held up as an example of the liberated woman, she herself wanted most to be considered a lady."[3] Above all else, she was a showman who knew how to present a winning package, including the girlish pout she put on when she (usually on purpose) missed a shot, followed by the back kick she gave before hitting the target, and the kisses she blew to the audience as she gracefully entered the arena. She was a tiny, fragile-looking, yet athletic woman succeeding in what had previously been an exclusively all-male enterprise, yet she never lost her sense of being a lady.

In some ways, what was most impressive about Annie according to everyone who knew her was her self-confidence, perhaps a result of her "doin' what comes naturally," as Irving Berlin put it. Like Berlin's music, which has a kind of simple inevitability, she was doing what she was born to do, what she'd been doing from the age of six. She was fearless. One of the most telling descriptions of her skills as a competitor came from Johnny Baker, a young sharpshooter whom Annie mentored and who eventually took over her role in Buffalo Bill's show.

> You know the ordinary person has nerves. They'll bob up on him in spite of everything; he'll notice some little thing that distracts his attention, or get fussed by the way a ball travels through the air. Or a bit of light will get on the sights—or seem to get there, and throw him

off. I wasn't any different from the average person, but Annie was. The minute she picked up a rifle or a shotgun, it seemed that she made a machine of herself—every action went like clockwork. . . . To tell the truth . . . it would have made a better show if I could have beat her every few performances. But it couldn't be done.[4]

Annie's confidence and fierce competitiveness were her most distinctive traits, and they are crucial to understanding why *Annie Get Your Gun* and Annie's actual life were forced to diverge. But truly understanding what the musical did with Annie's story requires a grasp of where Berlin, the Fieldses, the Broadway musical, and America were when the team began work on the show.

Looking back in 1975 on his wartime experiences, Richard Rodgers wrote in *Musical Stages*, "The world outside was still torn by devastating warfare, but my little world within the theatre in 1943 brought me nothing but happiness."[5] As noted, Rodgers had tried to obtain an Army commission, but because of a limit on civilian commissions he was unable to serve. While writing *Oklahoma!* (1943) and *Carousel* (1945), he did support the war effort, along with his wife Dorothy, through work for the Red Cross, the Writers' War Board, and the USO, but he claimed to feel guilty sitting at home on his "plush behind" while soldiers were "wallowing in mud."[6] Irving Berlin, on the other hand, had a very different wartime experience. Perhaps being a first-generation American who had risen from nothing to extraordinary wealth and success was a contributing factor, but whatever the reason, Berlin was intensely patriotic. In 1941, before America even entered World War II, Berlin wrote several patriotic songs, including "Any Bonds Today?," "Angels of Mercy" (for the Red Cross), and "Arms for the Love of America" promoting the Lend-Lease Act. Shortly after Pearl Harbor, Berlin approached the War Department and offered to do what he could to help.

They suggested a revival of *Yip! Yip! Yaphank!*, his World War I revue, but instead Berlin decided to write a new revue called *This Is the Army*. All proceeds went to benefit Army Emergency Relief.

Though Berlin was already fifty-three years old, he not only wrote and produced *This Is the Army*, he then spent most of the next three years touring the show worldwide while often coming dangerously close to the front line. In between performances he visited wounded soldiers, hospitals, rank-and-file troops, and ultimately raised about $10 million for Army Emergency Relief in a display of patriotism that earned him the presidential Medal for Merit for "the performance of extraordinary service to the United States Army." His impact on the country's morale was further enhanced by the release of the movie *Holiday Inn*, which had been filmed in September 1941—before Pearl Harbor—but was not released until August 1942. The film contained the now-legendary performance by Bing Crosby of "White Christmas," which would provide enormous comfort to the troops and their families during their first Christmas away from home. (It was also, for fifty years, the best-selling record in history.) And when you consider the emotional impact of Kate Smith's 1938 recording of "God Bless America"—dropped from *Yip! Yip! Yaphank!* twenty years earlier—it is safe to say that, more than any other single songwriter, Irving Berlin was the voice of America during World War II.

Berlin's involvement in the war effort meant that he actually composed very little other music. When the war was over and the tours of *This Is the Army* finally ended, Berlin was completely exhausted. But when his close friend Jerome Kern, who was supposed to write the score for *Annie Get Your Gun*, died suddenly in the fall of 1945, Dorothy and Herbert Fields, as well as Rodgers and Hammerstein, begged Berlin to take over the job. Berlin initially rejected their offer for two interesting reasons. While he was away, Rodgers and Hammerstein had written *Oklahoma!* and *Carousel*, and integrated musicals were all the rage. Berlin, however, preferred the more traditional revue format, which he felt freed the composer from plot and character. He came from the world of Tin Pan Alley, where stand-alone hit songs were the goal.* The Fieldses, however, wanted a book musical with a story, and they set about adapting Annie's life to fit the narrative demands of a post-*Oklahoma!* musical.

For Rodgers and Hammerstein, producing a musical based on a famous heroine from the pioneer days of the Wild West seemed like a logical follow-up to *Oklahoma!* and *Carousel*, but Berlin claimed he had no idea how to write what he called "hillbilly music." Hammerstein's famous response, which reveals how little authenticity mattered to him, was that all Berlin needed to do was drop the *g*'s.† At this point, the origin story of *Annie Get Your Gun* sprouts as many different versions as the spelling of Annie Oakley's birth name. Having reached an impasse, Rodgers told Berlin to take the script home and work on it for a while to see if it felt like a good fit. Depending on which of the countless versions you believe, Berlin either went off for a weekend, a week, or a couple of weeks—either to the Catskills or Atlantic City—and came back with either one, three, or six great songs, and the show was on its way.

Dorothy and Herbert Fields knew from the beginning that they were inventing their own Annie Oakley. Dorothy Fields once joked, "We did a lot of research on Annie Oakley and Frank Butler and both of them apparently were about the dullest people in the world. Annie Oakley in real life used to sit in her tent and knit for God's sake!"[7] This offhand comment captures the challenge of turning Annie's life into a musical since, aside from the inherent drama of Annie and Frank's initial meeting and shooting contest,

---

* Buffalo Bill's Wild West show itself, with its vaudeville-like sequence of largely independent acts, was similar to the aesthetic of the kinds of musical revues Berlin preferred.

† This seemed to be Hammerstein's generic solution to all dialect issues beginning with his own lyrics for *Show Boat*. Whether western or southern, dropping the *g*'s was all that was required.

their relationship was, for all intents and purposes, utterly without drama. At heart, *Annie Get Your Gun* is a traditional book musical:

1. *Boy meets girl*—Annie and Frank "meet cute" (to use modern terminology) at the shooting match, fall in love, and she joins his act.
2. *Boy loses girl*—Annie outshoots Frank and loses him in time to create suspense at the end of Act I.
3. *Boy gets girl*—Annie overcomes her pride and deliberately loses the final shooting match to win Frank back.

Boy meets girl, boy loses girl, boy gets girl is the engine that has driven and continues to drive the plots of traditional Broadway musicals, and the Fieldses created a first-rate version. The only problem (though no one at the time would have considered this to be a problem) is that it bears not the slightest resemblance to Annie and Frank's actual relationship, which, though dull in Dorothy's view, was interesting in ways that a traditional musical could not possibly address.

In fact, Annie and Frank's relationship was almost an inversion of the one portrayed in the musical, and, given the conventional morality of the times, strikingly liberated. Though the musical portrays Frank as an arrogant, proud, "big swollen-headed stiff," in reality, from the moment he lost his initial shooting encounter with Annie, he realized he was outclassed, and once Annie joined Buffalo Bill's Wild West show, Frank happily took a back seat and became Annie's manager. Annie was the star and breadwinner, and by all accounts Frank (completely unlike the vain, egotistical Frank Butler in the musical) slid into his behind-the-scenes role without the slightest hesitation for the more than forty years of their seemingly happy marriage. Though there was plenty of theatrical drama during Annie's shooting act, aside from the ten minutes she spent performing each day, Frank and Annie's lives were, in fact, incredibly dull. Annie didn't swear, smoke, or drink hard liquor. Because of her extreme poverty as a child, she was incredibly tight with money, even though she was being paid superstar wages.* Like so many gifted athletes and musical virtuosi, all her energy went into working obsessively at her one, unique skill—sharpshooting—to which everything else took a back seat. The only real drama in her otherwise repetitive regimen came in 1903 when two of the Hearst newspapers in Chicago published a false story claiming that she had been jailed for buying cocaine. Though she demanded and quickly obtained a retraction, she spent the next five years suing all fifty-five newspapers that had printed the story for libel in an effort to clear her name and won judgments in all but one of the cases. In court, as in shooting contests, Annie did not like to lose.

The real Annie was a complicated woman, one whose complexities were not easy to render in the broad strokes of an Irving Berlin musical. Though as Shirl Kasper points out, in later years many people tried to hold her up as an example of a liberated woman, she does not easily fit into any simple political agenda. In many ways, she exhibited what today would be called feminist traits, succeeding as a diminutive woman in what was traditionally a rough-and-tumble male domain. When she first joined Buffalo Bill's Wild West show, she was the only white woman in the company, traveling with cowboys and Mexican vaqueros who had anything-but-great reputations, yet she reportedly put them in their place in short order and earned their respect. Her marriage was certainly something any feminist would be proud of, with her as the principal breadwinner and superstar celebrity supported by a subservient husband. She shocked Secretary of War Newton D. Baker when she offered to create a women's regiment to fight in World War I, and she also volunteered her services to the government during the Spanish-American War. But no issue made her sound like more of a feminist than her staunch belief that women should carry guns

---

* She was the highest-paid member of the troupe and in 1900 received the equivalent of approximately $4,000 dollars a week in today's dollars. This is not counting the considerable amount of money she earned from the frequent private shooting matches she engaged in arranged by her husband.

and learn to shoot. She claimed to have taught 15,000 women to shoot and said, "I would like to see every woman know how to handle them [firearms] as naturally as they know how to handle babies."[8] She wanted women to keep guns by their beds and carry them when they went out alone, and she actually suggested to the New York legislature that every school in the state should have a shooting range and teachers for both boys and girls. In spite of all of these beliefs, she was unwilling to support the country's growing women's movement in any way. Though Buffalo Bill was a strong supporter of women's suffrage, Annie was not, claiming she couldn't be sure that "only the good women" would vote.[9] In many ways her actions were those of a strong, independent, feminist woman, but she remained old-fashioned and conservative in spirit and attitude.

Clearly conveying a woman as complex as Annie in a musical would require far more of Berlin than simply having her drop her *g*'s. No one seems to have wondered where Berlin got the idea that Annie Oakley was an illiterate hillbilly. Nor, for that matter, has anyone wondered why Hammerstein didn't simply explain that Annie wasn't a hillbilly at all. In some ways, Berlin's misconceptions about Annie were understandable. Her legend grew during her years of touring with Buffalo Bill, and like his Wild West show, she became the living embodiment of the Old West—a sharpshooting, western cowgirl—even though she grew up in Ohio and had never traveled west of the Mississippi River until she started touring. Though she never lied about where she grew up, she also never made an effort to correct people's image of her. Berlin made her an illiterate hillbilly by turning standard English—"Doing What Comes Naturally"—into Hammerstein's hillbilly English—"Doin' What Comes Natur'lly"—from the moment he first began working on the score. Though Berlin has an uneducated Annie sing "Folks like us could never fuss / With schools and books and learnin'," in fact Annie learned to read at the Infirmary and later harshly criticized her rival sharpshooter Lillian Smith for her poor grammar.

Perhaps the greatest liberty the musical takes, and the one that has proved most difficult to make palatable for audiences, has to do with the show's final shooting contest. Though the Fieldses were faithful to how Oakley and Butler met, they invented two important plot points: at the end of Act I, Annie humiliates Frank with her trick shooting, causing him to quit the show: and at the end of Act II, Annie intentionally loses the final shooting match with Frank on Governor's Island so she can win back her man.

It's hard to imagine a more strikingly antifeminist conclusion than this, and it's inconceivable that the real Annie Oakley would have ever contemplated throwing a match for anyone, least of all Frank Butler. When she was in Europe and Prince Edward arranged a shooting contest with Grand Duke Michael of Russia, she had no hesitation about beating him 47 birds to 36. She was intensely competitive and took great pride in her shooting— in real life she won Frank Butler by beating him, not by losing.* In fact, as the century progressed and attitudes toward women's rights shifted, the show's ending proved harder and harder for audiences to accept. In much the same way that Hammerstein's original opening line of *Show Boat*, "Niggers all work on de Mississippi," became unacceptable to later generations and was changed first to "Colored folks work on de Mississippi," then "Here we all work on de Mississippi," and finally in the Lincoln Center revival eliminated completely, in the 1999 revival of *Annie Get Your Gun*, Peter Stone rewrote the book, and in a victory for equal rights, the final shooting match ends in a tie. Though this might be a far more satisfying ending for modern sensibilities, it is important to understand the context of the original 1946 ending.

The movement for women's rights in America began as early as 1848 with Elizabeth Cady Stanton as its leader at the Women's Rights Convention in

---

* The combative spirit of the challenge song, "Anything You Can Do" actually comes much closer to Annie's actual spirit than the scene that follows, in which she loses the shooting match on purpose.

Seneca Falls, New York. By 1878 the movement had grown in strength, and with Susan B. Anthony leading the charge, a proposed right-to-vote amendment to the Constitution was introduced into Congress. After forty years of protests, demonstrations, parades, it was finally ratified as the 19th Amendment in 1920, six years before Annie Oakley's death. During the Depression, however, feminism as an active political movement largely fell silent. Jobs were scarce, and it seemed inappropriate for women to take the few that were available. America's entry into the war in 1941, however, changed all that. Because of the huge need for personnel, women were allowed in the military as something other than nurses for the first time in American history, and approximately 350,000 women served in the Armed Forces in some capacity during the war.* With so many men fighting abroad, women took over an enormous amount of the war work in factories at home, symbolized most famously by the image of Rosie the Riveter. For many women, this was their first experience in the working world. They learned new skills, earned real wages, and developed a new sense of themselves. More than 6 million women joined the American workforce during World War II, and when the men came home, they assumed they would take back "their" jobs. This caused considerable conflict as working women were unhappy about returning to homemaker roles that no longer seemed as attractive as they once did. The ending of *Annie Get Your Gun*, in which conventional morality triumphs and a woman sacrifices herself in the service of a man's ego, was actually written at a time when that very morality was under siege. A time when newly empowered women threatened to follow the lead of the real Annie Oakley and proudly defeat their personal Frank Butlers rather than pretend to be less than they were in order to preserve male egos and prerogatives, like the Annie in the musical.

---

* The Army had the Women's Army Corps (WACs), the Navy had the Women's Reserve (WAVES), the Coast Guard had the SPARs, and the Army Air Forces had the WASP. Though women did not fight, they had extensive office jobs, served as gunnery instructors, flight instructors, repair workers, and transport pilots.

So what then, did Berlin get right? Given its almost complete inauthenticity, what makes *Annie Get Your Gun* one of the most beloved musicals ever written? In the end, what is remarkable about *Annie Get Your Gun* is that, although the Annie Oakley it depicts bears almost no resemblance to the real one, Berlin's music brings her to life in a vibrant and vital way that is true to her essence if not to her actual biography. Berlin may have gotten almost all the facts wrong, but he got the spirit behind the facts right, and no song captures that better than Annie's great hymn of gratitude, "I Got the Sun in the Morning."

In Act II, Pawnee Bill hosts a reception for Buffalo Bill's troupe at the Hotel Brevoort. Pawnee Bill's troupe is on the brink of bankruptcy, but he assumes that Buffalo Bill's has made a fortune touring Europe and hopes a merger will save his company, not realizing that Buffalo Bill's troupe is broke as well and plotting a merger for the same reasons. Once it becomes clear that both troupes are in the same mess, the plan to merge falls apart until Annie comes to the rescue and offers to sell the shooting medals she won in Europe to finance the merger. Charlie Davenport, the manager of the Wild West show, warns Annie that she is giving up her only bankroll, but Annie says, "Shucks I don't care . . . I got what I had when I started. Don't you fret, Charlie, I'm doin' fine. . . ."

Like so many children who grew up in abject poverty, Annie in real life (like Irving Berlin himself) was extremely careful with money and would probably never have considered giving up her bankroll for anyone, but she wasn't materialistic either. Other than the money she spent on her fancy costumes, her tastes were quite simple, and the conclusion of the song's opening lyric, "The things I've got will keep me satisfied," accurately conveys her basic attitude.

This attitude has been beautifully set up by the scene preceding the song. When Annie first enters the ballroom, the society ladies are dazzled by her shooting medals. As they ooh and ah, Annie deflates their upper-class pretensions. After each one greets her either with "Charmed!" or

"Enchanted," one guest changes the pattern and says, "Delighted," to which Annie replies, "Oh, no, you gotta be charmed or chanted!" When an over-solicitous, hovering waiter asks her if she'd like more salad, she says, "I'd love some more—after I've had some." Though she enjoys the upper-class frills her celebrity has provided, as the scene so clearly shows, at heart she is "just folks." She sees the shallowness of society life, pokes fun at it, and is satisfied with "the things she's got."

From the beginning, when America first decided to refer to George Washington as Mr. President and not his Excellency, this anti-aristocratic strain has been at the core of American values. Like Annie, our heroes are plainspoken, direct, and unpretentious, and like *Oklahoma!* and *Carousel*, *Annie Get Your Gun* reminded Americans of these traditional values. Her down-to-earth, unpretentious humor is pointedly contrasted with the society pretension surrounding her in the ballroom and already establishes her character before the song makes her philosophy explicit.

It should come as no surprise that Berlin was the perfect songwriter to turn this philosophy into music, as in many ways Annie's situation and character paralleled Berlin's own. Like Annie, he had risen from childhood poverty through natural talent and hard work and had made his way into high-society, celebrity circles that would have seemed unimaginable in his youth. His music was as direct, humorous, and unaffected as Annie herself. It never put on airs or tried to be more than what it was. Yet beneath its deceptively simply surface, there was surprising intelligence. Neither Annie nor Berlin, nor "I Got the Sun in the Morning" were as simple as they appeared to be, and it is the song's many unexpected touches that make the difference between simple and seemingly simple and bring both the music and Annie to life.

The number begins almost conversationally with Annie putting celebrity, fame, and money in perspective as she takes stock of her situation in life: of what she has and what she hasn't (Ex. 13.1).

Yet even this seemingly straightforward opening is not as simple as it appears. For example, if one were to put "normal" chords underneath

Example 13.1 "I Got the Sun in the Morning," opening

"Taking stock of what I have and what I haven't," it would sound like Example 13.2.

Instead of a simple F chord in measure 1 and measure 3, Berlin adds an extra note* for warmth (a D), softening Annie's character while sliding the opening chord down a step to an unusual, glowing chord in measure 2 before returning to the opening chord in measure 3 (Ex. 13.1). Berlin was a master at fitting his songs to his singers, and the leap up to repeated C's to finish the thought on "What do I find" is perfectly written for Ethel Merman's belt voice.†

---

* For musicians, an added sixth chord in measures 1 and 3 and a substitute dominant in measure 2 produced by sliding all voices down by step—F–C–A–D/E♭–B♭–G–C.

† Mary Martin, who replaced Merman on the national tour of the show, had a completely different kind of voice and energy from Merman, and lines like "What do I find" were perfectly written for Merman's distinctive belt voice. Ironically, though she might have been hired for her unique power and energy, Merman always claimed that it was Berlin who had gotten her out of her "tough broad" image and let her be more vulnerable. It was Berlin's lyrics, she claimed, "that made a lady out of me." See Benjamin Sears, *The Irving Berlin Reader* (Oxford University Press, 2012), 111.

Example 13.2 "I Got the Sun in the Morning," Kapilow version

The sunny optimism of the remaining lyrics in this short verse—"Checking up on what I have and what I haven't, What do I find? A healthy balance on the credit side."—is perfectly reflected in the music (Ex. 13.3). Rather than simply repeating the first 4 measures, the excitement rises as the phrase repeats higher and in a new key. Berlin then uses the same belt notes on the repeated words, "What do I find?" but changes the harmony underneath, and the result of her optimistic discovery (She's got a "healthy balance on the credit side") generates the swing rhythm that leads into the chorus.

In Berlin's "Nine Rules for Writing Popular Songs," rule number 8 was "Your song must be perfectly simple," and that is a perfect description of this classic chorus. It is as clear and direct as anything Berlin ever wrote but as always seemingly, but only seemingly, simple. A single, unusual chord repeated three times (Ex. 13.3, mm. 9–11)* accompanies a repeated melody that perfectly captures everything Annie *doesn't* have (that is, no diamonds and no pearls).

As her thinking changes from what she doesn't have to what she *does* have—"still I think I'm a lucky girl"—the harmony changes, leading to a punch line kicked off by the same belted C's ("I got the sun") from the introduction's "What do I find." This moment is a beautiful hymn of gratitude.

---

* For musicians, a striking, C7/♭5 with the ♭5 in the bass.

Example 13.3 "I Got the Sun in the Morning," transition to chorus

The vocal line moves straight down a scale from the phrase's highest note—the repeated C's—C, B♭, A, G, F, conveying a universal, age-old truth with simple, hymnlike harmony:* "I got the sun in the morning and the moon at night."

The piece's form is as simple as Annie's philosophy, and following the time-honored 32-bar song form, the second 8 measures repeat the music of the first 8 with new lyrics: "Got no mansion, got no yacht, Still I'm happy with what I've got, I got the sun in the morning and the moon at night."

The B section (Ex. 13.4) is equally straightforward, but one note in each chord is the difference between simple and seemingly simple and makes

Example 13.4 "I Got the Sun in the Morning," B section

---

* For musicians, notice the two lovely 9–8 suspensions on "sun in" and "morn-ing," which give warmth and a hymnlike quality to the phrase and decorate what otherwise is essentially two measures of parallel octaves; as both melody and bass fundamentally descend B♭–A–G–F with the two 9–8 suspensions, and the rhythmically anticipated F, therefore avoiding parallels.

Example 13.5 "I Got the Sun in the Morning," chord comparison

Annie's happiness that much happier. Example 13.5 compares Berlin's two fantastic chords with two more ordinary chords that might have accompanied "Sunshine gives me a lovely day," showing the power of changing a single note.

The same music repeats lower with the same great chords for "Moonlight gives me the Milky Way," followed by the expected return of the opening music for "Got no checkbooks, got no banks, / Still I'd like to express my thanks. I got the sun in the morning and the moon at night." Berlin's second rule for writing popular songs was, "The title must be planted throughout the song via use of repetition," and having now repeated the title for the third time, he could easily have followed the standard 32-bar form and ended the song as in Example 13.6.

No one knew how to finish a song better than Berlin, so instead he adds a short epilogue perfectly summing up Annie's philosophy in 4 measures (Ex. 13.7). Verse after verse has itemized all that she doesn't have—silver,

Example 13.6 "I Got the Sun in the Morning," Kapilow version

Example 13.7 "I Got the Sun in the Morning," epilogue

gold, diamonds, pearls, mansions, yachts, heirlooms, checkbooks, and so on—but she finally decides that "with the sun in the morning and the moon in the evening, I'm all right." The long notes on the final three words emphatically conclude Annie's anthem, with Berlin's wonderful syncopation on the word "I'm" summing up her spirit in a single, surprising, yet ultimately inevitable rhythm. In "I Got Rhythm" in 1930, Merman had reassured Depression-era Americans that all they needed was rhythm, music, and "a man." Now in 1946, she assured an America recovering from World War II that all they needed was the "sun in the morning, and the moon at night," and they too would be "all right." Sadly, in the post-Hiroshima, nuclear age, that would not be quite enough.

Since the invention of photography in the nineteenth century, we have gradually become more capable of convincingly portraying reality. At the same time, our interest in purely imaginative versions of reality seems to have diminished. In a period film today, every costume, fish fork, and hairstyle has to be reproduced, after meticulous historical research, exactly as it was in its time period. The importance of authenticity in visual style is taken for granted, and movies based on actual events that take excessive liberties with historical facts—like *Argo*, *Lincoln*, and *Selma*—frequently become the subject of intense academic debate and controversy. At the time of this writing, *Hamilton,* the most talked-about commercial blockbuster musical of recent memory, is literally drawn from a major scholarly book on Alexander Hamilton and is being lauded not only for its entertainment value but also for its authentic, educational presentation of American history.

Authenticity is, of course, not only an important concern in musicals and movies, but also in the world of classical music, where the authentic-performance-practice movement and use of period instruments has been perhaps the most significant development in the field in the past twenty-five years. Because of the extraordinary focus on authenticity today, it can be easy to forget how unique this emphasis is to modern times. Shakespeare was certainly not concerned with fidelity to the facts of English history any more than Copland was concerned with fidelity to the facts of Billy the Kid's life, or Berlin and the Fieldses were concerned with fidelity to the facts of Annie Oakley's. Facts were a spur to invention. Artists were more interested in essence. Berlin and the Fieldses may have gotten many things wrong about Annie's life, but they got her spirit right—her determination, self-confidence, straightforwardness, energy, and vitality.

In "There's No Business Like Show Business," the show's most famous anthem (and a song that Berlin almost dropped because he thought Rodgers didn't like it), Berlin manages to perfectly capture not only Annie's spirit, but his own as well. Ultimately, beyond all her talents as a sharpshooter, Annie, like Berlin, was a showman. A performer. A trouper who lived for show business. A maker of myths. By all accounts, in her years of touring with Buffalo Bill, she only missed five performances, four of which occurred when she had such a serious ear infection that she almost died. Even at its worst, when she could barely stand up, she still tried to ride in the parades on tour. Though she was not an overtly emotional person, somehow Berlin managed to capture, better than she could ever express it herself, what she felt about show business, perhaps because it was so close to what he felt. "There's No Business Like Show Business" sums up the miraculous transformation that a life in the theater made possible for both of them. The music's thrilling energy and excitement captures what Annie must have felt about her remarkable journey from the poverty of Darke

County to her dressing room—where they did in fact "hang a star." She was a show person who "smiled when she was low," and much like Irving Berlin, who as an immigrant Jew had started with nothing and transformed himself into the voice of American popular music, Annie started with nothing as a poor backwoods girl from Ohio and transformed herself into America's image of a sharpshooting cowgirl from the Wild West. Though the Annie that Berlin created might be only tangentially related to the real one, it is Berlin's Annie that has survived, and it is Berlin's Annie that has become an American icon. Berlin invented Annie and gave her a voice, and America brought that voice to the world.

14

Fantasy in New York

Leonard Bernstein's "Tonight"

Though Stephen Sondheim was by far the youngest and least famous member of the creative team responsible for *West Side Story*, he brought a distinct perspective to the collaboration. His outsider status as the only member of what might be thought of for our purposes as the fourth generation of Broadway creators (Berlin and Kern were the first generation; Porter and Rodgers the second; Bernstein, Arthur Laurents, and Robbins were third) allowed him to see aspects of the show to which the other collaborators were largely blind.

When Bernstein first began to work on *West Side Story*, he fully intended, like Porter and Berlin, to compose both the music and the lyrics himself. But when he realized how much ballet and symphonic music he would have to write while fulfilling the overwhelming demands of his conducting career, he agreed to take on a cowriter. At the time, Sondheim was an almost completely unknown twenty-six-year-old composer-lyricist. He'd previously met *West Side Story*'s book writer, Arthur Laurents, at an audition of *Saturday Night*, one of Sondheim's early shows. Some months later the two ran into each other again at a party. Laurents told Sondheim he was working on an updated musical version of *Romeo and Juliet*, and that they were looking for someone to write lyrics since Comden and Green, Bernstein's lyricists for *On the Town* and *Wonderful Town*, were unavailable. But when Laurents explained that they intended to reset Shakespeare's play in the present-day world of Puerto Rican street gangs in New York City, Sondheim instantly said that he was the wrong man for the job since "I've never been that poor and I've never even *known* a Puerto Rican."[1]

Perhaps the most common advice of writers' manuals is to write what you know, so Sondheim's reaction intuitively makes sense. For everyone else on the creative team, their lack of experience didn't seem to matter. It never struck them as odd that four upper-class white Jewish gay men were writing a musical about poor, tough, inner-city Puerto Rican gangs, though in many respects, the reality of New York City gang life was as remote from their personal experience as Elizabethan life in Shakespeare's London. Like the Mississippi River for Kern, Catfish Row for Gershwin, the Wild West for Copland, and Annie Oakley for Berlin, the New York City street gangs depicted in *West Side Story* ultimately existed nowhere but in Bernstein's, Robbins's, Sondheim's, and Laurents's imaginations. Yet to understand the show and the effect it had requires an understanding of the context within which it was created and the New York City reality that inspired their invention.

In 1917, Congress passed the Jones-Shafroth Act, which allowed Puerto Ricans to travel between Puerto Rico and the United States without a passport. Migration quadrupled in the next decade, and the arrival of cheap air travel in the late 1940s launched what has become known as the Great Migration of the 1950s. By 1955 nearly 700,000 Puerto Ricans were living in New York City.[2] Like so many immigrant groups before them, they tended to band together, forming distinct communities in the Bronx, Brooklyn, and East Harlem. At the time, large areas of New York City had in effect been divided into distinct areas, each turf run by different, ethnically defined young gangs very much like the Sharks and Jets in *West*

Side Story. East Harlem was run by the Dragons, Red Wings, and Egyptian Kings, while Washington Heights was split between the Jesters and the Amsterdams.

Racism, a lack of work, and poor living conditions created frustration and tension among young people, and as a former gang member named Bobby put it, "All you had was your turf, there was nothing else. All you had was this pride in being an hombre, in being bad and taking care of your people. It was like you were trying to say to the world, 'This is me, man, I'm alive, you dig? And I got somethin' and I live in this community, and I'm somebody here. I'm a leader."[3] Different gangs defined themselves by their clothing. War councils, where gangs met on neutral turf to decide on weapons and locations for rumbles—like the war council in Doc's store in *West Side Story*—actually took place. Any incursion onto a rival gang's turf was cause for a beating or a knifing. Gang violence intensified throughout the fifties. The *New York Herald Tribune*, the *New York Mirror*, and the *Daily News* constantly published stories about gang shootings, stabbings, and murders often with garish, sensationalist photos attached, and many people believed that next to Communism, juvenile delinquency, which had doubled between the 1940s and the opening of *West Side Story*, was the greatest single problem facing the United States.

It was this reality—experienced secondhand almost exclusively through newspaper accounts, books, and magazine articles*—that ultimately inspired *West Side Story*. As with so many great projects, different collaborators tell different stories about the early stages of the creative process. Robbins claimed that he began thinking about the idea when actor Montgomery Clift asked him for help preparing the role of Romeo, sparking the idea of somehow setting the play in the present. A fellow dancer, Janet

---

* Julia Foulkes's book *A Place for Us:* West Side Story *and New York* (University of Chicago Press, 2016) does document a "research trip" Robbins made wandering through the Puerto Rican portions of Harlem, interviewing gang members at a school dance, and watching how they moved. Robbins described it "like going into a foreign country" (p. 67).

Reed, thinks the idea might have come from an acting-class improvisation she did with Robbins on the Romeo and Juliet theme, with Robbins as a Jewish boy and Reed as a Catholic girl.[4] Robbins danced the parts of both Mercutio and Benvolio in Anthony Tudor's setting of Prokofiev's *Romeo and Juliet* in the mid-forties, and it is certainly possible that some initial spark might have been ignited during that experience. It is of course also possible that all of these events provided inspiration. Whatever the case, in 1949 Robbins brought the idea of doing a modern version of *Romeo and Juliet* to Arthur Laurents and Bernstein. At the time, the plan was to set the story on the East Side of New York, not the West Side, with a Jewish Maria and an Italian-Catholic Tony at the time of Easter and Passover. The original conflict was intended to be religious rather than ethnic, somewhat closer to the actual experiences of Robbins, Laurents, and Bernstein. A story propelled by anti-Semitism was something they could all immediately relate to.

Though the idea of a Jewish/Catholic *East Side Story* seemed promising, reality refused to cooperate. The entire team was anxious to create a piece that would seem fresh and relevant, but when they began to look closer into setting *Romeo and Juliet* in the tenement world of the Lower East Side, they discovered that that world had already vanished. Even worse, the long-running play *Abie's Irish Rose* (1922), which had been re-released as a film in 1946, covered similar terrain with its story of a marriage between a Jewish boy and an Irish-Catholic girl. Multiple professional commitments on the parts of Bernstein, Robbins, and Laurents then made scheduling impossible, and the project was temporarily shelved.

That it was a serendipitous reading of a newspaper article that brought the project back to life is appropriate, as it was this kind of secondhand information from the media that became the prime source material for *West Side Story*. In the summer of 1955, Bernstein and Laurents happened to be sitting by the pool at the Beverly Hills Hotel when Bernstein glanced over at a copy of the *Los Angeles Times* sitting on a deck chair and saw a head-line about rioting Chicano gangs on the streets of Los Angeles. The idea of turning an outdated, Jewish-Catholic *East Side Story* into a ripped-from-the-headlines *West Side Story* set in the middle of New York City's Puerto Rican gang warfare grabbed both Bernstein and Laurents. They immediately telephoned Robbins, who was equally thrilled by the idea, and with the later addition of Sondheim, the team was off and running.

But were they all headed in the same direction, and where exactly did they think they would end up? For Jerome Robbins, the goal was clear:

> The aim was to see if all of us—Lenny who wrote "long-hair" music, Arthur who wrote serious plays, myself who did serious ballets, Oliver Smith who was a serious painter—could bring our acts together and do a work on the popular stage. . . . The idea was to make the poetry of the piece come out of our best attempts as serious artists; that was the major thrust.[5]

It is no accident that the word "serious" occurs four times in Robbins's statement, along with the words "long hair" and "poetry," while "popular" occurs only once. Nor is it surprising that Bernstein often referred to the piece in what sounds like oxymoronic terms as "a tragic musical comedy." Though *On the Town* and *Wonderful Town* had included some serious, sophisticated compositional writing in their scores, both shows exuberantly and enthusiastically embraced the world of musical comedy. The shows bubble over with Bernstein's love, facility, and affection for the popular music of the time, and they show a complete mastery of nearly every existing Broadway style. Having proved that he could succeed in commercial theater, Bernstein now wanted to do more. Early in the 1950s, he made two problematic, commercially unsuccessful stabs at bringing a popular-music sensibility into more serious musical forms with his short opera *Trouble in Tahiti* in 1952 and his unclassifiable operetta-musical *Candide* in 1956. (The 1974 *Candide* directed by Hal Prince was, however, a huge commercial success.) In *West Side Story* Bernstein clearly wished to reverse the process, bringing the serious into the popular.

Though time has perhaps dulled our appreciation of some of *West Side Story*'s originality, the idea of turning a true tragedy into a musical was essentially unprecedented, and no one was more aware of the challenge of doing so than Cheryl Crawford, the show's first producer, who ultimately resigned from the project when she was unable to find backers for a show with such bleak box office potential. Not only did the show have three murders at the core of its plot, it also had no stars (the creators were determined to cast the production with young, unknown talent), no Broadway pizzazz, and anything but a typical Broadway happy ending. The show eventually found financing when Hal Prince came on as a producer, but in truth the backers that he ultimately recruited to finance the show had no real belief that it would succeed commercially. They simply hoped that it would allow them entrée into Prince's future shows, where they thought they could earn back the money they would surely lose on *West Side Story*.

What could Bernstein have thought back in 1949 when, excited by the idea of reinterpreting *Romeo and Juliet*, he spoke of "making a musical that tells a tragic story in musical-comedy terms, using only musical-comedy techniques, never falling into the 'operatic' trap"?[6] *Carousel* had a death in its story, but Rodgers and Hammerstein made it acceptable by transforming *Liliom*'s original downbeat ending into an uplifting Broadway finale. *Show Boat* also had its darker moments and dealt with serious topics like miscegenation and alcoholism, but it too ultimately had a conventionally happy ending. In spite of Bernstein's claim that he wanted to avoid the operatic trap, the very idea of telling a tragic story in musical terms comes straight out of the opera world—something Bernstein, a great opera conductor, surely understood. Tragedy has been opera's lifeblood since its inception, fueling masterpieces from Purcell's *Dido and Aeneas* to Verdi's *La Traviata*, Puccini's *La Bohème*, Benjamin Britten's *Peter Grimes*, and countless others, including twenty-seven operatic versions of *Romeo and Juliet*. Though in 1949, Bernstein might have thought about avoiding opera, by 1957 when the show was in tryouts in Washington, D.C., he was complaining in a letter to his wife about being depressed with the show precisely because "all the aspects of the score I like best—the big poetic parts—get criticized as 'operatic'—and there's a concerted move to chuck them." And again a few days later, "All the things I love most . . . are slowly being dropped—too operatic."[7] For Bernstein, who had always had ambitions to write the great American opera (Gershwin's *Porgy and Bess*, one of Bernstein's favorite pieces, would forever haunt him as something to emulate), opera's vocabulary was a natural response to a classic Shakespearean tragedy like *Romeo and Juliet*, and the search for the perfect balance between opera and musical theater that the collaborators struggled to find would not be resolved for Bernstein even when the show was completed.

Though the casting of the initial production came down definitively on the side of musical theater, with actors chosen primarily for their dancing and acting ability rather than their vocal talent, in 1985 Bernstein recorded *West Side Story* with an all-operatic cast, claiming that this was the way he had always thought the music should be sung. Whatever his initial reservations about the show's operatic side had clearly been dispelled; however, the recording's mixed results show that the struggle to balance musical theater with opera was central to the show's success. In many ways it was the multiple creative tensions at the heart of the collaboration that were the source of its uniqueness, and the fact that none of these tensions were ultimately resolved helped to give the show its singular energy and vibrancy.

Perhaps the single most important tension at the heart of *West Side Story* was between realism and poetry. Sondheim claimed he wasn't the right lyricist because he believed the show should be written by someone familiar with the lives of poor Puerto Rican teenagers. And in fact that was one of the main problems for the show's first producer, Cheryl Crawford. The social issues at the heart of *West Side Story* were of great concern to her, and as Sondheim himself pointed out, "the essential reason she was withdrawing from the show was, she wanted us to explain why these kids were the way they were. We are making a poetic interpretation of a social situation, but she wanted it to be more realistic."[8] Though the show was inspired by the real world and the creators were excited to update a classic play, they ultimately were not trying to present a realistic portrayal of Puerto Rican gang life in New York City. Laurents was clear about the purposes of the show saying, "I think the reality [of the show] should be an emotional one, not a factual one."[9] The musical tries to walk a fine line between reality and stylization (a line that became even more challenging when the show was transferred to the more inherently realistic medium of film). Before it had ever been a show about Puerto Rican gangs, as Robbins put it, it had been about the collaborators coming together to "do a work on the popular stage" and make "the poetry of the piece come out of our best attempts as serious artists." Poetry and art were the real inspirations behind *West Side Story*, not the reality of Puerto Rican gang life in New York City.

The very essence of the show's struggle between its operatic and musical-theater impulses was epitomized by the struggle between the diametrically opposed personalities of its two lyricists—Sondheim and Bernstein. Because Sondheim was so young when he wrote *West Side Story*, he has had many opportunities to reflect on the experience, and the word he has most often used to describe the show's lyrics is "embarrassing." In one of many similar interviews, he told an ABC news reporter in 2010[10] that he found his lyrics "thrilling but embarrassing. It's very hard for me to listen to some of those songs." It's interesting that, after nearly half a century, Sondheim's reaction is so emotional. To actually be *embarrassed* after so many years by lyrics that have become iconic is, I believe, a reflection of how deeply opposed Bernstein and Sondheim's temperaments were. When Sondheim said that he wasn't right for the project, he was really expressing a fundamental aesthetic point of view that he would retain throughout his career as a lyricist—in spite of the unreal nature of all musical theater, characters on stage should inhabit a believable reality and speak a language that grows naturally out of their situations in life.

From the beginning, Sondheim knew that in working with Bernstein he "was getting into a collaboration with someone whose idea of poetic lyric writing was the antithesis of mine,"[11] and for Sondheim, the lyrics that he and Bernstein were writing for Tony and Maria were simply not believable. No young girl who had just gotten off the boat from Puerto Rico, he often said, could possibly sing lyrics like "It's alarming how charming I feel," or "today the world was just an address, a place for me to live in." In his hugely entertaining and insightful book of collected lyrics and commentary, *Finishing the Hat*, Sondheim says of one of Bernstein's favorite lines— "Tonight there will be no morning star"—that though "Tony is supposed to be a dreamy character . . . it's unlikely he's even seen a morning star (you don't see stars in Manhattan except at the planetarium), much less that he would be inclined to use it as an image."[12] The difference between Bernstein's fondness for purple prose and Sondheim's cooler, more "realistic" writing is often attributed simply to their different temperaments. There is no doubt that Bernstein's wildly demonstrative public personality and Sondheim's out-of-the-limelight private lifestyle are reflected in their very different lyrics. But it was more than that. Sondheim's body of work, though sophisticated, erudite, and seemingly light-years removed from the musicals of Kern and Berlin, is still at heart animated by the same basic impulse that inspired the creation of the American musical in the first place: a rejection of European operettas and their make-believe worlds in favor of an art form that grew out of American realities and spoke the vernacular language of real people in real situations. The American musical's language was conversational, its music was accessible, operatic sopranos were replaced by actresses who could communicate, and it tried to bring the elite, highbrow, artificial, stylized world of operetta down to earth and ground it in American life. Sondheim's work presents an extremely literary, highbrow version of this aesthetic, but it is still grounded in a concern with reality, with believable people, communicating in believable ways, in believable if often highly unusual situations and locales (*Pacific Overtures, Sweeney Todd,* etc.). In fact, in a work like *A Little Night Music,* it is the tension between the operetta-like artificiality of the show's setting and the utterly human thoughts and feelings of its characters that is at the heart of the musical's poignancy and power.

Bernstein, however, was fueled by fundamentally different impulses. Though energized by the vitality, informality, and accessibility of musical theater, he could never quite rid himself of his love for the soaring lyricism and exaggerated passions of opera. He loved the sounds of operatic voices, the extreme emotionalism of operatic drama, and the stylized reality that it represented—a reality that seemed to resonate at the same frequency as his own personality as a musician and a public figure. Because Bernstein's impulses continually gravitated toward the operatic, Sondheim's coolness and restraint provided crucial balance. But the reverse was also true. Bernstein's operatic impulses often infused Sondheim's lyrics with a passion they might otherwise never have attained. Though the clash of their temperaments might have made for painful collaborative moments and might ultimately have led to lyrics that Sondheim would later find embarrassing, the diversity of their approaches—the checks and balances they provided—proved crucial to the show's success, and no song better illustrates this push and pull than one of *West Side Story*'s most iconic songs: "Tonight."

It is extraordinary how smoothly Shakespeare's Montagues and Capulets become *West Side Story*'s Jets and Sharks—a white, "American" street gang and their Puerto Rican rivals. Like so many musicals that followed *Oklahoma!,* dance became an essential component of the show, and the opening danced Prologue brilliantly indicates the bitter tension between the two gangs. The plot is set in motion when Riff, the leader of the Jets, decides to challenge Bernardo, the leader of the Sharks, to a rumble that night at a dance in the gym. Riff's best friend Tony, the cofounder of the Jets, has been trying to distance himself from the gang, but when Riff asks for his help, out of loyalty he agrees.

Bernardo's sister Maria has just arrived in New York from Puerto Rico in order to marry his friend Chino, and the dance at the gym—a settlement-house gymnasium converted into a dance hall—is to be her first social event in America. Shortly after the two gangs arrive, they begin what Laurents calls a "challenge dance" that gets more and more frantic until everyone is dancing and shouting wildly. As the frenzy reaches its peak, Tony and Maria suddenly see each other from opposite sides of the hall. Laurents's poetic stage directions read:

> Now as they see each other, their voices die, their smiles fade, their hands slowly go to their sides. The lights fade on the others, who disappear into the haze of the background as a delicate cha-cha begins and Tony and Maria slowly walk forward to meet each other. Slowly, as though in a dream, they drift into the steps of the dance . . . completely lost in each other; unaware of anyone, any place, any time, anything but one another.[13]

These stage directions are a perfect example of what Laurents meant when he said, "I think the reality should be an emotional one, not a factual one." Though what was happening onstage may have been inspired by what was happening in New York City's streets, the expressive core of the show, like Tony and Maria's first meeting, takes place out of time and place. In a magical, love-at-first-sight dreamworld created by Laurents, Bernstein, Sondheim, and Robbins.

After the dance, Tony goes off to meet Maria in the show's famous balcony scene, which Laurents updates to Maria's fire escape. The entire scene, in a sense, grows out of the idea of visibility. As Tony calls to Maria to open the scene, their first spoken exchange consists of three words:

> **MARIA:** Ssh!
> **TONY:** Maria!!
> **MARIA:** Quiet![14]

We are instantly made aware of the danger that the lovers might be seen or overheard at any moment. First by Maria's parents, who continually call for her to come inside, and then potentially by Bernardo, who shortly will be coming home from the dance. Though Maria's fear of Tony being seen repeatedly leads her to cry "Ssh!" and attempt to cover his mouth, Tony, in fact, wishes to be seen, believing that if he is, Maria's parents will like him and he will like them. Maria, however, says that her father is like Bernardo—afraid—but then laughs and says, "Imagine being afraid of you!" Tony replies, "You see?"—using "see" to mean "understand." Maria then touches Tony's face and says, "I see you," the word now having the sense of seeing another person as they truly are. Unlike her friends and family, who because of prejudice cannot see beyond ethnic hatred, Maria can actually *see* Tony. The tragedy of *West Side Story* grows out of this very inability to see other people as individuals.

It is the shift in meaning of the word "see" from Tony's casual usage to Maria's deeper, poetic usage that moves the scene from speech to song. Bernstein's musical underscoring transitions from quoting the melody of "Maria" (Tony's serenade outside her bedroom window) to introducing the bass line that will accompany the opening of "Tonight" underneath Maria's spoken words "I see you." The scene deepens emotionally when Tony picks up on her poetic usage and says, "*See* only me." As the dialogue ends, the actual song begins with precisely this image. Maria responds with the first sung phrase, wedding their fates eternally by giving the word an infinite, temporal meaning: "Only you, you're the only thing I'll *see forever*." The shift from the casual to the emotional is a superb example not only of the way Sondheim and Bernstein raided Arthur Laurents's book for their song lyrics, but of how the collaborators took the image of seeing that is at the heart of the scene—and ultimately the entire show—and transformed it from the mundane to the poetic, seamlessly merging scene and song.

The song begins with a beautiful introductory phrase for Maria that is classic Bernstein. The 2-bar introduction, with its bass line descending in four slow, graceful steps (B♭–A–G–F♯), starts us out not in the reality of New York City but in a slow-motion dreamland. Like the moment in the gym when Tony and Maria first see each other, it's a moment outside of time, barely moving, barely breathing. Three slow notes in the vocal line on "Only you" (labeled x in Ex. 14.1) generate a hesitant rhythm—Maria's demure shyness. Then the same three notes faster show her urgency on "You're the on–" generating an expressive upward run filled with Bernstein-esque passion, slowing down exquisitely on "forever," when the orchestra begins to pulse, as if the word had made her heart beat.

Like a classical composer, Bernstein develops this tiny, three-note motive (x). B♭–C–D becomes D–E–F for "in my eyes," then F–G–A for "in my words," and once again that three-note kernel generates an even higher, more passionate run on "and in ev'rything I *do*," repeated once to set the rhyme, "nothing else but *you*." The phrase then concludes elegantly with a leap down from C–G (labeled y) on "ever," beautifully balancing the earlier leap from B♭–F on "for-ever" to set the phrase's only other rhyme.

In this one opening phrase we can already see how far Bernstein had come from *On the Town* in his development of a unique style that fuses classical techniques with the world of the musical theater. Not only does he manipulate small musical motives like a classical composer, but the vocal range and style of Maria's phrase artfully blends his operatic and musical-theater impulses. Within 5 measures, Maria ascends a full octave

Example 14.1 "Tonight," opening

and a fifth—an operatic vocal range—with a passionate arpeggio in measures 7 and 8 that rises to a high F; it would be extremely difficult for any soprano without classical training to negotiate this. The phrase is harmonically sophisticated as well, changing keys within 8 measures and ending without a resolution. Finally, though the phrase has the gestural clarity of a

Broadway introduction, it is an abbreviated 7-bar phrase—not the standard 8—because Tony's passion will not allow him to wait an extra measure.*

After Tony's vocal entrance, the song continues its complex mix of operatic and musical-theater languages. Bernstein follows Maria's irregular, opening 7-bar phrase with an equally irregular 5-bar phrase for Tony, and after descending in pitch to a first "low Maria" on C–G (using the same motive that ended Maria's phrase on "ever"), Tony crescendos and soars in pure operatic fashion to a high G and a "high Maria" on G–D (Ex. 14.2).

What happens next takes Bernstein's operatic impulses to the next level. After Maria urgently says, "Tony, Tony" (Ex. 14.2), he begins to repeat her opening phrase, shown in Example 14.3. However, after copying her vocal line for 2 measures on "Always you, ev'ry thought I'll ever know" (Ex. 14.4), passion pushes them past this opening version to a fantastic operatic climax (passion pushing the tempo faster as well) where they sing together for the first time (requiring Bernstein to add an extra beat to make a $\frac{3}{2}$ measure), and right on the words "you and me" they sing in unison and hold high notes as the melody of "Tonight" seamlessly slides in underneath to connect to the main body of the song.

If *On the Town* and *Wonderful Town* served as Bernstein's apprenticeship in the language and techniques of the contemporary Broadway musical, *West Side Story* shows him using what he learned in a remarkably fluid, sophisticated manner. Though the music of the opening sounds unconventional, it sets the scene for the chorus to follow with free, more conversational rhythms, significantly expanding what a chorus in a Broadway musical can contain.

Though it might seem impossible to remember a time when we didn't know the opening of this chorus (Ex. 14.5) by heart, its familiarity can sometimes make us overlook its superb craft.

---

* In Sondheim's discussion of *West Side Story* in *Finishing the Hat*, he says that one of the things he learned from working with Bernstein was to free himself from the squareness of Broadway's 4- and 8-bar phrases. To "ignore the math. Four bars may be expected, but do you really need them all? How about three bars?" (p. 29). This 7-bar opening phrase is a perfect example.

Example 14.2 "Tonight"

Example 14.3 "Tonight"

This opening accompaniment perfectly conveys the lovers' excitement. The opening tempo marking is Andantino, poco a poco accelerando (a relaxed moderate tempo, speeding up little by little). By the time the introductory music climaxes on "All the world is only you and me," the tempo has sped up to Allegro with a marking to accelerate still more, until the opening of the chorus is marked Molto allegro (Very swift). At the same time, the

Example 14.4 "Tonight"

Example 14.5 "Tonight," chorus

harmony breathlessly goes back and forth essentially between two chords, as in Example 14.6A. However, Bernstein adds one extra exciting dissonant note to each chord. Instead of Example 14.6B, Bernstein writes Example 14.6C. Instead of Example 14.6D, Bernstein writes Example 14.6E. This driving right-hand figure combines with a propulsive bass line in the left hand above which a sustained whole-note line glues the texture together, creating a fully orchestrated, detailed, pulsing accompaniment that propels the song forward (Ex. 14.6F).

Example 14.6A "Tonight," alternating chords

Example 14.6B "Tonight,"
Kapilow version

Example 14.6C "Tonight,"
Bernstein version

Example 14.6D "Tonight,"
Kapilow version

Example 14.6E "Tonight,"
Bernstein version

Example 14.6F "Tonight"

The repeat of this opening phrase is a perfect example of how the sensibilities of musical theater and classical music can intertwine. How Bernstein internalized the standard procedures of the contemporary Broadway musical while expanding their possibilities for his own expressive purposes. The chorus begins, like nearly every other chorus in this book, with a regular 8-bar phrase (Ex. 14.5). (As always, call it A.) Like a standard Broadway song, the melody then begins to repeat, but like a classical composition, it repeats in a different key and begins to be varied and developed (Ex. 14.7).

Example 14.7 "Tonight"

The craft here is so subtle that it is easy to miss. If he had copied the opening vocal line from "Tonight, tonight, it all began tonight" on "Tonight, tonight, there's only you tonight" (in the new key), the melody would have gone as in Example 14.8A. But instead, Bernstein takes the last two notes of "There's only you tonight" (F–E♭) and does them an octave higher (Ex. 14.8B), turning the earlier version into the far-more-passionate Example 14.8C.

The phrase finishes in this high, operatic register only to have Tony pick up Maria's final high note (F) and push it even higher (with a crescendo) to a G♭ and yet another new key to begin the B section (Ex. 14.9). In spite of Bernstein's 1949 vow to avoid the operatic trap, the gestures, vocal writing, range, and expression here are utterly operatic while still operating squarely within musical-theater traditions. Following the traditional 32-bar form, Bernstein

Example 14.8A "Tonight," Kapilow version

Example 14.8B "Tonight,"   **Example 14.8C** "Tonight,"
Bernstein version   Bernstein version

Example 14.9 "Tonight," B section

then repeats this music a second time with new words for 8 measures, but like a classical composer, the repeat is in a new key with development and variation of the material. The B section begins with Tony's "today, all day I had the feeling" and continues with a clear 8-bar phrase. Bernstein repeats Tony's vocal idea (z) three times in a descending sequence with a long note on "right" to complete the thought. The way that the section temporarily cools the emotional temperature of the song by repeating the same short idea lower and lower has the clarity and dramatic rightness of musical theater at its best.

The way the chorus ends is magical in itself, but what is important to understand is the way Bernstein will ultimately use this ending as part of an extended, ongoing, elaborate scene that owes as much to opera as it does to *Carousel*'s "If I Loved You." Though the tempo changes, vocal style, range, and emotionalism of the song to this point owe a great deal to Bernstein's operatic impulses, formally speaking, the chorus has been a perfect example of a 32-bar Broadway song. An 8-bar A section, immediately repeated with new words for 8 bars (A'), then an 8-bar B section with new material, and what seems to be a return to A for a final statement to end the song. For comparison's sake, the original 8-bar melody is shown in Example 14.10.

Bernstein's return feels like a repeat of this opening, yet it is actually a brilliant variation. Bernstein copies the original melody (Ex. 14.10) for two and a half measures, but then he skips to measure 5, ascending B–C–D rather than B descending to D–C an octave lower (see asterisks in Ex. 14.11).

Then, instead of copying the opening A section ("went away") on "is a star" (Ex. 14.12), he goes rapturously higher to a high F, where he remains for 4 full operatic measures (Ex. 14.13).

If this were a standard, 32-bar Broadway song, the form would now be complete, and the song would be over. However, this moment is actually part of a much larger scene. It functions not as an ending but as a transition.

Example 14.10 "Tonight," A section

Example 14.11 "Tonight"

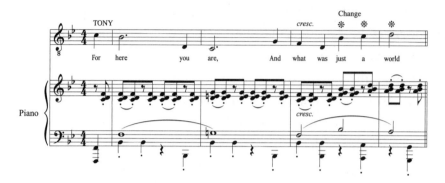

Example 14.12 "Tonight," Kapilow version

Example 14.13 "Tonight," Bernstein version

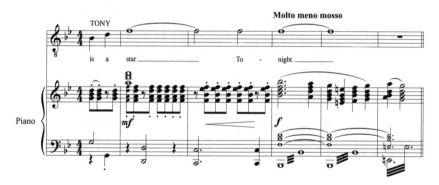

Though both singers have participated in this opening 32-bar chorus, they have not yet sung together, only in alternation. As Tony holds his high F, the tempo slows to Andante and the music magically changes key. Over shimmering strings, celesta, and vibraphone, Maria and Tony breathlessly begin to sing the chorus in unison—together for the first time— incredibly softly, *pianissimo* ("Tonight, tonight, / The world is full of light"). After 4 measures the tempo picks up, the full orchestra reenters, and they sing the entire chorus in unison now—they're together emotionally and musically—in this new key. As before, they come to the ending and repeat the same note twice (now an E) on the final words, "Tonight."

Then, yet again the tempo slows. Like Rodgers and Hammerstein in "If I Loved You," Bernstein is composing a scene, not a song. In this slower tempo, as Maria briefly goes inside to answer her parent's call, Tony sings the opening 8 bars alone in yet a third key, which smoothly transitions into a dialogue scene with string underscoring.

Maria, fearful of being caught, begs Tony to leave. He reluctantly agrees, and they make a plan to meet the next day at the bridal shop where she works. She asks him what the name Tony stands for, and when he says Anton, she says "Te adoro, Anton" in Spanish, to which he replies, "Te adoro, Maria." This brief exchange is deeply meaningful in its symbolism. Maria has pushed past Tony's surface; she "sees" Anton whereas the rest of the world sees Tony. And when they both declare their love in Spanish, they transcend the racial prejudice and linguistic barriers that the gang members cannot. Their love speaks a shared language, and having reached this magical place, they return one last time, in a third key and a slow, adagio tempo to the chorus's closing 8 bars: "Good night, good night, / Sleep well and when you dream, / Dream of me, / Tonight."

In both the opening version and the unison duet version, the vocal line has always finished this phrase by repeating the same note on the two syllables of "Tonight." Tony repeats two F's; the duet version, two E's. We now expect the song to end as before, with a repeated note on the final "Tonight"—two E♭'s as in Example 14.14.

Instead, in a deeply moving moment surely inspired by Mimi and Rodolfo's floated high notes at the end of Act I in the Puccini opera *La Bohème*, the two singers float operatically in falsetto and head voice to an exquisitely high A♭ (Ex. 14.15). To an otherworldly vocal region that perfectly represents the only place where Tony and Maria could

Example 14.14 "Tonight"

Example 14.15 "Tonight," ending

ever be together. Outside this world, far away, or as the orchestra tells us in the perfect musical foreshadowing played under this ethereal high Ab—"somewhere."

In Joy Kasson's *Buffalo Bill's Wild West: Celebrity, Memory, and Popular History*, she talks about the way that Buffalo Bill's Wild West show presented a vision of frontier life that, despite containing some authentic elements of reality, was largely drawn from dime novels and sensational journalism, thereby allowing audiences who would never have any real experience of the Wild West to have contact with a fictionalized version that ultimately became a substitute for the real thing. *Annie Get Your Gun* continued this process by inventing an almost completely fictionalized version of Annie Oakley who ultimately became, as her reality faded, a substitute for the real thing. Something similar happened with *West Side Story*, but with far more dangerous consequences.

The original stage version of *West Side Story* was quite successful, running for 732 performances and receiving six Tony Award nominations (*The Music Man* beat out *West Side Story* for Best Musical), but it was the European tour, the original Broadway cast album (at the time, the best-selling album in history), and the 1961 film that turned the show into a worldwide sensation. The film not only won ten Academy Awards—the most for any musical film—it held the attention of the viewing public for an astonishing length of time. A Paris theater ran it for three years, the Rivoli Theatre in New York City for two and a half, and the movie was so popular with teenagers in Japan that law enforcement used its three-year run to help deter juvenile delinquency.[15] Because of the musical's unprecedented popularity, people who would never have any real contact with or knowledge of New York City gang life began to view it, like Buffalo Bill's Wild West show, as a substitute for the real thing. In her book *West Side Story: Cultural Perspectives on an American Musical*, Elizabeth Wells describes a sociological phenomenon that has been labeled *West Side Story* Syndrome, referring to the way the musical's romanticization and glittery portrayal of gang life has caused the government and the media to actually divert their attention away from the real problems of gang culture. She quotes a *New York Times* article from 1978 with the title "True Story of City Gang Life No Glittery *West Side Story*," describing two estranged teenage sisters in love with rival gang members who say, "This is no *West Side Story*. This is the real thing."[16]

And of course, *West Side Story* was *not* the real thing. In reality, the music teenagers danced to in gyms was rock and roll, not Bernstein's sophisticated reworking of adult, Latin American dance music, and their dance moves bore no real resemblance to the ones Jerome Robbins invented. The street slang that the Sharks and the Jets used in the musical—"Cut the frabbajabba" and "Chung! Chung!" for example—was actually invented by Laurents so that the piece would sound neither dated (though that is precisely how it now sounds) nor *too* authentic. So that it would *not* be mistaken for reality.

In the libretto, right before the chorus of "Tonight," Laurents writes an extraordinarily poetic stage direction—"And now the buildings, the world fade away, leaving them suspended in space." Though *West Side Story* was inspired by New York City gang life, and though a great deal of the critical discussion at the time of the premiere focused on this aspect of the show, Laurents's stage direction offers the real location where the story takes place: an imaginary world where the buildings and the city have faded away. Where Tony and Maria could use the kind of stylized language Sondheim found unbelievable, where Bernstein's operatic impulses could flourish, and where Robbins's gangs could move with the precision of City Ballet dancers. One of the reasons it was so easy to switch the show from being an *East Side Story* about Jews and Catholics to a *West Side Story* about Puerto Ricans and Americans is that the show was never ultimately about gang life. From the beginning, Bernstein said, "Prejudice will be the theme of the new work,"[17] and on the first page of his copy of *Romeo and Juliet* he scrawled, "An out and out plea for racial tolerance," which is really the key to the show's emotional power and its remarkable ability to continue to engage widely divergent audiences more than sixty years after its premiere.

Though neither Laurents, Robbins, nor Bernstein had any firsthand experience with gang life, they all had considerable firsthand experience with prejudice and intolerance as Jewish, gay men, with leftist politics in the conservative 1950s of Eisenhower, the Cold War, and Joseph

McCarthy's fanatical anti-Communist crusade. Bernstein had to deal with anti-Semitism at Harvard, where there were quotas for Jewish students. Laurents, who served during World War II as a writer of training films and propaganda scripts, dealt directly and brutally with anti-Semitism in the Army in his play *Home of the Brave*, and his refusal to hide his homosexuality made prejudice a lifelong reality. Both Bernstein and Laurents were blacklisted in Hollywood and had their passport renewals held up by the State Department. The FBI investigated Bernstein and Robbins and maintained extensive files on them throughout the 1970s, and in one of the most chilling episodes in his life, Robbins was summoned to testify before the House Un-American Activities Committee in 1953, where he admitted to being a member of the Communist Party and named names—an action for which Laurents never forgave him.[18] Ed Sullivan, the host of the most popular television show of the era, refused to have Robbins on his show and threatened to reveal his homosexuality if he did not cooperate with the FBI.[19]

Prejudice and intolerance in the 1950s was by no means limited to gay men, Jews, or leftists. It was rampant throughout the country and the world at large. The battle over civil rights that was unleashed by the Supreme Court's desegregation decision in *Brown v. Board of Education* in 1954 reached a climax the day before the opening of *West Side Story*, when President Eisenhower was forced to send federal troops to Little Rock, Arkansas, to escort nine black schoolchildren into Central High School to start their first full day of classes on September 25, 1957. The struggle between blacks and whites was mirrored on an international level by the entire Cold War struggle between the United States and the Soviet Union. As a response to the United States dropping the first atomic bomb on Hiroshima in 1945, the Soviet Union accelerated their nuclear program and successfully tested their first atomic bomb in 1949. Tensions were ratcheted up further by the United States' development of a hydrogen bomb in 1952, followed by a Russian version in 1955. The possibility that the two countries might engage in a nuclear war that could destroy the human race at any moment—a "nuclear rumble"—created a sense of uncertainty and fear that was felt by nearly everyone throughout the decade, and when the Russians launched *Sputnik* eight days after the opening of *West Side Story*, the country was plunged into a terrifying space age unprecedented in history.

Bernstein got it right when he said that prejudice would be the theme of *West Side Story*. Though the particular form that prejudice took in the show was between Puerto Ricans and white Americans, on a fundamental level the same fear and hatred of an "other"—be it a Montague, a Capulet, a Jew, a homosexual, a leftist, an African American, or a Russian—lay behind all prejudice. What made the show so powerful was not its specificity but its universality. In basing their show on Shakespeare's timeless tale, they elevated their story beyond a particular situation at a particular moment in time to something that would be meaningful in all situations for all times.

Perhaps the biggest difference between *Romeo and Juliet* and *West Side Story* is the fact that Maria does not die in the end. In the show's powerful final scene—which Bernstein, after many attempts, finally gave up trying to turn into a song—Maria rises from Tony's dead body, takes Chino's gun, points it at the two gangs, and shouts "WE ALL KILLED HIM; and my brother and Riff. I, too. I CAN KILL NOW BECAUSE I HATE NOW." Moved by the depth and honesty of Maria's grief, the two gangs lift up Tony's body and process out together: rifts healed by the tragedy they have all witnessed. The instrumental music underscoring this procession could not be more perfect. The orchestra first plays the anguished music of "I have a love" (from the duet "A Boy Like That—I Have a Love"), followed by four, poignant, soothing bars of "Somewhere," and then a final, sophisticated, ambivalent cadence* denying closure. Denying resolution.

---

* For musicians, a resolution to a C-major chord in the upper parts undercut by a questioning, dissonant, F♯ bass note underneath.

In a sense, this ending, like so much of *West Side Story*, perfectly fuses Bernstein's operatic impulses with the world of the commercial theater. Though this scene clearly feels like the ending of an operatic tragedy, in many respects it also functions as an uplifting if not upbeat Broadway ending, "an out and out plea for racial tolerance." In spite of the tragic, operatic element of Tony's death, that death has allowed the community to reach a new space—a new communion. The world has faded away, and they have at least for a brief moment reached a place that is suspended in time and space. It is a place Bernstein strove to reach over and over again in the ending of theater pieces like *Mass* ("Pax: Communion"), and *Candide* ("Make Our Garden Grow"), as well as in his famous performance of Beethoven's Ninth Symphony when the Berlin Wall fell in 1989. A place where *"Alle Menschen werden Brüder"*—where all men shall be brothers. Where difference and prejudice are overcome. Where we are all connected.

It is a place that America and the rest of the world were desperately trying to reach at that moment in 1957. A place where blacks and whites might overcome racial prejudice, connect, and become brothers; where Russians and Americans might end a planet-threatening arms race, and where Jews and Arabs might find peace and reconciliation in the Mideast. Like so much about Bernstein, his hope for the future was larger than life, yet it grew out of a fundamental idealism that has always been at the heart of the American identity—the belief in America as a possibility. A belief that someday we shall overcome what divides us and find what unites us.

In a profound sense, it was this desire for connection that drove Bernstein's creative life as an educator, conductor, composer, and collaborator, and was at the center of his entire personality. Perhaps it was only in his art that this kind of connection could be perfectly realized, and perhaps it was only in the artificial world of a musical that the prejudice so omnipresent in the society at large could be overcome, but a belief in its possibility—a belief that there is a "somewhere" where this kind of connection can happen—is, in its own way, a happy ending.

15

Rock and Roll, Broadway, and the Me Decade

Stephen Sondheim's "Send in the Clowns"

When *West Side Story* opened in London, a review in the *London Sunday Express* exclaimed:

> The musical comedy has grown up! *West Side Story* is no mutation freak. It isn't just marvelous music, superb dancing, better singing, and better acting than we're used to. It is *different*. So different and so *much* better that there will be no going back to sentimental flimsiness. The usual musical's anemic, happy-ever-after plot will be as impossible now as women's magazine stories after *War and Peace*.[1]

In spite of this reviewer's enthusiastic proclamation of a rosy new millennium where the Broadway musical would be as transformed by *West Side Story* as literature was by *War and Peace*, there were of course women's magazine stories after *War and Peace* and sentimental musicals with happily-ever-after plots after *West Side Story*. Interestingly enough, no one disagreed with the London reviewer's assessment of the show's influence more profoundly than Sondheim himself, who said:

West Side Story hasn't influenced anything at all. Because it's, as far as I'm concerned, sui generis. I mean, name me a musical that's been influenced by *West Side Story*. I can't think of one. . . . There are shows that are originals and there are shows that are dead ends, in and of themselves, because they respond only to the requirements—as *West Side Story* does—of that particular story.[2]

Though as we shall see, Sondheim's own musicals were, I believe, profoundly influenced by *West Side Story* in ways that Sondheim himself may have been unaware of, the immediate history of the post–*West Side Story* Broadway musical in the 1960s would surely seem to support Sondheim's point of view. The decade was filled with traditional musicals—*Oliver!*, *The Fantasticks, Funny Girl, Hello Dolly, Zorba*, and *1776*—that blissfully ignored *West Side Story*'s legacy and generated huge audiences. Even the few darker, more serious shows like *Cabaret* (1966) and *Fiddler on the Roof* (1964) never approached the musical complexity or tragic drama of *West Side Story*.

Two shows that in essence bracketed the decade, *Bye Bye Birdie* (1960) and *Hair* (1968),* however, dealt with a revolution in the musical world that would not only have profound repercussions for the future of the Broadway musical but for American society as a whole. *Bye Bye Birdie* is the fictional story of Conrad Birdie, the world's most famous rock and roll superstar, who is about to be drafted into the Army. His agent concocts a final publicity stunt where Conrad will kiss his biggest fan, Kim McAfee of Sweet Apple, Ohio, on the decade's most popular television show, *The Ed Sullivan Show*, before being inducted. Birdie was obviously based on Elvis Presley, who had been inducted into the Army in March 1958 and served as a regular soldier for two years, until a month before *Bye Bye Birdie* opened on Broadway.

---

* *Hair* actually opened Off Broadway at the Public Theater in October of 1967 but did not open on Broadway until April of 1968.

Though Presley has now become almost a camp figure, largely known to the public through impersonators and his Graceland estate, it is almost impossible to overestimate his impact on both American music and culture. White Americans had been appropriating black music throughout the first half of the century, transforming "race music" into "rhythm and blues" and spreading it throughout the country on radios, car radios, transistor radios, jukeboxes, and records. But Elvis Presley took this to a completely new level while adding a sexually provocative performance style that earned him the nickname "Elvis the Pelvis," as he, more than any other artist, turned rhythm and blues into rock and roll and made race music mainstream. Bill Haley's "Rock Around the Clock" (a classic 12-bar blues) had spent twenty-four weeks on the *Billboard* chart in 1955* and was popular with young people all over the world, but it was really 1956 that marked the indisputable arrival of rock and roll. In the nine months between April and December of that year, Presley astonishingly had four No. 1 hits: "Heartbreak Hotel," "I Want You, I Need You, I Love You," "Don't Be Cruel/Hound Dog," and "Love Me Tender."† He continued his extraordinary run in 1957 with four more number-one hits, including "All Shook Up" and "Jailhouse Rock." Once Presley opened the door, others followed quickly, and by the end of 1957, forty of the top sixty records and every entry in *Billboard*'s Top 10 was a rock song.[3] A *Billboard* magazine article that succinctly summed up the generational impact of the rock and roll revolution was headlined TEEN-AGERS DEMAND MUSIC WITH A BEAT, SPUR RHYTHM-BLUES, and went on to point out that "the teen-age tide has swept down the old barriers which kept this music restricted to a segment of the population."[4]

The reaction of parents and community leaders to this new, overtly sexual, music (spoofed in *Bye Bye Birdie*) was violent and extreme. Put simply,

---

* Interestingly enough, it was the placement of the song underneath the opening credits of the film *The Blackboard Jungle* that really made "Rock Around the Clock" popular, and Jerome Robbins listed the film in his early planning notes for *West Side Story* as one of the films on gang life that were currently popular.

† "Love Me Tender" was actually inspired by the American Civil War song "Aura Lee."

rock music and the frenzied response it generated among young people terrified adults. Echoing earlier reactions to the supposed immorality of the Roaring Twenties and songs like Porter's "Let's Do It," the older generation saw rock and roll as an affront to public morality and common decency that would lead, according to *Variety* magazine, to "juvenile violence and mayhem." Presley's swaying hips provoked moral outrage on the part of parents who saw his sexuality and the frenzy it created as a threat to the very fabric of "decent" society. Rock and roll belonged exclusively to young people, and it threatened to complete a generational split between teenagers and their parents that had been developing in America for decades.

The very notion of "teenagers" as a separate group was relatively new. The word did not even appear in the *Oxford English Dictionary* until 1941, and it was only in the 1950s that a market for teen movies, teen magazines, and, once rock and roll entered the picture, teen music really began to exist. The postwar economic boom gave teenagers billions of dollars to spend, and as they became an identifiable consumer entity with different tastes from their parents, businesses and media were quick to respond. Completing a process that had begun as early as the 1920s when the proliferation of cars allowed young people to separate from their parents, teenagers and their parents now occupied distinct worlds with their own distinct cultures. Adults are almost completely absent from *West Side Story*, and Arthur Laurents's final stage direction after Tony's death could serve as a metaphor for the generational split: "The adults—Doc, Schrank, Krupke, Glad Hand—are left bowed, alone, useless. The Curtain Falls."

Rock and roll had a profound impact on American music, and in many ways signaled the end of the so-called Golden Age of the Broadway Musical. Broadway's most traditional practitioners immediately felt the threat that rock and roll represented, and Meredith Willson, composer of *The Music Man*, spoke for many when he exploded: "The people of this country do not have any conception of the evil being done by rock 'n' roll; it is a plague as far reaching as any plague we have ever had. . . . My complaint is that it just isn't music. It's utter garbage and it should not be confused in any way with anything related to music or verse."[5]* For nearly a half-century the music of Broadway had been the music of America, but the arrival of rock and roll at the end of the 1950s created an enormous schism between Broadway and commercially popular music. Broadway would ultimately move in new directions and find new audiences, but its music would never again be America's music. Though many of the great songwriters of Broadway's Golden Age were still alive—Arlen died in 1986, Rodgers in 1979, Ira Gershwin in 1983, and Berlin in 1989—that unique period when the music of Broadway had been completely in sync with the larger American culture had passed, and the older generation of songwriters no longer felt like they had anything to contribute. Listening to Broadway and listening to America were no longer the same thing, and Leo Robin, the lyricist of *Gentlemen Prefer Blondes*, summed up the new cultural divide when he said, "I don't think the kids are writing for anyone except themselves. They don't really want to reach anyone else. It's as if they're saying, 'This is a music for *us*. This is our music.' "[6] Rock and roll had created a wedge between the generations, and the arrival of the Beatles and Beatlemania in 1964 made the split permanent. Broadway was no longer everyone's music; it had become your parent's music.

As the Golden Age of Broadway came to an end, the turmoil of the 1960s enveloped nearly every aspect of American society. The Vietnam War, the assassinations of two Kennedys and Martin Luther King Jr., the Civil Rights struggle, the Black Power movement, and the hippies of the counterculture left Americans more polarized than at perhaps any other time in the country's history. On Broadway, the decade ended with an

---

* It is striking how similar Willson's tirade against rock and roll sounds to the reaction to rap and hip-hop music in its early days.

attempt on the part of Galt MacDermot to write a rock musical, *Hair: The American Tribal Love-Rock Musical,* that would be relevant to the times and would reflect the enormous changes America had gone through. Ironically, the most significant developments in musical theater would not come from rock and roll but from a composer and lyricist who for all practical purposes ignored the turmoil and music surrounding him: Stephen Sondheim.

As the son of upper-middle-class Jewish parents, Sondheim grew up in New York City till he was twelve years old. After his parents separated, he moved to Doylestown, Pennsylvania, to live with his mother. His childhood and adolescence were lonely and painful, and Sondheim describes himself as "the boy in the bubble":[7] protected by money and insulated from others. He had an extremely difficult relationship with a mother he called psychologically abusive who wrote him a horrific, now-infamous letter in which she claimed her only regret in life had been giving him birth. He spent most of his adolescent years in a luxurious yet isolated environment in rural Pennsylvania with little human contact followed by elite schooling at the New York Military Academy, George School, and Williams College. He was fortunate to develop a lifesaving relationship with his musical mentor and surrogate father, Oscar Hammerstein II, who had a summer home nearby in Doylestown, and he later had fruitful postgraduate studies in composition with the brilliant avant-garde composer Milton Babbitt.

West Side Story established Sondheim's Broadway credentials at the age of twenty-seven, but it immediately pigeonholed him as a lyricist. Though it initially seemed like his next project, *Gypsy,* would give him the opportunity to make his Broadway debut as a composer as well, Ethel Merman insisted on a more experienced songwriter, and Sondheim was again forced into the role of lyricist—this time to Jule Styne. It was not until 1962, five years after *West Side Story*, that Sondheim finally got the chance to write both the music and lyrics for a Broadway show, and he made the most of the opportunity with his first Tony Award–winning musical,* *A Funny Thing Happened on the Way to the Forum*.

The show opened on May 8, 1962. John F. Kennedy was almost a year and a half into his presidency, some 9,000 American troops were in Vietnam, and the embargo against Cuba that would lead to the Cuban missile crisis was three months old. The civil rights movement, which had sent shockwaves through the country the previous year when angry mobs attacked freedom riders in the South, would heat up even further on October 1 when President Kennedy was forced to send federal troops to Mississippi to stop the violence and rioting surrounding James Meredith's enrollment at the University of Mississippi as its first black student. Sondheim, the "boy in the bubble," took no more notice of this than he did of the rock and roll revolution. Instead, he went his own way, and with the significant help of Burt Shevelove and Larry Gelbart wrote a vastly entertaining, bawdy, low-comedy farce inspired by the ancient Roman playwright Plautus, complete with slamming doors, silly disguises, cases of mistaken identity, pun-filled lyrics, and a hilarious, jam-packed plot. The show's run of 964 performances was the longest of Sondheim's original Broadway productions; however, its success was largely due to the hilarity of its book and lyrics, not Sondheim's score. Though Sondheim's music was competent and occasionally inspired, it would take eight more years for his real voice as a composer to emerge with the first of his landmark scores: *Company* in 1970.

The eight years between *Forum* and *Company* were difficult ones for Sondheim. *Anyone Can Whistle* in 1964 followed *Forum*'s success with the worst failure of Sondheim's entire career: a Broadway run of only nine performances. *Do I Hear a Waltz?* in 1965 relegated Sondheim once again to the role of lyricist, this time to Richard Rodgers. The 1966 film version of *A Funny Thing Happened on the Way to the Forum* included almost none of

---

* The show won the Tony Award for Best Musical, though Sondheim did not even receive a nomination for Best Original Score.

Sondheim's songs, and nothing else of Sondheim's appeared on Broadway until 1970. It is interesting that one of Sondheim's many failed projects during this time was a Jerome Robbins/John Guare/Leonard Bernstein collaboration designed to turn Bertolt Brecht's play *The Exception and the Rule* into a musical. According to Guare, the plan was to create an updated version of the play that "was supposed to deal with the idea that in 1968 having 'good intentions' was not enough and that it was presumptuous and hilarious to expect that showing man's inhumanity to man would change anything in the world. I guess we still had illusions."[8] For Sondheim, the show was perhaps the closest he ever came to creating something directly connected to contemporary, political, real-world events, but he despised Brecht's didacticism, bluntness, and lack of humor, and to his great relief, the project fell apart. No longer fettered with illusions or good intentions of any kind, he returned to his bubble and created his first distinctive show, *Company*, directly out of his own imagination and experience.

Company, based on a book by George Furth, almost immediately established Sondheim as the most inventive composer in the contemporary musical theater, as well as someone who brought a new level of seriousness to the genre. The show itself, however, like so much of Sondheim's future work, produced polarized responses. Though no one could deny its innovative style and theatrical brilliance, its sour tone and bitter view of marriage alienated many listeners. Clive Barnes's opening night review in the *New York Times* described the show's main characters:

> These people are just the kind of people you expend hours each day trying to escape from. They are, virtually without exception . . . trivial, shallow, worthless and horrid. Go to a cocktail party before the show, and when you get to the theater you can have masochistic fun in meeting all the lovely, beautiful people you had spent the previous two hours avoiding. You might enjoy it. At least this lot goes away with the curtain, and doesn't know your telephone number.

There had occasionally been antiheroes in a Broadway musical, like Joey in Rodgers and Hart's *Pal Joey*, but this was the first time a show had been populated by almost entirely unsympathetic characters. In William Goldman's insider book about Broadway, *The Season*, he says, "Whatever you call it, the thing that characterizes Popular theatre is this: it wants to tell us either a truth that we already know or a falsehood we want to believe in. . . . The Popular Theater whatever else it may be, can never be unsettling."⁹ Sondheim, however, felt quite differently: "If I consciously sat down and said I wanted to write something that would send people out of the theater really happy, I would not know how to do it. Ambivalence is my favorite thing to write about, because it's the way I feel, and I think the way most people feel."¹⁰ For a genre like the Broadway musical that, according to Goldman, must above all never be unsettling, Sondheim's love of ambivalence was a direct attack on basic principles. Though discussions about what made *Company* so new have often focused on its role in establishing the so-called concept musical, what may have been far more important was the way it brought a uniquely personal, sophisticated, adult sensibility into the world of the Broadway musical for the first time. Sondheim's characters were troubled, complex, and neurotic—perfect embodiments of the self-absorbed mentality of the "Me Decade"—and he reveled in expressing their contradictions and ambivalence in songs like "Sorry-Grateful": "You're scared she's starting to drift away, / And scared she'll stay."

Company ultimately manages to muster a grudgingly ambivalent version of a happy ending. After watching the original, negative, final number "Happily Ever After" fail completely with the out-of-town audience in Boston, Sondheim added "Being Alive" at the last minute to give the show at least a semblance of a positive ending. Yet even this upbeat anthem is filled with ambivalence, as Bobby* begs for someone to "need me too much,"

---

* Bobby, the show's protagonist, was a thirty-five-year-old bachelor unable to commit to a relationship of any kind. In many ways he is a perfect personification of Tom Wolfe's "Me Decade." He's self-absorbed, narcissistic, and unconnected. A complete opposite of the communitarian hippie of the 1960s.

because "alone, is alone, Not alive." This was about as far from a traditional Broadway ending as could possibly be imagined. For a show like *Company*, the goal was no longer to have the audience leave the theater happily singing songs that would become *Billboard* hits, but instead, as Sondheim often said, to have them laugh uproariously and then go home and not be able to sleep.

❧

Company began an extraordinary run for Sondheim, during which he won the Tony Award for Best Original Score for an unprecedented three consecutive years in 1971, 1972, and 1973 with *Company, Follies*, and *A Little Night Music*, while *Company* and *A Little Night Music* also won Best Musical. One of the most striking aspects of Sondheim's work throughout his career has been his willingness to not only create musicals out of wildly diverse and unusual source materials, but also to fanatically avoid any kind of repetition from project to project. It is hard to imagine three shows that are more different than *Company*—an experimental, plotless musical about the state of contemporary marriage—*Follies*—a pastiche-style musical about a reunion of former Ziegfeld-style showgirls at the about-to-be-demolished theater where they used to perform—and *A Little Night Music*, described on the original cast recording as "a fairy tale for adults, a stylish celebration of romantic love set in the enchanted birch groves of Sweden at the turn of the century."

At first glance, it's difficult to think of a less likely subject for an American musical that opened a month after Roe v. Wade, in the middle of Watergate, as the final peace pacts ending the Vietnam War were being signed, than *A Little Night Music*. The original idea was for Hal Prince, Arthur Laurents, and Sondheim to turn Jean Anouilh's play *Ring Round the Moon* into a musical. As Prince put it, "We wanted to do something based on the kind of material that's called a 'masque.' Something that deals with encounters in a country house, love and lovers and mismatched partners.

Such masques frequently have people of all ages from a child to an old lady who's seen it all, and there are lots of foolish crises. Love and foolishness tied in with age."[11] *Company* and *Follies* had been critical but not commercial successes, and it is clear that the collaborators were interested in doing something that would repay their investors and have broad commercial appeal, but it is by no means obvious that composing a masque inspired by Anouilh's play would be the solution. *Ring Round the Moon* includes a pair of antithetical twins, mismatched lovers, fast-paced wit, satire of the upper classes, and a fairy-tale conclusion in which everything turns out for the best. The play is infused with a kind of artificiality that, at least on the surface, would seem to be a better inspiration for a European operetta than for a Broadway musical. Whether or not the adaptation would work quickly became a moot point as Anouilh turned the collaborators down—twice. But Sondheim was determined to find similar masque-like material, and he finally narrowed the choice down to two films, Jean Renoir's *Rules of the Game* (1939) and Ingmar Bergman's *Smiles of a Summer Night* (1956). Both contain remarkably similar elements and, like Anouilh's play, operate in upper-class, sophisticated, artificial worlds of country estates, mistresses, maids, romantic liaisons, and constantly shifting amorous partners. Mistaken identities and shuffled couplings ensue at a dizzying pace until the correct pairs of lovers finally end up together with no one's emotions too painfully damaged by the experience.

After much debate, the team ultimately chose Bergman's film. Though it has a romantic heart, it is anything but sentimental, and it couches its deep wisdom and humanity within the formality and restraint of its comedy-of-manners setting. Like an eclipse of the sun that can only safely be viewed indirectly, Sondheim chose to look at love in *A Little Night Music* from an angle, avoiding the direct glare that had proved so problematic for audiences in *Company*. The distancing inherent in the show's turn-of-the-century, Swedish setting with a score consciously based on time signatures that were all multiples of three—an apotheosis of the nineteenth century's defining dance, the waltz—allowed Sondheim, like Bergman, to contain his own romantic impulses within an ironic, stylized framework that gives the show* an unparalleled poignancy perhaps most perfectly expressed by its most famous song, "Send in the Clowns."

The clever and sophisticated book for *A Little Night Music* was written by Hugh Wheeler, an English-born playwright, screenwriter, and librettist who would go on to work on the 1974 version of *Candide*, was the sole librettist for *Sweeney Todd*, and contributed additional material to *Pacific Overtures*. Wheeler shared Sondheim's love of mystery novels (Wheeler had written several of them under a *nom de plume*), and the satisfying way that *A Little Night Music*'s plot eventually works itself out has much in common with the kind of neat and tidy resolution offered by conventional mysteries. Wheeler was remarkably faithful to Bergman's screenplay, reproducing not only its outline but also large portions of scenes and individual lines almost verbatim.

The central relationship in the show is between Desiree Armfeldt, a well-known actress of a certain age, and Fredrik Egerman, a lawyer and Desiree's former lover. After splitting up many years earlier (Fredrik is unaware of the child he has fathered with her—a boy named Fredrik in Bergman's film, a girl named Fredrika in *Night Music*), Desiree has decided to rekindle their relationship and marry Fredrik, only to discover that he has just married an eighteen-year old girl named Anne. Adding further complications to the plot, Fredrik's son Henrik is also in love with Anne (though he doesn't yet know it), Desiree has her own lover who has his own jealous wife, and they all end up at Desiree's mother's country estate for a weekend in which each person who is initially paired with the wrong partner eventually finds their way to the right one.

The brief scene that leads up to "Send in the Clowns" is one of the most

---

* Sondheim's decision to name the show *A Little Night Music*, with its reference to Mozart's famous serenade, is meant to convey a sense of operatic lightness that pervades the entire musical.

moving in the musical, and it provides such a superb dramatic frame for the song (Rodgers and Hammerstein's integrated musical taken to a whole new level) that any performance outside the context of the show inevitably loses multiple layers of emotional richness and meaning. The scene begins in Desiree's bedroom. Flirtation is in the air. She invites Fredrik to sit next to her as she sews her hem, and they laugh about the tryst they had a week before while acknowledging that it won't be repeated—surely not with all of the guests visiting for the weekend. As they make fun of Desiree's current lover, the tone is light, like two old friends gossiping, but even as they laugh they are also revealing truths about themselves to each other. In an exchange that captures the show's unique mixture of honesty, stylization, irony, and truth, Desiree says, "What in God's name are we laughing about? Your son was right at dinner. We don't fool that boy, not for a moment. The One and Only Desiree Armfeldt, dragging around the country in shoddy tours, carrying on with someone else's dim-witted husband. And the Great Lawyer Egerman, busy renewing his unrenewable youth." To which Fredrik replies, "Bravo! Probably that's an accurate description of us both."[12]

Though written by Wheeler, this exchange could easily have come from Sondheim himself. What makes Sondheim's characters so compelling—even when they are as grotesque as the characters in *Sweeney Todd* and *Assassins*—is their self-awareness and psychological acuity. Like Sondheim himself (after more than two decades in therapy), they know who they are, are aware of their faults, but often simply cannot bring themselves to do better. Desiree knows her relationship with her "dragoon lover" is absurd, just as Fredrik knows that his unconsummated marriage to an eighteen-year-old girl is a ridiculous attempt to renew "his unrenewable youth." However, when Desiree finally brings herself to ask Fredrik if they might try to get back together again,* he

---

* She asks in the most indirect way imaginable, asking not if they might marry, or fall in love again, but instead if they might "find some sort of coherent existence after so many years of muddle."

is unable to give up the illusion that his young wife offers, even though he is all-too aware that it *is* an illusion. In a speech that encapsulates Sondheimian ambivalence, Fredrik responds to Desiree's offer by saying:

> When my eyes are open and I look at you, I see a woman that I have loved for a long time, who entranced me all over again when I came to her rooms…who gives me such genuine pleasures that, in spite of myself, I came here for the sheer delight of being with her again. The woman who could rescue me? Of course.
>
> (Pause)
>
> But when my eyes are not open—which is most of the time—all I see is a girl in a pink dress teasing a canary, running through a sunlit garden to hug me at the gate, as if I'd come home from Timbuktu instead of the Municipal Courthouse three blocks away. . . .

Fredrik feels two contradictory emotions, and both are true. When his eyes are open and his better, more adult self is present, he sees clearly that Desiree is the appropriate partner for him, but when his eyes are not open—which he ruefully acknowledges is the case most of the time (as it is for most of us)—he cannot help but be seduced by Anne's youth. As soon as Desiree recognizes the truth of the situation, she interrupts Fredrik's speech mid-sentence and says, with the poignant mixture of anger, sadness, hurt, and regret that only song can add to words,

> *Isn't it rich?*
> *Are we a pair?*
> *Me here at last on the ground,*
> *You in mid-air. Send in the clowns.*

One of the things that Sondheim learned from working on *West Side Story* was how important it is for all of the collaborators on a project to be on the same page creatively, writing the same show, and the seamless way Desiree's song emerges from this scene is a testament to Sondheim and Wheeler's shared sensibility. An unaccompanied clarinet plays the opening phrase of "Send in the Clowns" as underscoring at the moment in Fredrik's speech when it seems like the lovers might reunite: "The woman who could rescue me? Of course." This delicate touch adds a new color to the scene, giving Desiree a sliver of hope. For a brief moment, it seems as if she could be the woman to rescue him. But as the speech continues and it becomes clear that Fredrik is still caught in Anne's spell, the solo clarinet line assumes a lonely, sad color. Once Desiree has truly acknowledged her defeat, the full orchestra enters with the song's opening accompaniment, and the power of this rich harmony after the sparse texture of solo clarinet beautifully conveys everything that Desiree feels before a single note has been sung.*

"Send in the Clowns" was clearly written with Glynis Johns's limited vocal ability in mind. She had initially been hired to play Desiree because of her theatrical glamor, and Sondheim had assumed that the vocal burden of the show would be placed on everyone else. It turned out that she did have a very musical, breathy voice, but she couldn't sustain a note. Though Sondheim, like many great songwriters, has been remarkably adept at tailoring songs to individual performers, before writing music or words, he nearly always begins with character. He is famous for the notecards and notepads on which he generates rich background histories for his characters

---

* Where to start the song when performing it outside the context of the show is always problematic. Option one—playing the unaccompanied clarinet melody without Fredrik's words—doesn't work, as the unaccompanied melody sounds empty and meaningless without its dramatic context. Option two—playing the clarinet line while saying Fredrik's final words—also doesn't work, as his cue makes no sense without the speech that precedes it. Option three—simply starting with the three beats of accompaniment before the voice enters (or adding an extra repeat of the measure to make the vocal entry less abrupt)—makes the opening sound merely like a conventional introduction to a conventional Broadway song rather than the superb recognition and acceptance of Desiree's situation that it represents when the scene is done in its entirety.

as well as theatrical contexts and subtexts for individual songs, even though this material might never appear in the actual song. In the case of "Send in the Clowns," Sondheim points out that much of the song's unusual imagery grew directly out of Desiree's character:

> I wanted to use some theater images because she is an actress. I was aware that I had to use irony to prevent it from becoming sentimental, because she is not a sentimental character and the show, while full of sentimentality, is ultimately ironic, because it's about flirtation rather than love. There's a light, dry quality about it, rather than a sweet quality. That made me think she should ask questions rather than make statements. . . . I started with short phrases, partly because I thought someone who was wounded wouldn't speak in long phrases. Also, Glynis's voice is most effective in short phrases. But it most of all had to do with Desiree being someone who doesn't want to give in to the depth of her feelings.[13]

Once he knew he was going to work with short phrases and questions, he began to write lyrics.

> By the time I got to the second or third or fourth lyric sheet, I already had the rhythm of phrases that went da-da-da-dum. . . . And from having that rhythmic pattern, I had a series of short ironic questions, with comments on the questions. Desiree's a lady who comments on herself as she goes along. The rhythm also suggested the melody. Glynis can handle an octave and two or three notes more, but she can't sustain. And that was another reason for the short phrases. She's not a lyric singer, more of a chanteuse.[14]

One of Sondheim's fundamental artistic principles, emblazoned in large type on the inside cover of his book *Finishing the Hat*, is "less is more," and what he is able to create out of a short, four-note, rhythmic idea—da-da-da-dum (a lyrical, triple-time version of the short-short-short-long opening rhythm of Beethoven's Fifth Symphony, or perhaps more pertinently Johann Strauss's *Blue Danube* waltz)—and a series of ironic questions is remarkable.

The song begins with two ironic questions—"Isn't it rich?" (a theatrical phrase) and "Are we a pair?"—both sung to the same da-da-da-dum rhythm, the same four notes establishing a musical pattern (Ex. 15.1). The melody sits low in the voice, and the pause between the two questions gives the opening a conversational feel, as if Desiree is speaking rather than singing.* What happens next goes to the heart of how Sondheim was able to create sentiment without sentimentality, turning Glynis Johns's vocal limitations into powerful yet understated expression.

In Example 15.2, I have written a continuation that keeps Sondheim's basic outline and melody, maintaining the da-da-da-dum rhythm for each group of words, while slightly changing the chords in the piano part as well as one important note in the melody. Since my version uses the same rhythm for both Desiree's questions and her answers, we hear the same rhythmic idea five times. However, instead of my version—"me on the ground" (da-da-da-dum)—Sondheim adds three extra notes and three extra words— "me *here at last* on the ground" (da-da-da-da-da-da-dum), creating a subtle, emotional push that reflects Desiree's heightened emotion as she reflects on her situation and reacts to her own questions.

What happens next is a perfect example of Sondheim's distinctive compositional craft. Great songwriters ultimately do not set words to music, but rather the feelings behind the words. What Sondheim is really setting to music here is the bittersweet emotion of missed opportunity. Desiree finally knows what she wants. She's "here at last on the ground," ready to commit. But Fredrik is lost in a fantasy; not on the ground but "in mid-air." The way Sondheim expresses this musically is as powerful as it is subtle. Instead of

---

* For musicians, notice how much difference a single note makes. If the melody of "Isn't it" had been G♭– B♭–D♭ with a B♭ not an A♭ in the accompaniment as well, the phrase would have been far less poignant.

Example 15.1 "Send in the Clowns," opening

my **descending** vocal line (Ex. 15.2, mm. 2–3) on "you in mid-air, Sond-heim has the voice rise from F **up** to A♭ (Ex. 15.1, m. 4) with the highest note of the phrase on the word "in," emphasized by a tenuto mark (a musical symbol instructing the performer to hold the note slightly longer). This high note is followed by a full-octave leap down to the next note (low A♭ on "mid"), which literally leaves the note, like Fredrik, hanging in mid-air.

Example 15.2 "Send in the Clowns," Kapilow version

As beautiful as this melody line is, it is actually the harmony that makes the moment so heart-stopping. Sondheim's version of "you in" differs from mine by only one note (Exx. 15.3A and 15.3B), but that one note gives his second chord a deeply expressive, minor color that sets up the heart-rending chord on "mid-air." My chord (Ex. 15.3C) is plain, without emotion, but Sondheim's is exquisitely dissonant, filled with ambiguity and open-endedness (Ex. 15.3D).

The accompaniment then goes further and literally sets Desiree's heartache to music. As she holds her note on "air," the accompaniment becomes her inner thoughts—her feelings about choosing Fredrik too late—and one note is the difference between reflection and longing. My version (Ex. 15.3E) simply repeats B♭ on the beat four times, but Sondheim's one higher, yearning note—the dissonant C on beat three—shows us wordlessly all that Desiree is feeling (Ex. 15.3F).

Example 15.3A Kapilow version   **Example 15.3B** Sondheim version

Example 15.3C Kapilow version   **Example 15.3D** Sondheim version

Example 15.3E Kapilow version   **Example 15.3F** Sondheim version

W. H. Auden said that great poetry is "clear thinking about mixed feelings," and it is hard to imagine a more perfect description not only of this song but of Sondheim's art in general. This great opening chorus ends with yet another theatrical image and the song's title words—"Send in the Clowns." Sondheim could easily have ended the section neatly, with clear harmony and clear feelings, as I did in Example 15.2. But instead of my straightforward, D♭ chord under "clowns," Sondheim uses a wonderfully ambiguous, thoughtful, reflective, open-ended chord (Ex. 15.1, mm. 6–7).* Desiree sees clearly the absurdity and irony of their situation, yet this

---

* For musicians, a dominant-7th chord over an open-fifth, tonic pedal.

awareness in no way diminishes her sense of anger, sadness, and regret. She feels all of these emotions, and they are all true. Clear thinking about mixed feelings has rarely sounded more beautiful.

Though Sondheim was one of the greatest innovators in the history of the musical theater, his innovations were, in many ways, deeply grounded in theatrical tradition, and the standard, 32-bar, AABA song form that dominated Broadway's first half-century is deeply embedded in Sondheim's compositional DNA. Because of the gently fluid $\frac{12}{8}$ meter* as opposed to the squarer, more propulsive $\frac{4}{4}$ or cut-time signature that was standard in Broadway songs, the opening phrase feels utterly unlike a simple, predictable Broadway song, and the section lasts for only 6 measures as opposed to the typical 8. However, just like a standard AABA song, the second section (beginning with the words, "Isn't it bliss?") repeats the music of the opening A section exactly (with a beautiful new countermelody added to the accompaniment) except for a slight alteration at the end to make a clear, section-ending cadence.

Formally speaking, the song continues to follow the standard Broadway model with two A sections followed by a contrasting B section, but though the form might be traditional, the content is anything but. This B section is as great as anything Sondheim would ever write, and its opening measure takes us to a completely different emotional space (Ex. 15.4). Though it might not be immediately obvious to the listener, the entire piece up to this point has used only two bass notes—D♭ and G♭ (Ex. 15.1). And other than a momentary minor color on "You in mid-air," the harmonies in the piece have all been major chords. The emotional vocabulary of the song develops slowly as we get to know Desiree's feelings. After hearing only two bass notes and major chords for 13 measures, the B section starts with a brand-new bass note (an F), and our first true minor chord (an F-minor chord). It feels as if we are

---

* As well as the asymmetrical $\frac{9}{8}$ bar for "last on the ground" (Ex. 15.1, m. 4). Shifting meters in music has the same effect as shifting line lengths in poetry. It makes the metrical flow less formal, less organized, less controlled, and more conversational.

suddenly entering a deeper, richer, more passionate world. As if artifice, wit, and irony are being put aside, and Desiree is finally telling us how she really feels. The B section's move to a new key with an expanded harmonic palette is a move to a new psychological space. Content and form are one.

The harmony in this section is superb and deeply moving. For the purpose of comparison, I have written a version of this passage using standard harmony in Example 15.5.

Sondheim's first harmonic surprise is the dark minor chord he puts under the word "opening,"* (Ex. 15.4, m. 2), which immediately adds depth and intensity to the song, but what follows takes us deeper and deeper into Desiree's psyche, beginning with the extraordinary chord underneath the

Example 15.4 "Send in the Clowns," opening of B section

---

* For musicians, a modal, C-minor 7th chord, rather than the standard, C dominant-7th chord.

Example 15.5 "Send in the Clowns," Kapilow version

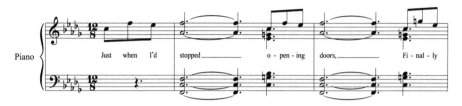

word "finally." Instead of my version (Ex. 15.5), Sondheim writes a highly unusual, wonderfully dissonant, mixed chord that begins major yet ends minor (E♮ clashing with E♭ in Ex. 15.4, m. 3).*

Sondheim's words are lyrical and again express deeply felt emotions "sideways"—so to speak—from an angle. Rather than simply saying "You were the one I always wanted," he uses a metaphor—a distancing technique. "Just when I'd stopped opening doors, Finally knowing the one that I wanted was yours." After years of moving from lover to lover (opening door after door), Desiree is finally ready to stop. She has now realized that Fredrik is the one. Sondheim takes this rare moment of honesty and confession and turns Desiree's yearning into music through heart-stopping harmony.

Right next to "less is more" on the inside cover of *Finishing the Hat* is another one of Sondheim's key artistic principles—"God is in the details"—and superb details make all the difference in this extraordinary passage. In Examples 15.6A and 15.6C, I have written standard versions of the passage with the bottom note in the right hand staying the same in both examples.

---

* For musicians, a split-third chord.

Example 15.6A "Send in the Clowns," Kapilow version

Example 15.6B "Send in the Clowns," Sondheim version

Example 15.6C "Send in the Clowns," Kapilow version

Example 15.6D "Send in the Clowns," Sondheim version

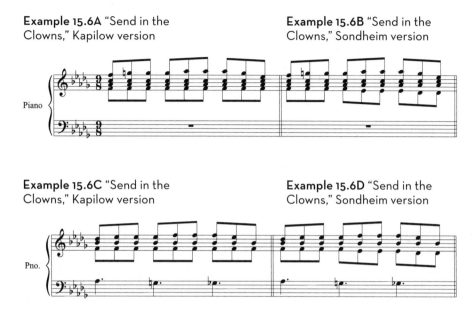

Sondheim's powerful version (Exx. 15.6B and 15.6D) changes the harmony not once but twice in each fragment, and the "wanting" catches Desiree—and us—by surprise.*

If "clear thinking about mixed feelings" could be summed up by a single chord, the next chord would be it. The text reads, "sure of my lines," and a straightforward setting of those words that was, so to speak, "sure of its lines" (how Desiree used to be) would sound like Example 15.7A. Sondheim instead uses a wonderfully ambivalent, dissonant chord† that is anything but "sure of its lines" (Ex. 15.7B).

This is not just an interesting, unusual chord chosen for its purely musical effect, but rather a representation of who Desiree has become. A

---

* The vocal melody enhances the emotional effect of the harmony. After singing nothing but short, breathless, five- and seven-note phrases, Desiree now sings two 13-note phrases ("Finally knowing the one that I wanted was yours" and "Making my entrance again with my usual flair"), which, in the song's restricted melodic universe, feels like an outpouring of passionate melody.

† For musicians, an oddly spelled D♯ half-diminished 7th chord.

Example 15.7A "Send in the Clowns," Kapilow version   **Example 15.7B** "Send in the Clowns," Sondheim version

woman who has always been in control but who has now lost her footing. A woman who has been undone by real pain. Once again, the piano becomes Desiree's inner thoughts, and once again "God is in the details." In Example 15.8 I have written a version of this measure, which is nothing more than emotionless filler and simply repeats the same figure in the right hand three times.

Sondheim's version (Ex. 15.9), however, yearns exquisitely for two beats with two dissonant B♭'s (the third and sixth notes of the measure), and then, in a subtle depiction of resignation, through a single note falls back to A♭, a note that is consonant to the chord underneath, a note that accepts the reality of her situation. Desiree may now be "sure of her lines," but—and there is nothing more horrible on every level for a woman who has been a superlative actress both on stage and off—"no one is there."

Her journey from anger, regret, irony, despair, and humiliation to a hard-won acceptance is complete, and there is nothing left but to return

Example 15.8 "Send in the Clowns," Kapilow version

Example 15.9 "Send in the Clowns," Sondheim version

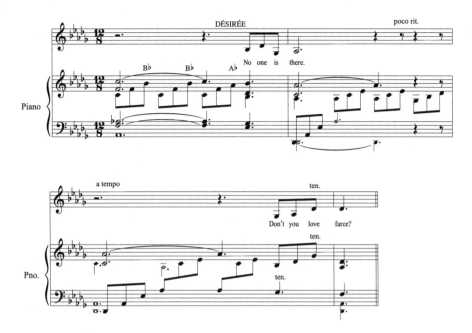

to farce. Looking directly at the sun for too long can be dangerous, and it is time to turn away. In a theatrical image for an utterly theatrical woman, there is nothing left to do but "send in the clowns."

"Send in the Clowns" has without a doubt become Sondheim's most famous song. By his own count there have been more than five hundred separate recordings. Though there has probably never been anyone who has written more intelligently about the art of songwriting than Sondheim, he seems to have always been baffled by the song's popularity. In *Finishing the Hat* he makes his befuddlement clear: "Why so many fine (and not so fine) singers have recorded 'Send in the Clowns' is a mystery to me. Not that I don't think the song is eminently worth singing, but why this ballad of all the ones I've written?"[15] After positing that Judy Collins's and Frank Sinatra's recordings were fundamentally responsible for its success, he expresses his amazement that Collins's recording won a Grammy Award for Song of the Year in 1976 against rock and pop contenders, and in an acknowledgment of the bubble within which he and Broadway continue to exist, points out that it was the last time a song from a musical won Song of the Year. He finally gives up any attempt at explanation and concludes, "The success of 'Send in the Clowns' is still a mystery to me."

That someone as insightful as Sondheim should be so baffled by his most famous song perhaps suggests that something deeper might be at work, and Hal Prince hints at a potential explanation when he describes the first time he heard the song. "We were doing a run-through for an invited audience at the Shubert, and we met early in the morning and Steve delivered the song. *Very* apologetically. He said, 'I don't know what I think of this,' and then muttered to me, 'Sounds like a piano bar song.' . . . Steve always suspected it was too pretty, too easy to remember, too whatever."[16]

It is interesting that many of the world's most famous pieces of music, like "Send in the Clowns," have been created at a whirlwind pace, either as a result of an impending deadline or a sudden burst of inspiration. In the classical music world, Saint-Saëns's *Carnival of the Animals*, Prokofiev's *Peter and the Wolf*, and Shostakovich's Eighth String Quartet were all written at blinding speed, and they are among each composer's most iconic works. Writing quickly tends to reduce self-criticism and self-consciousness, and in each of these cases, it perhaps allowed these composers to bypass inner critics and access aspects of their musical personalities that they might normally have rejected. Saint-Saëns considered *Carnival of the Animals* to be nothing more than a joke for a party, and its success caused him such embarrassment that he refused to allow it to be published during his lifetime.* Prokofiev's *Peter and the Wolf* was written for children's amusement—as a kind of musical holiday—and like *Carnival of the Animals*, tapped into a kind of humor and accessibility present in almost none of Prokofiev's other music.

---

* He did allow one movement—"The Swan"—to be published but suppressed the rest.

Shostakovich's Eighth Quartet was written as a reaction to the bombed-out city of Dresden he visited while working on a film score. Like *Carnival of the Animals* and *Peter and the Wolf*, the quartet, written in a white-hot burst of inspiration, has a visceral directness of expression and accessibility that is noticeably absent from his other works.

Perhaps something similar is true of "Send in the Clowns." Written in a single night, in a state of near-exhaustion, after the show was nearly complete, under the pressure of a deadline, constrained by the limitations of Johns's vocal abilities, it is possible that the song bypassed some of Sondheim's famous self-censorship and self-criticism and accessed emotional aspects of his carefully controlled musical personality that might otherwise have been unavailable.* Sondheim refers to Desiree as "being someone who doesn't want to give in to the depth of her feelings," and this description could apply equally to Sondheim himself. Perhaps being exhausted and under enormous pressure, Sondheim allowed a part of himself—a depth of feeling—to escape his control and enter the song causing him, like Saint-Saëns, to be embarrassed and apologetic afterward. For having written a "piano bar song" that was "too pretty, too easy to remember, too whatever." Perhaps the very depth of feeling that embarrassed Sondheim is actually at the heart of what makes the song so special, and his inability to acknowledge his own depth of feeling leaves him unable to explain the song's universal appeal.

There is something wonderfully ironic about the fact that the song Sondheim is most embarrassed about should be his only song to have successfully crossed over to the Billboard Pop Singles chart, where Judy Collins's recording spent twenty-seven weeks and earned her a Grammy nomination for Best Pop Vocal Performance. Once rock and roll took over the popular-music scene in the late 1950s and early '60s, Broadway and

---

* Sondheim was extremely conscious of the struggle with his own mental censors that writing entailed and spoke openly about his use of liquor and marijuana as loosening agents.

commercially popular music went down completely different paths. Broadway songs almost never appeared on the Billboard Pop charts (Louis Armstrong's recording of "Hello, Dolly!" being a notable exception), and until the twenty-first century brought jukebox musicals and Disney scores onto Broadway, rock composers were almost completely absent from Broadway theaters. Yet somehow Judy Collins—the quintessential folk singer of the Woodstock era—transformed Sondheim's dramatically subtle, conversational, theater song about missed opportunities into a lyrical, melodic ballad that bridged what at the time seemed like an unbridgeable chasm between Broadway and Billboard. Removed from the theatrical context for which it had been created, the song somehow retained its emotional core, its "too-whatever" quality. Somehow, for one brief moment in the Me Decade, Sondheim's clear thinking about mixed feelings brought the country together and turned a nation of me's into an America of we's.

16

New Directions On and Off Broadway

Stephen Sondheim's "Finishing the Hat"

Stephen Sondheim is probably the most decorated composer in the history of the musical theater. He has won the Tony Award for Best Musical six times, the Grammy Award for Best Show Album six times, an Oscar for Best Song in a Film, a Pulitzer Prize, he has been elected to the American Academy and Institute of Arts and Letters, appointed as a Visiting Professor of Contemporary Theatre at Oxford University, and received a National Medal of Arts from the National Endowment for the Arts. Given his iconic status today, it can be difficult to remember how controversial his work was in the 1970s and '80s. However, three successive Tony Award–winning musicals—*Company* (Best Musical, Best Original Score, 1971), *Follies* (Best Original Score, 1972), and *A Little Night Music* (Best Musical, Best Original Score 1973)—seemed finally to have won over critics and to some degree the popular audience. It also created what might be called a "Sondheim moment" in the cultural conversation, an acknowledgment of the new level of sophistication, seriousness, and art that he brought to musical theater. Feature articles were written about him in prestigious publications like the *New York Times Magazine*, and the *New Yorker*, and he was pictured on the cover of *Newsweek*. He appeared on television countless times on programs like *Charlie Rose, Larry King Live, 20/20, Good Morning America, The MacNeil/Lehrer Newshour, and 60 Minutes*, and Leonard Bernstein himself anointed Sondheim "the most important force in the American musical theater."[1] Though neither *Company, Follies*, nor *A Little Night Music* sounded like *West Side Story* in any way, the artistic intent, integrity, and erudition of these three shows was inspired by the earlier collaboration and spoke to a similar if limited audience for this new kind of sophisticated work. The headiness of this post–*Night Music* moment and the self-confidence that it generated emboldened Sondheim to continue his artistic experimentation, and he ended the decade with two shows—*Pacific Overtures* (1976) and *Sweeney Todd* (1979)—that pushed the boundaries of musical theater beyond anything Bernstein had ever imagined.

Sondheim knew he was breaking new ground with these shows, and in an interview in the *New York Times* before *Pacific Overtures* opened, he proudly described it as "the most bizarre and unusual musical ever to be seen in a commercial setting."[2] (Not exactly the best pitch for investors.) Who but Sondheim and Harold Prince, the show's director, would have thought that a complex story about Commodore Perry's 1853 visit to open Japan to Western influence, told from the Japanese point of view, in a Kabuki style, with men playing women's parts would make a good idea for a musical? And who but Sondheim, Prince, and the show's book writer John Weidman could have been surprised that the show would receive horrific reviews, find no audience, close after only 193 performances, and lose its entire financial investment?

A great deal of critical writing about the Broadway musical over the past fifty years has focused on the so-called "concept musical"—a musical in which a unifying concept or theme replaces a conventional plot as a show's basic organizing principle—with the Sondheim-Prince team usually described as one of the principal creators of the genre. Ironically, Prince himself hated the label, and though thousands of pages have been spent trying to define what a concept musical is, it is hard to imagine a more perfect example than *Pacific Overtures*, which Sondheim succinctly describes as a musical that tried "to tell a story that has no characters in it at all, that is entirely about ideas."[3] The concept had proved viable in *Company* and would resurface in *Sunday in the Park with George*, but in *Pacific Overtures* it completely failed to resonate with audiences. It seemed that Sondheim's moment as Broadway's darling had ended as abruptly as it began.

One of the most remarkable aspects of Sondheim's career has been its resilience. In spite of the failure of *Pacific Overtures*, he continued to defiantly pursue his own aesthetic agenda seemingly without a thought of commercial viability, choosing to base his next major musical on Christopher Bond's play *Sweeney Todd, the Demon Barber of Fleet Street*. Its melodrama of revenge and cannibalism made the plot of *Pacific Overtures* seem audience-friendly in comparison. The horrific story, brilliantly adapted by Hugh Wheeler (the book writer for *A Little Night Music* and *Candide*) centers around Benjamin Barker, a Victorian-era barber wrongly imprisoned by a lecherous judge who lusts after Barker's wife. After fifteen years in prison, Barker escapes, takes on a new identity as Sweeney Todd, and bent on revenge, joins forces with a woman named Nellie Lovett, who bakes and sells meat pies. Before long Todd is murdering everyone in sight, and as the bodies pile up, Mrs. Lovett turns them into meat pies that she sells to the unsuspecting public. In the musical's chilling final scene, Todd slits the throat of a beggar woman who turns out to be his own wife. Realizing what he has done, he then murders the judge and Mrs. Lovett in a state of delirium, and the tragedy ends with Todd's own murder at the hands of Mrs. Lovett's young assistant, Toby.

It is hard to imagine less likely material for a Broadway musical than this, or two more fundamentally despicable main characters. Though the body count vastly exceeds *West Side Story*'s and the plot is infinitely more grotesque, *Sweeney Todd* is one of the rare examples of a Broadway musical that, like *West Side Story*, is a true tragedy. In Sondheim's view, "Todd is a tragic hero in the classic sense that Oedipus is. He dies in the end because of a certain kind of fatal knowledge: he realizes what he has been doing."[4] For Sondheim the musical is about obsession and revenge, and not only does it risk alienating the traditional Broadway audience by ending with tragedy, it goes one step further than *West Side Story*: the show's finale has the entire company sing, "No one can help, nothing can hide you—Isn't that Sweeney there beside you? . . . There! There! There! There!" The company then points directly at individual audience members, essentially demanding that each spectator acknowledge that they have the same capacity for obsession and revenge as Sweeney. In Sondheim's chilling view, we are all Sweeney Todd.

Even for Sondheim, who had grown used to the polarizing responses to his work, the reaction to *Sweeney Todd* was extreme. "Most of the musicals I've been connected with have been received at first with extreme reactions, both good and bad, the barometer leaning toward the negative. . . . None, however, elicited the extravagant accolades and contemptuous rage that *Sweeney Todd* did."[5] To some critics, the show marked the high point of the Sondheim/Prince collaborations. *Sweeney* was nominated for ten Tony Awards and won nine, including Best Musical and Best Score. Yet to other critics, the show was "repellent, sick, and loathsome" and represented the "death of the American musical." Sondheim himself acknowledges that the show was "a resounding commercial failure both on Broadway and in the West End," and as if things could not get any worse, on March 27, 1979, three weeks after opening, he suffered a near-fatal heart attack.

Though the attack was terrifying, in a strange way it may have saved his life. Scared by the experience, he completely changed his lifestyle. He bought an exercise bike and vastly reduced his consumption of red meat and alcohol. Shortly after being released from the hospital, he was plunged into a blinding depression, and it seems hard to believe that the glimpse of mortality he'd experienced, and his ensuing depression were unrelated to his next project, *Merrily We Roll Along*. Based on the 1934 play by George S. Kaufman and Moss Hart, Sondheim and George Furth (author of *Company*) updated it to tell the story of Franklin Shepard, a gifted composer of Broadway musicals who has sacrificed his friendships and talent to become a shallow but famous commercial film producer. The show's principal innovation was to tell the story backward, beginning in 1976 with Franklin at the height of his empty success, and gradually traveling back in time to a younger, happier Franklin at the beginning of his promising career in 1957. Though the show was by no means auto-biographical, it seems hardly coincidental that its endpoints, 1957 and 1976, were the years of Sondheim's euphoric debut with *West Side Story* and the debacle of *Pacific Overtures*. *Merrily* is filled with longing for a happier, more innocent, pre–heart attack, pre–*Pacific Overtures* past. In "Like It Was" Mary sings, "Why can't it be like it was? I liked it the way that it was." This nostalgic tone infuses not only the entire book of the show, but its score as well.

In *Finishing the Hat,* Sondheim discusses the problem he faced writing a musical in 1981 that would convey the world of young songwriters in the 1950s. His conceptual solution was to write anachronistic, 32-bar, AABA songs in the Rodgers and Hammerstein storytelling tradition, which had been the mainstay of Broadway scores until the 1950s, but which were now part of both his and Broadway's past.

> By 1981 the musical and theatrical language of Broadway had evolved considerably, but I hoped to write the score of *Merrily We Roll Along* as if I still believed in those conventional forms as enthusiastically as I had twenty-five years earlier, before I and my generation had stretched them almost out of recognition. . . . In truth, like the characters in the show, I was trying to roll myself back to my exuberant early days, to recapture the combination of sophistication and idealism that I'd shared with Hal Prince, Mary Rodgers, Jerry Bock and Sheldon Harnick, John Kander and Fred Ebb, and the rest of us show business supplicants, all stripped back to our innocence.[6]

The combination of the bitter attacks on *Pacific Overtures* and *Sweeney Todd* and his frightening confrontation with mortality and depression could not help but make Sondheim nostalgic for his "exuberant early days," and the idea of a show cast exclusively with young actors (updating *Babes in Arms*) that would roll time backward seems like a thinly veiled form of artistic wish fulfillment. Though Sondheim creates an elaborate, intellectual justification for writing old-fashioned songs with witty, smart lyrics, it ultimately seems like a sophisticated way to conceal a simple desire to avoid the commercial failures of *Pacific Overtures* and *Sweeney Todd* by writing a score that would actually be hummable, or as Sondheim puts it in the show's autobiographical song, "Opening Doors," "a tune you go bum-bum-bum-di-dum" that had "a melody" that let audience's "tap their toes a bit."

Whatever the explanation, the tactic didn't work. *Merrily* was a humiliating failure, as confused audiences and blisteringly negative reviews forced the show to close after only sixteen performances. The attacks in the press were viciously personal and led to the abrupt, unhappy end of Sondheim's eleven-year collaboration with Hal Prince. Sondheim became bitter and depressed, telling interviewers that he was seriously thinking about leaving musical theater behind in order to write mystery novels. Three years later, Frank Rich looked back on this moment in a retrospective *New York Times* article and said that the failure of *Merrily* seemed to bring "the Sondheim era of the musical to an end. He had run through the dance musical [*Gypsy*], the operatic musical [*Sweeney Todd*], and the musical play [*A Little Night Music*]—only to end up, in *Merrily*, with an insular, self-martyring diatribe that blamed Broadway and possibly even Hammerstein for his own creative and commercial frustrations."[7] Rich concluded: "It took the fiasco of the 1981 *Merrily We Roll Along* to jolt Sondheim into *Sunday in the Park. . . .* *Sunday in the Park with George* grows directly out of the ashes of *Merrily* and rebels against it."

Though Rich might be correct in this conclusion, the "jolt" had actually been coming for some time, the result of forces that were not only psychological and creative, but also cultural and economic. In spite of the limited commercial success of most of his shows, Sondheim had always been quite comfortable financially, able to rest in his Turtle Bay bubble without significant concern about the ups and downs of the country's economy. Even when his shows were not commercially successful, they carried enormous prestige, and there seemed to always be producers and investors willing to support his idiosyncratic artistic vision. Over time, however, the cost of producing a Broadway show had dramatically increased and finding investors willing to fund Sondheim's experimentation became more and more challenging. In the 1920s, '30s, and '40s, the financial risk involved in backing a show was minimal, and if a Gershwin, Porter, or Kern musical failed, composers, lyricists, producers, and investors simply picked themselves up and moved on to the next show with barely a second thought.* But by the time *Merrily* failed in 1981, the situation had changed, and the financial stakes were significantly higher on both sides of the footlights. Now, it was not only investors and producers who were unwilling to support experimentation, it was theatergoers as well. Ticket prices had soared to match the higher costs of production, and audiences were no longer willing to spend the significant amount of money required to go to a show for an evening of experimental work like Sondheim's. A Gershwin show in the 1920s could easily have repaid its backers after 150 performances, but a Sondheim show like *Sweeney Todd* that ran for 558 performances barely recouped half of its investment. By the 1980s, musicals were no longer being funded primarily by individual investors and "angels" who were deeply committed members of the theatrical community, but rather by corporate sponsors who carefully

---

* As Richard Rodgers put it in *Musical Stages*, a three-month run "was pretty good in those days. . . . In 1920 a Broadway production needed no more than six months to make it one of the major hits of the season."

monitored shows for their return on investment. In order to do the kind
of long-term business that these costly shows required, spectacle and mass
appeal became essential, and it was Andrew Lloyd Webber's *Evita* (1979)
and *Cats* (1981), not Sondheim's *Sweeney Todd* (1979) and *Merrily We Roll
Along* (1981) that spoke to an audience whose concept of entertainment was
shaped by pervasive exposure to television and movies.

Unfortunately, or perhaps fortunately, the situation reached a crisis
state for Sondheim after the failure of *Merrily*. The real world impinged
on his sequestered existence and forced him to fundamentally rethink his
approach to creating theater. In August 1981, President Reagan signed his
Economic Recovery Tax Act into law, massively cutting personal and corporate income tax rates and reducing government spending while simultaneously initiating one of the largest military buildups in American history.
By the fall of 1982, the country had been plunged into the worst reces-
sion in fifty years. In November of that year, unemployment reached nine
million—the highest number since the Depression. Businesses failed at
alarming rates, farmers lost their land, and the numbers of poor and homeless rose to shocking heights. The impact on Broadway was immediate and
devastating. Attendance during the 1982–83 season dropped a full 22 percent from the previous year, while gross ticket receipts dropped 13 percent.
Due to the precipitous decline in business, fifteen of thirty-nine theaters—
nearly 39 percent—were dark.[8] Under these conditions, Sondheim could
not hope to find support for his kind of experimental work on Broadway,
and he was forced to explore new possibilities in the Off Broadway, not-for-
profit world that would both reinvigorate his career and create a working
model for the next generation of musical-theater composers.

૭૦

In his follow-up volume to *Finishing the Hat* entitled *Look, I Made a
Hat*, Sondheim talks about how "unexpected significant moments,
moments which happen entirely by chance, keep life surprising and

sometimes change its direction permanently,"[9] and Sondheim's meeting with the young writer-director James Lapine turned out to be one of those moments. In 1982, Sondheim saw *Twelve Dreams*, a play written and directed by Lapine at the New York Shakespeare Festival. Deeply impressed by the production, Sondheim immediately thought of collaborating with Lapine on a musical but did nothing to further the possibility. In the midst of perhaps the blackest period of his career, mired in depression and bitterness, Sondheim unexpectedly got a telephone call from a producer friend who asked him if he would be willing to meet with Lapine about a potential project. Sondheim called the moment kismet, not coincidence, and though the potential project turned out to be unworkable, the meeting brought the two together and began a collaboration that gave Sondheim new life, leading to *Sunday in the Park with George* in 1984.

Lapine was twenty years younger than Sondheim and had grown up outside of the Broadway bubble where Sondheim had spent his entire career. *Sweeney Todd* was actually the first Broadway musical that Lapine had ever seen, and at the time of their meeting, he was largely uninterested in the genre. As Lapine put it, "I wasn't a culture vulture in the past. I was a photographer and a designer and I just never went to the theater until the late Seventies. And I was more into the avant-garde stuff . . . the visual theater, not stuff that was reliant on a text."[10] Lapine's sensibility was abstract and visual, and he had created all of his work in the not-for-profit, Off Broadway world, whereas Sondheim was deeply interested in words and had spent his life in the commercial world of Broadway. Like all of the songwriters of his generation, Sondheim had "produced work under the pressures of unions, reviews, and the obligation to pay investors back."[11] Lapine, however, had a connection with Playwrights Horizons—an Off Broadway, not-for-profit theater—and Sondheim and Lapine were able to develop *Sunday in the Park* there through a workshop process utterly different from the development of a Broadway show.

Over time, Broadway has been both a physical location, a way of doing business, and a state of mind.[12] Traditionally, Broadway shows took place in the geographical region surrounding Times Square (from 40th Street to 54th between Sixth and Eighth Avenues), in large proscenium theaters with approximately 1,000 seats or more, and they were funded by investors hoping for a long-running hit that would repay their investment. Because these shows required union membership on the part of musicians, actors, and stagehands, productions were extremely expensive and of the highest quality. Initially, major newspapers would only review Broadway-level work, and their opening-night reviews were crucial to a show's survival. On a psychological, aspirational level, Broadway represented the major leagues of theater. It was the brass ring that directors, composers, performers, and designers all strove for, and it represented the dreams, hopes, and fantasies of everyone who had ever performed in their high-school or college musical.

Though Broadway was the center of the theatrical universe, theater, of course, took place outside of Broadway as well, and beginning in the 1950s, people began to refer to the wide variety of non-Broadway productions in New York as "Off Broadway." If Broadway represented the major leagues of theater, then Off Broadway was initially viewed as the minor leagues. Because theaters were smaller and Broadway unions were not involved, productions could be put on for far less money, allowing for much greater experimentation. However, as Off Broadway productions like *The Threepenny Opera* (1954–60) and *The Fantasticks* (1960–2002) enjoyed long runs and others were quickly moved to Broadway, the qualitative distinction between the two became less rigid. By the 1970s, major Broadway productions like *Man of La Mancha*, *Hair*, and *A Chorus Line* were being developed not only Off Broadway in New York but also in regional theaters like the Goodspeed Opera House in Connecticut, and this vibrant, experimental, Off Broadway world would resuscitate Sondheim's career and become his home for the next chapter of his artistic life.

Developing *Sunday in the Park with George* at Playwrights Horizons was a freeing experience for Sondheim. Like so many Off Broadway theaters, Playwrights Horizons ran their productions for a limited time period as opposed to Broadway's open-ended runs. Reviewers were not even invited to see shows until their runs were nearly over, as there was no need to generate audiences with tickets already sold to subscribers. In addition, Sondheim no longer had to deal with the nightmare of finding investors willing to put up the enormous sums required to mount a long-running Broadway show; the workshop's minimal sets and costumes and vastly lower performer's salaries brought the show in at a fraction of the cost of a Broadway production. The workshop version presented in 1983 consisted almost exclusively of Act I (the second act had not been finished in time), yet the theater's subscription audience was willing to accept this kind of work in progress in a way that would have been impossible on Broadway. The experimental atmosphere of the workshop process proved liberating for Sondheim, and he claimed that this new environment affected all of his subsequent scores. And as the first major Broadway songwriter of his generation to work Off Broadway, he created a template that became the norm for the next generation of young theater composers.

Lapine's uniquely visual approach, informed by his work as a photographer and graphic designer, opened up new creative possibilities for Sondheim as well. In *Look, I Made a Hat*, Sondheim points out that one of the things that differentiated him from Lapine was the fact that Lapine's generating ideas, unlike his own, were primarily visual, and that was no doubt crucial in their surprising decision to base an entire musical on George Seurat's landmark 1884 painting of city dwellers lounging, strolling, sailing, and fishing in a park on an island in the River Seine—*A Sunday Afternoon on the Island of La Grande Jatte*. Though *Merrily We Roll Along* features TV anchors announcing historical events like the end of the Vietnam War to convey the backward passage of time and connect the show to the real world, Sondheim's art has never truly been inspired by current events. His imagination seems most powerfully stimulated by remote realities, allowing him to comment on people and relationships obliquely. Settings like the vanished past of *Follies*, the Victorian world of *Sweeney Todd*, the turn-of-the-century Sweden of *A Little Night Music*, the imperial Japanese court of *Pacific Overtures*, the nineteenth-century French world of *Sunday in the Park*, and the fairy-tale dream of *Into the Woods*. *Sunday in the Park with George* may have been inspired by the facts of Seurat's biography as well as his famous painting, but Sondheim and Lapine viewed both Seurat and his art askew, focusing on what was missing. Sondheim said, "All those people in that painting. You speculate on why none of them are looking at each other. . . . Maybe someone was having an affair . . . or one was related to someone else. And then Jim said, 'Of course, the main character's missing—the artist.' When he said that I knew we had a real play."[13] What attracted Sondheim and Lapine was the opportunity to invent their own reality out of the cipher-like individuals in the painting and the cipher-like identity of Seurat himself. Because so little was actually known about Seurat's short life—he died at the age of thirty-one—Sondheim and Lapine felt free to invent him in whatever way they pleased.

One thing we do know is that Seurat was highly stimulated by new discoveries in optical and color theory. Under their influence he created a unique style of painting called pointillism, in which objects were rendered by means of tiny, precise brushstrokes of different colors that were placed next to each other so that they would blend together at a distance. Sondheim describes Seurat's paintings as "composed of hundreds of thousands of daubs of color . . . [with] no outlines as such, the figures and landscape being delineated by the juxtaposition of the colored daubs."[14] Inspired by Seurat's theories of painting and color, Sondheim devised a kind of parallel musical universe of dots, squiggles, and swirls that offered radically new possibilities for powerfully emotional expression. However, though the musical techniques that Sondheim used in *Sunday in the Park* were influenced by Seurat's visual vocabulary as well as the minimalism of contemporary classical composers like Philip Glass and Steve Reich, they grew naturally out of his already-existing compositional style, a style markedly different from other Broadway composers.

> I always start with motifs. Always. That's partly because of my training with Milton Babbitt, who taught me the long-line technique of musical development, whereby small musical ideas are expanded into large structural forms, and the point is to make the most out of the least and not vice versa. I've always taken that to be the principle of art. If you look at a Bach fugue you see this gigantic cathedral built out of these tiny little motifs. I've always composed that way, and I think that's why I'm attracted to the kind of musical I'm attracted to—the kind that offers opportunities to take characters and assign motifs to them which can grow with them.[15]

To slightly oversimplify, there might be said to be a continuum of approaches to composition with one endpoint represented by what one might call "melodic composers"—Verdi, Puccini, and Tchaikovsky, famous for their expressive, long-lined, vocally conceived melodies—and the other endpoint represented by "motivic composers"—Beethoven and Haydn, who constructed their works primarily out of short, continually developing musical fragments. (Though of course on occasion Beethoven wrote beautiful, singable melodies and Verdi worked with short, musical motives, their fundamental compositional approaches might still be said to be motivic and melodic.) From this perspective, Sondheim might be said to be the most significant motivic composer in a genre—the Broadway musical—dominated since its inception by melody. His approach, which reached perhaps its fullest flowering in *Sunday in the Park*, has led to years of criticism and misunderstanding of just what it is that makes his music so subtle, moving, and great.

Sunday in the Park with George tells two very different but thematically connected stories in its two acts. The musical's opening twelve words powerfully sum up the challenge of both Seurat's and Sondheim's entire life's work. George, on a white stage, looks at his sketchpad and says, "White. A blank page or canvas. The challenge. Bring order to the whole." We then see George sketching his mistress and model, Dot (could there be a more apt name for a character in a musical about a pointillist painter?), in a park on the Island of La Grand Jatte: a park we watch him literally will into existence out of his imagination. Though Dot wants George to see her as a woman and a person, he sees her only as a model. As something to draw. Art, not relationships, are what ultimately matter to George.

In a series of short vignettes, Sondheim introduces the various characters in the painting while fluidly moving back and forth between the park and George's studio. As George and Dot interact, it becomes clear that though she truly sees George for who he is and loves him, his complete absorption in his work ultimately leaves no room for her. The inevitable end of their relationship is handled with elegant economy. In order to placate Dot, George has promised to take her to the Follies, and we watch Dot primp excitedly for their evening out. Then in a moment that beautifully sets up and foreshadows the show's central song, "Finishing the Hat," George refuses to go, saying he must stay in his studio, work on his painting, and "finish a hat." Realizing that his art will always come first, Dot leaves in a rage.

Sondheim claims that he never thought of himself as Seurat or as any of the characters in his shows. Instead, he says that what he is doing when he writes is acting. Infusing himself into the character.

> So when I'm writing the song "Finishing the Hat," half of it is writing about what I, Steve, feel, and the other is what Seurat feels. And I'm aware of both going on at the same time. I'm able to get into Seurat's head because there's a part of me that knows something about this. . . . I think all writers get attracted to stories that resonate in them."[16]

It is possible that no single character in any of Sondheim's shows resonated more completely with him than Seurat, and no single song dealt more directly with that resonance than "Finishing the Hat." It is surely no coincidence that Sondheim chose the title of this song as the title of his book of collected lyrics, as "finishing the hat" is as perfect a summation of his obsessive life's work as a composer and a lyricist as it is of Seurat's as a painter. Like Seurat, Sondheim has been criticized for art that was "all mind and no heart." Mandy Patinkin, who played George in the original production of *Sunday in The Park*, said, "The character of Seurat was the hardest for Sondheim to write because George was Sondheim and 'Finishing the Hat' was the story of Sondheim's life. It was much easier to write about what George observed. The harder thing for Steve was to write what George was feeling."[17] Sondheim describes "Finishing the Hat" as a song about what he calls "trancing out—that phenomenon of losing the world while you're writing (or painting or composing or doing a crossword puzzle or coming to a difficult decision or anything that requires intense and complete concentration),"[18] but on another level it is a song about the conflicting demands of a life obsessed with art and a life among people. About having to choose (to use the song's images) between the voices that come through the window—the world of people—and finishing the hat—the world of art.

Once Dot has left George, she quickly takes up with Louis the baker: someone far less charismatic than George, but someone who adores her, supports her, and needs her. Moments before "Finishing the Hat" begins, Dot, now with Louis, has an awkward yet poignant encounter with George in the park where he is sketching. After she leaves, George remains in the park alone. His complex feelings over all he has lost are expressed in both verbal and musical fragments.

Given Sondheim's compositional style based on motifs rather than melodies, the idea of creating an invented, musical universe made out of fragments that would parallel Seurat's pointillism must have been irresistible, and Sondheim extended this idea to his lyrics as well. In *Look, I Made a*

Hat, he points out that "Finishing the Hat" has a stream-of-consciousness lyric without a single complete sentence until the final stanza. The song begins with snippets of thought, interspersed with pauses, in halting rhythm (Ex. 16.1). With stabs of feeling. Pointillist dots of emotion jumping from hurt to hurt. As George looks at the place where Dot has exited, he thinks, "Yes, she looks for me," followed by a musical pause that allows his

Example 16.1 "Finishing the Hat," opening

Example 16.1 "Finishing the Hat," opening (*continued*)

resentment to emerge and express itself in a single word—"good." Another pause sets off a third fragment—"Let her look for me to tell me why she left me"—and the painful words, "she left me," subtly generate the song's rhythmic accompaniment (m. 5).

The fragmented lyrics of these opening 4 measures are matched by an equally fragmented vocal line that uses only four notes—B♭, D♭, E♭, and F. If Desiree Armfeldt in *A Little Night Music* was "someone who doesn't want to give in to the depth of her feelings," George, in this respect, could easily be Desiree's French cousin. Nothing in the short fragments of this opening vocal line, like the fragments of Desiree's opening vocal line, lets us know how George feels about Dot; however, the two yearning chords that alternate in the accompaniment beautifully convey the feelings he cannot bring himself to express or even acknowledge. These two heartfelt chords recur throughout the musical, and they continually represent the deep feelings that George and Dot have for each other. Feelings that are hidden beneath the tensions or arguments occurring on the surface of the scene. The chords show us what is true between them, though this truth is sadly and poignantly unreachable for them as a couple. The first chord yearns while the second resignedly accepts the reality that Dot is gone forever (Ex. 16.1, mm. 1–2).

What happens next shows Sondheim at his most creative and most subtle, demonstrating the power of his unique, motivic approach to composition. The vocal line's four notes (B♭, D♭, E♭, and F) become a short motive—not a melody—and as in "Send in the Clowns," the motive repeats twice for "As I always knew she would," and "I had thought she understood" (labeled "and–a–1–2–3–4–5 on Ex. 16.1). The blending of music and lyrics here is superb. The two fragments of lyrics represent two completely separate thoughts. First George says he always knew that Dot would leave him. Five beats let the lyric register emotionally before he moves on to the next thought—"I had thought she understood." Though the vocal melody (and–a–1–2–3–4–5) is identical for both fragments, each thought is paired with a different bass note, creating a different chord and conveying a different emotion.

George then takes the thought to a larger, more universal level. "She" becomes "they"—all the people who have never understood him—and both the vocal line and the accompaniment reflect this change. Instead of repeating the vocal motive a third time, the first two notes ("They have") are higher and longer—more expressive—and the bass line changes a third time, moving even lower (from B♭, to E♭, to C♭), as the emotion becomes more intense and more heartfelt (Ex. 16.1, mm. 8–9).

This leads to the climax of the song's introductory section created by a subtle manipulation of this opening idea. The notes George sings on the words "always knew she would," "thought she understood," "never understood," and "reason that they should" are identical (1–2–3–4–5). The only notes that change in these four statements are the two pickup notes (and–a).

The first two times, the pickup notes rise to the third note ("As I al-" and "I had thought"). The third time ("They have nev-") lengthens and changes the pickup notes so that the idea now *descends* to its third note (G♭, A♭, down to F) (Ex. 16.1, mm. 8–9). The fourth time repeats the same pickup notes only quicker ("And no rea-") (Ex. 16.1, mm. 9–10).

Then, in a truly extraordinary moment made possible by Sondheim's unique motivic art, the words "But if anybody could" (i.e., if anyone could have understood him) cause the melody to rise up in pitch (G♭, A♭ up to B♭) and change the motive's ending for the first time (Ex. 16.1, mm. 11–12). And as the music resolves exquisitely to a major key and the vocal line reaches the opening section's highest note (B♭), we feel everything that Dot has meant to him. Only she might have understood him. Only she might have allowed him to connect with another human being. (Only she might have caused the motive to go up to a B♭ rather than down to an F.) The effect, within George's constricted emotional universe, perfectly matched by the music's restricted motivic universe, is heartrending. But Sondheim's art, like Seurat's, is an art of restraint, and the sentence "But if anybody could" is never completed. The thought simply hangs in the air for eight, poignant, hope-filled beats, and this beautifully understated revelation ends the opening section's emotional journey while simultaneously serving as a seamless entry into George's world. The world of art. The world of finishing the hat.

The accompaniment to the main body of the song creates a musical language out of the flickering colors of Seurat's pointillism (Ex. 16.2). The right hand is made exclusively out of primary colors: three pairs of notes (F–A♭, E♭–G♭, and D♭–F) arranged in constantly shifting patterns. The left hand is also made of primary colors: four individual notes (G♭, D♭, A♭, and B♭) also arranged in shifting patterns. When the two hands combine, they create a Seurat-like effect of flickering light in music. Constantly shifting combinations of the same few notes, or colors. Though the accompaniment flickers on the microscopic level—every beat is different—the overall effect of the

Example 16.2 "Finishing the Hat"

repeated, 2-measure pattern and single harmony* is static, like Seurat's, and blends when looked at from afar.

Above this pointillist accompaniment is an equally pointillist melody. Each fragment begins with the same five notes ("Finishing the hat," "How you have to fin-," "How you watch the rest'). "Finishing the hat" states the motive in its pure, five-note form. "How you have to finish the hat" begins with the same five notes and adds three more. "How you watch the rest of the world from a window" keeps the previous versions and adds four more notes (a subtle, Seurat-Sondheim version of a "punch line"), including the only new, climactic note of the entire phrase. The emotional high point on "window" (C♭), as George pauses and feels what it's like to watch the rest of the world from a window (Ex. 16.2, m. 8). Once again, the power comes from Sondheim's restraint. So much feeling is contained in this one new note and brief pause. But George, like Desiree, doesn't want to give in to his feelings, and the swirling accompaniment stops for only a single measure. The emotion is held in check. George quickly turns away from the distractions of watching "the rest of the world through a window" in order to return to the safety of his art—the vocal line's original notes, and the original accompaniment.

Although this opening and the song as a whole feels fluid, new, and experimental, it is still shaped formally like a conventional 32-bar song. The opening 12-bar verse (plus a 4-bar connector) is followed, as in a traditional Broadway song, by an 8-bar A section (beginning at "Finishing the hat"), which is then repeated with new words, beginning at "Mapping out a sky."

Like "Send in the Clowns," "Finishing the Hat" has an extraordinarily heartfelt B section (Ex. 16.3). The pitch of the song vocally has been rising higher and higher as George's frustration and unhappiness mounts, and all of his pent-up emotion bursts forth as he now sings in a new high register with a brand-new, dissonant accompaniment figure underneath. This new accompaniment alternates back and forth with the A section's accompaniment,

---

* For musicians, a G♭ 9th chord.

Example 16.3 "Finishing the Hat," B section

Example 16.3 "Finishing the Hat," B section (*continued*)

blending the two sections as George tries to control his emotions and get back to the world of art, to the A section's accompaniment.

Sondheim uses subtle transitions and extensions to adapt the 32-bar song form to his expressive needs, and the gradual return to the opening music after this intensely passionate B section beautifully parallels George's emotional transition (Ex. 16.3, mm. 9–13, summarized in Ex. 16.4). The

Example 16.4 "Finishing the Hat"

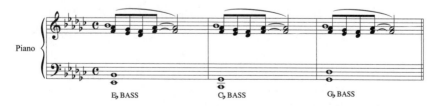

right hand of this returning passage repeats virtually identically three times (there is a slight alteration the third time), but the left hand changes each time, with the three different bass notes giving each repeat a new emotional color. The musical transition perfectly matches George's psychological transition, and the passage gives the song a beautiful sense of symmetry, as these three bass notes (E♭, C♭, G♭) are the same ones that originally ended the introduction. What is important to understand is that the return to the opening music here is not simply a standard return to a standard A section, but rather a return to a space far away from the confusing emotions aroused by Dot's departure. A return to the only place where George, Desiree, and ultimately Sondheim himself could find safety. In the world of art. In the world of finishing the hat.

The Off Broadway production of *Sunday in the Park with George* opened at Playwrights Horizons in July of 1983 and ran for twenty-five performances. In a process unthinkable on Broadway, the second act was not finished until the final three performances. This workshop/public performance process would become a new creative template not only for Sondheim's future productions but for other Broadway composers as well. *Sunday in the Park with George* moved to Broadway in May of 1984 where it ran for 604 performances, but in spite of its critical success, like so many Sondheim shows, it still lost money.* In his book *Finishing the Hat*, Sondheim laments the fact that "live theater itself is at most an ancillary part of American culture these days." Lyrics today, he continues, have only "a tiny impact on what is currently coming out of people's earphones or the bar down the block or the car blasting by. The lyrics of contemporary popular song, of rock and rap and country, are the ones that reflect the immediacy of our world, much as theater songs did in the first half of the twentieth century. They are the sociologist's totems."[19] As Sondheim points out, though

---

* In a strangely symmetrical way, as *West Side Story* was beaten out by the more conservative, hummable *Music Man* for the Tony Award for Best Musical in 1958, *Sunday in the Park with George* was beaten by the more conservative, traditional, hummable *La Cage aux folles* in 1984.

Broadway musicals may have other things to offer, they are no longer the place where one goes to listen for America. Its songs no longer hold potent material for the sociologist intent on discovering the way, as Irving Berlin put it, "songs make history and history makes songs." The unique moment in time in which the Broadway musical was in sync with and reflected the American zeitgeist—a moment when the songs heard on Broadway were the songs heard and sung throughout the country—has passed and will probably never to be recaptured. Musicals no longer "reflect the immediacy of our world," however, in the hands of great artists like Sondheim they may do something equally powerful.

In "Move On," the radiant final song of *Sunday in the Park with George*, George's great grandson, an artist also named George, has returned to the island where Seurat painted his famous painting, seeking to find a way out of his own artistic crisis. Dot appears to him in a vision and tells him to stop worrying about his doubts, his critics, and other people's opinions. "Just keep moving on. Anything you do, Let it come from you. Then it will be new." These brief words point directly to the ultimate source of Sondheim's artistic inspiration. His work was fundamentally created not by turning to the outer world but rather by turning inward. Toward his own, idiosyncratic reaction to the singular people, places, situations, and stories that moved him. Emerging out of the Me Decade of the 1970s, Sondheim relocated the center of the Broadway musical within the subjective imagination of each individual artist, challenging each creator to make their unique vision powerful enough to move others. To connect—as George continually tells himself throughout *Sunday in the Park*. Sondheim's entire career has been based on a belief in Dot's words, "Let it come from you, then it will be new." But what makes this belief not simply one man's personal, solipsistic vision is the song's final line, which beautifully captures the essential impulse behind all of Sondheim's art, and its challenge for all future artists: "Give us more to see." That is exactly what Sondheim has done. By looking deeply inside himself and turning what he found there into art, he has given us all more to see. In his comments on "Sunday," the song that brilliantly concludes Act I of *Sunday in the Park*, Sondheim remarks that "Once during the writing of each show, I cry at a notion, a word, a chord, a melodic idea, an accompaniment figure. . . . In this show it was the word 'Forever' in 'Sunday.' I was suddenly moved by the contemplation of what these people would have thought if they'd known they were being immortalized, and in a major way, in a great painting."[20] Sondheim continues this process of immortalization, and through his uniquely personal reaction to Seurat's painting, turns a distant, seemingly unreachable past into an ecstatically moving present, opening up his own inner world to all of us and joyously giving us all "more to see. Forever."

Epilogue
The Broadway Musical
Goes Global

In 1971, the same year that Sondheim gave us his poignant, valedictory valentine to Broadway's past in *Follies*, Andrew Lloyd Webber and Tim Rice made their first appearance on Broadway with *Jesus Christ Superstar*, inaugurating a British invasion that would transform Broadway in the late 1970s and '80s. With Webber's high-tech megamusicals *Evita* (1979), *Cats* (1982), *Song and Dance* (1985), *Phantom of the Opera* (1986), and *Starlight Express* (1987), and the French pair, Claude-Michel Schönberg and Alain Boublil's *Les Misérables* (1987), and *Miss Saigon* (1991), the Broadway musical, which for decades had been a quintessentially American genre, suddenly became a European import. Both Webber's and Schönberg's musicals were not only phenomenally successful on Broadway; they also earned astounding profits globally with multiple long-running productions throughout the world. A Broadway production was still important for the purposes of prestige and legitimacy, but it was no longer the ultimate goal. The worldwide triumph of these European shows in the late seventies and eighties challenged the fundamental nature of the Broadway musical in ways that continue to reverberate today. As Andrew Lloyd Webber's biographer John Snelson put it:

> A musical no longer has to be, or aspire to be, American. In itself, this is a significant redefinition of the "Broadway musical," moving it toward a global art form, with expressions of national identity becoming a more localized coloring than an essential element of the musical's identity.[1]

For decades, the music heard on Broadway, like jazz, country music, and rock and roll, had been America's music. It spoke in the American vernacular, grew out of our history, and it was embraced by a huge portion of the country. The arrival of the Beatles in 1964, and the countless British rock groups that followed, ended America's monopoly on rock and roll much as the British invasion begun by Andrew Lloyd Webber and Tim Rice in 1971 ended America's monopoly on the Broadway musical. Shows like *Cats*, *Evita*, or *Phantom of the Opera* no longer "reflected the immediacy of our world," nor were they exclusively designed to appeal to American sensibilities. Their audience was and continues to be a global one, not a local one. The Broadway musical, which had once been a national art form, now became transnational.

Once it became clear how much money there was to be made from these new global, megamusicals, corporations and entertainment conglomerates like Livent and SFX were quick to enter the scene. The kinds of spectacle required to compete with *Phantom* and *Miss Saigon* required enormous sums of money, and the financing of Broadway shows through small groups of committed insider theater "angels" who had traditionally underwritten musicals in the past was no longer feasible. Deep pockets were required, and one of the direct side effects of the European invasion was an almost total corporatization of Broadway.

One of the biggest corporations to enter the Broadway arena was the Walt Disney Company, and its impact has been enormous. Disney not only changed the content, marketing, production, and financing of Broadway musicals, it changed the physical state of Broadway itself. Through a huge financial investment in the neighborhood in the 1990s, the company helped turn what had become a sleazy, dangerous section of Manhattan into a safe, middle-class entertainment zone and a mecca for tourists.

Since the beginning of sound films, Hollywood had looked to Broadway for musicals that could be turned into films. Disney reversed this process, taking their hugely successful animated films like *Beauty and the Beast* and *The Lion King* and turning them into high-tech, blockbuster musicals that were more than a match for the European megamusicals that had dominated the eighties. The huge sums of money required to underwrite these productions posed no problem for a multinational company like Disney, and the synergistic possibilities inherent in these shows led to staggering profits. A successful animated movie like *Beauty and the Beast* generated huge audiences for the Broadway version, which generated customers for theme park rides, T-shirts, merchandise, ice shows, recordings, and global tours. Like the megamusicals of Andrew Lloyd Webber, the audience for Disney's musicals was global, and they expanded the Disney brand worldwide. What was most fundamentally American about Disney's shows was not their content but the corporatization of culture that they represented.

The huge success of Disney's "movicals" inspired others to copy their model, and shows like *Sunset Boulevard* (1994), *Big* (1996), *The Full Monty* (2000), *Hairspray* (2002), *Spamalot* (2005), and *Billy Elliot* (2008) also turned movies into musicals with equally stunning results. With the costs of Broadway productions rising ever higher, the need for finding safe, well-known properties with a built-in audience became greater and greater. Creating a new show from scratch was not only an expensive proposition; it was a risky one as well, and in addition to hit movies, one of the places producers turned to in the search for safe, audience-friendly material was the past in the form of jukebox musicals and revivals.

Before the rock revolution, the music heard on Broadway was not fundamentally different from the music on the pop charts, and songs from shows regularly became Top 40 singles. Jukeboxes were stocked with Broadway hits, Broadway's music was America's music, and parents and their children danced to the same songs. Rock and roll's arrival in the late 1950s and '60s, however, pushed Broadway music out of the mainstream, leaving it to pursue a limited path for a more limited audience. Rock and pop became the country's lingua franca: the common language that united the nation musically. The explosion of the LP market, followed by cassettes and CDs, helped pop hits reach huge numbers of listeners, and if the 1920s began a Golden Age for Broadway, the 1960s began a Golden Age for rock and pop music. For the generation that grew up during this era, its songs were the soundtrack of their youth, and over time they became a source of immense nostalgia. Producers at the turn of the millennium, looking for precertified material with built-in audience appeal, began to repackage these hit songs as Broadway shows, and the early 2000s saw an influx of jukebox musicals like *Mamma Mia!* (2001) based on the music of ABBA, *Movin' Out* (2002) based on the music of Billy Joel, and *Jersey Boys* (2005) based on the music of Frankie Valli and the Four Seasons. Their very genre locates their source in the past—an era of diners and jukeboxes—and the audience for these largely nostalgic enterprises has primarily been an older one for whom these songs were already familiar. As with Disney's movicals, the jukebox musicals reverse the traditional relationship between Broadway and popular music. In the 1930s, '40s, and '50s, music from Broadway filled jukeboxes. Now music from jukeboxes fills Broadway.

Beginning in 1977, the Tony Award for Best Revival was given to either a play or a musical that had already appeared on Broadway in a previous production, but a deluge of revivals in the 1990s made it necessary in 1994 to split the category into Best Revival of a Musical and Best Revival of a Play. Like the influx of movicals and jukebox musicals, the proliferation of revivals was a response to the need for safe properties with instant, brand-name recognition, and classic shows from the so-called Golden Age of musicals perfectly fit the bill.

Nearly all important artistic movements follow a similar progression over time. They begin as a vibrant, often radical response to contemporary conditions; develop, flourish, and spread; and eventually die and become canonic. Impressionist art, for example, arose as a radical rejection of French Salon art, flourished and spread, was superseded by Neo-Impressionism and other artistic movements, and today has become canonical. Even rock and roll, which began as a defiant rejection of everything mainstream, has now reached classic status with a Hall of Fame in Cleveland and "classic rock" radio stations throughout the country. And though it would surely have shocked songwriters like Berlin, Kern, and Gershwin who created their shows for an ephemeral present with no thought of the future, the best of the Broadway musicals from its Golden Age have now acquired the status of classics. Like classics of literature that merit reinterpretation by each new generation, "classic shows" are now revived over and over again, living exhibits in a Broadway museum. Musicals like *Carousel, Annie Get Your Gun, Kiss Me, Kate, The King and I,* and *Show Boat* have entered the musical theatre's canon of great works. They have become the Beethoven symphonies of the Broadway musical, and their prestige mounts with each new revival.[2]

In spite of this ever-increasing focus on the past, there has, of course, been significant new work, work that once again has been created by listening for America. For example, the 2015, Jeanine Tesori/Lisa Kron musical, *Fun Home,* based on Alison Bechdel's graphic memoir, was the first Broadway musical with a lesbian as the central character. The work clearly reflects a contemporary American world where same-sex marriage, LGBT rights, and gender issues have become central preoccupations of the culture. The fact that a musical centered around the complex relationship of a homosexual father (who may or may not have committed suicide) and his lesbian daughter could win the Tony Award for Best Musical shows what it is still possible to achieve on Broadway.

Though it is always dangerous to write about recent events, as only time can tell what their long-term significance will be, as this book is being written, Lin-Manuel Miranda's phenomenon of a show, *Hamilton* (2015 on Broadway), has had an earth-shattering impact on the Broadway musical. Based on Ron Chernow's 2004 biography of Alexander Hamilton, the musical tells the story of one of America's Founding Fathers in a sung-through, or more aptly put, a rapped-through style. It manages to mix street hip-hop verbal virtuosity with an astonishing variety of other styles including rhythm and blues, pop music, and traditional show tunes alongside references to Gilbert and Sullivan, *West Side Story*, Rodgers and Hammerstein, Stephen Sondheim, and *1776*.[3] In addition to its purely musical content, the conscious decision on the part of the creative team to cast people of color as the Founding Fathers as well as the show's decidedly pro-immigration, pro-diversity message has given the production an extraordinary resonance at a moment in America's history when anti-immigration sentiments and border walls are central tenants of the country's ruling party.

It is far too soon to tell whether *Hamilton* will be a unique, one-time phenomenon or the beginning of a new direction for the Broadway musical; however, it is the first show in recent memory that has been so successful at bridging the gap between the popular music of the day and the music heard in a Broadway theater. *Hamilton* speaks recognizably the same language as the music heard in the streets and on pop radio stations, and it has been embraced by everyone from inner-city teenagers to ultrasophisticated Broadway insiders.* Though the show recounts some of America's oldest stories, with a cast dressed in eighteenth-century costumes, it reinvents that past, and reinterprets our foundational myths in an unmistakably vibrant contemporary way. It allows us to listen to America then, in a way that speaks directly to America now.

---

* As the ultimate testament to the show's inclusivity, then–President Obama said, "In fact, *Hamilton*, I'm pretty sure, is the only thing that Dick Cheney and I agree on."

In *Poetics of Music*, Stravinsky says, "Tradition is a living force that animates and informs the present. Far from implying the repetition of what has been, tradition . . . appears as an heirloom, a heritage that one receives on condition of making it bear fruit before passing it on to one's descendants."[4] The Broadway musicals discussed in this book are part of a uniquely American artistic tradition, but for that tradition to bear fruit, each generation must make it their own. Today's musicals cannot repeat what has been done in the past because the America of the past is not the America of the present. To be meaningful, they must reflect what Leonard Bernstein called "our speech, our tempo and our moral attitudes."[5] But speech, tempo, and moral attitudes are continually in flux, and today's composers, directors, and performers must adapt their work to an ever-changing world. They must listen for the realities of a new America and a new world. Only then will they be able to create a new tradition, a new heirloom that they might leave for the future.

ACKNOWLEDGMENTS

n Thich Nhat Hanh's *The Miracle of Mindfulness*, he asks the reader to:

> Consider the example of a table. The table's existence is possible due to the existence of . . . the forest where the wood grew and was cut, the carpenter, the iron ore which became the nails and screws, and countless other things which have relation to the table, the parents and ancestors of the carpenter, the sun and rain which made it possible for the trees to grow. If you grasp the table's reality then you see that in the table itself are present all those things which we normally think of as the non-table world. If you took away any of those non-table elements and returned them to their source . . . the table would no longer exist.[1]

Similarly, *Listening for America* was made possible by an enormous number of "non-book elements," without which it would never have come into being. On the simplest level, had my devoted and doggedly persistent literary agent, Henry Thayer, not believed so strongly in this book, I would have abandoned it before it even got started. He not only helped shape the overall concept for the book in its early stages, but he continually encouraged me to write something that would not only look at the American Songbook in purely musical terms but also in the context of the broader society and culture within which it arose and flourished. It was he who first believed (even before I did) that simultaneously exploring both musical and historical perspectives on this repertoire was not only possible, but essential.

I am fortunate that Henry found an equally enthusiastic and committed partner in this enterprise in the person of Michael Fauver, my brilliant editor at W. W. Norton/Liveright, without whom not a single sentence in this book would ever have been written. The care and effort that Michael put into reading every word of text and every measure of music was extraordinary. I cannot thank him enough for his consistently thoughtful, carefully crafted comments that were invariably accurate and to the point. Somehow, he managed to convey his thousands of corrections and suggestions with such unfailing enthusiasm for the project that I was never discouraged, only encouraged. I cannot imagine having a more perfect editor for this book, and I can never thank him enough for the magnificent work he did keeping me on track and positive over the past five years. Also at Liveright I am indebted to Bob Weil for his enduring support, as well as Marie Pantojan, Cordelia Calvert, Pete Miller, Nick Curley, Steve Attardo, David Bradley, Becky Homiski, Fred Wiemer, and Debra Nichols.

I am deeply grateful to two remarkable scholars. Robert Kimball, the eminent historian of the American musical theater and artistic advisor to the Ira and Leonore Gershwin Trusts and the Cole Porter Estate, carefully read all but the final chapters of the book. His comments and corrections were invaluable (though any remaining errors are exclusively my responsibility), and his overwhelmingly positive response as the book's first outside reader meant more than I can say. In addition, his enthusiasm for a Cole Porter program I did at Lincoln Center in 2012 and his willingness to introduce me to several heads of the various estates involved in this project was a key factor in my deciding to move ahead. His support for the past seven years has been unwavering, and for that, as well as for his peerless scholarship, I am deeply grateful.

I was also fortunate to have Geoffrey Block, an equally brilliant and distinguished historian, read the later chapters of the book. His broad background, encyclopedic knowledge, and insightful comments were enormously helpful to me, and his thought-provoking remarks continually led me down new and exciting paths.

It has always been important to me that my books can be read, understood, and heard by anyone, regardless of whether or not they can read music. To that end, recordings of every example synced to scrolling notation appear online thanks to the technical wizardry of my extraordinary engineer, Spencer Shafter. His work has been invaluable in making this book accessible to everyone.

And of course, none of this website material would have been possible without the superb performances by my two wonderful singers, Michael Winther and Sally Wilfert, who recorded all of these examples with myself at the piano. Sally and Michael have been my partners for all of the American Songbook programs of the past fifteen years, and working with them brought these songs to life for me. I would like to thank them, not only for the enormous effort involved in recording the musical examples, but also for our decade-and-a-half long collaboration in exploring this material.

To include all of the musical examples in the book required getting permission from publishers, a lengthy process I could never have completed without Kathleen Karcher. Her diligence, persistence, and professionalism were, put simply, a godsend.

I would also like to thank my manager, Lee Prinz, who continually supported my work on this book even though it took me completely away from performing for months at a time, year after year. Without his understanding and selfless belief in the importance of the project, I would never have been able to put aside the time necessary to finish it.

Finally, and perhaps most importantly: the audiences at all of my American Songbook "What Makes It Great" programs. From the moment I began to deconstruct this repertoire at Lincoln Center, it was the audience's astonishment at discovering how much they had missed in songs they had heard all of their lives that drove me to write *Listening for America*. As they discovered, along with me, the riches of this quintessentially American repertoire, their enthusiasm drove me to dig deeper and research further. Without these "first responders"—these listeners who first helped bring this music to life for me—this book would never have been written. Thank you.

NOTES

PREFACE

1. S. J. Woolf, "Sergeant Berlin Re-enlists," *New York Times*, May 17, 1942.
2. John Williams, "Of God and War," *New York Times,* Sept. 22, 2017.

PROLOGUE: NOTHING COMES FROM NOTHING

1. *The Wisdom of George Santayana* (Philosophical Library, Open Road Media, 2010), Q-560.
2. John Bush Jones, *Our Musicals, Ourselves: A Social History of the American Musical Theatre* (Brandeis University Press, 2003), 28.
3. John Strausbaugh, *Black Like You: Blackface, Whiteface, Insult & Imitation in American Popular Culture* (Jeremy P. Tarcher/Penguin, 2007), 102–103.
4. Leslie M. Alexander and Walter C. Rucker Jr., eds., *Encyclopedia of African American History* (ABC-CLIO, 2010), 161.
5. Frank Cullen, Florence Hackman, and Donald McNeilly, *Vaudeville Old & New: An Encyclopedia of Variety Performances in America,* vol. 1 (Psychology Press, 2007), xii.
6. Bill Messenger, *Great American Music: Broadway Musicals* (Teaching Company, 2006), 43.
7. Anthony Slide, *New York City Vaudeville* (Arcadia Publishing, 2006), 8.
8. *Western New York Heritage,* vol. 8 (Western New York Heritage Institute, 2005), 40.
9. Cynthia Brideson and Sara Brideson, *Ziegfeld and His Follies: A Biography of Broadway's Greatest Producer* (University Press of Kentucky, 2015), 237.
10. Bill Messenger, *Great American Music: Broadway Musicals* (Teaching Company, 2006), 67.
11. The Associated Press, "Florence Ziegfeld Dies in Hollywood After Long Illness" (*New York Times,* July 23, 1932).

12. Linda Mizejewski, *Ziegfeld Girl: Image and Icon in Culture and Cinema* (Duke University Press, 1999), 24.

13. Perhaps more than any other individual before Kern and Berlin, George M. Cohan, as a performer, playwright, producer, theater owner, and composer, was the first person to bring a truly American voice to the Broadway musical. Though he was an immigrant like so many of the composers in this book, songs like "The Yankee Doodle Boy," and "You're a Grand Old Flag" were consciously and unmistakably American in content and spirit in a way that completely rejected European influence.

14. Daniel Hardie, *The Ancestry of Jazz: A Musical Family History* (iUniverse, 2004), 184.

15. Mark Sullivan/Dan Rather, *Our Times: America at the Birth of the Twentieth Century* (Scribner, 1996; original 1926), 411.

16. Howard Pollack, *George Gershwin: His Life and Work* (University of California Press, 2007), 49.

17. Sean Dennis Cashman, *America Ascendant: From Theodore Roosevelt to FDR in the Century of American Power, 1901–1945* (NYU Press, 1998), 72.

1. INVENTING AMERICA

1. Edna Ferber, *A Peculiar Treasure: An Autobiography* (Vintage Books, 1938), 302.

2. Though she never saw the Mississippi River, according to William G. Hyland (*The Song is Ended: Songwriters and American Music, 1900–1950* [Oxford University Press, 1995]), Ferber did visit an actual showboat for research—the James Adams Floating Palace Theatre on the Albemarle Sound in North Carolina. Kern and Hammerstein limited their research to about an hour. They went to see a performance on a showboat in Maryland, but found its amateurism so depressing that they left before the show had even ended. Gerald Bordman, *Jerome Kern: His Life and Music* (Oxford University Press, 1990).

3. The basic biographical facts of Kern's life are drawn from the two major Kern biographies: *Jerome Kern: His Life and Music* by Gerald Bordman (Oxford University Press, 1990), and *Jerome Kern* (Yale Broadway Masters Series, Yale University, 2006) by Stephen Banfield.

4. The Princess Theatre musicals were a series of shows composed by Kern for the small (299-seat) Princess Theatre between 1915 and 1918. The first two, *Nobody Home* and *Very Good Eddie*, were written by Kern and Guy Bolton, with P. G. Wodehouse joining the team for *Oh, Boy!*, *Leave It to Jane*, and *Oh, Lady! Lady!* Because of the theater's size, these shows replaced the spectacle and grandeur of other contemporary musicals with a new kind of intimate, small-scale, literate musical comedy that featured sophisticated, witty, coherent plots, set in the contemporary New York world of the 1910s. Kern's songs grew naturally out of the shows' plots and characters and spoke in a casual, American voice. Dorothy Parker famously called Bolton, Wodehouse, and Kern her "favorite indoor sport," and the Princess Theatre shows created a new set of possibilities for the Broadway musical.

5. Banfield, *Jerome Kern*, 155, quoting Miles Kreuger. Also see Larry Stempel, *Showtime: A History of the Broadway Musical Theater* (W. W. Norton, 2010), 194–201.

6. The standard, AABA, 32-bar Broadway song form is the form of many of the songs in this book and an enormous number of musical theater songs in general. It begins with an 8-measure idea (A), followed by a repeat of the same music with new words (A), then a move to a contrasting B section (also 8 measures), and a return to A to finish. In short, AABA, 8 + 8 + 8 + 8, or a 32-measure form in which 24 measures repeat the same music.

2. THE NEW SEXUAL MORALITY

1. The blog site Darwination has a post on May 6, 2012, that includes extensive scans of a rich profusion of original source material from a large number of Flapper magazines. The material in this paragraph is drawn from the scans of these fascinating primary-source documents.

2. Frederick Lewis Allen, *Only Yesterday: An Informal History of the 1920s* (Perennial Classics, 2000, originally published by Harper & Row, 1931), 87.

3. Daniel Pope, "Making Sense of Advertisements," *History Matters: The U.S. Survey Course on the Web*, http://historymatters.gmu.edu/mse/ads/, June 2003.

4. Ads from *Flapper's Experience,* Oct. 1925.

5. Stephen B. Oates, *Portrait of America: From Reconstruction to the Present* (Houghton Mifflin, 1994), 225.

6. Peter C. Engelman, *A History of the Birth Control Movement in America* (Praeger, 2011), 144.

7. Allen, *Only Yesterday*, 83.

8. Allen, *Only Yesterday*, 56.

9. Stephen Citron, *Noel & Cole: The Sophisticates* (Hal Leonard, 2005), 78–79.

10. William McBrien, *Cole Porter: A Definitive Biography* (HarperCollins, 1998), 137.

11. McBrien, *Cole Porter*, 121.

12. Brad Leithauser, "He's the Top!" *New York Review of Books*, Nov. 5, 1998.

3. AIRBRUSHING THE DEPRESSION

1. Deena Rosenberg, *Fascinating Rhythm: The Collaboration of George and Ira Gershwin* (University of Michigan Press, 1991), 188.

2. Donald R. McCoy, *Coming of Age: The United States During the 1920's and 1930's* (Penguin Books, 1973), 178.

3. Gordon Theisen, *Staying Up Much Too Late: Edward Hopper's Nighthawks and the Dark Side of the American Psyche* (Macmillan, 2007), 170.

4. David E. Kyvig, *Daily Life in the United States, 1920–1939: Decades of Promise and Pain* (Greenwood Publishing Group, 2002), 137.

5. A. A. Brill, M.D., *Amos 'n' Andy Explained*, *Popular Science Monthly*, June 1930, 22.

6. See Frederick Lewis Allen, *Since Yesterday: The Nineteen-Thirties in America* (Harper & Brothers, 1940), 204–5.

7. Howard Pollack, *George Gershwin: His Life and Work* (University of California Press, 2006), 237.

8. Pollack, *George Gershwin*, 237.

9. Kathleen Riley, *The Astaires: Fred & Adele* (Oxford University Press, 2012), 62.

10. Richard B. Manchester, *Amazing Facts: The Indispensable Collection of True Life Facts and Feats* (Sterling Publishing Co., 1991), 115.

11. William E. Leuchtenburg, *The Perils of Prosperity, 1914–1932* (University of Chicago Press, 1958), 241.

12. Herman Edward Krooss, *Executive Opinion: What Business Leaders Said and Thought on Economic Issues, 1920s–1960s* (Doubleday, 1970,) 118.

13. Pollack, *George Gershwin*, 467.

14. Rosenberg, *Fascinating Rhythm*, 190.

15. Pollack, *George Gershwin,* 16.

16. Philip Furia and Graham Wood, *Irving Berlin: A Life in Song* (Schirmer Books, 1998), 91.

17. George Gershwin, "Jazz Is the Voice of the American Soul," reprinted in Robert Wyatt and John Andrew Johnson, *The George Gershwin Reader* (Oxford University Press, 2004), 91–94.

4. SEGREGATION AND OPPORTUNITY IN HARLEM

1. Ed Jablonski, *Harold Arlen: Rhythm, Rainbows, and Blues* (Northeastern University Press, 1996), 315.

2. Walter Rimler, *The Man That Got Away: The Life and Songs of Harold Arlen* (University of Illinois Press, 2015), 6.

3. Rimler, *The Man That Got Away*, 6.

4. David Lehman, *A Fine Romance: Jewish Songwriters, American Songs* (Schocken Books, 2009), 71.

5. Jablonski, *Harold Arlen*, 27.

6. Barbara S. Glass, *African American Dance: An Illustrated History* (McFarland & Co., 2007), 226.

7. Jablonski, *Harold Arlen*, 40.

8. Quoted in Jablonski, *Harold Arlen*, 51.

9. Nathan Miller, *New World Coming: The 1920s and the Making of Modern America* (Scribner, 2003), 271.

10. Cary D. Wintz and Paul Finkelman, eds., *Encyclopedia of the Harlem Renaissance,* vol. 2 (Routledge, 2004), 845.

11. Paul Buhle, *Jews and American Popular Culture: Volume 2, Music, Theater, Popular Art, and Literature* (Praeger Publishers, 2007), 134.

12. Jablonski, *Harold Arlen*, 53.

13. Lee Foster Hartman and Frederick Lewis Allen, *Harper's Magazine,* vol. 220 (1960): 44.

14. *Moody's Governments,* vol. 5 (Moody's Investors Service, 1933), 1438.

15. Murray Newton Rothbard, *America's Great Depression* (Ludwig von Mises Institute, 2008), 330.

16. Hollis R. Lynch, *The Black Urban Condition: A Documentary History, 1866–1971* (Crowell, 1973), 205.

5. APPROPRIATION OR INSPIRATION?

1. Michael Brim Beckerman, *New Worlds of Dvořák: Searching in America for the Composer's Inner Life* (W. W. Norton, 2003), 128.

2. Lynn Abbott and Doug Seroff, *Out of Sight: The Rise of African American Popular Music, 1889–1895* (University Press of Mississippi, 2002), 273.

3. Howard Pollack, *George Gershwin: His Life and Work* (University of California Press, 2007), 183. Pollack's extremely thorough biography of Gershwin is my primary source for the biographical details surrounding the *Porgy and Bess* project in this chapter.

4. Pollack, *George Gershwin*, 568.

5. Pollack, *George Gershwin*, 574.

6. Ellen Noonan, *The Strange Career of Porgy and Bess: Race, Culture, and America's Most Famous Opera* (University of North Carolina Press, 2012), 9. This excellent book is the source of many of the basic facts and material about DuBose Heyward in this chapter.

7. *The Wisdom of George Santayana* (Philosophical Library, Open Road Media, 2010), Q-560.

8. Noonan, *The Strange Career of Porgy and Bess*, 22.

9. James M. Hutchisson, *Dubose Heyward: A Charleston Gentleman and the World of Porgy and Bess* (University Press of Mississippi, 2000), 53.

10. Noonan, *The Strange Career of Porgy and Bess*, 26.

11. Noonan, *The Strange Career of Porgy and Bess*, 23.

12. C. Vann Woodward, *Origins of the New South, 1877–1913* (Louisiana State University Press, 1951), 154–55.

13. Du Bose Heyward, *Porgy* (Read Books, 2013), Part IV, p. 3.

14. Noonan, *The Strange Career of Porgy and Bess*, 43.

15. Robert Wyatt and John Andrew Johnson, eds., *The George Gershwin Reader* (Oxford University Press, 2004), 205.

16. Pollack, *George Gershwin*, 577.

17. Pollack, *George Gershwin*, 578.

18. Pollack, *George Gershwin*, 578.

19. Pollack, *George Gershwin*, 578.

20. Noonan, *The Strange Career of Porgy and Bess*, 155.

21. Noonan, *The Strange Career of Porgy and Bess*, 147.

22. Noonan, *The Strange Career of Porgy and Bess*, 120.

23. Noonan, *The Strange Career of Porgy and Bess*, 147.

24. James Standifer, *"The Tumultuous Life of Porgy and Bess," Humanities,* vol. 18, issue 6 (Nov./Dec. 1997): 11.

25. Richard Kostelanetz, *Virgil Thomson: A Reader: Selected Writings, 1924–1984* (Routledge, 2013), 151.

26. Michael J. O'Neal, *America in the 1920s* (Infobase Publishing, 2009), 51.

27. Wyatt and Johnson, *The George Gershwin Reader*, 200.

28. Pollack, *George Gershwin*, 589.

29. Joseph Horowitz, *"On My Way": The Untold Story of Rouben Mamoulian, George Gershwin, and Porgy and Bess* (W. W. Norton, 2013), 151.

30. Mark C. Carnes, *Invisible Giants: Fifty Americans Who Shaped the Nation but Missed the History Books* (Oxford University Press, 2003), 150.

31. Joanne Gordon, *Art Isn't Easy: The Theater of Stephen Sondheim* (Da Capo Press, 2009), 13.

32. Pollack, *George Gershwin*, 667.

33. Joan Peyser, *The Memory of All That: The Life of George Gershwin* (Billboard Books, 1998), 155.

6. IMMIGRATION AND THE AMERICAN VOICE

1. Eugene Labovitz and Annette Labovitz, *A Sacred Trust: Silver Age of Poland* (Isaac Nathan Publishing Co., 1996), 417.

2. Hans Rogger, *Russia in the Age of Modernisation and Revolution 1881–1917* (Routledge, 2014), 200.

3. Edward Jablonski, *Irving Berlin: American Troubadour* (Henry Holt & Co., 1999), 4.

4. Gerald Sorin, *A Time for Building: The Third Migration, 1880–1920* (John Hopkins University Press, 1992), 33.

5. Mordecai Paldiel, *Churches and the Holocaust: Unholy Teaching, Good Samaritans, and Reconciliation* (KTAV Publishing House, 2006), 239.

6. Christina Reis and Yehuda Baruch, eds., *Careers Without Borders: Critical Perspectives* (Routledge, 2013), 298.

7. Elliott Robert Barkan, ed., *Immigrants in American History: Arrival, Adaptation, and Integration,* vol. 1 (ABC-CLIO, 2013), 44.

8. John F. May, *World Population Policies: Their Origin, Evolution, and Impact* (Springer Science+Business Media, 2012),189.

9. Catherine Cocks, Peter C. Holloran, and Alan Lessoff, *Historical Dictionary of the Progressive Era* (Scarecrow Press, 2009), xx.

10. Mark Sullivan, *Our Times, 1900–1925: Over Here, 1914–1918* (Scribner, 1972), 484.

11. Kenneth K. Lee, *Huddled Masses, Muddled Laws: Why Contemporary Immigration Policy Fails to Reflect Public Opinion* (Praeger Publishers, 1998), 45.

12. Tim Coles and Dallen J. Timothy, eds., *Tourism, Diasporas, and Space* (Routledge, 2004), 97.

13. Felice Batlan, *Women and Justice for the Poor: A History of Legal Aid, 1863–1945* (Cambridge University Press, 2015), 91–92.

14. Quoted in Norman H. Finkelstein, *Heeding the Call: Jewish Voices in America's Civil Rights Struggle* (Jewish Publication Society, 1997), 57.

15. The basic biographical facts of Berlin's life are drawn from Alexander Woollcott, *The Story of Irving Berlin* (William Press, 2013), and Edward Jablonski, *Irving Berlin: American Troubadour* (Henry Holt & Co., 1999).

16. Walter LaFeber, Richard Polenberg, and Nancy Woloch, *The American Century,* vol. 1: *A History of the United States from 1890 to 1941* (M. E. Sharpe, 2013), 74.

17. *The Theatre: Illustrated Monthly Magazine of Dramatic and Musical Art,* vol. 21 (1915): 9.

18. Steve Turner, *The Band That Played On: The Extraordinary Story of the 8 Musicians Who Went Down with the Titanic* (Thomas Nelson, 2011), 133.

19. Frank Ward O'Malley, "Irving Berlin Gives Nine Rules for Writing Popular Songs," *American Magazine 90* (Oct. 1920): 36–37, 239–46.

20. Laurence Bergreen, *As Thousands Cheer: The Life of Irving Berlin* (Da Capo Press, 1990), 85.

21. Benjamin Sears, ed., *The Irving Berlin Reader* (Oxford University Press, 2012), 138.

22. Bergreen, *As Thousands Cheer*, 222.

7. HOW THE OTHER HALF LIVED

1. David R. Roediger and Philip Sheldon Foner, *Our Own Time: A History of American Labor and the Working Day* (Greenwood Press, 1989), 243. However, as the government did not keep unemployment records at the time, all unemployment figures during the Depression are estimates.

2. James Kirby Martin, *America and Its Peoples: A Mosaic in the Making,* vol. 2 (Prentice Hall, 2001), 707.

3. Glenda R. Balas, *Recovering a Public Vision for Public Television* (Rowman & Littlefield, 2003), 62.

4. *The Conference Board Bulletin,* vols. 7–10 (National Industrial Conference Board, 1933), 95.

5. Steven M. Gillon and Cathy D. Matson, *The American Experiment: A History of the United States Since 1865* (Houghton Mifflin, 2004), 673.

6. Barry D. Karl, *The Uneasy State: The United States from 1915 to 1945* (University of Chicago Press, 1983), 124.

7. Jonathan Alter, *The Defining Moment: FDR's Hundred Days and the Triumph of Hope* (Simon & Schuster Paperbacks, 2006), 93.

8. All of the details of Porter's onboard routine are drawn from William McBrien, *Cole Porter: A Definitive Biography* (HarperCollins, 1998), 176.

9. *Evening Sun*, Mar. 29, 1916.

10. George Chauncey, "A Gay World, Vibrant and Forgotten," *New York Times*, June 26, 1994.

11. Stanley Green, *Broadway Musicals of the 30s* (Da Capo Press, 1971), 120.

12. McBrien, *Cole Porter*, 188.

13. McBrien, *Cole Porter*, 99.

14. McBrien, *Cole Porter*, 186.

15. McBrien, *Cole Porter*, 189.

8. LOVE IN NEW YORK

1. Robert Gottlieb, "Rodgers and Hart's Dysfunctional Partnership," *The Atlantic*, Apr. 2013.

2. William G. Hyland, *Richard Rodgers* (Yale University Press, 1998), 3.

3. Richard Rodgers, *Musical Stages* (Random House, 1975), 4.

4. Meryle Secrest, *Somewhere for Me* (Alfred A. Knopf, 2001), 28.

5. Dorothy Hart, *Thou Swell, Thou Witty: The Life and Lyrics of Lorenz Hart* (Harper & Row, 1976), 15.

6. Secrest, *Somewhere for Me*, 33.

7. Hyland, *Richard Rodgers*, 18.

8. Ethan Mordden, *Make Believe: The Broadway Musical in the 1920s* (Oxford University Press, 1997), 11.

9. Rodgers, *Musical Stages*, 130.

10. Rodgers, *Musical Stages*, 164.

11. Hyland, *Richard Rodgers*, 98. O. O. McIntyre—short for Oscar Odd McIntyre—was one of the most famous columnists of the 1920s and '30s, and his daily column about New York, "New York Day by Day," ran in more than five hundred U.S. newspapers. To small-town America, his column represented New York as an exotic, exciting place, yet the fictional version of New York he created bore little resemblance to the actual New York of the times.

12. Hyland, *Richard Rodgers*, 117.

13. Rodgers, *Musical Stages*, 218.

14. Ben Yagoda, *The B-Side: The Death of Tin Pan Alley and the Rebirth of the Great American Song* (Riverhead Books, 2015), 56.

15. Hyland, *Richard Rodgers*, 38.

16. Rodgers, *Musical Stages*, 180.

17. Rodgers, *Musical Stages*, 180.

18. Hyland, *Richard Rodgers*, 110.

19. Hart, *Thou Swell, Thou Witty*, 185.

9. THE IMPACT OF RECORDED SOUND

1. Michael Campbell, *Popular Music in America: The Beat Goes On* (Schirmer Cengage Learning, 2006), 29.

2. Benjamin Sears, ed., *The Irving Berlin Reader* (Oxford University Press, 2012), 35.

3. Deena Rosenberg, *Fascinating Rhythm: The Collaboration of George and Ira Gershwin* (University of Michigan Press, 1991), 39.

4. *Brooklyn Daily Eagle Almanac* (Brooklyn Daily Eagle, 1918), 577.

5. Colin Symes, *Setting the Record Straight: A Material History of Classical Recording* (Wesleyan University Press, 2004), 20.

6. Michael Miller, *The Ultimate Digital Music Guide* (Pearson Education, 2012), 14.

7. Douglas Kellner, *Television and the Crisis of Democracy* (Westview Press, 1990), 27.

8. Robert J. Gordon, *The Rise and Fall of American Growth: The U.S. Standard of Living Since the Civil War* (Princeton University Press, 2016), 192.

9. Gwenyth L. Jackaway, *Media at War: Radio's Challenge to the Newspapers, 1924–1939* (Praeger Publishers, 1995), 87.

10. Gerald Bordman, *Jerome Kern: His Life and Music* (Oxford University Press, 1990), 249–50.

11. Oscar Hammerstein II, *The Complete Lyrics of Oscar Hammerstein,* ed. Amy Asch (Alfred A. Knopf, 2008), 244.

12. Marvin E. Paymer and Don E. Post, *Sentimental Journey: Intimate Portraits of America's Great Popular Songs, 1920–1945* (Noble House Publishers, 1999), 369.

10. AMERICA GOES TO THE MOVIES

1. John Buntin, *L.A. Noir: The Struggle for the Soul of America's Most Seductive City* (Harmony Books, 2009), 18.

2. *Australian Journal of Screen Theory*, issues 13–16 (1983): 168.

3. Gregory Albert Waller, *Main Street Amusements: Movies and Commercial Entertainment in a Southern City, 1896–1930* (Smithsonian Institution Press, 1995), 194.

4. Historical National Population Estimates, www.census.gov, 2000.

5. Laurence E. MacDonald, *The Invisible Art of Film Music: A Comprehensive History* (Ardsley House, 1998), 8–9.

6. Robert Sklar, *Film: An International History of the Medium* (Prentice Hall, 1993), 173.

7. Scott Eyman, *The Speed of Sound: Hollywood and the Talkie Revolution, 1926–1930* (Simon & Schuster, 1997), 141.

8. Eyman, *The Speed of Sound*, 160.

9. Edwin M. Bradley, *The First Hollywood Musicals: A Critical Filmography of 171 Features, 1927 Through 1932* (McFarland & Co., 1996), 12.

10. Harvey Green, *The Uncertainty of Everyday Life: 1915–1945* (Harper Collins, 1992), 206.

11. Laurence E. MacDonald, *The Invisible Art of Film Music: A Comprehensive History* (Scarecrow Press, 1998), 28.

12. James W. Cook, Lawrence B. Glickman, and Michael O'Malley, eds., *The Cultural Turn in U.S. History: Past, Present, and Future* (University of Chicago Press, 2012), 188.

13. Aljean Harmetz, *The Making of The Wizard of Oz* (Chicago Review Press, 2013), 63.

14. Harmetz, *The Making of The Wizard of Oz*, 62.

15. Edward Jablonski, *Harold Arlen: Happy with the Blues* (Doubleday, 1961), 120.

16. Harmetz, *The Making of the Wizard of Oz*, 81.

17. Harold Myerson and Ernie Harburg, *Who Put the Rainbow in the Wizard of Oz? Yip Harburg, Lyricist* (University of Michigan Press, 1993), 2.

18. *The Eddie Mannix Ledger* (Margaret Herrick Library, Center for Motion Picture Study, 1962).

19. Harmetz, *The Making of The Wizard of Oz*, 290.

11. WORLD WAR II AND THE INTEGRATED MUSICAL

1. Raymond Knapp, Mitchell Morris, and Stacy Wolf, eds., *The Oxford Handbook of the American Musical* (Oxford University Press, 2011), 98.

2. Knapp, Morris, and Wolf, *The Oxford Handbook*, 98.

3. Richard Rodgers, *Musical Stages* (Random House, 1975), 227.

4. Knapp, Morris, and Wolf, *The Oxford Handbook*, 98–99.

5. Rodgers, *Musical Stages*, 229.

6. Stanley Green, *The World of Musical Comedy* (Da Capo Press, 1980), 58.

7. Rodgers, *Musical Stages*, 118.

8. Quoted in Knapp, Morris, and Wolf, *The Oxford Handbook*, 102.

9. Quoted in Knapp, Morris, and Wolf, *The Oxford Handbook*, 102.

10. Quoted in Knapp, Morris, and Wolf, *The Oxford Handbook*, 100.

11. Jason Van Bergen, "Great Company or Growing Industry?" *Investopedia*, Aug. 20, 2014.

12. Rodgers, *Musical Stages*, 227.

13. William G. Hyland, *Richard Rodgers* (Yale University Press, 1998), 157.

14. Rodgers, *Musical Stages*, 238.

15. Rodgers, *Musical Stages*, 238.

16. Rodgers, *Musical Stages*, 239.

17. Rodgers, *Musical Stages*, 240.

18. Ian Bradley, *You've Got to Have a Dream: The Message of the Broadway Musical* (Westminster John Knox Press, 2005), 74.

12. AMERICA GETS A CLASSICAL VOICE

1. Richard Rodgers, *Musical Stages* (Random House, 1975), 210.

2. Humphrey Burton, *Leonard Bernstein* (Doubleday, 1994), 135.

3. Burton, *Leonard Bernstein*, 4.

4. Duke Ellington, *The Duke Ellington Reader,* ed. Mark Tucker (Oxford University Press, 1995), 326.

5. Carol J. Oja, *Bernstein Meets Broadway: Collaborative Art in a Time of War* (Oxford University Press, 2014), 21.

6. Oja, *Bernstein Meets Broadway*, 29.

7. Oja, *Bernstein Meets Broadway*, 32.

8. Oja, *Bernstein Meets Broadway*, 56.

9. Burton, *Leonard Bernstein,* 130.

10. *Jazz in America*, Thelonious Monk Institute of Jazz Resource Library, Boogie Woogie, 2000, is the source of the boogie-woogie historical material.

11. Oja, *Bernstein Meets Broadway*, 13.

13. WILL THE REAL ANNIE OAKLEY PLEASE STAND UP?

1. Shirl Kasper, *Annie Oakley* (University of Oklahoma Press, 1992), 22.

2. Larry McMurtry, *The Colonel and Little Missie: Buffalo Bill, Annie Oakley, and the Beginnings of Superstardom in America* (Simon & Schuster, 2005), 161.

3. Kasper, *Annie Oakley*, 49.

4. Kasper, *Annie Oakley*, 13–14.

5. Richard Rodgers, *Musical Stages* (Random House, 1975), 229.

6. William G. Hyland, *Richard Rodgers* (Yale University Press, 1998), 134.

7. Kathryn Kalinak, *Music in the Western: Notes from the Frontier* (Routledge, 2012), 105.

8. Kasper, *Annie Oakley*, 214.

9. McMurtry, *The Colonel and Little Missie*, 216.

14. FANTASY IN NEW YORK

1. Although the participants' recollections of the show's genesis are slightly different depending on who is speaking and in what setting, the general consensus I've described comes from *Broadway Song & Story: Playrights/Lyricists/Composers Discuss Their Hits*, edited by Otis L. Guernsey Jr. (Dodd, Mead & Company, 1985), 42–43, and Craig Zadan, *Sondheim & Co.* (Harper & Row, 1986), 11–14.

2. Migration statistics are drawn from José L. Vázquez Calzada, *La población de Puerto Rico y su trayectoria histórica* (Escuela Graduada de Salud Pública, Recinto de Ciencias Médicas, Universidad de Puerto Rico, 1988), p. 286 and statistics from the Library of Congress data.

3. The quote is from Eric C. Schneider, *Vampires, Dragons, and Egyptian Kings: Youth Gangs in Postwar New York* (Princeton University Press, 2001), 125. Other material on 1950s gangs in this paragraph is drawn from Paul Kendall, "50 Years of West Side Story: The Real Gangs of New York," *The Telegraph*, July 2008.

4. Elizabeth A. Wells, *West Side Story: Cultural Perspectives on an American Musical* (Scarecrow Press, 2011), 29.

5. Humphrey Burton, *Leonard Bernstein* (Doubleday, 1994), 275.

6. Burton, *Bernstein*, 187.

7. Burton, *Bernstein*, 271.

8. Wells, *West Side Story*, 189.

9. Julia L. Foulkes, *A Place for Us:* West Side Story *and New York* (University of Chicago Press, 2016), 63.

10. John Berman, Deborah Apton, and Victoria Thompson, "Sondheim: *West Side Story* Lyrics 'Embarrassing,'" ABC News, Dec. 28, 2010.

11. Stephen Sondheim, *Finishing the Hat: Collected Lyrics (1954–1981) with Attendant Comments, Principles, Heresies, Grudges, Whines, and Anecdotes* (Alfred A. Knopf, 2010), 26.

12. Sondheim, *Finishing the Hat*, 26.

13. Arthur Laurents et al., *West Side Story* (Random House, 1957). All lyrics in this discussion come from the published libretto.

14. Laurents et al., *West Side Story*, Act I, Scene V.

15. Wells, *West Side Story*, 237.

16. Wells, *West Side Story*, 209.

17. Burton, *Bernstein*, 18.

18. For a more complete discussion of this, see Foulkes, *A Place for Us,* Chapter 1.

19. Foulkes, *A Place for Us*, 35.

15. ROCK AND ROLL, BROADWAY, AND THE ME DECADE

1. "The Theatre: A Musical That Makes the Others Look Pale," *London Sunday Express*, Jan. 12, 1959.

2. Stephen Sondheim, interview by Steven Swayne, in "Hearing Sondheim's Voice" (Ph.D. diss., University of California, Berkeley, 1999), 346–47.

3. Sondheim, interview by Swayne, 178. See Ben Yagoda, *The B-Side: The Death of Tin Pan Alley and the Rebirth of the Great American Song* (Riverhead Books, 2015), Chapter 7, for an in-depth discussion of the advent of rock and roll from which this material is drawn.

4. Yagoda, *The B-Side*, 177.

5. Yagoda, *The B-Side*, 179.

6. Yagoda, *The B-Side*, 222.

7. Meryle Secrest, *Stephen Sondheim: A Life* (Alfred A. Knopf, 1998), 228.

8. Secrest, *Stephen Sondheim*, 188.

9. William Goldman, *The Season: A Candid Look at Broadway* (Harcourt, Brace & World, 1969), 273.

10. Joanne Gordon, *Art Isn't Easy: The Theater of Stephen Sondheim* (Da Capo Press, 2009), 17.

11. Secrest, *Stephen Sondheim*, 244.

12. Hugh Wheeler, Stephen Sondheim, and Harold S. Prince, *A Little Night Music* (Dodd, Mead & Co., 1973), 152. All quotations from the show come from this published libretto.

13. Samuel G. Freedman, "The Words and Music of Stephen Sondheim," *New York Times*, April 1, 1984.

14. Ibid.

15. Stephen Sondheim, *Finishing the Hat: Collected Lyrics (1954–1981) with Attendant Comments, Principles, Heresies, Grudges, Whines, and Anecdotes* (Alfred A. Knopf, 2010), 278.

16. Secrest, *Stephen Sondheim*, 251.

16. NEW DIRECTIONS ON AND OFF BROADWAY

1. *Newsweek,* "Broadway's Music Man," Apr. 23, 1973.

2. *New York Times*, January 24, 1976.

3. Meryle Secrest, *Stephen Sondheim: A Life* (Alfred A. Knopf, 1998), 282.

4. Secrest, *Stephen Sondheim*, 245.

5. Stephen Sondheim, *Finishing the Hat: Collected Lyrics (1954–1981) with Attendant Comments, Principles, Heresies, Grudges, Whines and Anecdotes* (Alfred A. Knopf, 2010), 375–76. (The other Sondheim comments in this paragraph are drawn from the same source.)

6. Sondheim, *Finishing the Hat*, 381.

7. Frank Rich, "A Musical Theatre Breakthrough," *New York Times*, Oct. 21, 1984.

8. Secrest, *Sondheim*, 323. The basic facts surrounding the show are drawn from Chapter 17 of this book.

9. Stephen Sondheim, *Look, I Made a Hat* (Alfred A. Knopf, 2011), 3.

10. Craig Zadan, *Sondheim & Co.* (Harper & Row, 1986), 296.

11. Sondheim, *Look, I Made a Hat*, 5–6.

12. See Chapter 12 of Larry Stempel's *Showtime: A History of the Broadway Musical* (W. W. Norton, 2010) for an extended discussion of the history of Off Broadway.

13. Secrest, *Sondheim*, 327.

14. Sondheim, *Look, I Made a Hat*, 3.

15. Joanne Gordon, *Art Isn't Easy: The Theater of Stephen Sondheim* (Da Capo Press, 2009), 265.

16. Secrest, *Sondheim*, 348.

17. Secrest, *Sondheim*, 335.

18. Sondheim, *Look, I Made a Hat*, 27.

19. Sondheim, *Finishing the Hat*, xxi.

20. Sondheim, *Look, I Made a Hat*, 33.

EPILOGUE: THE BROADWAY MUSICAL GOES GLOBAL

1. John Snelson, *Andrew Lloyd Webber* (Yale University Press, 2004), 188.

2. Larry Stempel, *Showtime: A History of the Broadway Musical* (W. W. Norton, 2010), 646. See Chapters 14–16 for a much more thorough discussion of these trends.

3. See Jesse Green, "Theater Review: Lin-Manuel Miranda's 'Hamilton' Is Worth Way More than $10," vulture.com, Feb. 17, 2015.

4. Igor Stravinsky, *Poetics of Music in the Form of Six Lessons* (Harvard University Press, 1970), 57.

5. Leonard Bernstein, *The Joy of Music* (Simon & Schuster, 1959), 170.

ACKNOWLEDGMENTS

1. Thich Nhat Hanh, *The Miracle of Mindfulness: A Manual on Meditation*, rev. ed. (Beacon Press, 1987), 47.

CREDITS

Jerome Kern's "Can't Help Lovin' Dat Man": Lyrics by Oscar Hammerstein II. Music by Jerome Kern. Copyright © 1927 Universal–Polygram International Publishing, Inc. Copyright renewed. This arrangement copyright © Universal–Polygram International Publishing, Inc. All rights reserved. Used by permission. Reprinted by permission of Hal Leonard LLC.

Cole Porter's "Let's Do It (Let's Fall in Love)" (from *Paris*): Words and music by Cole Porter. © 1928 (Renewed) WB Music Corp. All rights reserved. Used by permission of Alfred Music.

George Gershwin's "I Got Rhythm": Music and lyrics by George Gershwin and Ira Gershwin. Copyright © 1930 (renewed) WB Music Corp. and Ira Gershwin Music. All rights administered by WB Music Corp. All rights reserved. Used by permission of Alfred Music.

Harold Arlen's "Stormy Weather (Keeps Rainin' All the Time)": Words by Ted Koehler. Music by Harold Arlen. Copyright © 1933 Fred Ahlert Music Group, Ted Koehler Music Co. and S.A. Music Co. Copyright renewed. Copyright © 1933 (renewed) Fred Ahlert Music Corporation / Ted Koehler Music (administered by BUG) and S.A. Music. Canadian rights controlled by EMI Mills Music Inc. (publishing) and Alfred Publishing Co., Inc. (print). All rights reserved. Used by permission of Alfred Music. This arrangement copyright © 2018 Fred Ahlert Music Group, Ted Koehler Music Co. and S.A. Music Co. All rights for Fred Ahlert Music Group and Ted Koehler Music Co. administered by BMG Rights Management (U.S.) LLC. All rights reserved. Used by permission. Reprinted by permission of Hal Leonard LLC.

George Gershwin's "Summertime": Music and lyrics by George Gershwin, DuBose and Dorothy Heyward and Ira Gershwin. © 1935 (Renewed) Nokawi Music, KMR Music Royalties II SCSP, Frankie G. Songs, Dubose and Dorothy Heyward Memorial Fund Publishing, and Ira Gershwin Music. © 1935 (renewed) Ira Gershwin Music, DuBose and Dorothy Heyward Memorial

INDEX